"*Comparative Public Opinion* provides a comprehensive and modern coverage of one of the major areas of political science research. It brings together leading authors in the field and takes a very broad and rigorous view of public opinion. The textbook provides a priceless insight into the field."

Ignacio Lago, *Universitat Pompeu Fabra, Barcelona, Spain*

COMPARATIVE PUBLIC OPINION

This book presents a comprehensive examination of public opinion in the democratic world.

Built around chapters that highlight key explanatory frameworks used in understanding public opinion, the book presents a coherent study of the subject in a comparative perspective, emphasizing and interrogating immigration as a key issue of high concern to most mass publics in the democratic world.

Key features of the book include:

- Covers several theoretical issues and determinants of opinion such as the effects of personality, age and life cycle, ideology, social class, partisanship, gender, religion, ethnicity, language, and media, highlighting over time the effects of political, social, and economic contexts.
- Each chapter explores the theoretical rationale, mechanisms of effect, and use in the scholarly literature on public opinion before applying these to the issue of immigration comparatively and in specific places or regions.
- Widely comparative using a nine-country sample (Australia, Canada, France, Germany, Italy, Portugal, Switzerland, the United Kingdom, and the United States of America) in the analysis of individual-level determinants of public opinion about immigration and extending to other countries like Belgium, Brazil, and Japan when evaluating contextual factors.

This edited volume will be essential reading for students, scholars, and practitioners interested in public opinion, political behaviour, voting behaviour, politics of the media, immigration, political communication, and, more generally, democracy and comparative politics.

Cameron D. Anderson is Associate Professor in the Department of Political Science at the University of Western Ontario, Canada.

Mathieu Turgeon is Associate Professor in the Department of Political Science at the University of Western Ontario, Canada.

Comparative Public Opinion

Edited by
Cameron D. Anderson
and Mathieu Turgeon

Routledge
Taylor & Francis Group

LONDON AND NEW YORK

Cover image: © Getty Images

First published 2023
by Routledge
4 Park Square, Milton Park, Abingdon, Oxon OX14 4RN

and by Routledge
605 Third Avenue, New York, NY 10158

Routledge is an imprint of the Taylor & Francis Group, an informa business

© 2023 selection and editorial matter, Cameron D. Anderson and Mathieu Turgeon; individual chapters, the contributors

British Library Cataloguing-in-Publication Data
A catalogue record for this book is available from the British Library

Library of Congress Cataloging-in-Publication Data
A catalog record has been requested for this book

ISBN: 978-0-367-64069-9 (hbk)
ISBN: 978-0-367-64060-6 (pbk)
ISBN: 978-1-003-12199-2 (ebk)

DOI: 10.4324/9781003121992

Typeset in Sabon
by Deanta Global Publishing Services, Chennai, India

Contents

Figures

Tables

Contributors

Kathrin Ackermann is Assistant Professor at the Institute of Political Science at Heidelberg University, Germany.

Cameron D. Anderson is Associate Professor in the Department of Political Science at the University of Western Ontario, Canada.

Frédérick Bastien is Associate Professor in the Department of Political Science at Université de Montréal, Canada.

Katrine Beauregard is Senior Lecturer in the School of Politics and International Relations at the Australian National University, Australia.

Éric Bélanger is Professor in the Department of Political Science at McGill University, Canada.

João Carvalho is guest Assistant Professor in the Department of Political Science and Public Policy at ISCTE, Instituto Universitário de Lisboa, Portugal.

Philippe Chassé is a PhD student in the Department of Political Science at Université de Montréal, Canada.

Ruth Dassonneville is Associate Professor and Chair of the Canada Research Chair in Electoral Democracy in the Department of Political Science at Université de Montréal, Canada.

Paul A. Djupe is Associate Professor in the Department of Political Science at Denison University, USA.

Jan Eckardt is an MA student at the Institute of Political Science at Heidelberg University, Germany.

Ana Espírito-Santo is Assistant Professor in the Department of Political Science and Public Policy at ISCTE, Instituto Universitário de Lisboa, Portugal.

Nadjim Fréchet is a PhD student in the Department of Political Science at Université de Montréal, Canada.

Allison Harell is Professor in the Department of Political Science at Université du Québec à Montréal, Canada.

Robert A. Hinckley is Associate Professor in the Department of Politics at SUNY Postdam, USA.

John Kennedy is a PhD candidate in the Department of Political Science at the University of Western Ontario, Canada.

Anthony Kevins is Lecturer in Politics and International Studies at Loughborough University, UK.

Baowen Liang is a PhD student in the Department of Political Science at Université de Montréal, Canada.

Ryan Lloyd is Research Coordinator in the Population Research Center at the University of Texas at Austin, USA.

Tetsuya Matsubayashi is Professor in the Osaka School of International Public Policy at Osaka University, Japan.

Amâncio Jorge de Oliveira is Professor at the Institute of International Relations at the Universidade de São Paulo, Brazil.

Tyler Romualdi is a PhD student in the Department of Political Science at the University of Western Ontario, Canada.

Laura B. Stephenson is Professor in the Department of Political Science at the University of Western Ontario, Canada.

Mathieu Turgeon is Associate Professor in the Department of Political Science at the University of Western Ontario, Canada.

Stephen White is Associate Professor in the Department of Political Science at Carleton University, Canada.

Masateru Yamatani is a PhD student in the Department of Political Science at Texas A&M, USA.

Acknowledgements

An edited volume like this is the result of many individuals' hard work and commitment. We start by thanking the contributors to this volume – without whom there would be no book! Each bought in to our philosophical approach to this project and made outstanding contributions to the book through their individual chapters. We are also extremely grateful to Andrew Taylor and Sophie Iddamalgoda at Routledge. They provided wise and patient counsel as we navigated the review and publication process, and the resulting book is better because of their involvement. We also thank Andrew Malvern for planting the seed of the concept of this volume within the minds of the editors. Last, we would like to thank our colleague Laura Stephenson for encouraging us to pursue this book project and our Department Chair Matt Lebo for his constant support.

PART 1

Public opinion in a comparative perspective

CHAPTER 1

Introduction

....

Cameron D. Anderson and Mathieu Turgeon

INTRODUCTION

This book is about public opinion on immigration – one of the defining issues of the 21st century. This book explores how we think about, understand, and make sense of people's opinions of immigrants and immigration. The discussion in this book is motivated by many related questions. These include: how are we to define and measure public opinion about immigration? What factors explain public opinion about immigration? How and why do these factors influence the shape of opinion about immigrants and immigration? Does public opinion about immigration differ between countries?

All of this said, the book opens with two chapters that have little to do with public opinion about immigration. Rather, the first two chapters are designed to introduce the reader to longstanding debates and contemporary issues in the study of public opinion. We start with positioning the study of public opinion within broader philosophical debates about democracy and the role of the citizen in democratic practice. We then explore the historical development of the concept and study of public opinion. We attempt to answer the question of why we study public opinion and we close by providing an overview of the sections and chapters that follow in this volume. Chapter 2 concerns itself with the definition and measurement of public opinion.

PUBLIC OPINION AND THEORIES OF DEMOCRACY

While this book is largely concerned with the empirical study of public opinion about immigration, we start with a treatment of the normative foundations of the relationship between democracy, citizens, and the role of public opinion in democracy. Among many definitions of democracy, the simplest might be "rule by the people." Theorists of democracy, as well as scholars of public opinion, have long

DOI: 10.4324/9781003121992-2

concerned themselves with the question of what does "rule by the people" mean? Among various answers to this question, debates have arisen around who constitutes "the people" (or citizenship rules), how the people should be involved in governing and collective decision-making as well as how capable and competent citizens are for extensive involvement in matters of the state. We start our discussion here by sketching some democratic theories that articulate different conceptions of the appropriate role of the public in matters of democratic government and policy-making. While there are many variations of democratic theory, the approaches we consider include classical democratic theory, democratic elitism, and participatory democracy. We should note that we don't purport to provide an exhaustive review of these theoretical approaches to democracy but rather provide skeletal outlines exemplifying the ideal type features of each.

We start with classical democratic theory. Classical democracy finds its intellectual origins in the fledgling democracies of the city-states of ancient Greece. In these early accounts, all citizens were theorized to have an active role in governing decisions of the city-state. While citizenship was limited to non-slave men (a membership criterion that is itself problematic for contemporary conceptions of democratic citizenship) in the ancient Greek democracies, this approach prized the active participation of citizens in decisions of the Assembly (Thucydides, 1991). Classical democratic theory conceives of citizens in particular ways. It values citizen attention to and interest in political matters and holds in high regard the intellectual capacity of citizens to engage with politics. Further, classical theorists take the view that citizens' motivation in public affairs will be driven by the general interest rather than the narrow advancement of one's self-interest. Based on these conceptions of citizens as publicly minded and capable, classical democratic theory assigns a prominent role for the involvement of citizens and their opinions in collective decision-making. Stated differently, classical democratic theory holds a central place for citizens and the inclusion of public opinion in the successful practice of democratic decision-making.

Democratic elitism, by contrast, does not allocate citizens a direct or central role in governmental decision-making. Rather, the public is understood as exerting its collective influence indirectly through the election of representatives who then are tasked with making decisions about public policy. In this account, representatives gain office through winning competitive elections and are to govern with the interests of the public in mind because of the accountability incentives associated with electoral democracy. In this conception of democracy, it is the elected representatives who are understood, by their knowledge and expertise, as being best placed to make public policy decisions rather than citizens. In part, theories of democratic elitism are borne out of empirical observations that citizens may not be up to the task that classical democratic theorists laid out for them. In particular, citizens may not be as knowledgeable about or interested in politics as classical democratic theorists would hold (Delli Carpini and Keeter, 1996; Achen and Bartels, 2017). Further, citizens may be more apathetic and less participatory than the classical account would have (Hibbing and Theis-Morse, 2002). For these reasons, theories of democratic elitism emerged to reconcile the imperatives of democratic self-government with the mores of citizens in democracies who may not quite measure up to theoretical expectations. In the words of one notable theorist of Democratic elitism, Joseph Schumpeter, "the electoral mass is incapable of action other than a stampede" (1976). Indicative of this approach, citizens were thought to be capable of little more than voting in elections and the complexities of governing and public policy decisions should be left to democratically elected elites. Beyond the citizen capacity arguments, democratic elite theory holds that elites tend to be more supportive of democratic norms and values and are better positioned than the public to weigh the rights and interests of minority and disadvantaged groups within society. For all of these reasons, in the view of democratic elite theory, citizens' individual opinions and those of the collective public should not have a prominent role in the conduct of democratic decision-making.

Related to democratic elitism is pluralism as a theory of democracy. While pluralists share the pessimistic views of citizen capabilities and the importance of competitive elections in the theory and practice of democracy, they, unlike democratic elitists, position a central role for groups within the democratic decision-making process. Interest groups are "collections of like-minded individuals that attempt to influence elected officials and other governmental decision makers regarding issues of concern to them" (Clawson and Oxley, 2017, pp. 7–8). According to the pluralist approach, interest groups function as an aggregator of public and citizen opinion about politics and these interests are expressed by interest group leadership to the elected governing elites between elections. In this way, interest groups are thought to aggregate diverse interests and present compromise positions to politicians as part of the policy process. In the view of pluralists, then, the role of public opinion in democracy is less central because interest groups are the vehicle through which opinion, interest, and policy positions are conveyed within the democratic political system.

Critics of the democratic elitist and pluralist schools of thought have emerged from many corners of the discipline. Some, such as the participatory democracy theorists (who we look at next), suggest that their dim view of citizens' participatory capacity (knowledge, interest, apathy) is misplaced. Others point out that not all interest groups are treated the same by governments or have the same level of influence on public policy decision-making – governments can choose who to listen to and who not to listen to (e.g. Lindblom, 1977). Another line of criticism is that resources (in terms of money, expertise, and access) are not evenly distributed throughout interest groups in any one democracy and usually it is the most well-endowed interest groups who are most successful in influencing the policy-making process. Based on these criticisms, a last line of democratic theory is considered – participatory democracy theorists – to consider the theoretical relationship of public opinion and democracy.

Participatory democracy assigns a central role to citizens in the practice of democracy. While committed to the features of representative democracy (such as elected politicians and competitive elections), participatory democracy advocates for a larger role for citizen involvement in democracy. This approach emerged in the 1960s as a response to the prevailing positions of democratic elitism and pluralist thought dominating political science in the mid-20th century. While participatory democracy theorists acknowledge the relative lack of knowledge, interest, and participatory impulses of the average citizen, they suggest a different diagnosis of the problem. Writing in the 1980s, Barber suggested that "people are apathetic because they are powerless, not powerless because they are apathetic" (272). He went on to argue that American history is full of examples of citizens participating in politics when given the opportunity. The argument is extended to suggest that participation in political matters begets more participation. It is suggested that this path occurs because participation facilitates the accumulation of political knowledge and interest as well as civic skills and resources (like public speaking, organizational skills, and a sense of personal efficacy in the political sphere). Beyond skill acquisition, participation may also foster an awareness of interests other than one's own and the ability to see a collective good in public policy decision-making and outcomes. In sum, political participation is theorized to have the potential to produce better democratic citizens (Clawson and Oxley, 2017; Barber, 1984).

Of course, there are critics of the participatory democracy approach as well. Some have found that, when presented with greater opportunities to participate in politics, citizens have not taken advantage of these moments. For instance, when barriers to electoral participation in the United States have been lowered, electoral turnout has not increased (Rugeley and Jackson, 2009). Further, some argue that the assumptions made by participatory democracy theorists are unrealistic and the average citizen may simply dislike politics and not wish to pursue further involvement (Clawson and Oxley, 2017). So, while there may be democratic benefits for citizens from greater participation and interaction with each other, the fact of the matter is that many citizens may simply not be that interested.

Taken together, these various theories of democracy posit different assumptions, expectations, and demands of citizens within a functioning democracy. Our task is not to determine which approach has it right. Rather it is to highlight how different theoretical approaches to democracy position a role for citizens in different ways. Depending on our preferred approach, we may come to have very different views about the role of public opinion within democratic practice.

HISTORICAL REFLECTIONS ABOUT PUBLIC OPINION

When we consider the topic of public opinion we often reference the latest opinion polls about the most recent pressing issue, public controversy, or political scandal. Despite the immediacy of how we consume and think about public opinion in popular media or conduct the scholarly study of public opinion with the latest data set or sophisticated methods, there is a long historical lineage within which the current practice and study of public opinion should be situated. We wish to take some time in the introductory chapter to understand some of this tradition to better understand where we are now.

The concept of public opinion arose in the ancient civilizations of Greece and Rome. While referred to by names other than public opinion (e.g., "vox populi"), consideration of the opinion of the citizenry was part of the decision-making process in these earliest forms of limited democratic government. In the Greek city-states, citizens' opinion was a respected part of the political sphere despite the fact that membership and participation were limited to only some men. As Herbst notes, political life in the Greek city-states included many venues (e.g., theatre, public speaking, festivals, and juries) through which public opinion could be expressed and ultimately conveyed a form of community (2012). Of course, beyond the collective practices and expression of public opinion within the fledgling Greek democracies, great philosophical thinkers such as Plato and Aristotle took positions on the proper role and place of the citizens in collective decision-making. While Plato was more sceptical of the public's capacity for involvement in politics, Aristotle was decidedly more optimistic about this role and articulated an early vision of the public as a collection of individuals and the value of the collective judgment of the public in politics (Minar, 1960). Taken together, the experience of the ancient Greek city-states demonstrates the earliest examples of popular opinion being brought to bear on political decision-making.

Despite these early beginnings, the history of public opinion doesn't meaningfully develop until the Renaissance period of European history (Herbst, 2012). While citizens held and expressed views about government and politics, the toil of daily life and the relative difficulty of transferring ideas and opinions across geography larger than the local community rendered the development of mass publics nearly impossible. The invention of the printing press changed all of this. Through the publication of books, pamphlets and newspapers, the printing press allowed for the widespread diffusion of ideas across geography and facilitated the development of new conceptions of democracy, citizenship, and political identities such as nationhood (Anderson, 1983; Hobsbawm, 2012). The invention of the printing press allowed for the diffusion of ideas, attitudes, opinions, and identities to be geographically dispersed and for the beginnings of a collective consciousness extending beyond the confines of one's local community. In this sense, the printing press can be seen as the technological conduit through which an early modern public opinion emerges.

Perhaps the clearest inklings of the concept of mass public opinion emerged in pre-revolutionary France of the late 17th and 18th centuries (but also in other countries in Europe). During this period, print communication in newspapers and pamphlets facilitated an increase in knowledge and awareness about citizenship and its public expression. But beyond the printed matter, discussions, conversations, and debates were increasingly taking place in collective venues in pre-revolutionary France. Coffee houses, salons, and taverns, which had, of course, already been in existence, became sites for public dissemination of news and opinion (owing to the cost of individual purchase) and debate of the issues, ideas, and conflicts written about in newspapers and pamphlets. Journalists and editors who wrote in these newspapers mingled with owners, business people, and regular customers in these collective venues. The interactive debate between these groups of people helped to drive the content and opinion of their newspapers and pamphlets and thereby disseminated the new and changing ideas about politics and government beyond those immediately in attendance. As Habermas notes, these 18th-century coffee houses created a "public sphere" outside that of the royal court and the private realm of one's home (1991). Collectively, these coffee houses were part of and facilitated the emergence of a vibrant public debate about politics and government in this period.

While the coffee houses and taverns were more open, the salons of 18th-century Paris also had an important role in the development of public opinion in this period (Goodman, 1989). Salons were elite gatherings of politicians, philosophers, writers, wealthy business people, and other opinion leaders that were held in the homes of well-to-do women. These events consisted of performative oratory (such as plays and argument) in which participants debated the existence of God, politics, theories of social life, and engaged in criticism of the King of France. While these events occurred amongst a tiny elite, they, along with the more open coffee houses, fostered an ideational landscape that was ripe for the eventual revolutionary overthrow of the French monarchy in 1789. While somewhat different in appearance, similar dynamics in the expression and evaluation of public opinion such as town halls were percolating in the revolutionary period and early years of the United States of America.

Together the American and French examples ushered in a modern era of public opinion. Facilitated by the invention of the printing press and revolutionary fervour in the United States and France, public discussion and debate about political regimes fostered the emergence of an active public with evident opinions about politics.

Writing about the United States in the late 19th century, British author James Bryce noted that "in no country is public opinion so powerful as in the United States." He also observed that "the obvious weakness of government by opinion is the difficulty of ascertaining it" (Bryce, 1900). In the 19th century, the United States experienced profound economic, social, and political change through massive developments in manufacturing, immigration, communication, and transportation. These complex changes made it extremely difficult to accurately identify public opinion, as Bryce observed. As a means of getting an accurate handle on public opinion, politicians and their political party operatives, journalists, and average citizens increasingly took to quantitative means to understand and assess what this new complex public was thinking. These early efforts at polling and getting measurements of opinion were largely of the straw poll variety – polls in which a measure of opinion is taken from a convenience sample such as parishioners in a church, workers in a factory, readership of a newspaper or magazine, or students in a classroom, for example. As Chapter 2 makes clear, sampling procedures and good questionnaire design are pivotal to establishing a reliable estimate of opinion on any topic. Straw polls, no matter how widespread their deployment and use for political ends, would not suffice for accurately assessing public opinion.

It wasn't until the 1930s when George Gallup correctly predicted the outcome of the 1936 US presidential election that more scientific methods of collecting opinion were widely adopted. Famously, in the leadup to the 1936 election, a magazine called the *Literary Digest* asked their readership who they were going to vote for in the upcoming presidential election. With thousands of responses, the *Literary Digest* confidently predicted that Alf Landon would win the presidency. By contrast, using his fledgling and more sophisticated polling methods including methods to draw more representative samples, George Gallup predicted that Franklin Roosevelt would win. The election result showed that Gallup was right and consequently a commercial polling industry developed in the United States modelled on Gallup's early scientific methods.

Since the days of Gallup's first public opinion polls in the 1930s, commercial (market research), political (for both government and partisan purposes), and academic use of public opinion polls has skyrocketed. Born out of this early collective interest in public opinion polling, the American Association of Public Opinion Research (AAPOR) and its sister organization the World Association of Public Opinion Research (WAPOR) were founded in 1947 by leading public opinion researchers of the day. Since their founding, AAPOR and WAPOR have concerned themselves with developing and maintaining best practices regarding survey question wording, sampling methods, modes of conducting surveys (e.g., in-person, mail, phone, internet), as well as professional and ethical standards by which polling firms abide. Chapter 2 provides a thorough discussion of how public opinion polling is conducted today.

WHY STUDY PUBLIC OPINION?

Thus far, we've tried to situate the study of public opinion in a larger theoretical and historical context. This discussion fleshes out some of the historical nuances in the development of the study of public opinion and why it has been studied from theoretical and historical perspectives. All of this said, there are many reasons that can be identified for why it remains important to study public opinion. For these, we draw on five reasons that were articulated by Glynn et al. in their volume on public opinion (2004).

The first of these reasons is that "policy, in democratic states, should rest on public opinion" (Glynn et al., 2004). While there can be debate about how closely public policy should reflect public opinion, there is broad agreement that the public should have some say in the nature of policy decisions. There are two central means through which public opinion can be seen to influence politics – political institutions and public policy.

The first is in the public's opinion about democratic political institutions. Pippa Norris conceptualizes five different political objects toward or about which we can have opinions (1999). Ranging from the more general to the more specific, the public can hold opinions about *political community* through questions of allegiance, identity, and rules for membership. Here political community can include the rules for community membership (citizenship), the priority of identity when there are multiple and overlapping community memberships (national vs. subnational vs. local). For instance, public opinion might be relevant to the question of establishing or changing the rules for determining residency in a new country for immigrants or refugees and the criteria by which citizenship is granted. A little more specific than the political community is *regime principles*. At base, is the political community governed by democratic principles or some other principle of governing (authoritarian, communist, etc.)? As the countries included in this volume are all democracies, we might consider public opinion about democratic values such as freedom, equality and the rule of law in a democracy as well as the appropriate role of the state. Beyond regime principles, lies *regime performance*. Here the central question might be how well does democracy, as a set of regime principles, work in your country? It is very possible that public opinion might be divided on the performance of the democratic regime. Next are the specific *institutions* that comprise the democratic state. These could include the national legislature, subnational legislatures, the legal system, police and law enforcement, as well as electoral institutions. How confident is the public in the performance of the political institutions that govern your country? The last institution identified is that of specific *political actors*. How much trust, confidence, approval does the public have for political leaders, politicians, candidates, etc.? Across each of these parts of the institutional matrix of a country, it is arguably important to know and understand the nature of public opinion about them.

The second means of thinking about the statement that "policy, in democratic states, should rest on public opinion" is just that – the connection of policy and public opinion. While there may be theoretical debates about political representation and whether politicians should lead public opinion on policy issues or vice versa, it is important that political leaders in a democracy be to some extent aware of public opinion as they design and implement public policies.

A second reason to study public opinion is that "respect for public opinion is a safeguard against demagoguery" (Glynn et al., 2004). In countries around the world, there is always the possibility (however remote) that a single individual will assume all power of the state. Being aware of public opinion is not a sure-fire means of preventing the rise of a dictator, public opinion is a potentially effective check on political leadership within a democracy. In more mundane circumstances than an individual seizing political power, public opinion can be a contributing factor in determining the course of events when political leaders show bad judgement, are incompetent, or are corrupt. Often times, whether a politician weathers those storms or not is shaped by the tenor of public opinion.

"Public opinion can provide clues about culture" (Glynn et al., 2004). Another reason for studying public opinion is that its study helps us to understand the prevalence of collective identities, beliefs, and values in democratic publics. Knowing these cultural values through public opinion research assists in understanding how and why publics respond to certain events, threats, or scandals. For instance, think of the experience of the COVID-19 pandemic in different countries around the world. Each country has sought to meet the public health challenges of the pandemic in different ways. Arguably, knowing about the unique political culture in each of these contexts assists in understanding variation in the nature of public health responses on such things as "lockdowns," capacity limits, mask mandates, and vaccine passports.

A fourth reason for studying public opinion is the argument that "public opinion must, at times, be mobilized" (Glynn et al., 2004). In this approach, public opinion is a tool to be used by politicians in support of political initiatives. Historically conceived of in the context of war, understanding public opinion and how it can be shaped or influenced is important to building widespread support for major policy initiatives such as declaring war on another state, introducing significant expansion or retrenchment of the public sector, or committing to international environmental agreements.

A final reason for studying public opinion is that "public opinion can set the boundaries of acceptable action" of public authorities (Glynn et al., 2004). While related to some of the earlier reasons for studying public opinion, this reason suggests a relationship between the public and the political class. Knowing the public's position on existing issues as well as new or emerging issues gives politicians a sense of what the possible range of actions might be that are acceptable or plausible in the mind of the public. For instance, every few years, thousands of representatives from countries around the world attend the Conference of the Parties (COP) meetings under the United Nations Framework Convention on Climate Change to discuss a comprehensive plan to combat climate change. In 2021, COP26 met in Glasgow, Scotland. Arguably public opinion in the home country of each national group of representatives serves to set the boundary range within which these participants negotiate. While this may make finding agreement more difficult, it also helps to understand where and when agreement might be found.

WHY THIS VOLUME (AS OPPOSED TO OTHER EXISTING VOLUMES)?

Given the scope of the public opinion field, there are many excellent introductory books about public opinion. These books do a nice job outlining the history, methods, context, and uses of public opinion and its academic and professional study. However, through our collective experience of teaching and researching in the field of public opinion over the last 20 years, we observed a commonality amongst all of these books – each one was empirically focussed on the United States. It is certainly true that the United States has been *a* if not *the* leading democracy over the last 200 years of human history and that the academic study of public opinion and political behaviour within universities and colleges in the United States has flourished unlike anywhere else in the world. Indeed, as referenced above, the founder of modern public opinion survey methods, George Gallup, was American. We know, however, that countries all around the world have publics who develop and express opinions about politics as well. Yet little has been written and published on other countries in a truly comparative manner. This gap in accessible, published academic work on public opinion is the central opening in the academic marketplace that this book aims to fill. What follows is a comprehensive, high quality, edited book about public opinion in the democratic world *inclusive of but not exclusive to the United States*. Democratic publics that make a prominent appearance in this book include Australia, Belgium, Brazil, Canada, Germany, France, Italy, Japan, Portugal, Switzerland, the United Kingdom, and the United States. We believe that this edited volume makes an independent and important scholarly contribution to the study of public opinion while simultaneously being appropriate for adoption in undergraduate and graduate courses on comparative public opinion and political behaviour.

WHY IMMIGRATION AS A POLICY FOCUS?

In today's world, mass publics could be concerned about numerous issues and many of them would be good candidates to illustrate and explain public opinion. Indeed, as editors of this book on comparative public opinion, we felt that we needed to identify an issue that would be important and salient in countries around the world. We could look at immigration, the environment and climate change, globalization of economies and international trade, the COVID-19 pandemic response and recovery, etc.

Ultimately, we settled on immigration and, more specifically, how mass publics perceive immigrants for a couple of reasons. The first is that immigration and perceptions of immigrants continue to be a timely issue. For instance, since the early 1970s, the number of international migrants has increased threefold (McAuliffe and Khadria, 2019). According to the latest available figures, there were over 281 million international migrants in 2020, representing 3.6% of the world's population. This degree of migration has massive political, economic, and social implications for both the countries from which migrants have left as well as the countries where migrants plan to or hope to settle. Beyond the scale of the qualitative implication of immigration, virtually every country around the globe is impacted either as a source country of migrants, as a temporary site of transition for migrants on the move, or as a settlement country. Simply put, immigration affects all countries and regions of the world. For decades, it has shaped domestic and global politics and stirred important societal debates. The issue has become a cornerstone for many political parties and voters and is not likely to recede anytime soon. Given the prominence, ubiquity, and longevity of the immigration issue, we believe that this issue constitutes an excellent candidate around which to explore the dynamics of public opinion.

Additionally, we needed a policy issue for which there was good comparative data on public opinion. We wanted this volume to have both individual country case studies and also truly comparative analyses. Among the range of possible policy issues we mention, we could only locate good data for the issue of immigration. In particular, Module 5 of the Comparative Study of Electoral Systems (CSES) contained some excellent questions on immigration that were asked in many countries (see the discussion in Chapter 3 of the value and utility of this data set). As a result, armed with a pressing issue of public policy and good comparative data with which to explore it, we chose to focus on the issue of immigration.

PLAN FOR THE BOOK

This volume is comprised of three separate parts. Part 1 includes this chapter (the introduction) as well as a chapter on defining and measuring public opinion. Together these chapters are intended to provide a thorough introduction to central topics in the study of public opinion and how to go about ascertaining what public opinion is.

The second part of the book is composed of nine chapters that are centrally organized around a common approach. Almost every chapter in Part 2 includes a comparative analysis of public opinion on immigration from a set of nine countries (Australia, Canada, France, Germany, Italy, Portugal, Switzerland, the United Kingdom, and the United States). Each of these chapters draws, in whole or in part, on a unifying dataset (Module 5 of the Comparative Study of Electoral Systems – CSES). Module 5 of the CSES has a battery of three very good questions about immigration that have been asked of representative samples of voters in all nine countries listed above, making it possible to explore the determinants of public opinion about immigration in a unifying way. Note that the data from Module 5 were also collected in the past two to three years making the contributions of the volume both timely and relevant. Part 2 is also organized in a way to examine the determinants of public opinion about immigration through adopting a theoretical lens that covers not only demographic (age, gender, ethnicity, and religion) and socioeconomic (class and income) determinants of public opinion, but also the role of ideology, partisanship, and personality. As such, each chapter dedicates time to provide a thorough literature review of their determinant of interest before conducting a straightforward empirical analysis (using the CSES data) that is communicated in easy-to-interpret figures. The main comparative figures have been centrally produced by the editors and follow the same format in all chapters. Depending on the chapter, some of the author(s) of the Part 2 chapters have chosen to delve more deeply into exploring some of the country differences or other aspects particular to one or two country cases. However, preceding these "determinant-specific" chapters of Part 2, an introductory chapter introduces the policy area of interest (immigration), discusses the specific measures used in the CSES on immigration opinion, and explores the distribution of opinion on these questions in the set of nine countries.

The third part of the volume continues the emphasis on understanding immigration opinion and some chapters also consider opinions on environmental protection and the globalization of the world economy. These chapters are united in two features. The first is that these chapters deepen our understanding of public opinion by highlighting the additional influence of context and attitudinal complexity on public opinion about immigration and these related issues. In particular, these chapters consider the effects of partisan polarization, locally experienced immigrant diversity, labour market vulnerability, linguistic cleavage, media coverage, and racial attitudes. Secondly, beyond deepening our theoretical understanding, these chapters are united in their use of more sophisticated statistical analyses to consider these relationships.

The last section of the volume consists of a concluding chapter. This chapter includes a comprehensive model including most of the factors considered by individual chapters from Part 2 on immigration opinion. The concluding chapter closes by summarizing central themes and findings from the volume, highlighting contributions and identifying some potential limitations of the work.

SUMMARY POINTS

- The chapter began with positioning the study of public opinion in broader philosophical debates about democracy (including classical democracy, democratic elitism, and participatory democracy) and the role of the citizen in democratic practice.
- The chapter briefly considered the historical development of the concept and study of public opinion from the ancient Greeks to the coffee houses of 17th-century France to the contemporary practices of public opinion research.

SUGGESTED FURTHER READINGS

Achen, C.H. and Bartels, L.M., 2017. *Democracy for realists*. Princeton: Princeton University Press.
Held, D., 1996. *Models of democracy*. Stanford, CA: Stanford University Press.
Shapiro, R.Y. and Jacobs, L.R., eds., 2011. *The Oxford handbook of American public opinion and the media*. Oxford: Oxford University Press.

SOURCES

Achen, C.H. and Bartels, L.M., 2017. *Democracy for realists*. Princeton: Princeton University Press.
American Association of Public Opinion Research. Available from: https://www.aapor.org/ [Accessed 26 November 2021].
Anderson, B., 1983. *Imagined communities*. London: Verso.
Barber, B., 1984. *Strong democracy: Participatory politics for a new age*. Berkeley, CA: University of California Press.
Bryce, J., 1900. *The American commonwealth*. New York: Macmillan.
Carpini, M.X.D. and Keeter, S., 1996. *What Americans know about politics and why it matters*. New Haven, CT: Yale University Press.
Clawson, R.A. and Oxley, Z.M., 2017. *Public opinion: Democratic ideals, democratic practice*. 3rd ed. Thousand Oaks, CA: CQ Press.
Glynn, C., Herbst, S., O'Keefe, G., Shapiro, R., and Lindeman, M., 2004. *Public opinion*. Boulder, CO: Westview.
Goodman, D., 1989. Enlightenment salons: The convergence of female and philosophic ambitions. *Eighteenth-Century Studies*, 22(3), 329–350.
Habermas, J., 1991. *The structural transformation of the public sphere: An inquiry into a category of bourgeois society*. Cambridge, MA: MIT Press.
Herbst, S., 2012. The history and meaning of public opinion. In: A. Berinsky, ed. *New directions in public opinion*. London: Routledge, pp. 19–31.
Hibbing, J.R. and Theiss-Morse, E., 2002. *Stealth democracy: Americans' beliefs about how government should work*. New York: Cambridge University Press.
Hobsbawm, E., 2012. Introduction: Inventing traditions. In: E. Hobsbawm and T. Ranger, eds. *The invention of tradition*. New York: Cambridge University Press, pp. 1–14.
Lindblom, C.E., 1977. *Politics and markets*. New York: Basic Books.

McAuliffe, M. and Khadria, B., 2019. Report overview: Providing perspective on migration and mobility in increasingly uncertain times. *World Migration Report 2020*, McAuliffe and Khadria, pp. 1–14.

Minar, D.W., 1960. Public opinion in the perspective of political theory. *Western Political Quarterly*, 13(1), 31–44.

Norris, P., 1999. Introduction: The growth of critical citizens? In: P. Norris, ed. *Critical citizens: Global support for democratic government*. New York: Oxford University Press, pp. 1–30.

Rugeley, C. and Jackson, R.A., 2009. Getting on the rolls: Analyzing the effects of lowered barriers on voter registration. *State Politics & Policy Quarterly*, 9(1), 56–78.

Schumpeter, J., 1976. *Capitalism, socialism and democracy*. 5th ed. London: Allen and Unwin.

Thucydides., 1991. *History of the Peloponnesian War, books I and II*, trans. Charles Smith. Cambridge, MA: Harvard University Press.

CHAPTER 2

Defining and measuring public opinion

....

Cameron D. Anderson and Mathieu Turgeon

INTRODUCTION

At the outset of this volume, we think it imperative to address some topics of central concern to the study of public opinion. One of these is the appropriate definition and understanding of the term "public opinion." The second is to consider the process of and issues around measuring public opinion. Both of these topics have elicited a wide range of responses in the literature and it is our intent to shed some light on these discussions and debates. We start with the definition of public opinion before treating issues of measurement.

DEFINING PUBLIC OPINION

While the concept of public opinion is essential in democratic theory and practice, it is not particularly easy to define. When the term "public opinion" is thrown out in media or popular discourse, there is often a presumption of the correct understanding of the term. In this vein, the notion of public opinion as the "voice of the people" can often come to mind. Under this "voice" assumption, public opinion is referenced as a certain percentage of an identified population dis/agree with a particular statement about politics or a public issue. For instance, in the age of the COVID-19 pandemic, we might see reporting on public support or opposition to "vaccine passports." In this case, there might be public opinion polling reports of some percentage of the population who "agree" or "strongly agree" with the adoption of a common form of documentation to demonstrate one's vaccination status. So how we understand public opinion is extremely important when we think about how the concept of public opinion can be used and drawn upon in public and policy discourse.

Scholarly treatments of the concept of public opinion have originated from many different disciplines within the social sciences and each tends to bring its own

DOI: 10.4324/9781003121992-3

definitional understanding of the concept. As a result, it is difficult to arrive at one commonly accepted definition. As such, at the outset, it is particularly important to consider our definitions and understandings of public opinion. In so doing, we think it is helpful to consider the constituent terms of "public" and "opinion" initially.

Public

We start with the term "public." What constitutes the public? One way to approach answering this question is to consider some other groupings of people and to explore how they differ. As such, we will explore what is meant by "public" in contrast to the concepts of "crowd" and "mass."

In the early 20th century, a new science of crowd psychology developed. One of the central questions asked by this work was how people were collectively enticed to do things that they would never dream of doing alone. One of the earliest theories of crowd psychology emerged from a French academic named Gustave Le Bon (1948). Le Bon proposed that there were three features of a crowd that elicited this changed human behaviour: (1) the anonymity of being in a crowd loosened civil restrictions over one's baser instincts, (2) emotions and actions could spread rapidly spontaneous imitation and contagion, and (3) the "conscious personality vanishes" under the influence of a crowd. Starting with Le Bon's work and extending out over the 20th century, the concept of crowd has come to be defined by a "unity of emotional experience" and the sense that a "crowd develops in response to shared emotions." To put it into plain terms, think of yourself at a sporting event or rock concert of your favourite band or artist. At these events, we easily get caught up cheering (or booing!), singing, and/or dancing along with everyone else at the event. Of course, standing at the bus stop and trying to get other transit users to cheer wildly when the bus arrived would make little sense and probably be quite awkward!

While crowds are defined by a shared emotional experience, masses of people are defined by interpersonal isolation. Herbert Blumer notes that a mass "is composed of separate detached and anonymous individuals who engage in very little interaction or communication and who respond to events based on their own needs" (1946). A mass of people is extremely heterogeneous. It includes people from all strata of society and all walks of life. The concept of mass entails geographical dispersion and loose organization such that members of the mass are unable to act collectively. There is little beyond immediate self-interest or need that ties people together. We might think of masses as including people who are affected (perhaps excited or concerned) by events of national or international importance or interest.

One way of thinking about a mass, is in the answer to the question of "where were you when"? For Americans old enough to remember, one could ask, where were you when you first found out about the 9/11 attacks in New York City and Washington? In other countries, there might be a significant athletic accomplishment in the Olympics and one could ask, where were you when you watched or heard about the event? Regardless of the specific example, the idea of the mass in response to major events is that we experience and respond to these events in emotional and geographic isolation, the response is experienced regardless of your economic or social position in society and there is virtually no ability to collectively act in response to some event.[1]

We now consider the definition of a public in contrast to that of a crowd and a mass. When assessing the concept of a public against that of a crowd, both the crowd and the public are characterized by a kind of collective force (or will). However, where the crowd is marked by a unity of emotional experience (everyone cheering the home team!), the public is characterized by opposition and rational discourse. Whereas the crowd develops in response to shared emotions, the public organizes in response to an issue. Put another way, participating in the crowd only requires one's ability to feel and empathize with others. By contrast, joining the public additionally requires the ability to think and reason with others. For the difference between public and mass, the central difference is the public is "self-aware," unlike a mass. Additionally, individuals within a public are as capable of expressing opinions as they are of receiving them. Taken together then, we follow Blumer in defining public "as a group of people who are confronted by an issue, who are divided in the ideas as to how to meet the issue and who engage in discussion over the issue" (1948).

While we can provide this kind of definition of public, we can also draw on the work of Vincent Price to consider "types of publics" (1992). Price works to disentangle the concept of public into types of publics and we think that this helps to provide a little more context and specificity to understanding the concept of public. The first type of public is the "general public." This notion refers to a given population in its entirety whereby the general public is usually circumscribed by some form of political jurisdiction or geographical boundary. Here we might think of a general public as the population of an entire country, a subnational region (province, state, Lander), or even a local region like a city or municipality.

We might also conceive of public as the "voting public." This conception of the public makes a distinction between the general public and some smaller subset of the public that turns out to vote in elections – "the electorate." While turnout rates vary cross-nationally and across levels of government within a state, the designation of a voting public makes an important distinction between individuals based on a minimum level of political involvement. Of course, the voting public is going to be a subset of the general public because turnout rates are well below 100% in most jurisdictions.

A further distinction is to identify something called the "attentive public." The attentive public might best be understood as those individuals interested in policy problems and who constitute the relevant audience for policy elites such as politicians, political parties, think tanks, etc. The attentive public is distinguished from the voting public by its attention to and knowledge about politics. Despite the fact that the voting public minimally participates in politics, not all members of the voting public will pay close attention to and be knowledgeable about politics. Some estimates place the attentive public at between 30–50% of the general population (Price, 1992).

Beyond the attentive public, a further delineation of the concept highlights the "active public." The active public is characterized by actual engagement in public affairs through both formal means such as contributing to political parties, being a member of a political party, attending rallies or protests, as well as information participation such as public discussion and debate with others. By some measures, the active public constitutes about 15% of the attentive public and we might refer to the active public as elites. These elites could include political elites (such as party leadership and their party operatives, elected representatives, etc.), bureaucratic elites (those working with or within government bureaucracies), interest elites (leaders and members of interest and protest groups), and communication elites (members of the mass media). This type of public clearly designates a subset of individuals who are qualitatively more interested, knowledgeable, and involved than the attentive public.

The last kind of public identified by Price is an "issue public." The concept of an issue public arises from the observation that there can be variation in the extent of interest and attentiveness across policy issues and through time. There are two ideas here. The first is that public discussion and debate can ebb and flow on the same issue over time and that at any one time there may be more or less focus on a particular issue. For instance, think about the Brexit debates in the UK over the last number of years. While there have always been Eurosceptics within British society and public opinion, the attention of British public opinion became focussed on the Brexit issue in the leadup to a referendum on the issue and the aftermath of dealing with the result. The second is that depending on the issue at hand there is likely some variation in the importance of the issue across the general public and the likelihood of taking an opinion position on the issue. For example, think of an issue like gun control. In some countries and for some people this is a very salient issue. In the United States, there is a public issue around the topic of gun control with many people ardently in favour of stricter gun controls and many others equally opposed to gun control legislation. The public issue emerges in the self-selection of individuals into the taking of opinions on either side of the issue.

This discussion of the term "public" has articulated how we think of the concept – what it is and what it is not. As well, we have tried to nuance the term "public" by thinking about how we might consider variations in types of publics. We now turn our attention to exploring the concept of opinion.

Opinion

The second key term to define is that of "opinion." In everyday discourse, we easily talk about having opinions on all manner of things. Whether it be your favourite movies or music groups or whether you like a new restaurant in your city or whether your favourite sports team is likely to do well in the upcoming season, we have opinions about everything. It's helpful though to think a little bit about how we understand the concept of an opinion.

In the world of political behaviour and public opinion research, the words "opinion" and "attitude" are often used interchangeably. While we will do the same throughout this volume, as the words are clearly related, we think it helpful to articulate how we conceive of these words differently in the effort to define what we think an opinion is. When looking to define opinion, we think that it is helpful to start with the concept of an attitude. The field of psychology has long concerned itself with understanding attitudes – what they are and how they operate – and so we draw on some work from that field to commence our discussion. Two useful definitions of an attitude are the following: "Attitude is a psychological tendency that is expressed by evaluating a particular entity with some degree of favor or disfavor" (Eagly and Chaiken, 1993) and "a general and enduring positive or negative feeling about some person, object or issue" (Petty and Cacioppo, 1981).

Based on these definitions, there are a couple of key things to highlight about the concept of an attitude. The first is that there is a focus on the attitude. Whether it be an "entity" or a "person, object or issue," an attitude develops in response to some kind of target. In the world of politics and public opinion, attitudes may be held towards political parties, politicians (generally or specific individuals), institutions of government (legislatures, courts, bureaucracies as well as national/subnational and supranational institutions), not to mention specific issues of public policy (from trade and foreign policy to health and criminal justice and everything in between), and even events.

The second feature of an attitude evident from these definitions is that an attitude involves an affective orientation towards a target. This entails an evaluation of the target that is either positive or negative; liking or disliking. For example, you might have positive evaluations of the governing political party and members from that party and negative evaluations of the opposition parties and their members. Or you might have a positive evaluation of a longstanding public policy. In Canada, for example, publicly funded health care has been around since the 1960s and most Canadians view this policy so favourably that it is often considered part of the national fabric of Canada. We should also note that attitudes might also be affectively neutral in that one doesn't have a strong positive or negative response to some political target. Or that you view some aspects of a target positively and some aspects negatively and as such the balance cancels out to an effectively neutral position. A third feature of these definitions is slightly more subtle but no less important to our understanding of what an attitude is. This is that an attitude is a "psychological tendency" or an "enduring feeling." In this vein, the concept of attitude lies in the unspoken and underlying orientations that each of us holds about the world around us.

Based upon this discussion outlining what an attitude is, we suggest that there might be three ways in which to disentangle the concept of opinion from attitude. The first is that opinions can be considered as observable responses (verbal or otherwise) to an issue or question while attitudes are covert, psychological predispositions or tendencies. The key difference here is in the expressing of the sentiment – attitudes are underlying orientations and opinions are expressions of those attitudes. While both attitudes and opinions imply approval or disapproval towards some target (e.g., person, institution policy issue), for many a second point of difference is that attitudes generally refer to affect (fundamentally liking or disliking something) and opinion is more characterized by cognition and a conscious decision to support or oppose the aforementioned target. While debatable and admittedly subtle, the key difference is that attitudes relate more to emotional orientations and opinions more to thoughtful and conscious deliberation. The last point of difference is that attitudes can be thought of as globally enduring orientations to a general class of targets while opinions might be more viewed situationally, as pertaining to a specific issue in a particular setting. In this way, attitudes are thought of as being continually held and opinions denote the focussed and specific application of those underlying attitudes to a delimited target.

As an example to illustrate the differences noted here, think of responding to an online public opinion survey about political support in your country. As you enter into completing the survey, you no doubt hold a range of underlying and enduring psychological predispositions and orientations (or attitudes) towards politics, politicians, the political system, and the functioning of government in your country. As you complete the public opinion survey, one question asks you to rate the job performance over the past year of your country's Prime Minister or President on a scale from 0 to 10 where 0 denotes a "bad job" and 10 indicates a "great job." As you consider your answer to this question, the transition from attitude to opinion becomes evident. The first is that your answer is an observable expression of your sentiment about the politician's job performance. Second, you have considered your answer and have indicated your rating of job performance. Third, you have taken what are perhaps enduring but general predispositions about politics, politicians, and the political system and applied them to a specific target and within a specific context.

To summarize, opinions and attitudes are clearly related. The terms will be used interchangeably at times throughout this book as they are in political science and public opinion literatures more generally. This said, we think that in trying to highlight some potential differences between the concepts of attitude and opinion we have given a more precise understanding of each.

Before closing this discussion, we would be remiss not to consider heterogeneity in the concept of opinions. In the first instance, opinions clearly vary based on the direction of the sentiment. Taking our example of PM or Presidential approval, very simply, do you think the PM/President is doing a good job (6–10 on the scale), a bad job (0–4), or neither good nor bad (5)? Beyond the basic direction is the extremity of the opinion position taken. This is to say, how far from the neutral position is your opinion on the job performance of the PM/President? Do you moderately approve (6–7) or moderately disapprove (3–4) of the job performance of the political leader? Conversely, do you take a much more extreme position and think that they are doing a really great job (9–10) or a really bad job (0–1)? The last feature is the importance or salience of the issue or topic. Here the question is how important the topic is to you. There are lots of topics about which you might have opinions but it isn't necessarily the case that you'll have strong opinions on every single issue (Miller and Peterson, 2004).

MEASURING PUBLIC OPINION

> Polls are the worst way of measuring public opinion and public behavior, or of predicting elections – except for all the others.
>
> Humphrey Taylor, chairman of *The Harris Poll*

Now that we have defined public opinion, we can address the issue of how to measure it. There is not a unique way of measuring public opinion, but there is clearly a dominant one. Mass protests, elections, referendums, and plebiscites can inform us about public opinion, but the opinion poll is by far the preferred and most frequently used means of measuring public opinion. Conducting an opinion poll – or survey – is not an easy task and requires researchers and pollsters alike to make many decisions, including *who* to interview, *how* to interview, and *what* to ask of those being interviewed. Below, we address these concerns that must be considered to assess adequately the public will.

The first question of interest in conducting an opinion poll is *who* should be interviewed? The answer to this question depends on the population of interest about which we would like to learn about: Canadian voters, Paris residents, Bavarian adults, American college students, etc. Frequently, the population of interest is too large to conceivably interview all of its members. Censuses – the procedure to systematically survey all members of a population of interest – are very expensive and time-consuming. Instead, pollsters draw a sample of respondents from the population of interest to make inferences, that is, generalizations, about the larger population (with a degree of uncertainty). Good samples, that is, samples that carry as close as possible the characteristics of the population of interest, are not easily drawn. Many hurdles present themselves and each must be passed successfully to achieve a representative sample of respondents.

The first hurdle concerns the selection of respondents to form a survey sample. Respondents should be chosen following a procedure that involves chance – that is, respondents should be chosen randomly – where each member of the population has an *equal* chance of being included in the sample. This procedure is called simple random sampling (SRS) and is easily performed when there exists an exhaustive list of all members of the population of interest. In that case, a computer can easily select respondents by simple random sampling to build a survey sample. In most situations, however, such a list does not exist, and pollsters must proceed differently. To select a representative sample of Australian voters, for example, one could use information from the last national census to decide first how many respondents should be interviewed from each of Australia's states and territories. More populous states should proportionately include more respondents in the survey sample. We frequently refer to these units as the primary sampling units (PSUs). Within each PSU, one can follow the same procedure using a smaller geographical unit to define, again, how many respondents should be selected from these subunits. This procedure commonly ends at the city block or rural area where residential units and respondents within the residential units are chosen randomly.

Random digit dialling (RDD) is also another procedure that can be used, although it is less frequently used now that most people have mobile phones instead of land-lines. The idea behind RDD is simple: randomly select phone numbers and once a household is reached, randomly select a member of that household to be interviewed. Random digit dialling was extensively used when most households had landlines – meaning most members of a population of interest could be easily reached – but before they were replaced by mobile phones. The main issue with mobile phones is that most national legislations prohibited pollsters from calling them, given the high costs associated with their use. Also, some people have more than one mobile phone (or chip in their mobile phone), increasing their probability of being selected in the sample and thus violating the property of equal chance of being drawn in the sample.

Random digit dialling or selecting respondents from primary sampling units maintains the idea that each procedure selects respondents *randomly*, only that each is adapted, in part, to the mode by which respondents will respond to the survey questions (although this is not necessary). Distortions in the representativity of the sample are introduced when some potential respondents are systematically excluded or are simply harder to reach than other respondents. For example, random digit dialling excludes all households who do not have a phone. Homeless people, for their part, will systematically be excluded from samples that use primary sampling units to select residential units. Similarly, rich people living in gated communities are also very hard to reach, if not inaccessible.

Random sampling is desirable because it produces samples that are more repre-sentative of the population of interest than would non-random samples, for exam-ple. Moreover, random sampling also allows the quantification of uncertainty about one's sample by calculating sampling errors and confidence intervals for estimates of interest. Despite the known advantages of random sampling, we have observed in recent years a notable increase in the use of non-random samples, especially for opin-ion polls conducted online. Most online samples seek representativeness by adopt-ing quotas from what we know about the population's characteristics (obtained via census). If a population has 20% of its people with a college degree, then the sample should also have 20% of its respondents with that level of education. Quota samples frequently rely on population characteristics like gender, age, income, education, and region. Convenience samples are also non-random samples and are composed of members of the population of interest that are easy to reach or contact like sub-scribers of a magazine. Convenience and quota samples, however, are generally not as representative as random samples and do not afford to quantify the uncertainty around them.

A second important hurdle concerns respondents agreeing to be interviewed. In recent decades, we have seen an important drop in respondents' willingness to par-ticipate in surveys.[2] Specifically, it is not uncommon to see response rates as low as 10%! The problem is that those that refuse to be interviewed (labelled unit nonre-sponses) frequently share common characteristics, meaning that they do not refuse to participate at random. In other words, there is a relationship between their atti-tudes and the decision to partake in a survey. In general, survey nonrespondents, when compared to respondents, have busier lives, are more educated, have higher income, etc. Their exclusion from the sample introduces important distortions in the representativeness of the sample. The same happens when some respondents accept to participate but fail to complete the survey or refuse to answer some questions (labelled item nonresponses).

Pollsters are fully aware of these hurdles and know how negatively they affect the representativeness of their samples. To recover some of the losses in representativeness, pollsters commonly use weights. For example, if women are overrepresented in a sample, pollsters can give less weight to women in their analyses to correct for such overrepresentation. Pollsters can compare the characteristics of their sample with those from the latest census to evaluate if some groups of respondents are over or underrepresented in their sample and apply a correction before drawing descriptive and/or causal inferences. Weights are helpful but they are no panacea to a bad sample.

The next question is *how* respondents should be interviewed. There are essentially four modes to survey people. A first mode is face-to-face interviews, labelled FTF. In face-to-face interviews, interviewers ask questions in person and record their answers. FTF interviews can take place in many settings but are frequently conducted in the respondents' homes. A second common mode is telephone interviews where interviewers also ask questions, but, this time, over the phone. At times, automated voice calls ask the questions to respondents. A third mode, and one increasingly adopted by pollsters, is online surveys where respondents answer questions autonomously on their computers, tablets, or phones. Similarly, respondents can autonomously answer mail surveys by hand that they return, also by mail, to pollsters.

The choice between these different modes may depend on several considerations. One important consideration is cost. Online and mail surveys are cheaper than telephone surveys, which are themselves cheaper than face-to-face surveys. In choosing which mode to use, pollsters also have to consider how respondents will be reached, how questions are to be delivered to respondents to engage them to cooperate, the nature of the questions asked, and how respondents will provide answers. For example, face-to-face and telephone surveys are superior to both online and mail surveys to build *rapport* – that is, a feeling of connectedness and trust between the interviewer and the respondent – which, in turn, generally improves respondents' cooperation and attention to survey questions. Similarly, online and mail surveys are not adequate for some populations like those without a fixed address or access to the internet and those who do not know how to read and/or write. Online and mail surveys, however, provide for greater privacy in responses and are, consequently, superior to both face-to-face and telephone surveys when the questions tap sensitive issues or behaviours. In sum, each mode of interview has its advantages and shortcomings and, depending on the target population and nature of the survey, pollsters can choose wisely which mode is most adequate for their study.

The third and last question concerns *what* to ask of those being interviewed. As discussed earlier, pollsters frequently pursue three objectives: (1) describe some underlying characteristics of the target population like the popularity of a government; (2)

explain social phenomena like why some people support and others oppose state intervention in the provision of healthcare services; and (3) predict future outcomes like an upcoming election. To do so, pollsters need to elaborate questions that allow them to adequately measure concepts of interest like government popularity, support for healthcare services, and vote intentions, for example. This is a question of measure *validity*. Pollsters, however, must also be worried about the elaboration of questions that are *reliable*, that is, questions that elicit consistent and dependable answers. In other words, a question is reliable when, asked repeatedly of the same respondent, it produces the same answer each time (provided the same time period). Finally, respondents should have a common understanding of what questions to ask.

We can distinguish from two question formats: closed and open-ended questions. Closed-ended questions are questions for which respondents choose an answer from a pre-defined list of response options. These include questions with response answers like "Yes" or "No" and "True" or "False" but also others with more choices like, for example, one about marital status: "Single," "Married," "Widowed," "Divorced," etc. Other closed-ended questions are those where respondents indicate agreement on a scale. These scales, known as Likert scales, generally measure agreement from "strongly agree" to "strongly disagree" but not exclusively so. Other closed-ended questions ask respondents how they "feel" about some elected officials, political parties, or groups of people on scales of varying length (e.g., 0–7, 0–10, 0–100) where the lower and upper bounds indicate extreme dislike and likeability, respectively. They can also be placement questions where respondents place themselves on a scale like one on ideology from, say, "Extreme-left" to "Extreme-right."

Open-ended questions are questions where respondents are asked to provide an answer freely without having to choose from a pre-defined list of response options. This question format is appropriate when the list of response options is excessively long or when it is impossible to dress an exhaustive list of options. It is also adequate when respondents are asked to provide a specific value. For some types of questions, like questions tapping knowledge, for example, offering response options may encourage respondents to guess. Moreover, open-ended questions may elicit more spontaneous answers than closed-ended questions. In such circumstances, open-ended questions can sometimes be more desirable.

Closed-ended questions, however, are generally preferred to open-ended questions for four reasons. First, it is conceivable to elaborate a relatively short but exhaustive list of response options for most survey questions such that presenting these questions as open-ended makes little sense. Second, by pre-defining the response options, pollsters have greater clarity as to what the answers mean. Third, closed-ended questions are less prone to error, both at the data collection and interpretation (coding) stages of the research. Fourth, and finally, closed-ended questions are easier to analyze than open-ended questions. Not surprisingly, pollsters are generally more likely to rely on closed-ended questions in their surveys.

There are other notable features of survey questions to consider when elaborating them so that they are valid, reliable, and are equally well understood by survey respondents. In particular, survey questions should be clear, unambiguous, and objective. This means that survey questions should avoid sophisticated or rarely used words and loaded language. Preferably, survey questions should also be short and concise and avoid negatives, or worse, double negatives. Pollsters should also avoid double-barreled questions, that is, questions that tap on two or more issues while allowing for only one answer.

Pollsters should also be concerned about response bias in surveys. Response bias occurs when respondents lie or do not respond accurately to survey questions. For example, respondents may over or underrepresent their true opinions or preferences in order to portray themselves in a more favourable light. Respondents can exaggerate their level of interest in politics or news consumption, for example, because they know that such attitudes and behaviours are valued by society. Respondents can also lie about their true opinions to make them more in line with social norms, especially when it concerns socially sensitive issues like race, gender, or sexual orientation. Racially prejudiced respondents, for example, are not likely to respond honestly to questions about out-group members because it would not be socially desirable to do so. Instead, such respondents may portray themselves as free of prejudice. Survey researchers have proposed several solutions to circumvent response bias like providing respondents with greater anonymity in their responses or wording questions that avoid judgmental language. Others have also proposed more sophisticated techniques like the list experiment where opinions and preferences are measured indirectly at the aggregate level. Such techniques are particularly useful to uncover the "true" underlying opinions or preferences of a target population.

Somewhat relatedly, most questions in surveys are accompanied by a "Don't know" option so that respondents can select it when they simply don't know the answer to the question or to express unfamiliarity with a particular topic. There is a debate, however, about whether it is best to "force" respondents to provide a meaningful answer by not providing a "Don't know" option or simply present respondents with the option so that they can express a lack of knowledge or familiarity. This debate is particularly relevant for opinion and knowledge questions. The argument for not offering "Don't know" options to opinion questions is to encourage respondents to engage with the survey and thus avoid them going through the survey as quickly as possible. By withholding the "Don't know" option, respondents need to pay closer attention to the survey question and select the option that is closest to their opinion. Such a process requires greater effort from respondents. As for knowledge questions, the belief is that some respondents are less confident about the knowledge they hold and are more likely to select the "Don't know" option if offered to them. The presence of the "Don't know" option, therefore, would contribute to underestimating real knowledge.

Finally, pollsters should also be concerned about the length of the questionnaire and the order in which questions are asked. Short and concise questionnaires, when possible, are generally preferable to maintain respondents engaged and attentive to the questions. Pollsters want to avoid respondents putting minimal to no effort in answering questions, a tendency among survey respondents labelled satisficing. Moreover, a survey is like a discussion between an interviewer and an interviewee and thus transitions between the different sections of the questionnaire should be smooth, with language that highlights what the upcoming sections are asking about. For the same reason, intrusive and sensitive questions should also be presented late in the survey so that the interviewer can build a rapport with the respondents. As the survey progresses, respondents become more at ease and trustful and, consequently, more willing to share information that they would not otherwise.

The order in which questions are presented to respondents also matters a great deal. In particular, the answers to earlier questions can affect answers provided to questions that appear later in the questionnaire. For example, answers to two or more questions asked close to each other may encourage respondents to provide more consistent answers than they would otherwise. A notable example is the assimilation effect uncovered in the 1970s where American respondents were found to be substantially more inclined to let Soviet journalists come to the US and report the news as they see it if asked first about the Soviets letting American journalists into the Soviet Union (Hyman and Sheatsley, 1950). Similarly, earlier questions may elicit considerations that respondents would not have naturally recalled when answering later questions. Thus, vote intentions collected late in a survey, after questions about an electoral campaign and its candidates and parties, may look quite different than if asked earlier in the survey.

As the discussion above suggests, measuring public opinion through polls is no easy task. The possibilities for errors are numerous, and the sources of errors are to be found along the survey lifecycle (from the survey design to the analysis stage, including when respondents are selected into a sample and when questionnaires are applied). The Total Survey Error (TSE) approach or paradigm allows pollsters and researchers alike to evaluate survey quality. But there is more to assessing error in survey design. New challenges also emerge as technology progresses and societies evolve. Thankfully, pollsters have learned and continue to learn a great deal about how to mitigate errors in surveys and adapt to new challenges. One such new challenge concerns the growing interest in comparative public opinion research, where pollsters seek to uncover population characteristics, explain social phenomena, and predict future outcomes in more than one country. We conclude this chapter with a brief discussion of the challenges associated with measuring public opinion in a comparative perspective, also frequently referred to as "3MC" surveys (surveys conducted in multinational, multiregional, and multicultural contexts).[3] This discussion is helpful to understand the contributions to Part 2 chapters where we seek to explain public opinion towards immigration in nine countries using survey data from the Comparative Study of Electoral Systems (CSES).

The most fundamental challenge to 3MC surveys concerns the development of survey instruments that are comparable or equivalent across countries, cultures, or regions. Specifically, how can we make sure that respondents in one specific context, say France, understand a survey question the same way as a respondent from the Philippines would. The conceptual equivalency problem relates to the idea that a certain concept may not exist or have the exact same meaning across countries, cultures, or regions. Concepts that are culture-specific frequently do not have an equivalent in other contexts and the goal of measurement equivalency becomes, therefore, unachievable. For example, is there an equivalent concept in English for the Portuguese word *saudade* or the French word *dépaysement*? One could translate them as nostalgia and homesickness, respectively, but native Portuguese and French speakers would certainly tell you that their meaning is somewhat different. And there are, of course, problems associated with translation. Some words or expressions simply do not have their equivalent in other languages. Take, for example, the commonly used English word *feedback*. There is no equivalent in French or Portuguese. Instead, many French and Portuguese speakers use the same word – feedback – with their rather unique way of pronouncing it! In comparative public opinion research, perfect equivalency is impossible. Pollsters, instead, should seek to maximize it but acknowledge that comparisons are never perfect.

There exist other obstacles to comparative public opinion research that can arise at any stage of the survey lifecycle. Countries with very different social and economic structures, for example, may hinder pollsters' ability to draw similarly representative national samples. Cellular telephone use or literacy rates, for example, may be comparatively high or low in some countries. These dissimilarities are frequently compounded by the fact that national surveys are conducted by different organizations, each with its own internal procedures, capacities, and limitations. Similarly, face-to-face survey data collections may represent minimal risks to interviewers in low-crime countries but substantial ones in countries plagued with violence associated with narcotrafficking, inequalities or political instability. Respondents' cultural differences can also affect 3MC surveys. Smith (2010), for example, notes that East Asian respondents tend to avoid extreme responses. Finally, data collected from comparative public opinion surveys will require harmonization so that response categories speak to the same concepts of interest. This is particularly true of sociodemographic questions asking about income and education.

Thus, in addition to the Total Survey Error discussed above concerning "single-context" surveys, pollsters conducting 3MC surveys need to be concerned about the "comparison error" (Smith, 2011). Minimization of the "comparison error" comes, in part, from the standardization of the study design and the application of strict protocols across the different contexts. The implementation of said procedures and protocols all contribute to increasing the costs associated with conducting comparative public opinion survey research.

The discussion above about 3CM only scratches the surface of a growing field within survey research. It serves to illustrate, however, the complexities associated with survey research when one seeks to compare across populations. Just like "single-context" survey research comes with its own limitations (and virtues), multiple-context survey research adds an extra layer of difficulty. The return to researchers and policy-makers, however, might be worth the added trouble.

SUMMARY POINTS

- In contrast to a crowd and a mass, the chapter defined public as "a group of people who are confronted by an issue, who are divided in the ideas as to how to meet the issue and who engage in discussion over the issue" (Blumer, 1948).
- As different from the concept of attitudes, this chapter conceives of opinions as observable responses to an issue, characterized by cognition and thought and viewed as situationally applicable.
- Conducting an opinion poll – or survey – requires researchers and pollsters alike to make many decisions, including *who* to interview, *how* to interview, and *what* to ask of those being interviewed.

NOTES

1 Of course, social media may reduce the barriers to collective emotional experience and even collective action though the geographic isolation is likely still a feature of the mass in a social media world.
2 See this recent study from the Pew Research Center: https://pewrsr.ch/2XqxgTT.
3 For more on 3MC, see the recent American Association of Public Opinion Research (AAPOR) and World Association of Public Opinion Research (WAPOR) *Task Force Report on Quality in Comparative Surveys* (2021): https://wapor.org/resources/aapor-wapor-task-force-report-on-quality-in-comparative-surveys/.

SUGGESTED FURTHER READINGS AND RESOURCES

American Association of Public Opinion Research (AAPOR). Available from: https://www.aapor.org/

Lohr, S.L., 2019. *Sampling: Design and analysis.* New York: Chapman and Hall/CRC.

Schuman, H. and Presser, S., 1996. *Questions and answers in attitude surveys: Experiments on question form, wording, and context.* Thousand Oaks: Sage.

World Association of Public Opinion Research (WAPOR). Available from: https://wapor.org/

REFERENCES

Blumer, H., 1946. Collective Behaviour. New York: Barnes and Noble.

Blumer, H., 1948. *Collective behaviour.* New York: Barnes and Noble.

Eagly, A.H. and Chaiken, S., 1993. *The psychology of attitudes.* San Diego: Harcourt Brace Jovanovich.

Hyman, H.H. and Sheatsley, P.B., 1950. The current status of American public opinion. In J. C. Payne *The Teaching of Contemporary Affairs.* Washington, DC: National Council for the Social Studies, pp. 11–34.

Le Bon, G., 1948. *The crowd: A study of the popular mind.* London: Unwin.

Miller, J.M. and Peterson, D.A., 2004. Theoretical and empirical implications of attitude strength. *The Journal of Politics,* 66(3), 847–867.

Price, V., 1992. *Public opinion.* Vol. 4. Thousand Oaks: Sage.

Petty, Richard and Cacioppo, John, 1981. Attitudes and Persuasions: Classic and Contemporary Approaches. Dubuque: William C. Brown.

Smith, T.W., 2010. The globalization of survey research. In: Janet A. Harkness et al. (Eds.), *Survey methods in multinational, multiregional, and multicultural contexts.* Hoboken: John Wiley and Sons inc, 475–484.

Smith, T.W., 2011. Refining the total survey error perspective. *International Journal of Public Opinion Research*, 23(4), 464–484.

PART 2

The individual-level determinants of public opinion

Part 2 addresses common individual-level determinants of public opinion by focusing on a single issue: immigration. This section is organized to examine the determinants of public opinion about immigration through adopting a theoretical lens that covers demographic (age, gender, ethnicity, and religion) and socioeconomic (class and income) determinants of public opinion as well as the role of personality, ideology, and partisanship. The first chapter in this section (Chapter 3) presents the issue of immigration and public opinion about it in nine countries spanning three continents. The countries are Australia, the United Kingdom, Canada, France, Germany, Italy, Portugal, Switzerland, and the United States. Public opinion about immigration is measured through three survey questions that tap respondent attitudes toward immigrants and, more specifically, about how immigrants are perceived to affect one country's economy, culture, and crime. Chapter 3 illustrates how public opinion about immigrants varies among these nine countries but also how mass publics feel differently about immigrants depending on the issue (economy, culture, or crime). Chapter 3 sets the stage for the eight chapters in Part 2 that discuss, in turn, how age, gender, ethnicity, religion, class and income, personality, ideology, and partisanship affect public opinion and, in particular, public opinion about immigrants. These eight chapters all follow a similar organization. First, they review the literature about how their determinant of concern explains public opinion, in general, and more specifically about immigration. Second, they present a simple, bivariate empirical analysis that communicates in easy-to-interpret figures the relationship between the determinants and attitudes about how immigrants impact the economy, culture, and crime rates. The empirical analysis covers all nine countries except for when there is no measure for a determinant of interest. Lastly, each chapter delves a little deeper by exploring some of the country differences or other aspects particular to one or two country cases related to the determinant in question. Together, these chapters offer a general overview of how individual-level determinants shape public opinion. In Part 3, the focus turns to the contextual determinants of public opinion.

DOI: 10.4324/9781003121992-4

Public opinion about immigration and immigrants

....

Cameron D. Anderson and Mathieu Turgeon

INTRODUCTION

Mass publics are concerned about numerous issues and many of them would be good candidates to illustrate and explain public opinion. We settled on immigration and, more specifically, how mass publics perceive immigrants. This is a timely issue, given that the number of international migrants has increased threefold in the last five decades (McAuliffe and Khadria, 2019). According to the latest available figures, there were over 281 million international migrants in 2020, representing 3.6% of the world's population. Simply put, immigration affects all countries and regions of the world. For decades, it has shaped domestic and global politics and stirred important societal debates. The issue has become a cornerstone for many political parties and voters and is not likely to recede anytime soon. Given the prominence, ubiquity, and longevity of the immigration issue, we believe that this issue constitutes an excellent candidate around which to explore the dynamics of public opinion.

We explore public opinion about immigration and immigrants using data from nine countries dispersed over three different continents. Immigration has affected these nine countries in similar but also distinct ways, influencing domestic public debates and, more importantly for present purposes, public opinion about it. As we will see in the following sections, some mass publics have a more positive perception of immigrants while others do not. The focus of Part 2, however, is not inherently to explain between-country differences but instead to examine how individual-level characteristics vary in explaining attitudes towards immigrants in different contexts. This is the task taken up by the next eight chapters, each focusing on one set of individual-level characteristics to explain public opinion about immigration and immigrants. In what follows, we present the details about

DOI: 10.4324/9781003121992-5

the data employed in Part 2. We next present the questions used to measure public opinion about immigration. And, finally, we show how mass publics in our nine countries perceive immigrants.

DATA

The data come from Module 5 of the Comparative Study of Electoral Systems (CSES) project (CSES, 2020). Since 1996, researchers from different countries have teamed up to gather a common set of public opinion and electoral behaviour data. Country participants have agreed to include a series of common questions in their respective electoral national studies that are then combined into a single data source. The survey data is accompanied by other country-level data, including information about political parties and electoral rules. So far, the CSES has conducted five modules of data collection, each focusing on specific themes. We use the data from the last module – Module 5, 2016–2021 – that focuses, in part, on citizens' perceptions of immigrants (out-groups).

A total of 58 countries participated in the data collection for Module 5 of the CSES. We selected nine countries from that group. They are Australia, the United Kingdom, Canada, France, Germany, Italy, Portugal, Switzerland, and the United States. These countries were not chosen randomly. Instead, we chose them because the contributors to this book are familiar with the politics in these countries and, more importantly, because they represent a diverse set of cases to justify a comparative analysis in Part 2. The respondent samples from the nine selected countries are representative of their voting-age populations. Samples vary from 984 respondents (UK) to 4,595 (Switzerland), with an average of about 2,300 respondents in all nine studies. Note that the analyses reported here and in the subsequent chapters of Part 2 apply a weight variable to better reflect the population's characteristics in each of the nine countries.

Module 5 of the CSES included three questions of interest to us. All three questions are about perceptions of immigrants but differ in the issue with which immigrants are frequently associated. The issues are those of the economy, crime, and culture. Each of these issues and the impact of immigrants on them can be viewed through a lens of threat perception in which the presence of more immigrants in one's country can induce a response of concern based on economic, crime, or cultural dimensions. Specifically, respondents in Module 5 of the CSES were asked the extent to which they agree or disagree with the following three statements:

1. Immigrants are generally good for [country]'s economy.
2. Immigrants increase crime rates in [country].
3. [Country]'s culture is generally harmed by immigrants.

Respondents could indicate their agreement (or disagreement) with the above statements using a five-point scale ranging from strongly disagree to somewhat disagree, neither agree nor disagree, somewhat agree, and strongly agree.

PERCEPTIONS OF IMMIGRANTS

Figures 3.1–3.3 present the distribution of attitudes about immigrants in each of the nine countries. The figures are bar graphs that indicate the percentage of respondents selecting agreement (or disagreement) with the statements about immigration. Each country is presented as a separate panel in the three figures together with the mean score on the agreement (disagreement) scale in the upper right corner. In each of Figures 3.1–3.3, higher values indicate more negative perceptions about immigrants.

Let's start with the statement about immigrants' contribution to the national economy. The statement is framed positively where agreement with the statement indicates more positive perceptions about immigrants. Figure 3.1 presents the distribution of such perceptions from strong agreement (1) to strong disagreement (5) with the statement that immigrants are generally good for the country's economy. As the mid of neutral point of the response scale is (3), scores below (above) 3 indicate positive (negative) perceptions. The average score for all nine countries together is 2.57,

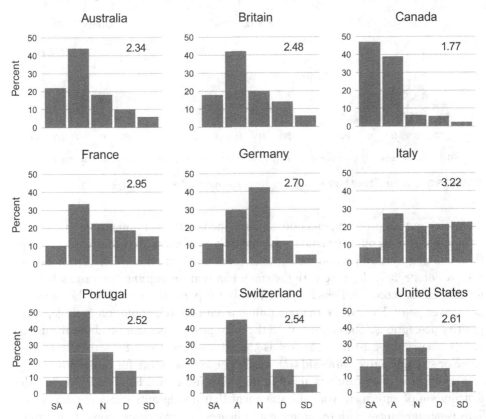

Immigrants are generally good for [COUNTRY]'s economy.

SA = Strongly agree (1); A = Agree (2); N = Neither agree nor disagree (3); D = Disagree (4); SD = Strongly disagree (5)

FIGURE 3.1 Attitudes about how immigrants are perceived to affect a country's economy.

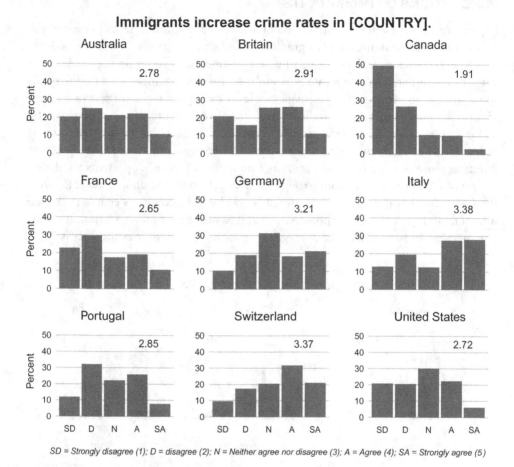

Immigrants increase crime rates in [COUNTRY].

SD = Strongly disagree (1); D = disagree (2); N = Neither agree nor disagree (3); A = Agree (4); SA = Strongly agree (5)

FIGURE 3.2 Attitudes about how immigrants are perceived to affect a country's crime.

indicating overall positive perceptions about the impact of immigrants on national economies. Among our nine countries, only Italy exhibits an overall negative perception of immigrants' impact on the national economy. More than 40% of respondents disagree or strongly disagree with the statement that immigrants are generally good for the Italian economy. French opinion is almost perfectly neutral on this question at an average of 2.95, while the remaining seven countries hold, on average, more positive perceptions. The country with the most positive perception about the immigrants' contribution to the economy is Canada, where about 85% of respondents agree or strongly agree with said statement. The average score for Canada is 1.77.

Moving next to perceptions about immigrants and crime, Figure 3.2 presents the distribution of agreement with the statement that immigrants increase crime rates. This time, agreement with the statement indicates negative perceptions about immigrants. Like with the issue of the economy discussed above, we find that Canadians hold the most positive perceptions about immigrants' impact on crime rates while

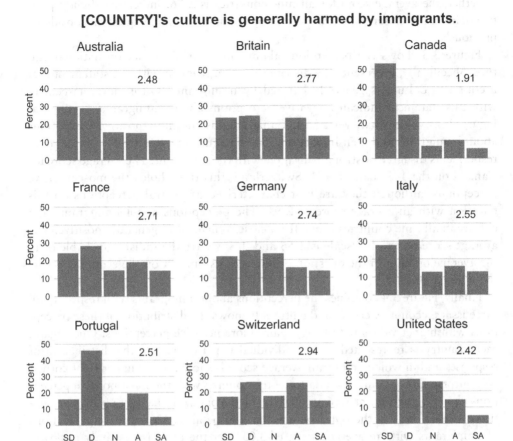

[COUNTRY]'s culture is generally harmed by immigrants.

SD = Strongly disagree (1); D = disagree (2); N = Neither agree nor disagree (3); A = Agree (4); SA = Strongly agree (5)

FIGURE 3.3 Attitudes about how immigrants are perceived to affect a country's culture.

Italians hold the most negative ones. Specifically, about 75% of Canadian respondents disagree or strongly disagree with the statement that immigrants contribute to increased crime rates while about 55% of Italians agree or strongly agree with that statement. The average scores for Canada and Italy are 1.91 and 3.38, respectively. However, in comparison to the economic issue, Italian respondents are not alone in holding more negative perceptions about immigrants and their impact on crime rates. For instance, Swiss respondents hold nearly identical negative views to Italians, with about 55% agreeing or strongly agreeing with the statement that immigrants increase crime rates. The average score for Switzerland is 3.37. The third country also exhibiting negative views on immigrants' impact on crime rates is Germany. The average scale score for German respondents was 3.21. The other five countries (Australia, the United Kingdom, France, Portugal, and the United States) all exhibited varying degrees of positive opinion about immigrants' impact on crime rates.

Together, the average score for all nine countries is 2.86, indicating slightly positive opinion but closer to neutral perceptions than the economy question considered previously.

Figure 3.3 shows the perceptions about immigrants' impact on national culture. Specifically, it presents the distribution of agreement with the statement that a country's culture is generally harmed by immigrants. Once more, agreement with this statement indicates negative perceptions about immigrants. Looking at Figure 3.3, we see that, yet again, Canada holds the most positive perceptions about immigrants and their impact on Canadian culture. Nearly 80% of Canadian respondents disagree or strongly disagree with the statement. The average score for Canada on the 1–5 scale is 1.91. Switzerland, this time, holds the most negative perceptions, although they are best characterized as neutral perceptions on this question with an average score of 2.94. The perceptions about immigrants and culture in all nine countries range from close to neutral to generally positive. The average score on the 1–5 scale is 2.56 and this is virtually indistinguishable from the average opinion in the question of immigrants' impact on the economy across these nine publics.

Finally, Figure 3.4 combines the perceptions about immigrants with respect to all three issues: economy, crime, and culture. It shows the distribution of these perceptions with higher values indicating, again, more negative perceptions. Once again, each country is represented by an individual panel displaying the distribution of responses and in which an overall average score is shown in the upper right corner. Not surprisingly, we find Canada to be the country with the most positive perceptions about immigrants at 1.86 and Italy to be the one with the least positive perceptions. In fact, Italy is the only country that, on balance, has negative perceptions of immigrants with an average score of 3.05 over the three issues. Italy is closely followed by Switzerland at 2.95. The remaining countries have, on average, more positive perceptions of immigrants across these issues with Australia being closest (but still distant) to Canada at a scale average of 2.53.

Overall, the results from Figures 3.1–3.4 show that most countries selected for our analysis have neutral or slightly positive perceptions about immigrants and that there are interesting differences between countries, with Canada and Italy being the most distinct. Canada is distinguished by consistently having more positive perceptions of immigrants in comparison to the other eight countries. We also find that perceptions differ somewhat depending on the issue at hand. In particular, most publics do not perceive immigrants to threaten or harm one's culture. The same can be said about the economy where most countries positively perceive immigrants' impact on the national economy. Views about immigrants, however, are substantially more negative with respect to crime. On this issue, opinion in three of these countries trends towards negative perceptions and many others hold rather neutral perceptions.

More importantly for present purposes, Figures 3.1–3.4 show that there is substantial variation worth explaining. This is the task taken upon in the following eight chapters (Chapters 4 to 11) where each chapter addresses a known individual-level

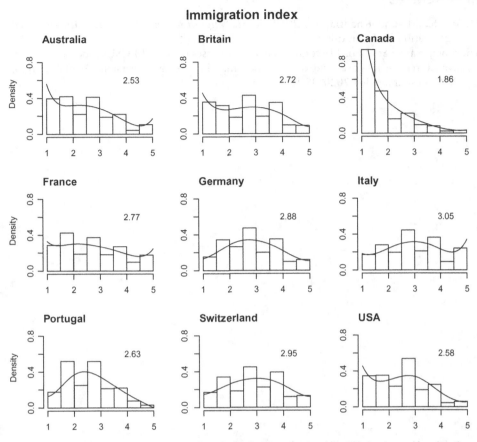

Values range from 1 to 5 with higher values indicating less favourable attitudes toward immigration.

FIGURE 3.4 Attitudes about how immigrants are perceived to affect a country's economy, crime, and culture (index).

determinant (or set of determinants) of public opinion and, in particular, public opinion about immigrants. In Chapter 4, Stephen White looks at age as a determinant of public opinion. The following chapter (Chapter 5) by Ana Espírito-Santo and João Carvalho examines the role of gender. Chapter 6 by Katrine Beauregard considers how ethnicity affects public opinion about immigrants. In Chapter 7, Tyler Romualdi, John Kennedy, and Cameron D. Anderson explore class as a determinant of public opinion. Religion, as a determinant of public opinion about immigrants, is examined next in Chapter 8 by Paul A. Djupe. Kathrin Ackermann and Jan Eckardt assess the role of personality in shaping public opinion in Chapter 9. Next, Philippe Chassé and Éric Bélanger explore ideology as a determinant of public opinion. And, finally, the last chapter of Part 2 by Laura Stephenson centres on how partisanship and partisan identity relate to public opinion.

REFERENCES

McAuliffe, M. and Khadria, B., 2019. *World migration report.* Geneva: International Organization for Migration.

The Comparative Study of Electoral Systems (www.cses.org). 2020 CSES module 5 second advance release [Dataset and documentation]. May 14, 2020 version. Available from: 10.7804/cses.module5.2020-05-14

CHAPTER 4

Age and public opinion

....

Stephen White

INTRODUCTION

The notion that political outlooks usually evolve with age long precedes the study of public opinion. Sometime in the century after the French Revolution, for example, French Premier and historian François Guizot (1787–1874) is believed to have coined the maxim "[n]ot to be a republican at twenty is proof of want of heart; to be one at thirty is proof of want of head" (Shapiro, 2006, p. 327). In his time, Guizot would have been referring to appreciably different stages in life: in late 18th-century France, life expectancy was somewhere around 30 years (Institut National Etudes Démographiques, 2021). The implication was that the motivations and interests – and consequently, the political orientations – of individuals in their "prime" were likely to differ from those of individuals relatively late in their lives: to support republicanism was a "progressive" position, to support monarchy was a conservative stance.

Indeed, there is considerable evidence that older people usually hold more conservative values and take more conservative political positions (Ray, 1985; Truett, 1993; Maltby, 1997; Robinson, 2013; Peterson, Smith, and Hibbing, 2020). This is true of opinions about immigration and across a variety of contexts (Quillian, 1995; Bauer, Lofstrom, and Zimmermann, 2000; Mayda, 2006; O'Rourke and Sinnot, 2006; Sides and Citrin, 2007; Gorodzeisky and Semyonov, 2009; Hainmueller et al., 2015). Typically, younger individuals are more inclined than their older counterparts to support immigration and to hold favourable views of immigrants.

Answering the question of *why* age matters is a more complex undertaking. "Age" can represent at least three quite distinct phenomena, each with unique effects on political attitudes. Ageing is associated with biological and, more particularly, socio-psychological changes, which exert broad influences on political orientations; these changes are believed to push older individuals to more conservative positions. At the

DOI: 10.4324/9781003121992-6

same time, ageing is also associated with movement through different stages of life and different contexts, prompting different considerations for individuals and exposing them to new ideas; depending on the particular life stage and the political issue, attitudes might become more conservative or less so. Both biological ageing and movement through the life course, despite very different influences on attitudes, are usually termed "age effects." However, age is also a proxy for something else entirely: the distinctive constellation of social, economic, and political forces that people experience, especially in their "formative years" between childhood and early adulthood. Political outlooks that take shape in the formative years are thought to deepen and stabilize in subsequent years, influencing political attitudes throughout life. These influences are usually termed "cohort effects" and political scientists often refer to these cohorts as "political generations." For reasons that will be clarified later, age and cohort effects are further distinguished from "period effects": the assortment of influences that structure the attitudes of individuals of all ages and cohorts at a particular point in time.

This chapter explores the relationship between age and public opinion, with a focus on opinions about immigration and immigrants. The chapter begins by sketching out the theories and empirical research that underpin three perspectives on age: socio-psychological development, movement through the life course, and political generations. I also discuss a methodological problem unique to studies concerning age: the challenge of disentangling age, period, and cohort effects. The chapter then turns to cross-national evidence from the nine countries under study (Australia, the United Kingdom, Canada, France, Germany, Italy, Portugal, Switzerland, and the United States). The results reveal substantial cross-national differences in age effects.

AGE AND INDIVIDUAL PSYCHOLOGICAL CHANGES

The idea that socio-psychological changes associated with ageing might produce age differences in political outlooks has endured for decades, but empirical research focused on demonstrating those changes and their connection to political attitudes is surprisingly few and far between. Early research mostly speculated that the ageing process itself might influence political orientations (Crittenden, 1962; Cutler, 1969; Glenn, 1974). Researchers have since identified a number of psychological changes that occur as people get older, which might be associated with systematic shifts in political attitudes towards more conservative positions (Peterson, Smith, and Hibbing, 2020). These changes happen within one or more of the "Big Five" dimensions of personality, which are presumed to influence a variety of political attitudes and behaviours (Mondak, 2010), as further discussed in Chapter 9. Chief among these is increasing conscientiousness, described as "socially prescribed impulse control that facilitates task- and goal-directed behavior, such as thinking before acting, delaying gratification, following norms and rules, and planning, organizing, and prioritizing tasks" (Gerber et al., 2010, p. 113). Conscientiousness increases from early adulthood to middle age (Srivastava et al., 2003; Soto et al., 2011), and Mondak and Halperin, finding that individuals exhibiting this trait tend to identify as conservative, propose this is because "the inclination towards conformity and against 'making waves' suggests a preference for the status quo and a corresponding reluctance to embrace change" (2008, p. 333). Gerber and his colleagues (2010) show conscientiousness is also linked to conservative economic and social policy attitudes.

Peterson, Smith, and Hibbing (2020) identify increasing conscientiousness, along with decreasing openness to new experiences, as one candidate explanation for the link between older age and conservative political stances. Yet, while they demonstrate that ageing is associated with conservative political positions, they do not empirically test the extent to which psychological changes are responsible for the relationship. Cornelis and her colleagues (2009), however, have shown that older people's diminished openness to new experiences – "people's openness in diverse areas such as fantasy, aesthetic sensitivity, intellectual curiosity, willingness to try new things, empathy, and psychological-mindedness" – does in fact account for much of the relationship between older age and conservative political orientations.

Individuals' stances on immigration matters have not been examined in the context of ageing and personality changes, and it is far from obvious what kind of relationship should be anticipated. On the one hand, an "inclination towards conformity" and "a corresponding reluctance to embrace change" (Mondak and Halperin, 2008) would appear consistent with opposition to immigration and antipathy directed towards immigrants. On the other hand, even if psychological changes due to ageing are generally associated with more conservative political attitudes, immigration attitudes might be different. Hellwig (2014), for example, shows that immigration issues cut across the traditional "left/right" economic and social issue cleavages in post-industrial democracies.

AGE AND THE LIFE COURSE

Ageing also involves transitioning in and out of different social roles and contexts, many of which may influence political attitudes (Glenn, 1974; Kinder, 2006). Political stakes change for people throughout life, as they partner and build families, establish and change jobs and careers, and settle in communities: they become more concerned about their families (Glenn, 1974), and with career mobility and greater financial resources they may become less supportive of state efforts at redistribution (Glenn, 1974, p. 180; Peterson, Smith, and Hibbing, 2020, p. 601). Kingston and Finkel (1987, p. 57) suggest that marriage and married life "may reflect or even create a preference for order and stability in one's domestic life, and this preference may be transferred to the political realm." They find that married individuals hold more conservative positions on a variety of political issues (ibid, p. 60). Edlund and Pande (2002) find that women in the United States were less likely to support the Democratic Party following marriage, but more likely to support the party following divorce, and, examining nine West European countries, Edlund and her colleagues (2005) find marriage and divorce, especially for those with children, have a significant impact on the policy preferences of women. There is also evidence that the kinds of occupations individuals have – particularly the level of authority and skill, and the kinds of tasks associated with the occupation – influence a wide range of political outlooks (Kitschelt and Rehm, 2014). Finally, in older age, individuals may have greater concerns about different priorities like state pensions (Campbell, 2002).

Most of these aspects of social ageing have not been considered in regard to immigration attitudes. To the extent that public opinion research has taken into account movement through the life course and its impact on immigration attitudes, the focus has largely been on the different effects of labour market competition from immigrants, and the fiscal impacts of immigration, on individuals of varying ages, as further discussed in Chapters 7 and 14. The most prominent theory concerning the effects of labour market competition argues that the magnitude and balance of supply of relatively low-skilled versus high-skilled immigrants in a country produces different "winners" and "losers" in the native-born population, shaping their views on immigrants accordingly: more low-skilled immigration leads to increased competition for low-skilled jobs and higher wages for high-skilled occupation, while more high-skilled immigration will have the opposite effect (Scheve and Slaughter, 2001). Evidence from some cross-national studies (Mayda, 2006; O'Rourke and Sinnot, 2006) but not others (Hainmueller and Hiscox, 2010) is consistent with this theory. One implication is that older people are more likely to be retired and out of the labour force, and thus labour market competition from immigrants is unlikely to be a consideration for them (Calahorrano, 2013; Schotte and Winkler, 2018). At the same time, immigration can have a number of fiscal implications that also affect individuals at different stages of life in different ways. From an economically self-interested perspective, working immigrants pay taxes and support public services, including state pensions. However, if immigration strains public services in a country, in particular its social assistance programmes, native-born individuals may view immigrants less positively (Schotte and Winker, 2018).

The evidence with respect to these life-course effects supports the idea that under some conditions, and particularly after taking into account cohort effects, older individuals are more likely to express positive outlooks concerning immigration. Bauer, Lofstrom, and Zimmermann (2000) show that across 12 OECD countries, older age is associated with the views that "immigrants take jobs away" and "immigration should be reduced," but also that "immigrants are generally good for the economy." Examining data from Germany between 1990 and 2010, Calahorrano (2013) finds that concerns about immigration decrease with age, when controlling for generation. Schotte and Winkler's (2018) study of 25 European countries between 2002 and 2014, also controlling for generational effects, shows that the older age is linked to pro-immigration attitudes in nine countries, and anti-immigration attitudes in only four countries.

POLITICAL GENERATIONS

To this point, we have considered the ways in which two groups of features associated with *chronological ageing* – socio-psychological changes and transitions through different stages in life – shape political outlooks in general and immigration attitudes in particular. However, at any given point in time, an individual's age is also inextricably linked to their accumulated social, political, and economic experiences, and those experiences depend on the historical period through which an individual has lived. Someone who is 75 years old today has had different experiences than someone who is 25 years old. At a minimum, the 75-year-old will have had firsthand exposure to events that the 25-year-old was not yet alive to witness; these might include periods of peace and conflict, profound social change, pandemics, and economic upswings and crises. More importantly, however, there is a widely accepted strand of research focused on *political generations*, which posits that variation in individuals' early experiences results in systematic differences in the long-term political outlooks of people who come of age in different historical periods.

The relevant point is that we expect people of varying ages to hold different views because they have not been subject to the same "formative events." There are countless specific theories about political generations, but they typically have in common three core features. First, early experiences leave a lasting impression on individuals' political outlooks (Mannheim, 1970; Easton and Dennis, 1965; Greenstein, 1965; Hess and Torney, 1967; Sears and Brown, 2013). Precisely what counts as "early" is a matter of considerable debate, but it is thought that events experienced somewhere between late childhood and early adulthood (Markus, 1979; Niemi and Jennings, 1991; Sears and Brown, 2013) powerfully influence a person's outlooks and that these outlooks then freeze in place, or "crystallize" – that is, they stabilize, are reinforced, and become less susceptible to change thereafter (Sears and Valentino, 1997; Valentino and Sears, 1998). Second, these stable outlooks will structure subsequent attitudes: they predispose individuals to respond to subsequent social and political events in predictable, consistent ways (Sears and Funk, 1999). Third, generational differences emerge when the early, significant experiences of a group of individuals born and raised at one point in time, a *birth cohort*, differ from those of individuals born and raised at other points of time (Inglehart, 1977; Jennings and Niemi, 1981; Alwin, Cohen, and Newcomb, 1991).

Despite the evidence that age is related to immigrant attitudes, until recently, few studies have examined the possibility of generational effects. Some of this research, primarily concerned with ageing effects, has treated generations as a control variable (Calahorrano, 2013; Schotte and Winkler, 2018); nevertheless, these investigations offer strong evidence in a variety of settings that more recent generations are inclined to show more favourable attitudes towards immigrants. A growing number of studies, however, have focused attention on generational effects in structuring attitudes towards immigrants. They emphasize three factors: economic competition with immigrants, exposure to and social interaction with immigrants, and education.

The most fruitful line of investigation has stressed the importance of labour market competition with immigrants in shaping different generations' attitudes and behaviours towards immigrants (see also Chapters 7 and 14 for discussions of labour market competition). If younger people first enter a labour market under conditions in which they have to contend with large numbers of immigrants for a limited supply of jobs, that competition might leave a lasting imprint on views about immigration. The earliest to examine such effects were Coenders and Scheepers (1998), in a study of Dutch attitudes between 1979 and 1993. Their core hypotheses concerned "ethnic conflict" – the idea that competition for scarce economic resources between the white, Dutch-born population and largely immigrant, ethnic minority populations would lead to negative attitudes and discrimination directed at minority populations (ibid). They found that high immigration and high unemployment levels during the period when most individuals were beginning to enter the labour force (16 to 20 years old) produced more widespread discrimination (ibid). Follow-up studies in the Netherlands, covering the period from 1979–2002, confirmed the earlier findings (Coenders et al., 2008), and a similar study in Germany demonstrated that high unemployment in the years when individuals were between ages 16 and 20 was associated with high levels of discrimination against ethnic minority immigrants (Coenders and Scheepers, 2008). Wilkes and Corrigall-Brown (2011) uncovered a similar, if more modest, relationship between "[coming] of age in poor economic times" and a range of anti-immigrant and anti-immigration attitudes in Canada between 1987 and 2008, using the eight-year average unemployment rate during the period in which individuals were 20–24 years old. More recently, Gorodzeisky and Semyonov (2018) showed that in European countries for which significant inflows of immigration are a relatively new phenomenon, generations who experienced high unemployment rates at the time they were entering the labour market were more likely to express anti-immigrant sentiments.

The above studies suggest that under poor economic conditions in the formative years, exposure to relatively higher numbers of immigrants might generate negative attitudes about immigrants and immigration. However, from another vantage point, the exposure of more recent generations to larger numbers of migrants from diverse origins may well result in enduring positive orientations towards immigrants. McLaren and Patterson (2020), examining 16 European countries between 2002 and 2014, demonstrate that more recent generations view immigrants more favourably than do earlier generations. Citing the work of Allport (1954) and others (McLaren, 2003; Pettigrew and Tropp, 2006) on the positive effects of intergroup contact, they suggest that larger migrant inflows "has facilitated intergroup contact and the prejudice-reducing possibilities this brings" (McLaren and Patterson, 2020, p. 668). Schotte and Winkler also provide indirect evidence that, in the handful of countries where *earlier* generations hold more positive attitudes than recent generations towards immigrants, greater early exposure to immigrants in the distant past might be responsible (2018, p. 1278).

A third line of investigation emphasizes the enduring effects of education on different generations' views about immigration (see Chapter 7 for more on education). Wilkes and Corrigall-Brown (2011) suggest that more recent generations might be less inclined to hold negative views about immigrants and immigration because they are typically more educated. Aside from possibly shielding individuals from perceived labour market competition from immigrants, higher levels of education are associated with less parochial views and greater tolerance for difference (Espenshade and Calhoun, 1993; Citrin et al., 1997; McLaren, 2001), which could therefore generate lasting, more positive attitudes towards immigrants (Hainmueller and Hiscox, 2007). However, there has been no evidence of this education effect in Canada (Wilkes and Corrigall-Brown, 2011). Moreover, Schotte and Winkler (2018, p. 1276) point to indirect evidence that increases in education have had minimal impact on recent generations in Europe. They note that "improvements in educational attainment between 1990 and 2000 are not correlated with cohort effects across groups of countries. In fact, countries where the new generations are less pro-immigration experienced the largest increase in educational attainment." These findings may be related to the emergence in many European countries of new political parties opposed to immigration. McLaren and Patterson hypothesized that higher levels of education would insulate younger generations from far-right mobilization (2020, p. 669), but they found that although more education mostly resulted in more positive attitudes towards immigrants, the effect was *weakest* among recent generations in countries where far-right political parties had the strongest support during individuals' formative years.

DISTINGUISHING AGE FROM GENERATION

In reviewing theories of the impact of age on public opinion and attitudes about immigration in particular, we detailed some of the different causal mechanisms and processes through which age can affect political attitudes (Imai et al., 2011). Distinguishing between these causal mechanisms is important, because effects associated with psychology, life course, and generation have very different implications when we consider aggregate trends in public opinion. Individuals advance in years, but sometimes entire societies also grow older through a combination of declining birth rates and increasing life expectancy. At the same time, the generational makeup of entire societies will also change over time. If either ageing or generational differences matter, then they have the potential to influence the trajectory of entire publics.

Importantly, ageing and generational differences do not have *equal* potential to shape whole publics. To the extent that age-related effects are rooted in either movement through the life course (social ageing) or psychological ageing, their aggregate impacts might depend on how much the age composition of a population changes across time. Those shifts tend to occur relatively slowly, if at all. Generational effects are different. The generational composition of a population will change inevitably – and usually more precipitously – as new generations are born and older ones recede and eventually disappear. For example, one of the more dramatic shifts in age composition in recent decades has occurred in Italy, where, between 1985 and 2015, the median age in Italy rose by just under ten years, from 35.5 to 45.4 (United Nations, 2019). During that period, the share of the Italian population aged 20 to 39 years old dropped from 40 to 28%, while the share of those aged 60 years and older grew from 26 to 34% (ibid). Far more striking, though, were the changes in the generational composition of the Italian population over that period. People born in 1925 or earlier, for example, represented 26% of the Italian population in 1985, but just 1%

by 2015, while those born in 1986 or later, of whom there were none at all in 1985, made up 35% of the population by 2015 (ibid).

Researchers who study public opinion and are interested in empirically distinguishing generational effects and the consequences of movement through the life course or psychological ageing run into a potential problem because it is a challenge to tell them apart. Two people born 30 years apart might belong to different generational cohorts, but they are also necessarily of different ages. How, then, can generation be disentangled from age? One technical approach to sorting these effects is to observe people at different points in time. For example, two people born in 1970 who are observed at different points in time many years apart will belong to the same generational cohort but will not share the same age. Conversely, two 20-year-olds observed at different points in time many years apart will share the same age, but will not belong to the same generational cohort.

That approach, however, introduces yet another problem. What if opinions vary over time because of changes in context that have nothing to do with people's ages, nor when they were born? These "period effects" potentially confound any effort to separate the effects of age and generation. Imagine, for example, that a researcher uses the above strategy in an effort to determine whether people's attitudes about immigration are shaped primarily by generational effects or ageing. In the hypothetical example presented in Table 4.1, the anti-immigration attitudes of six individuals of varying ages and generations are observed at various time points (the years in which they were observed are noted in parentheses). There appear to be both generational and age differences. On average, members of the more recent generational cohort express less negative attitudes than the earlier generation, and older individuals express less negative attitudes than younger individuals. Yet, examining the data in Table 4.1 more closely to take into account when people were observed, there is also evidence of a cross-time trend: the mean anti-immigration attitude score is 5.0 in 1990, 3.5 in 2000, 2.5 in 2010, and 1.0 in 2020. Is this trend merely the product of an ageing effect (that is, people have become more favourably predisposed to immigrants with the passage of time *because* they are getting older)? Conversely, is the apparent ageing effect the combined result of a common trend across time and

TABLE 4.1 Anti-immigration index (1–5 scale), by age and birth cohort

	20 years old	30 years old	40 years old	Mean score by generational cohort
Individual A, born 1970	5 (in 1990)			4
Individual B, born 1970		4 (in 2000)		
Individual C, born 1970			3 (in 2010)	
Individual D, born 1980	3 (in 2000)			2
Individual E, born 1980		2 (in 2010)		
Individual F, born 1980			1 (in 2020)	
Mean score by age	4	3	2	

Note: 1 indicates low anti-immigration attitudes and 5 indicates high anti-immigration attitudes.

a generational effect (that is, because members of the more recent generation are always younger, on average, than their predecessors)? This is but one example of the general identification problem with this methodological approach to disentangling ageing effects from generational effects (Glenn, 2005).[1] Any two of these three variables – age in years, year of birth, and year of observation – is a perfect predictor of the remaining variable.

A variety of other technical solutions have been proposed to deal with this problem, but none can get around it without relying on theories about ageing, generational, and period effects, as well as what Converse (1976) termed "side information" – or additional evidence that helps to make a case for the plausibility (or implausibility) of one or more of those theories.[2] More specifically, distinguishing generational, ageing, and period effects from one another requires theoretically informed conjectures about the nature of those effects and the mechanisms by which they operate. Approximately when is one generation assumed to end and another to begin, for example? Are ageing-related changes assumed to be continuous during the life course, or do they occur primarily earlier in life, middle age, or later in life? What are the intervening variables that link ageing or generational differences to particular political attitudes (for example, personality traits such as conscientiousness or openness; life course such as having children, building a career, or retiring; formative experiences such as high unemployment in one's youth)? Expectations grounded both in theories and in prior evidence are crucial to any efforts to determine why age is related to specific attitudes or behaviours.

In this respect, research concerning ageing and generational effects on immigration attitudes has made considerable advances. All but one of the aforementioned studies employ data that use a repeated cross-sectional design. This design is one in which the same variables are observed at different time points over long periods, thereby making it easier to empirically distinguish age from generation. The exception is Calahorrano (2013), who uses panel data from Germany to track not only the same variables but also the individuals across time. More importantly, these studies make effective use of "side information." Research on economic conditions in the formative years, which uses data on unemployment and immigration flows, is an excellent example of this. However, some studies (Gorodzeisky and Semyonov, 2018; Schotte and Winkler, 2018; McLaren and Patterson, 2020) have also exploited the cross-national aspect of their data to theorize and test explanations for country-by-country variation in generational effects. This approach provides additional leverage in assessing the plausibility of ageing and generational explanations. As the analysis of the CSES data in the next section shows, we can learn something from these cross-national comparisons.

AGE AND IMMIGRATION ATTITUDES IN NINE COUNTRIES

The evidence from the CSES suggests the relationship between age and attitudes about immigration is complex and contingent on both national context and which kinds of immigration effects are under consideration. For the most part, older people are more likely than the younger to express negative attitudes towards immigrants. However, the age gap varies considerably from country to country and is typically much smaller with respect to people's views about the economic consequences of immigration than their views about the effects of immigration on culture and crime.

Most studies have found older age is generally associated with more negative attitudes towards immigration and immigrants, but the CSES data reveal both unequivocal differences and other, subtler distinctions between different national contexts. Figures 4.1, 4.2, and 4.3 show the response distributions and mean scores for culture, crime, and economic indicators of anti-immigrant opinions, for three age groups in each country: 18- to 34-year-olds, 35- to 64-year-olds, and those aged 65 and older. They reveal striking differences. Age is related in broadly similar ways to opinions about the impact of immigrants on culture and crime rates (Figures 4.1 and 4.2, respectively). In general, people aged 65 and older are more likely than those aged 35 to 64 to hold negative opinions about the impact

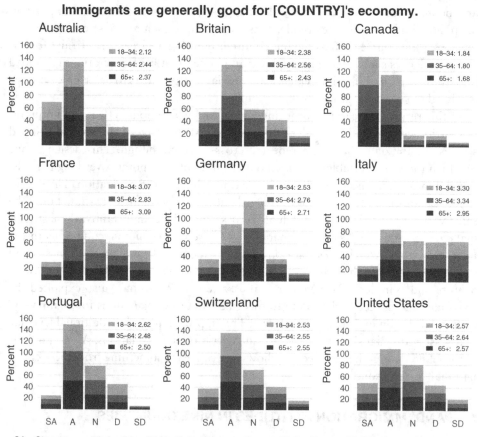

SA = Strongly agree (1); A = Agree (2); N = Neither agree nor disagree (3); D = Disagree (4); SD = Strongly disagree (5)

FIGURE 4.1 Attitudes about how immigrants are perceived to affect a country's economy, by age group.

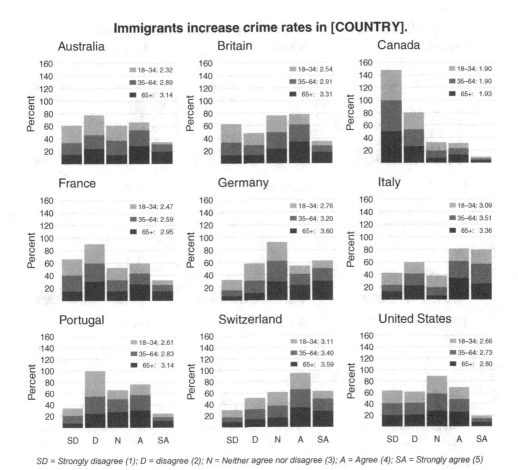

FIGURE 4.2 Attitudes about how immigrants are perceived to affect a country's crime, by age group.

of immigrants on culture and crime rates, and people aged 35 to 64 are more likely than those aged 18 to 34 to hold negative opinions. There are a number of instances of marked disparities between age groups. In Australia, for example, only 16% of 18- to 34-year-olds agree that "Immigrants increase crime rates in Australia," whereas 47% of people aged 65 or older agree with that statement. By the same token, while one-quarter of 18- to 34-year-old Germans agree that immigrants increase crime rates in the country, more than half – 53% – of those in the oldest age group agree. Canada and the United States, however, exhibit exceptionally small age group differences. The youngest are less likely than older groups to believe immigrants increase crime rates in the United States ($p < 0.05$), and 18- to 34-year-olds are less likely than 35- to 64-year-olds to believe Canada's culture is harmed by immigrants ($p < 0.05$), but no other age group differences in those two countries are statistically different from zero.

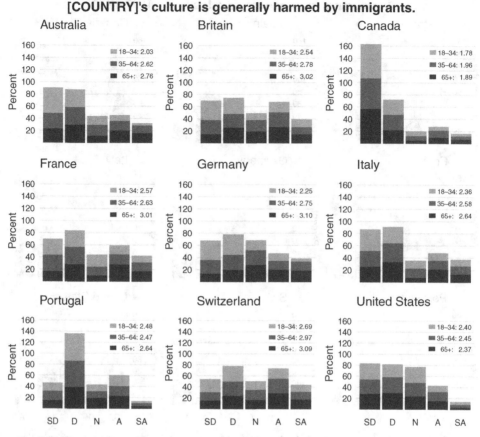

[COUNTRY]'s culture is generally harmed by immigrants.

SD = Strongly disagree (1); D = disagree (2); N = Neither agree nor disagree (3); A = Agree (4); SA = Strongly agree (5)

FIGURE 4.3 Attitudes about how immigrants are perceived to affect a country's culture, by age group.

In contrast to beliefs about the impact of immigration on culture and crime rates, the link between age and economic concerns about immigration is relatively modest (Figure 4.3). In fact, in Canada and Italy people aged 65 and older are significantly *more* likely than their younger counterparts (p < 0.05) to believe immigrants are *good* for the country's economy. The evidence from Italy is particularly striking, given the oldest age group expressed the most concern about the cultural impact of immigration. A little more than one-third (34%) of people aged 65 or older disagree with the statement "immigrants are generally good for Italy's economy," compared to 48% of 35- to 64-year-olds, and 42% of 18- to 34-year-olds.

The immigration index conceals the varied effects of age across different attitude dimensions, but it sheds light on the distinctive contours of the relationships between age and overall views about immigration in different countries (Figure 4.4). Older people are more likely than those who are younger to express anti-immigration

Immigration index by age groups

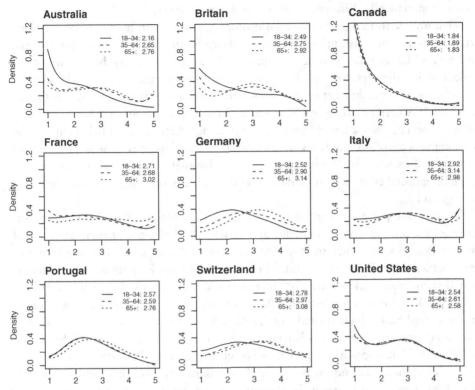

Values range from 1 to 5 with higher values indicating less favourable attitudes toward immigration.

FIGURE 4.4 Attitudes about how immigrants are perceived to affect a country's economy, crime, and culture (index), by age group.

attitudes in most, but not all, countries. In Australia, the United Kingdom, Germany, and Switzerland, people aged 65 and older are most likely to hold anti-immigration attitudes, 18- to 34-year-olds are least likely, and 35- to 64-year-olds are situated in the middle. All but two of the group differences in mean index scores are statistically different from zero (p < 0.05); the exceptions are the mean differences between 35- to 64-year-olds and people aged 65 and older in Australia (p = 0.36) and the UK (p = 0.07). In these four countries, the gap in mean scores on the immigration attitudes index between the youngest and middle age groups is generally larger than the gap between the middle and oldest age groups. France, Italy, and Portugal exhibit a different pattern. People aged 65 and older are more likely to hold anti-immigration attitudes than their younger counterparts in France and Portugal, but there are virtually no differences between 18- to 34-year-olds and 35- to 64-year-olds in either country. In Italy, the people in the middle age group are significantly more likely than those in the youngest group to express anti-immigration attitudes (p < 0.05), while those in the oldest group are not statistically different from either of the other two groups. In the two remaining countries, Canada and the United States, there are no discernible age patterns at all – none of the modest differences between age groups is statistically different from zero in either country.

What are we to make of these relationships? First, within many countries, there are systematic and substantial age group differences in attitudes about immigrants, and by and large, older people are more likely to hold negative beliefs about the impact of immigrants. Second, however, there is considerable cross-national variation in the relationship between age and attitudes about immigration. Third, the two North American countries, Canada and the US, stand apart from the rest by having especially weak age differences. Fourth, age differences in beliefs about the economic effects of immigration are comparatively modest. It is these last two points that we will explore further because they reveal something more about the importance of national context in understanding the link between age and attitude about immigrants.

Why are age patterns weakest in Canada and the United States? One clear difference between these two countries and nearly all of the rest is their histories of immigration. Both Canada and the United States are "traditional countries of immigrant settlement" (Freeman, 2006). These countries have long legacies of immigration that are essential features of their national self-images (Simonsen, 2016, p. 1157). As Martiniello and Rath (2010, p. 7) note, "Some countries such as Canada or the United States have hosted immigration for centuries, and their mental map and social fabric are consequently geared to accommodating newcomers." Simonsen (2016) finds that populations in settler societies are generally more inclusive with respect to immigrants and draw less rigid boundaries around their national identities. Regarding age differences in immigration attitudes, the relevant point about these legacies is that exposure to immigrants is not new in settler societies – even to the oldest generations.

However, the Australian evidence would appear to challenge any argument about the effects of historical immigration patterns. Australia, like Canada and the United States, is a traditional country of immigrant settlement, and yet it exhibits one of the strongest age patterns among the countries we have examined. Australia has a large foreign-born population that has risen steadily for nearly three-quarters of a century, from approximately 10% of the total population in the mid-1940s to 30% today (Australian Bureau of Statistics, 2021), and a longstanding immigrant selection policy that favours skilled immigrants. If legacies of immigration explain the weak effects of age in Canada and the United States, then why are those effects so pronounced in Australia?

One possible answer lies in political competition within these countries. In Canada, there has long been a cross-party consensus on immigration and multiculturalism at the national level (Marwah, Triadafilopoulos, and White, 2013). In the United States, "[s]trange bedfellow and rights-markets coalitions between the ideological left and right have historically played an important role in immigration policymaking," writes Wong (2017, p. 12). Only since the passage of the Border Protection, Antiterrorism, and Illegal Control Act of 2005 by the United States House of Representatives have bipartisan coalitions faded, with Republicans coalescing to support the legislation and Democrats opposing (ibid). In Australia, however, immigration and multiculturalism have been salient political issues for much longer, with clear partisan lines drawn between the Australian Labour Party (in favour) and the Liberal-National coalition (critical) since the 1980s (Jupp, 1995, 2002). Immigration has become an "easy" issue: a longstanding topic of debate that has become largely symbolic rather than technical, and for which the major parties and most voters have clear positions (Carmines and Stimson, 1980). Younger Australians are considerably less likely than their older counterparts to support the coalition parties (Cameron and McAllister, 2019), and it is quite possible the distinctive partisan preferences of Australians of different ages have shaped their views on immigration.

The CSES data support this interpretation. Figure 4.5 compares the effects of age on immigration attitudes in Australia to Germany, a country with an equally substantial age gap. The figure shows the estimated relationship between age and immigration index scores when people's ratings of the parties competing in the 2019 Australian election and 2017 German election are held constant (the solid lines), and when those ratings are not held constant (the dashed lines). In Australia, the relationship between age and immigration attitudes is weakened considerably when party ratings are controlled, suggesting partisan considerations go some way towards explaining the age gap in Australia. However, controlling for party ratings has virtually no effect on the relationship between age and immigration attitudes in Germany.

Why is age weakly related to economic anxieties around immigration, especially in light of the clear link between age and concerns about the impact of immigration on culture and crime rates? Recall that a prominent life course theory with respect to immigration attitudes suggests people's relative exposure to labour market competition from immigrants typically eases as they get older. It is reasonable to suppose that younger people, who are otherwise more inclined to support immigration, might express some doubts about the economic value of immigrants if they view newcomers as unwelcome competitors for scarce jobs. Conversely, those who are older and more inclined to oppose immigration because of concerns about culture or crime might be relatively less anxious about the economic consequences of immigration.

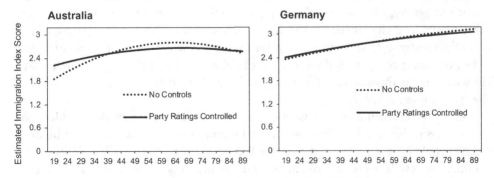

FIGURE 4.5 Estimated index score, by respondents' age in years (OLS regression).

TABLE 4.2 Unemployment rates, by country

	Unemployment rate		
	Overall	25- to 34-year-olds	Difference
Australia (2014–18)	5.5	4.9	–0.6
Canada (2014–19)	6.4	6.2	–0.2
France (2012–16)	10.2	12.3	2.1
Germany (2014–16)	4.6	5.4	0.8
Italy (2013–17)	11.6	17.5	6.9
Portugal (2014–18)	9.0	9.9	0.9
Switzerland (2014–18)	4.8	5.2	0.4
United Kingdom (2012–16)	5.4	5.1	–0.3
United States (2011–15)	6.3	6.5	0.2

Source: OECD.

The evidence from Italy offers some support for this line of reasoning. Italy is the only country in which the members of the youngest group were less likely than the oldest group to view the economic effects of immigration in positive terms: only 28% of 18- to 34-year-olds and 33% of 35- to 64-year-olds agreed that immigrants were good for Italy's economy, whereas 38% of people aged 65 and older agreed with the statement. If the labour market competition thesis is accurate, then these findings are perhaps unsurprising. As it happens, Italy's labour market showed considerable strain in the years leading up to the 2018 election – particularly for young people. Table 4.2 shows the average overall unemployment rate in the nine countries over the five years prior to the CSES election, as well as the corresponding unemployment rate among 25- to 34-year-olds. Italy's overall unemployment rate during this period was the highest of the nine countries examined, but the unemployment rate among 25- to 34-year-olds was even worse in relative terms.

CONCLUSION

Studying the effects of age on public opinion is a tricky enterprise. Indeed, relationships between political attitudes and nearly any sociodemographic characteristic – such as gender, income, social class, geographic location, or age – pose considerable interpretive challenges. In an important sense, these characteristics are empty containers; after all, what we really want to know is why they are related attitudes. The problem is compounded with respect to age because of the very different ways in which age is thought to influence attitudes and the difficulties in distinguishing between those influences.

Immigration attitudes are a case in point. The research literature shows older people are less inclined to view immigrants and immigration favourably. Is that because older people have personalities that predispose them to conservative positions on political issues? Is it because recent generations face less competition for jobs from immigrants? Is it because more recent generations are better educated, or have had more exposure to immigrants? If so, how do we square that with theory and evidence that younger people are relatively more likely to see immigrants as an economic threat? The entanglement of age, period, and cohort effects means that parsing the answers to these questions entails at least two things. First, it requires a lot of data: across time, and cross-nationally. Data across time are necessary to better isolate generation and age effects. Cross-national data are necessary because generational effects, and some age effects, are contingent on the setting. Second, it requires theories and careful interpretation of data in light of those theories. An overabundance of data is not on its own a solution to the fundamental problem that age, period, and cohort effects are logically linked to one another (Bell and Jones 2014, p. 338). In the absence of other information, researchers will not be able to determine the extent to which the relationship between age and immigration attitudes – or any other attitudes, for that matter – is shaped by generation or age. We require explanations and the kinds of data that will allow us to evaluate the plausibility of those explanations.

In the relatively short time that researchers have grappled with the relationship between age and immigration attitudes, they have made considerable advances in amassing data and using it to assess the plausibility of theories. Their evidence thus far suggests age-related effects are primarily generational, but with signs that ageing (via movement through the life course) also matters. Age effects are readily apparent when generation is controlled, and in ways that are quite consistent with theories about the effects of economic concerns at different stages of life. At the same time, there are clear generational effects, which appear to be linked to economic conditions and exposure to immigrants in the "formative years." Moreover, it is equally clear that context matters a great deal, and in ways that strengthen some claims about generational impacts: cross-national variations in economic contexts, and in the timing of immigration flows, are generally associated with generational differences in immigration attitudes in different countries.

The evidence from the CSES presented in this chapter is consistent with the research to date. Specifically, the pattern of relationships between age and immigration attitudes is consistent with generational explanations, but also the conjecture that all else being equal the labour market vulnerability of younger people makes them wary of immigration. The CSES data employed in this investigation are cross-national, but they are not a time series. Even so, careful consideration of age differences in response to different questions about the impacts of immigration (the economy, crime, culture), and the context in which those differences emerge, tells us a good deal in light of the theories outlined earlier in the chapter.

I will use the findings from Canada, the United States, and Italy to illustrate and emphasize this point. The evidence from either Canada or the United States reveals little in isolation: age is weakly related to immigration attitudes in both countries. However, taking into account the Canadian and American contexts and comparing them to other countries reveals much more. The findings with respect to Canada and the United States make more sense if generational differences are shaped by differential exposure to immigrants in the formative years. Likewise, immigration attitudes in Italy are puzzling at first blush, but are far more intelligible from a comparative perspective. If the labour market vulnerability of younger individuals makes them more circumspect about immigration, then it is unsurprising that Italian youth express a relatively high level of concern about the economic consequences of immigration given the high youth unemployment rate in that country.

The chapter began with the observation that answering the question of *why* age matters is a more complex undertaking than demonstrating empirically that it does matter. However, *where* age matters is an equally important question. Context is important for a couple of reasons. First, as shown in both the review of extant research and the investigation of the CSES data on the relationship between age and immigration attitudes, there are significant cross-national differences in the nature of that relationship. Second, theoretically informed cross-national comparisons can help us to evaluate the plausibility of age and generational explanations. Such comparisons are often rich sources of insight and may be particularly helpful because of the unusual challenge posed by age and generational effects.

SUMMARY POINTS

- The chapter presented the theory and empirical research that underpin three perspectives on the effects of age on public opinion: socio-psychological development, movement through the life course, and political generations.
- The chapter discussed the methodological problem associated with studies on the effects of age, that is, the challenge of disentangling age, period, and cohort effects.
- The chapter presented cross-national evidence that revealed substantial cross-national differences in age effects.
- The observed pattern of relationship between age and immigration opinion across different settings is consistent with both generational explanations and the argument that the labour market vulnerability of younger people makes them wary of immigration.

NOTES

1 Another possibility is to use panel data – observations of the same people at different points in time. This produces the exact same problem when, for example, the attitudes of two people from different birth cohorts change in the same direction over time. Under some conditions it is simply impossible to tell whether the change is a period effect or age effect.

2 Some are pessimistic about the possibility of correctly distinguishing between age, birth cohort, and period effects at all. Glenn (2005, p. 6) has described it as a "futile quest," and states that "[t]he continued search for a statistical technique that can be mechanically applied always to correctly estimate [age, period, and birth cohort] effects is one of the most bizarre instances in the history of science of repeated attempts to do something that is logically impossible." Bell and Jones (2014, p. 338) argue that "very solid theory … is required for such methods to be of any use, and unfortunately that theory is rarely forthcoming in applied research."

SUGGESTED FURTHER READINGS

Kinder, D.R., 2006. Politics and the life cycle. *Science*, 312(5782), 1905–1908.

Peterson, J.C., Smith, K.B., and Hibbing, J.R., 2020. Do people really become more conservative as they age? *The Journal of Politics*, 82(2), 600–611.

Sears, D.O. and Brown, C., 2013. Childhood and adult political development. In: L. Huddy, D.O. Sears, and J.S. Levy, eds. *The Oxford handbook of political psychology*. 2nd ed. Oxford: Oxford University Press, 59–95.

REFERENCES

Allport, G.W., 1954. *The nature of prejudice*. Reading, MA: Addison-Wesley.

Alwin, D.F., Cohen, R.L., and Newcomb, T.M., 1991. *Political attitudes over the life span: The Bennington women after fifty years*. Madison: University of Wisconsin Press.

Australian Bureau of Statistics, 2021. Migration, Australia: Statistics on Australia's international migration, internal migration (interstate and intrastate), and the population by country of birth. Available from: https://www.abs.gov.au/statistics/people/population/migration -australia/latest-release#australia-s-population-by-country-of-birth [Accessed 5 May 2021].

Bauer, T.K., Lofstrom, M., and Zimmermann, K.F., 2000. Immigration policy, assimilation of immigrants and natives' sentiments towards immigrants: Evidence from 12 OECD-countries. *Swedish Economic Policy Review*, 7, 11–53.

Bell, A. and Jones, K., 2014. Another 'futile quest'? A simulation study of Yang and land's hierarchical age-period-cohort model. *Demographic Research*, 30, 333–360.

Calahorrano, L., 2013. Population aging and individual attitudes toward immigration: Disentangling age, cohort and time effects. *Review of International Economics*, 21(2), 342–353.

Cameron, S. and McAllister, I., 2019. *Trends in Australian political opinion: Results from the Australian election study 1987–2019*. Canberra, ACT: The Australian National University.

Campbell, A.L., 2002. Self-interest, social security, and the distinctive participation patterns of senior citizens. *American Political Science Review*, 96(3), 565–574.

Carmines, E.G. and Stimson, J.A., 1980. The two faces of issue voting. *American Political Science Review*, 74(1), 78–91.

Citrin, J., Green, D.P., Muste, C., and Wong, C., 1997. Public opinion toward immigration reform: The role of economic motivations. *The Journal of Politics*, 59(3), 858–881.

Coenders, M., Lubbers, M., Scheepers, P., and Verkuyten, M., 2008. More than two decades of changing ethnic attitudes in the Netherlands. *Journal of Social Issues*, 64(2), 269–285.

Coenders, M. and Scheepers, P., 1998. Support for ethnic discrimination in the Netherlands 1979–1993: Effects of period, cohort, and individual characteristics. *European Sociological Review*, 14(4), 405–422.

Coenders, M. and Scheepers, P., 2008. Changes in resistance to the social integration of foreigners in Germany 1980–2000: Individual and contextual determinants. *Journal of Ethnic and Migration Studies*, 34(1), 1–26.

Converse, P.E., 1976. *Dynamics of party support: Cohort analytical party identification*. Beverly Hills, CA: Sage Publications.

Cornelis, I., Van Hiel, A., Roets, A., and Kossowska, M., 2009. Age differences in conservatism: Evidence on the mediating effects of personality and cognitive style. *Journal of Personality*, 77(1), 51–87.

Crittenden, J., 1962. Aging and party affiliation. *Public Opinion Quarterly*, 26(4), 648–657.

Cutler, N.E., 1969. Generation, maturation, and party affiliation: A cohort analysis. *Public Opinion Quarterly*, 33(4), 583–588.

Easton, D. and Dennis, J., 1965. The child's image of government. *The Annals of the American Academy of Political and Social Science*, 361(1), 40–57.

Edlund, L., Haider, L., and Pande, R., 2005. Unmarried parenthood and redistributive politics. *Journal of the European Economic Association*, 3(1), 95–119.

Edlund, L. and Pande, R., 2002. Why have women become left-wing? The political gender gap and the decline in marriage. *The Quarterly Journal of Economics*, 117(3), 917–961.

Espenshade, T.J. and Calhoun, C.A., 1993. An analysis of public opinion toward undocumented immigration. *Population Research and Policy Review*, 12(3), 189–224.

Freeman, G.P., 2006. National models, policy types, and the politics of immigration in liberal democracies. *West European Politics*, 29(2), 227–247.

Gerber, A.S., Huber, G.A., Doherty, D., Dowling, C.M., and Ha, S.E., 2010. Personality and political attitudes: Relationships across issue domains and political contexts. *American Political Science Review*, 104(1), 111–133.

Glenn, N.D., 2005. *Cohort analysis*. 2nd ed. Thousand Oaks: Sage.

Glenn, N.D., 1974. Aging and conservatism. *The Annals of the American Academy of Political and Social Science*, 415(1), 176–186.

Gorodzeisky, A. and Semyonov, M., 2009. Terms of exclusion: Public views towards admission and allocation of rights to immigrants in European countries. *Ethnic and Racial Studies*, 32(3), 401–423.

Gorodzeisky, A. and Semyonov, M., 2018. Competitive threat and temporal change in anti-immigrant sentiment: Insights from a hierarchical age-period-cohort model. *Social Science Research*, 73, 31–44.

Greenstein, F.I., 1965. Personality and political socialization: The theories of authoritarian and democratic character. *The Annals of the American Academy of Political and Social Science*, 361(1), 81–95.

Hainmueller, J. and Hiscox, M.J., 2007. Educated preferences: Explaining attitudes toward immigration in Europe. *International Organization*, 61(2), 399–442.

Hainmueller, J. and Hiscox, M.J., 2010. Attitudes toward highly skilled and low-skilled immigration: Evidence from a survey experiment. *American Political Science Review*, 104(1), 61–84.

Hainmueller, J., Hiscox, M.J., and Margalit, Y., 2015. Do concerns about labor market competition shape attitudes toward immigration? New evidence. *Journal of International Economics*, 97(1), 193–207.

Hellwig, T., 2014. The structure of issue voting in postindustrial democracies. *The Sociological Quarterly*, 55(4), 596–624.

Imai, K., Keele, L., Tingley, D., Yamamoto, T., 2011. Unpacking the black box of causality: Learning about causal mechanisms from experimental and observational studies. *American Political Science Review*, 105(4), 765–789.

Inglehart, R., 1977. Political dissatisfaction and mass support for social change in advanced industrial society. *Comparative Political Studies*, 10(3), 455–472.

Institut National Etudes Démographiques, 2021. Life expectancy in France. Available from: https://www.ined.fr/en/everything_about_population/graphs-maps/interpreted-graphs/life-expectancy-france/ [Accessed 5 May 2021].

Jennings, M.K. and Niemi, R.G., 1981. *Generations and politics*. Princeton, NJ: Princeton University Press.

Jupp, J., 1995. From 'White Australia' to 'part of Asia': Recent shifts in Australian immigration policy towards the region. *International Migration Review*, 29(1), 207–228.

Jupp, J., 2002. *From white Australia to Woomera: The story of Australian immigration*. New York: Cambridge University Press.

Kinder, D.R., 2006. Politics and the life cycle. *Science*, 312(5782), 1905–1908.

Kingston, P.W. and Finkel, S.E., 1987. Is there a marriage gap in politics? *Journal of Marriage and the Family*, 49(1), 57–64.

Kitschelt, H. and Rehm, P., 2014. Occupations as a site of political preference formation. *Comparative Political Studies*, 47(12), 1670–1706.

Maltby, J., 1997. The concurrent validity of a short measure of social conservatism among English students. *Personality and Individual Differences*, 23(5), 901–903.

Mannheim, K., 1970. The problem of generations. In: *Essays on the Sociology of Knowledge*, 57(3), 378–404.

Markus, G.B., 1979. The political environment and the dynamics of public attitudes: A panel study. *American Journal of Political Science*, 23(2), 338–359.

Martiniello, M. and Rath, J., 2010. Introduction. In: M. Martiniello and J. Rath, eds. *Selected studies in international migration and immigrant incorporation*. Vol. 1. Amsterdam: Amsterdam University Press.

Marwah, I., Triadafilopoulos, T., and White, S., 2013. Immigration, citizenship, and Canada's new Conservative Party. In: James Farney and David Rayside (Eds.), *Conservatism in Canada*. University of Toronto Press, 95–119.

Mayda, A.M., 2006. Who is against immigration? A cross-country investigation of individual attitudes toward immigrants. *Review of Economics and Statistics*, 88(3), 510–530.

McLaren, L.M., 2001. Immigration and the new politics of inclusion and exclusion in the European Union: The effect of elites and the EU on individual-level opinions regarding European and non-European immigrants. *European Journal of Political Research*, 39(1), 81–108.

McLaren, L.M., 2003. Anti-immigrant prejudice in Europe: Contact, threat perception, and preferences for the exclusion of migrants. *Social Forces*, 81(3), 909–936.

McLaren, L.M. and Paterson, I., 2020. Generational change and attitudes to immigration. *Journal of Ethnic and Migration Studies*, 46(3), 665–682.

Mondak, J.J. and Halperin, K.D., 2008. A framework for the study of personality and political behaviour. *British Journal of Political Science*, 38(2), 335–362.

Mondak, J.J., 2010. Personality and the foundations of political behavior. New York: Cambridge University Press

Niemi, R.G. and Jennings, M.K., 1991. Issues and inheritance in the formation of party identification. *American Journal of Political Science*, 35(4), 970–988.

O'Rourke, K.H. and Sinnott, R., 2006. The determinants of individual attitudes towards immigration. *European Journal of Political Economy*, 22(4), 838–861.

Peterson, J.C., Smith, K.B., and Hibbing, J.R., 2020. Do people really become more conservative as they age? *The Journal of Politics*, 82(2), 600–611.

Pettigrew, T.F. and Tropp, L.R., 2006. A meta-analytic test of intergroup contact theory. *Journal of Personality and Social Psychology*, 90(5), 751–783.

Quillian, L., 1995. Prejudice as a response to perceived group threat: Population composition and anti-immigrant and racial prejudice in Europe. *American Sociological Review*, 60(4), 586–611.

Ray, J.J., 1985. What old people believe: Age, sex, and conservatism. *Political Psychology*, 6(3), 525–528.

Robinson, O.C., 2013. Values and adult age: Findings from two cohorts of the European social survey. *European Journal of Ageing*, 10(1), 11–23.

Scheve, K.F. and Slaughter, M.J., 2001. Labor market competition and individual preferences over immigration policy. *Review of Economics and Statistics*, 83(1), 133–145.

Schotte, S. and Winkler, H., 2018. Why are the elderly more averse to immigration when they are more likely to benefit? Evidence across countries. *International Migration Review*, 52(4), 1250–1282.

Sears, D.O. and Brown, C., 2013. Childhood and adult political development. In: L. Huddy, D.O. Sears, and J.S. Levy, eds., *The Oxford handbook of political psychology*. 2nd ed. Oxford: Oxford University Press, 59–95.

Sears, D.O. and Funk, C.L., 1999. Evidence of the long-term persistence of adults' political predispositions. *The Journal of Politics*, 61(1), 1–28.

Sears, D.O. and Valentino, N.A., 1997. Politics matters: Political events as catalysts for preadult socialization. *American Political Science Review*, 91(1), 45–65.

Shapiro, F.R., ed., 2006. *The Yale book of quotations*. New Haven, CT: Yale University Press.

Sides, J. and Citrin, J., 2007. European opinion about immigration: The role of identities, interests and information. *British Journal of Political Science*, 37(3), 477–504.

Simonsen, K.B., 2016. How the host nation's boundary drawing affects immigrants' belonging. *Journal of Ethnic and Migration Studies*, 42(7), 1153–1176.

Soto, C.J., John, O.P., Gosling, S.D., and Potter, J., 2011. Age differences in personality traits from ages 10 to 65. *Journal of Personality and Social Psychology*, 100(2), 330–348.

Srivastava, S., John, O.P., Gosling, S.D., and Potter, J., 2003. Development of personality in early and middle adulthood: Set like plaster or persistent change? *Journal of Personality and Social Psychology*, 84(5), 1041–1053.

Hess, R.D. and Torney, J.V., 1967. *The development of political attitudes in children*. Piscataway: Transaction Publishers.

Truett, K.R., 1993. Age differences in conservatism. *Personality and Individual Differences*, 14(3), 405–411.

United Nations, Department of Economic and Social Affairs, Population Division, 2019. World population prospects 2019, custom data acquired via website. Available from: https://population.un.org/wpp/ [Accessed 5 May 2021].

Valentino, N.A. and Sears, D.O., 1998. Event-driven political communication and the preadult socialization of partisanship. *Political Behavior*, 20(2), 127–154.

Wilkes, R. and Corrigall-Brown, C., 2011. Explaining time trends in public opinion: Attitudes towards immigration and immigrants. *International Journal of Comparative Sociology*, 52(1–2), 79–99.

Wong, T.K., 2017. *The politics of immigration: Partisanship, demographic change, and American national identity*. Oxford: Oxford University Press.

CHAPTER 5

Gender and public opinion

....

Ana Espírito-Santo and João Carvalho

INTRODUCTION

This chapter aims to enhance our understanding of the effects of gender on public attitudes towards immigrants[1]. It provides a comprehensive literature review of the topic, complemented by a brief empirical analysis of the perception of the three aforementioned threats – economic, cultural, and security – in the nine countries presented in Chapter 3.

Throughout the years, great attention has been paid to the gender gap in political attitudes. Whereas the differences reported by scholars are not large, they are not negligible either. Consequently, the literature highlights the divergent preferences of women and men regarding such issues as public welfare spending and redistribution (Campbell, 2012; Howell and Day, 2000; Kamas and Preston, 2018) and crime and punishment (Applegate et al., 2002, Nellis, 2009; Toch and Maguire, 2014), not to mention issues that particularly affect women, such as gender quotas (Möhring and Teney, 2018). Similarly, women are usually reported to lean more towards the left of the political spectrum than men (Dassonneville, 2021), which has an effect on their vote choice (Abendschön and Steinmetz, 2014; Giger, 2009; Inglehart and Norris, 2003). Furthermore, several studies report that women are significantly underrepresented among radical right voters (for an overview, see Coffé, 2018). Yet, there are many political topics in which there is a lack of stable trends regarding gender effects.

This seems to be the case with attitudes towards immigration. As previous research concluded, gender interacts with opinions about immigrants in complex ways (Dancygier and Donnelly, 2014; Mudde, 2007). In fact, there are many inconsistencies and contradictions between the several studies that consider gender as a potential explanatory factor behind attitudes towards immigration. Thus, clear divergences between and trends for women or men are not easily perceptible, as we

DOI: 10.4324/9781003121992-7

describe in the next section. Curiously, among the pieces of research that analyze the perception of threats possibly associated with immigration, the outcomes are far more uniform. Women (as compared to men) tend to be more concerned about the immigrants' impact on their countries' economies (economic threat) but less so about the influence they might have on the national culture. Concerning the security threat, which, comparatively, has less often been the object of research, the results are, once again, rather contradictory. In general, what stands out is an absence of studies that focus specifically on the role of gender in attitudes towards immigration.

Notwithstanding the use of the "gender binary" classification (composed of women and men) in the field of political science, the concept of gender is much more complex and richer than that. In an effort to undermine biological determinism, the second-wave feminists have (successfully) endeavoured to disseminate the idea that "sex" should be defined as the biological aspects of being women and men. By contrast, "gender" should relate to what is culturally determined and to the roles and behaviours deemed typical of each of the sexes (Bittner and Grant, 2017, p. 1021). Accordingly, the term "gender" is generally preferred to "sex" in the social sciences, since it demonstrates that researchers are aware that not all differences between males and females are biologically determined (Pryzgoda and Chrisler, 2000, p. 555).[2]

Recent work seeks to raise awareness about the lack of accuracy and precision that the use of a binary sex variable as a proxy for gender provokes, besides denouncing its failure to include non-binary people. Alternative ways of conceptualizing and measuring gender/sex are being explored, and social and health scholars are being called on to shift towards the inclusive measurement of gender in quantitative research (Bittner and Grant, 2017; Fraser et al., 2020; Hyde et al., 2019, among others). Yet, this avenue is still in its infancy, and this chapter, which draws on secondary data (from the CSES), relies on the traditional and, so far, predominant binary gender/sex classification.

The chapter proceeds with a revision of the main trends about the association between gender and attitudes towards immigration, followed by an outline of the main theoretical mechanisms which might explain these associations. The following section presents an empirical analysis of the association between gender and attitudes about immigrants using data from the nine countries presented in Chapter 3. Lastly, we discuss and reflect on the implications of our main findings and suggest further avenues of research.

GENDER AND ATTITUDES TOWARDS IMMIGRATION

Most empirical research on the individual factors influencing public perceptions of the overall development of immigration includes gender/sex in its models, though usually in a secondary position. In other words, gender is seldom the focus of the research (but see Berg, 2010; Valentova and Alieva, 2014; Ponce, 2017). Instead, it usually simply assumes the role of a control variable.[3] We start by reviewing studies which have been most prominent in evaluating gender effects in political science and related social sciences.

Focusing on the factor being studied by each published piece, or on the dependent variable, we have identified three lines of research. The first focuses on a general measurement of attitudes towards immigrants and/or on the number of immigrants admitted annually. In these studies, immigrants are typically taken as a homogeneous group, without further specifications or implications. The second line of research explores variations in the public perception of immigrants according to their specific characteristics, which can refer to the immigrants' legal status (regular or irregular), to their geographic origin (rich vs. poor countries, and specific geographic areas), or to the type of immigration flow (labour, asylum, or irregular). Lastly, more recent work – to which this chapter relates – has aimed to disentangle the public's propensity to perceive immigrants according to specific threats, notably, economic, cultural, and security. The potential for perceiving threats by immigrants is important because the threat response can facilitate reactionary responses to the presence of immigrants (Immerzeel et al., 2015; Mayer, 2015). Even though the overall role of gender is not strong, gender differences are more likely to emerge when exploring the impacts of threat perception, as we elaborate below.

Regarding the first line of analysis, research conducted in the US during the 1990s indicated that females held more favourable views than male respondents with respect to larger intakes of immigrants (Chandler and Tsai, 2001). In a study of 24 countries, O'Rourke and Sinnot (2006) sought to assess the influence of socioeconomic and sociodemographic characteristics (including gender) and political attitudes on public opinion about immigration. This study explored a possible link between attitudes towards trade and those towards immigration and findings suggested that females held less anti-immigrant attitudes than males (although the coefficient is statistically insignificant).

By contrast, work in Canada came to the opposite conclusion. Wilkes et al. (2008) found that men were less likely than women to favour restricting immigration. Similarly, comparative research carried out in 1995–1997, covering 22 countries, also explored public perception of the intensity of inflows (number of immigrants). Regarding the role of gender, this investigation asserted that males were more likely than females to be more open to a greater intake of immigrants (Mayda, 2006).

Using the European context as a starting point and drawing on data extracted from the Eurobarometer, further cross-national analysis of public attitudes towards the general presence of immigrants originating in countries that were not member-states of the EU suggested that there were no gender effects (Kessler and Freeman, 2005). Also, Davidov and Meuleman (2012) addressed the willingness to allow immigrants into the country in several European countries and observed no difference between males and females. So, within this first line of work, the effects of gender on immigration opinion really are quite contradictory.

A second line of research on gender and immigration opinion focuses on the intrinsic characteristics of immigrants. For instance, a study in the US differentiated between legal and illegal immigrants and found that female respondents were more opposed than males to the rights and entitlements of legal immigrants and there was no gender difference in terms of anti-illegal immigrant attitudes (Chandler and Tsai,

2001). Yet, a more recent piece, also conducted in the US, reveals that male citizens are more in favour of an increase in "patrolling the border against illegal immigrants" (Mangum, 2019). It remains unclear if the disparity between both studies is due to the different wording of the questions or an effect of the passage of time.

In an article looking at the refugee status of immigrants in 24 countries, O'Rourke and Sinnot (2006) show that females seemed to exhibit attitudes which were significantly more pro-refugee than males. Analyses of public attitudes towards government policy on labour immigration highlighted that gender differences were not statistically significant (Freeman and Kessler, 2005; Mayda, 2006).

Considering the economic status of source countries, Hainmueller and Hiscox (2007) found that female respondents had a greater propensity than males to oppose immigration from richer countries but were significantly more inclined to support inflows from poorer countries.[4] Supported by a longitudinal approach (2002–2010), research on Europe suggested that males were more likely to support the admission of immigrants from poorer countries when the economic context was positive, but no overall effects were identified during periods of economic depression – if any, the statistical difference is in the opposite direction (Dancygier and Donnelly, 2014). Additionally, a study by Gorodzeisky (2011) found that males seemed more supportive of accepting immigrants from "richer countries" but did not differ from females in their exclusionary attitudes towards European immigrants from poorer countries.

One of the few studies to examine gender as the main explanatory variable explored the extent to which women have more negative attitudes towards Muslims than other immigrant groups (Ponce, 2017). This study concluded that gender differences were absent from attitudes towards poor immigrants, regardless of their origins (Ponce, 2017). However, female respondents were significantly more likely to hold a negative perception of Muslims compared to males. This finding was associated with the increased salience of gender egalitarianism in Europe and the recurrent stereotyping of Muslims as gender illiberal and irreconcilable with sex equality. Remarkably, the female gender effects towards Muslim immigration remained significant after controlling for a range of individual-level and country-level variables (Ponce, 2017).

The third line of work aims to disentangle survey questions which associate immigrants with specific threat perceptions, notably, economic, cultural, and security threats. Pichler (2010) focused on the perception of the impact of immigration in host societies in terms of the economic and cultural dimensions. Drawing on the data from the first three rounds of the European Social Survey (2002–2007), the research suggests that women and men followed a distinct pattern of threat perception with regard to immigration. While females held a stronger perception than males of the economic threat posed by immigrants, the opposite trend was observed regarding the cultural threat. From the author's perspective, these two opposing trends help explain the lack of gender effects in public perception of an overall threat from immigration (Pichler, 2010). Findings from other studies of gendered opinion on immigration threat coalesce around these trends – females were more likely to perceive immigration as an economic threat rather than a cultural one (Dancygier and Donnelly, 2014; Chasapopoulous and Williams, 2019).

Work conducted in the US explored the relationship between race/ethnicity and the public perception that immigration contributes to crime (Higgins et al., 2010). This study suggested that males demonstrated less inclination than females to view the relationship between immigration and crime as problematic. Thus, females held stronger perceptions of immigration as a crime threat (Higgins et al., 2010). Additional research conducted in the US evaluated public perception of immigrants' impact on job competition, immigrants' contribution to the national economy, and the perception of this social phenomenon as being a cause for the increase of crime rates. Females were more likely to disagree that immigrants take jobs from Americans but were also less inclined to perceive immigration as advantageous to the economy (Berg, 2010). Moreover, this study suggested that the perception of immigration as a cause for the increase of crime rates was weaker among females than males (Berg, 2010).

Another of the few available studies focused on gender differences explored the perception of immigration-related threats (crime, job market, and welfare) in the general population, as well as among residents with a migratory background (first- and second-generation immigrants), in Luxemburg in the late 2000s (Valentova and Alieva, 2014). Regarding the native population, this analysis highlighted a significant interaction between gender and the perception of a crime threat, as the general anti-immigrant attitudes of female respondents were strongly associated with the perception of crime threats. A lack of gender effects was found regarding the job and welfare threats (Valentova and Alieva, 2014). By contrast, the same study observed that first-generation immigrant women were more concerned about the cultural threat than men, who were more worried about the threat of the out-group size. The perception of immigration as a job threat was more significant among second-generation immigrant females than among males. The first trend was associated with the immigrant women's engagement with the education of their children, whilst the second trend was associated with the low levels of education and the occupation profile of the latter group (Valentova and Alieva, 2014).

In short, the available literature suggests that women hold attitudes which are generally less anti-immigrant than men, but that gender effects towards Muslim immigrants are very significant in Europe. However, other research emphasized the lack of gender effects on attitudes towards immigrants or that males were observed to have a higher predisposition to accept a larger intake of foreign citizens. The lack of gender effects or the existence of merely minor variations thereof were also identified regarding citizens' attitudes towards immigrants according to their regular/irregular status or the type of immigration flow (labour, asylum, irregular). Remarkably, the research on Europe contained contradictory conclusions concerning the gender effects on the citizens' acceptance of immigrants according to the income level of their country of origin. Regarding the levels of threat perception, gender effects seemed to be significant, as females tended to associate immigration with economic concerns, whilst males tended to perceive it as a cultural threat. Research in the US led to opposite conclusions regarding gender effects on the perception of immigration as a crime threat.

POTENTIAL THEORETICAL MECHANISMS BEHIND THE GENDER EFFECT

The growing literature on attitudes towards immigrants and immigration suggests that these are affected by both individual-level and country-level factors (Davidov et al., 2020, p. 554). Concerning the former (which is the main focus of this chapter and the other chapters in Part 2), the possible causal chain of factors that potentially explain opposition to immigration is extremely complex (Heath et al., 2020, Figure 1), and comprises a varied set of factors, ranging from sociodemographic characteristics (notably, education and socioeconomic position, as discussed in Chapter 7) to social distance from immigrants and perceived size of the immigrant population (see Chapter 13), perception of threats attributed to immigrants (see Chapter 14), and the weight of ideology (see Chapter 10), partisanship (see Chapter 11), and party choice (Davidov et al., 2020; Heath et al., 2020).

In an effort to organize several explanatory models, some authors have identified two main distinct intellectual traditions as dominant in accounting for anti-immigrant sentiments (e.g. Fietkau and Hansen, 2018; Hainmueller and Hopkins, 2014). The first approach, grounded in political economy, refers to the role of economic self-interest and to the competition over scarce resources between immigrants and natives – the so-called labour market competition hypothesis. The second model, rooted in political psychology, emphasizes the role of group-related attitudes and symbols in shaping attitudes towards immigrants. Possible conflicts emerge primarily in association with cultural, ethnic, and religious differences – the so-called sociotropic approaches or questions of identity (Fietkau and Hansen, 2018; Hainmueller and Hopkins, 2014).

The first approach tends to yield poor results (for instance, Dancygier and Donnelly, 2014; Fetzer, 2000; Malhotra et al., 2013 – but see Semyonov et al., 2008). Consequently, the available literature suggests that "there is little accumulated evidence that citizens primarily form attitudes about immigration based on its effects on their personal economic situation" (Hainmueller and Hopkins, 2014, p. 227). By contrast, the research outputs derived from the political psychology strand of analysis seems more encouraging. Within the latter tradition, opposition to immigration is found to be rooted in cultural concerns (e.g. Chandler and Tsai, 2001), in negative stereotypes/prejudices about immigrants or ethnic minorities (Kessler and Freeman, 2005; Lee and Fiske, 2006; Fiske, 2012), in the role of emotions (Gadarian and Albertson, 2014; Landmann et al., 2019), and/or in the function of cultural values (Davidov et al., 2020).

When we turn our attention to the mechanisms that are likely to be behind the effects of gender on public attitudes towards immigration, the same two general theoretical foundations apply, namely, the self-interest and the sociotropic approaches, though not necessarily with these labels. While, as previously mentioned, there is a relative dearth of work focusing specifically on gender and attitudes towards immigration, these two approaches are well documented and are even employed to explain slightly different factors, like the gender gap in the support for wealth redistribution and government spending (Shorrocks, 2020). By exploring these two large branches of theory, it appears reasonable to expect women to be both more in favour of and more opposed to immigrants (as compared to men), as we outline in the remainder of this section.

Drawing on the economic consequences derived from immigration, the development of inflows of low-qualified male workers will increase the supply of low-skilled labour in the host society. In light of higher rates of females' exclusion from the labour market, the expansion of job competition is more likely to be perceived as a direct threat by males than by females (Immerzeel et al., 2015). Consequently, the geographic areas with higher rates of unemployment and immigration will observe stronger levels of anti-immigration attitudes among male workers (Givens, 2004).

From a different perspective, in Europe, females tend to possess, on average, lower skills than males. They have been largely excluded from the top tiers of the labour market and are more economically vulnerable. Hence, from a job competition perspective, women could be expected to support immigration from countries with higher qualification levels to prevent enhanced competition – although that is not always the case (Hainmueller and Hiscox, 2007). Similarly, the less favourable attitudes towards immigration among females in Canada is associated with self-interest, as the females' higher representation in fragile and precarious labour market positions enhanced their vulnerability to the increase in competition from newcomers (Wilkes et al., 2008).

Another line of reasoning, greatly echoed in the literature since Gilligan (1982), argues that "women are more likely than men to think of themselves within interconnected relationships rather than in isolation and thus to develop an ethics of 'care'" (Shorrocks, 2020, p. 290). This trend supposedly reflects a concern for protecting the vulnerable and for accepting inequality as a cause of other problems such as violence (Wagnsson et al., 2020, p. 793). In the same vein, an old strand of literature has been claiming for decades that girls and boys are socialized differently, with important consequences on adult roles and functioning (Leaper and Friedman, 2007). Notably, female socialization experiences stress connection and concern for others from early childhood, whereas boys' socialization stresses separation, independence, and autonomy (Hurwitz and Smithey, 1998). This makes women more prone to share positive feelings towards immigrants.

There is another well-established stream of studies that relates gender with perceptions of the threat of crime. This branch of scholarship emerges as relevant for this chapter, since foreigners' impact on crime rates tends to be perceived as particularly negative (Semyonov et al., 2008) – although, over the last two decades, criminologists have proven the notion that immigrants increase crime to be false (McCann and Boateng, 2020). Two main conclusions are commonly reported: the first one states that women tend to report higher levels of fear of crime than men (Nellis, 2009; Toch and Maguire, 2014); the second argues that women tend to be less supportive of aggressive/violent actions (Applegate et al., 2002; Feldman and Stenner, 1997; Nellis, 2009). The explanations usually offered for the "women and peace hypothesis" are derived from the same kind of two-folded theories presented above. First, structural differences, such as the feminization of poverty or sexual aggression, can lead to women having more to lose from a war, for example. Second, social forces and gender roles are identified which harken back to the gendered social learning and socialization (Stevens et al., 2021). This mix of complex issues makes it difficult to predict gender behaviour regarding the relationship between attitudes towards immigrants and a perceived threat of crime.

GENDER GAP IN THREAT PERCEPTIONS IN NINE COUNTRIES

With the trend of international migration continuing to increase, analyzing public opinion on immigrants remains indispensable. It is rather common that immigrants (or foreigners) "are perceived as a threat to the social, political and economic order as well as a threat to the cultural homogeneity and the national identity of the state" (Semyonov et al., 2008, p. 6). Figures 5.1, 5.2, and 5.3 present gender differences regarding the economic, cultural, and security threats, respectively, as discussed in Chapter 3. For each threat, both the average and the percentages for each gender are shown in the upper corner of each country panel. Recall that the scale of possible answers ranges from 1 (lowest level of anti-immigration sentiment) to 5 (highest level of anti-immigration sentiment). Additionally, bivariate tests of women and men by country for each of the three threats were performed (data not shown).

Four main comments are warranted. First, in line with the literature, none of the three threat perceptions portrays very pronounced gender differences, which makes it difficult to discern trends from the figures by eye. This confirms that gender is not a very strong determinant of attitudes towards immigrants, in comparison to other individual-level determinants like social class or ideology, as discussed in Chapters 7 and 10, respectively.

Second, the traceable gender differences do not follow the same shape for all threat perceptions; in fact, at times, they follow opposite patterns. Whereas women tend to share more anti-immigrant opinions concerning the economic threat (Figure 5.1), this pattern is reversed when looking at the perceived crime threat (Figure 5.3), where it is the men who reveal, on average, a more negative position towards immigrants. In other words, women are less convinced (as compared to men) that immigrants are generally good for their country's economy, but they are also less convinced that immigrants increase crime rates in the respondents' country. As for the cultural threat (Figure 5.2), no clear trend emerges. Whereas in Australia, Germany, Switzerland, and the USA, men are more convinced that immigrants damage the countries' culture, in France, Italy, and Portugal the reverse is observed. But, of all nine countries, only for Switzerland and the USA are the differences of the bivariate tests significant, while between the UK and Canada there

Immigrants are generally good for [COUNTRY]'s economy.

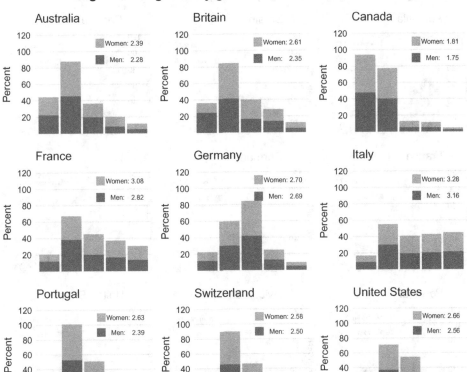

SA = Strongly agree (1); A = Agree (2); N = Neither agree nor disagree (3); D = Disagree (4); SD = Strongly disagree (5)

FIGURE 5.1 Attitudes about how immigrants are perceived to affect a country's economy, by gender.

is no gender distinction at all. The fact that we found contradictory results for the gender factor when analyzing the perceived threats reveals the potential inappropriateness of constructing an index aggregating the three threats – as done in the other chapters of this section.

Third, despite the fact that the gender gap – even with respect to the economic and security threats – is not very pronounced, our results are very consistent for these two threats across countries. Concerning the economic threat, the pattern previously described (tendency for women to be more anti-immigrant) can be observed in all countries, except for Germany, where the average is precisely the same for both men and women. As for the security threat, in all countries but Portugal, women are more pro-immigrant. Furthermore, five out of the nine countries show a significant gender gap for each of the two threat perceptions in the bivariate tests.

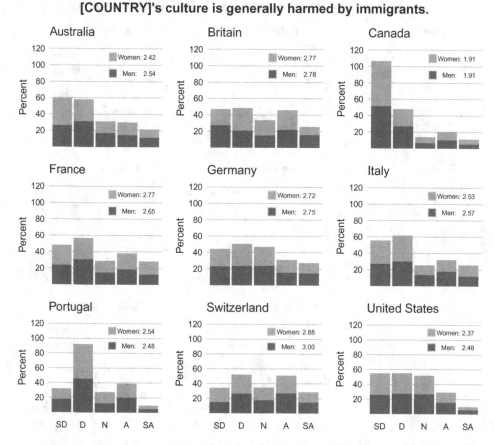

FIGURE 5.2 Attitudes about how immigrants are perceived to affect a country's culture, by gender.

The findings regarding the economic threat are in line with the very consistent outcomes of previous investigations, concerning both the US (Berg, 2010) and Europe (Chasapopoulous and Williams, 2019; Dancygier and Donnelly, 2014; Pichler, 2010; Valentova and Alieva, 2014). There does seem to be an overall – slight, yet consistent – tendency for women to be less inclined to perceive immigration as a contributing factor for the economy. By contrast, our results on the security threat are less in accordance with the literature, largely because the general outcome is much less consolidated concerning this threat. While some scholars report that women are less prone to associate immigration and crime rates (e.g. Berg, 2010) – which is in line with our findings – others come to the opposite conclusion (Higgins et al., 2010; Valentova and Alieva, 2014).

Concerning the cultural threat, our findings (Figure 5.2) are less consistent than previous research suggests. In fact, there seems to be a consensus in the literature

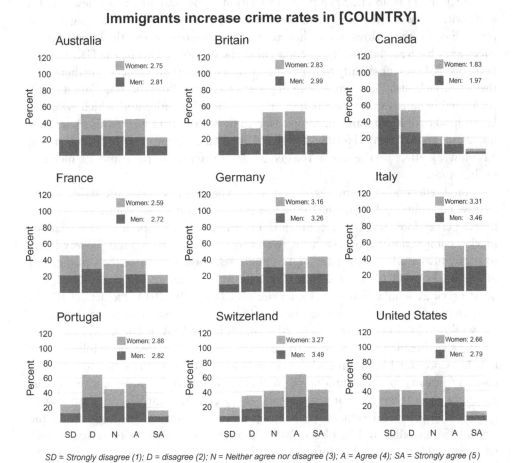

Immigrants increase crime rates in [COUNTRY].

SD = Strongly disagree (1); D = disagree (2); N = Neither agree nor disagree (3); A = Agree (4); SA = Strongly agree (5)

FIGURE 5.3 Attitudes about how immigrants are perceived to affect a country's security/crime, by gender.

around the idea that men (more than women) believe that culture is generally harmed by immigrants (Pichler, 2010; Chasapopoulous and Williams, 2019; Dancygier and Donnelly, 2014). This uniformity is not at all visible in our data. Moreover, our findings suggest a lack of overall effects from the 2015 asylum crisis in Europe and the subsequent political mobilization of gender nationalism over the intensity of gender effects regarding the perception of immigration as a threat to national culture (Hadj Abdou, 2017). Despite the claims made by Marine Le Pen (the leader of the *Rassemblement National* in France) in 2016, that the migratory crisis would signal the end of women's rights, the gender gap in the perception of a cultural threat is more evident in France than in other European countries included in this study and which received the largest number of asylum applications in 2018–2019 (Germany and Italy; Eurostat, 2021; Hadj Abdou, 2017).

Fourth, there is no clear gender gap variation across the nine countries. The US and Switzerland are the only countries where the gender differences are significant for each of the three threats, but they are *not* the countries where the largest differences are observed. For instance, concerning the economic threat, the UK, France, and Portugal present slightly greater (and also significant) differences. Furthermore, there is a lack of a clear pattern among settler nations (like the US, Canada, and Australia), where immigration is part of the national identity and which welcome larger intakes of immigrants in comparison to those countries where this social phenomenon is more recent (Hollifield et al., 2014). Thus, the timing of inflows seems to have a weak effect on the size of the gender gaps observed in the countries included in this study.

A final reflection is in order with respect to what might explain the stable results that we have obtained regarding the gender differences on the economic and security threat perceptions across the countries. Theoretically, the aforementioned labour market competition hypothesis, as it relates to economic self-interest, is very likely to partly justify why women are slightly more reluctant to assume that immigrants are generally good for their country's economy, not only in our data but also in most previous scholarship (e.g. Dancygier and Donnelly, 2014; Pichler, 2010). In fact, employment rates for women remain lower than those of men everywhere in the world – 12% lower in the EU in 2018; 8.1% in the USA in 2020.[5] Also, there is a generalized tendency for women to be overrepresented in precarious jobs.[6] These two facts presumably explain why women hold greater fear than men about newcomers from an economic standpoint (Wilkes et al., 2008). However, a dive into our data (not shown) reveals that respondents' socioeconomic status is not sufficient to explain the gender differences we find regarding this threat. This suggests, in the vein of Hainmueller and Hopkins (2014), that explanations of a more sociotropic nature should be pursued in future research. It is possible that economic issues go beyond the ethics of "care" that disproportionately characterize women, so other factors ought to be analyzed.

Concerning the perception of crime threat, we stated earlier that predictions were hard to draw, given the mixed possible mechanisms at play. However, our results (Figure 5.3) emerge as surprisingly stable across countries; in fact, more stable than previous scholarship would lead one to expect (Berg, 2010; Higgins et al., 2010). If women tend to have higher levels of fear of crime (Nellis, 2009; Toch and Maguire, 2014), why are they less concerned that immigrants increase crime rates? The most obvious answer is that the ethics of "care" renders women more likely to share positive feelings towards immigrants. But Stevens and his co-authors advocate two other rather interesting potential reasons. The first one is that women and men are likely to perceive threat and security differently – more self-centred in the male case, and more geared towards keeping the community in mind in the female case. The second one is that "women are more confident about government's ability to deal with security threats in the future" (Stevens et al., 2021, p. 47).

CONCLUSION

The nature of attitudes towards or beliefs about immigrants is complex and multi-faceted, and scholars are far from having an overall picture of what affects them. Hence, contradictory results between publications are rather common. One possible reason for this inconsistency is the lack of precision of the questions asked in questionnaires, implying that validity might be compromised. First, when surveyed about "immigrants", (only) one-fifth to one-third of the people consider immigrants in general, as opposed to immigrants of specific ethnicities, races or origins, implying that survey respondents do not often have "comparable" groups in mind (Braun et al., 2013). Second, the dimension of life that the researcher chooses to focus on as that which might be affected by the influx of immigrants is also likely to matter. In other words, some people might think that immigrants are beneficial in some dimensions of life (e.g. cultural) but not in others. The reversed gender pattern identified in this chapter regarding the economic and security threat perceptions is indicative of that. Having said this, making sure to specify all possible variations in every question would be a Herculean task, and the results would be equally unsatisfactory, only this time due to the high level of specificity of the dependent variable.

While these concerns apply to all scholarship on immigration attitudes, when we aim to tackle the role of gender, the imprecision of results may even increase. Women are a heterogeneous group, having less in common with each other than with similar groups of men (Campbell et al., 2010, p. 174), particularly when the issue at stake is not related to gender. Hence the reduced number of issues where some kind of gender gap is systematically encountered. And immigration is certainly not one of those. It is therefore no wonder that so few studies on immigration attitudes have gender as the central feature.

That being said, we found two light yet consistent tendencies across countries which are worth noting. First, in line with previous studies (e.g. Dancygier and Donnelly, 2014; Pichler, 2010), there is an overall tendency for women (as compared to men) to perceive immigration as a hindrance to the economy. While part of this might be attributed to women's lower economic conditions, further research is necessary to properly disentangle the mechanisms behind this outcome. Second, women seem to be less concerned about immigration's impact on crime, despite their higher levels of fear of crime (Nellis, 2009; Toch and Maguire, 2014). Although Stevens and co-authors (2021) have suggested good clues as to why that might be the case, we are far from fully comprehending this result, but the fact that it is less consistent in the literature makes understanding it a lower priority.

Finally, it remains unclear why our data do not confirm the tendency of women to positively appraise immigrants' influence on their countries' culture, which has been broadly suggested before (e.g. Berg, 2010; Dancygier and Donnelly, 2014; Pichler, 2010). But this is yet another sign that the relationship between gender and attitudes towards immigrants is inconsistent at best and mystifying at worst.

SUMMARY POINTS

- This chapter provided a comprehensive review of the literature on gender and public attitudes about immigrants showing that gender differences are neither large nor negligible.
- This chapter considered different explanatory mechanisms for a gender difference in immigration opinion including the political economy of self-interest and the group-related attitudes and identities.
- The chapter's findings suggested women (as compared to men) are more likely to perceive immigrants as a hindrance to the economy, which is in line with previous work, and that women are are less concerned than men about immigration's impact on crime – a less steady output in the literature.

NOTES

1 The English proofreading of this text was funded by the Fundação para a Ciência e a Tecnologia through R&D Unit UIDB/03126/2020.
2 There is a complex and multifaceted debate about the conceptions of sex and gender that is beyond the scope of this chapter. See these sources for a discussion (Butler, 1999; Hatemi et al., 2012; Bittner and Grant, 2017; Hyde et al., 2019).
3 A "control variable" means a variable that is included in a statistical analysis like multiple regression because it may influence the dependent variable of focus but is not theoretically prioritized in the analysis.
4 The authors nevertheless highlight that these coefficients were only flirting with conventional levels of significance in some cases.
5 https://ec.europa.eu/eurostat/web/products-eurostat-news/-/EDN-20200306-1; https://www.statista.com/statistics/192396/employment-rate-of-women-in-the-us-since-1990/ (accessed 21 February 2021).
6 https://ec.europa.eu/social/BlobServlet?docId=7925&langId=en (accessed 21 February 2021).

SUGGESTED FURTHER READINGS

Berg, J., 2010. Race, class, gender, and social space: Using an intersectional approach to study immigration attitudes. *Sociological Quarterly*, 51(2), 278–302.

Ponce, A., 2017. Gender and anti-immigrant attitudes in Europe. *Socius: Sociological Research for a Dynamic World*, 3, 1–17.

Valentova, M. and Alieva, A., 2014. Gender differences in the perception of immigration-related threats. *International Journal of Intercultural Relations*, 39, 175–182.

REFERENCES

Abendschön, S. and Steinmetz, S., 2014. The gender gap in voting revisited: Women's party preferences in a European context. *Social Politics*, 21(1), 315–344.

Applegate, B.K., Cullen, F.T., and Fisher, B.S., 2002. Public views toward crime and correctional policies: Is there a gender gap? *Journal of Criminal Justice*, 30(2), 89–100.

Berg, J., 2010. Race, class, gender, and social space: Using an intersectional approach to study immigration attitudes. *The Sociological Quarterly*, 51(2), 278–302.

Bittner, A. and Goodyear-Grant, E., 2017. Sex isn't gender: Reforming concepts and measurements in the study of public opinion. *Political Behavior*, 39(4), 1019–1041.

Braun, M., Behr, D., and Kaczmirek, L., 2013. Assessing cross-national equivalence of measures of xenophobia: Evidence from probing in web surveys. *International Journal of Public Opinion Research*, 25(3), 383–395.

Butler, J., 1999. *Gender trouble: Feminism and the subversion of identity*. New York: Routledge.

Campbell R., Childs S., and Lovenduski J., 2010. Do women need women representatives? *British Journal of Political Science*, 40(1), 171–194.

Campbell, R., 2012. What do we really know about women voters? Gender, elections and public opinion. *The Political Quarterly*, 83(4), 703–710.

Chandler, C. and Tsai H.-M., 2001. Social factors influencing immigration attitudes: An analysis of data from the general social survey. *The Social Science Journal*, 38, 277–288.

Chasapopoulous, P. and Williams, M., 2019. Immigrants' origin and skill level as factors in attitudes toward immigrants in Europe. *Journal of Identity and Migration Studies*, 13(2), 47–78.

Dancygier R. and Donnelly M., 2014. Attitudes toward immigration in good times and bad times. In: N. Bermeo and L. Bartels, eds. *Mass politics in tough times: Opinions, votes, and protest in the great recession*. Oxford: Oxford University Press, 148–184.

Dassonneville, R., 2021. Change and continuity in the ideological gender gap a longitudinal analysis of left-right self-placement in OECD countries. *European Journal of Political Research*, 60, 225–238.

Davidov E. and Meuleman B., 2012. Explaining attitudes towards immigration policies in European countries: The role of human values. *Journal of Ethnic and Migration Studies*, 38(5), 757–775.

Davidov, E., Seddig, D., Gorodzeisky, A., Raijman, R., Schmidt, P., and Semyonov, M., 2020. Direct and indirect predictors of opposition to immigration in Europe: Individual values, cultural values, and symbolic threat. *Journal of Ethnic and Migration Studies*, 46(3), 553–573.

Eurostat., 2021. Number of first-time asylum applicants (non-EU-27 citizens), 2018 and 2019. Available from: https://ec.europa.eu/eurostat/statistics-explained/index.php?title=File :Number_of_first-time_asylum_applicants_(non-EU-27_citizens),_2018_and_2019_ (thousands).png

Feldman, S. and Stenner, K., 1997. Perceived threat and authoritarianism. *Political Psychology*, 18(4), 741–770.

Fetzer J.S., 2000. *Public attitudes toward immigration in the United States, France, and Germany*. New York: Cambridge University Press.

Fietkau, S. and Hansen, K.M., 2018. How perceptions of immigrants trigger feelings of economic and cultural threats in two welfare states. *European Union Politics*, 19(1), 119–139.

Fiske, S.T., 2012. Managing ambivalent prejudices. *Annals of the American Academy of Political and Social Science*, 639, 33–48.

Fraser, G., Bulbulia, J., Greaves, L.M., Wilson M.S., and Sibley C.G., 2020. Coding responses to an open-ended gender measure in a New Zealand national sample. *Journal of Sex Research*, 57(8):979–986.

Gadarian S.K. and Albertson B., 2014. Anxiety, immigration, and the search for information. *Political Psychology*, 35(2), 133–164.

Giger, N., 2009. Towards a modern gender gap in Europe? *Social Science Journal*, 46(3), 474–492.

Gilligan, C., 1982. *In a different voice: Psychological theory and women's development.* Cambridge, MA: Harvard University Press.

Givens, T., 2004. The radical right gender gap. *Comparative Political Studies*, 37(1), 30–54.

Gorodzeisky, A., 2011. Who are the Europeans that Europeans prefer? Economic conditions and exclusionary views toward European immigrants. *International Journal of Comparative Sociology*, 52(1–2), 100–113.

Hadj Abdou, L., 2017. Gender nationalism': The new (old) politics of belonging. *Austrian Journal of Political Science*, 46(1), 83–88.

Hainmueller J. and Hiscox M., 2007. Educated preferences: Explaining attitudes toward immigration in Europe international organization. *International Organization*, 61(Spring 2007), 399–442.

Hainmueller, J. and Hopkins, D.J., 2014. Public attitudes toward immigration. *Annual Review of Political Science*, 17, 225–249.

Hatemi, P.K., Rose McDermott, J., Bailey, M., and Martin, N.G., 2012. The different effects of gen-der and sex on vote choice. *Political Research Quarterly*, 65(1), 76–92.

Heath, A., Davidov, E., Ford, R., Green, E.G.T., Ramos, A., and Schmidt, P., 2020. Contested ter-rain: Explaining divergent patterns of public opinion towards immigration within Europe. *Journal of Ethnic and Migration Studies*, 46(3), 475–488.

Higgins, G., Gabbidon, S., and Martin, F., 2010. The role of race/ethnicity and race relations on public opinion related to the immigration and crime link. *Journal of Criminal Justice*, 38, 51–56.

Hollifield, J., Martin, P., and Orrenius, P., 2014. *Controlling immigration: A global perspective.* Stanford, CA: Stanford University Press.

Howell, S.E. and Day C.L., 2000. Complexities of the gender gap. *Journal of Politics*, 62(3), 858–874.

Hurwitz, J. and Smithey, S., 1998. Gender differences on crime and punishment. *Political Re-search Quarterly*, 51(1), 89–115.

Hyde, J.S., Bigler, R.S., Joel, D., Tate, C.C., and van Anders, S.M., 2019. The future of sex and gender in psychology: Five challenges to the gender binary. *American Psychologist*, 74(2), 171–193.

Immerzeel, T., Coffé, H., and Lippe, T., 2015. Explaining the gender gap in radical right voting: A cross-national investigation in 12 Western European countries. *Comparative European Politics*, 13(2), 263–286.

Inglehart, R. and Norris, P., 2003. *Rising tide: Gender equality and cultural change around the world.* Cambridge: Cambridge University Press.

Kamas, L. and Preston A., 2018. Can empathy explain gender differences in economic policy views in the United States? *Feminist Economics*, 25(1), 58–89.

Kessler, A. and Freeman, G., 2005. Public opinion in the EU on immigration from outside the community. *Journal of Common Market Studies*, 43(4), 825–850.

Landmann H., Gaschler R., and Rohmann A., 2019. "What is threatening about refugees? Identifying different types of threat and their association with emotional responses and attitudes towards refugee migration. *European Journal of Social Psychology*, 49(7), 1401–1420.

Leaper, C. and Friedman, C.K., 2007. The socialization of gender. In: J.E. Grusec and P.D. Hastings, eds. *Handbook of socialization: Theory and research.* New York: The Guilford Press, 561–587.

Lee T.L. and Fiske S.T., 2006. Not an outgroup, not yet an ingroup: Immigrants in the stereotype content model. *International Journal of Intercultural Relations*, 30, 751–768.

Malhotra N., Margalit Y., and Mo C.H., 2013. Economic explanations for opposition to immigration: Distinguishing between prevalence and conditional impact. *American Journal of Political Science*, 57, 391–410.

Mangum, M., 2019. Revisiting economic threat and cultural concerns: Public opinion toward immigration and non-citizens by race. *Social Science Research*, 83, 102309

Mayda, A.M., 2006. Who is against immigration? A cross-country investigation of individual attitudes toward immigrants. *Review of Economics and Statistics*, 88, 510–530.

Mayer, N., 2015. The closing of the radical right gender gap in France? *French Politics*, 13(4), 391–414.

McCann, W.S. and Boateng, F.D., 2020. An examination of American perceptions of the immi-grant-crime relationship. *American Journal of Criminal Justice*, 45, 973–1002.

Möhring, K. and Teney, C., 2018. Equality prescribed? Contextual determinants of citizens' support for gender boardroom quotas across Europe. *Comparative European Politics*, 18, 560–589.

Mudde, C., 2007. *Populist radical right parties in Europe*. Cambridge: Cambridge University Press.

Nellis, A.M., 2009. Gender differences in fear of terrorism. *Journal of Contemporary Criminal Justice*, 25(3), 322–340.

O'Rourke, K. and Sinnott, R., 2006. The determinants of individual attitudes towards immigration. *European Journal of Political Economy*, 22, 838–861.

Pichler, F., 2010. Foundations of anti-immigrant sentiment: The variable nature of perceived group threat across changing European societies, 2002–2006. *International Journal of Comparative Sociology*, 51(6), 445–469.

Ponce, A., 2017. Gender and anti-immigrant attitudes in Europe. *Socius: Sociological Research for a Dynamic World*, 3, 1–17.

Pryzgoda, J. and Chrisler, J.C., 2000. Definitions of gender and sex: The subtleties of meaning. *Sex Roles: A Journal of Research*, 43(7–8), 553–569.

Semyonov M., Raijman R., and Gorodzeisky A., 2008. Foreigners' impact on European societies: Public views and perceptions in a cross-national comparative perspective. *International Journal of Comparative Sociology*, 49(1), 5–29.

Shorrocks, R., 2020. The attitudinal gender gap across generations: Support for redistribution and government spending in contexts of high and low welfare provision. *European Political Science Review*, 12(3), 289–306.

Stevens, D., Bulmer, S., Banducci, S., and Vaughan-Williams, N., 2021. Male warriors and worried women? Understanding gender and perceptions of security threats. *European Journal of International Security*, 6(1), 44–65.

Toch, H. and Maguire, K., 2014. Public opinion regarding crime, criminal justice, and related topics: A retrospect. *Journal of Research in Crime and Delinquency*, 51(4), 424–444.

Valentova, M., and Alieva, A., 2014. Gender differences in the perception of immigration-related threats. *International Journal of Intercultural Relations*, 39, 175–182.

Wagnsson, C., Olsson, E.-K., and Nilsen, I., 2020. Swedish opinions on crime, terrorism, and national security. *Gender & Society*, 34(5), 790–817.

Wilkes R., Guppy N., and Farris L., 2008. No thanks, we're full: Individual characteristics, national context and changing attitudes toward immigration. *International Migration Review*, 42, 302–329.

CHAPTER 6

Immigration status and public opinion

....

Katrine Beauregard

INTRODUCTION

In many established democracies, immigrants represent a growing share of the population. According to the UN DESA, 6.9% of Europeans were foreign-born in 1990 compared to 11% in 2019. In North America, the foreign-born population went from 9.9% in 1990 to 16% in 2019. Important variations also exist across countries where, in 2019, 30% of Australians were born in another country compared to 29.9% in Switzerland, 21.3% in Canada, 15.7% in Germany, 15.4% in the United States, 14.1% in the United Kingdom, 12.8% in France, 10.4% in Italy, and 8.7% in Portugal.[1] This increased immigration in many established democracies has led to growing debates on the impact of immigration on a country's culture and economy as well as debates about the desired levels of immigration.

While most research focuses on explanations for immigration attitudes of the native-born population, comparatively less is known about immigrants' opinions of immigration. Immigrants themselves tend to be more supportive of immigration than native-born citizens; however, there are important divisions among the former. Immigrants' countries of origin, their experience in the host country, and their attachment and identification to their ethnicity or country of origin are some of the factors that explain why some immigrants are more likely than others to have positive views of immigration.

The following sections first discuss the key definitions and measurements associated with immigration status before providing an overview of the theoretical mechanisms and findings in the literature detailing the effects of immigration status on immigration attitudes. The next section reviews differences in opinions between foreign-born and native-born respondents in eight established democracies. Finally, I test some of the explanations discussed in this chapter, using the 2019 Australian Election Study (AES).

DOI: 10.4324/9781003121992-8

KEY DEFINITIONS AND MEASUREMENTS

The literature on immigration status and public opinion employs three distinct concepts: group membership, group identification, and group consciousness (McClain et al., 2009; Czaja and Medenica, 2020). In most work, immigrant status is treated as group membership. McClain et al. (2009) stipulate that group membership "refers to the assignment of an individual into a particular group based on characteristics that are specific to that group, in accordance with widely held intersubjective definition" (p. 473). Generally, immigration status is measured through the place of birth of respondents (see Kang and Look, 2020; Just and Anderson, 2015; Strijbis and Polavieja, 2018). Respondents who are born outside of the host country are classified as immigrants while respondents who are born in the country of residence are natives or native-born. It is important to note that in some countries, native-born are not necessarily citizens. For example, Australian-born children of parents who are not citizens nor have permanent residency status are not Australian citizens.

Related to this measure of immigration status is the concept of immigrant generation, which is measured with a series of questions asking respondents where their parents (both mother and father) were born for the second generation and where their grandparents were born for the third generation. Second-generation immigrants are born in the country of residence but have at least one parent foreign-born (van der Zwan, Bles, and Lubblers, 2017; Strijbis and Polavieja, 2018) while third-generation immigrants are respondents who have at least one foreign-born grandparent (Strijbis and Polavieja, 2018). Surveys, however, rarely include a measure of grandparents' country of birth, meaning this third generation is little studied (Schneider and Heath, 2020). Schneider and Heath (2020) raise the concern that measuring immigration generation with the country of birth might lead to identifying as immigrants the children of native citizens who for different reasons have been born overseas.

The concept of group membership contrasts with two additional concepts that provide greater focus on the causal mechanisms linking immigration status to political attitudes: group identity and group consciousness (McClain et al., 2009). Group identification "refers to an individual's awareness of belonging to a certain group and having a psychological attachment to that group based on a perception of shared beliefs, feelings, interests, and ideas with other group members" (McClain et al., 2009, p. 474). Social identity theory (SIT) stipulates a relationship between group membership and group identification where identity is fostered by membership. Group consciousness, on the other hand, is "in-group identification politicized by a set of ideological beliefs about one's group's social standing, as well as a view that collective action is the best means by which the group can improve its status and realize its interests" (McClain et al., 2009, p. 476). The role of group consciousness in political attitudes has its origins in the specific experiences of African Americans in the United States. While the extent to which this concept can be applied to other groups is debated, group consciousness and group identification are investigated as mechanisms linking group membership to attitudes towards immigration (see Vega and Ortiz, 2018 for an example). See Chapters 8, 11, and 17 for further discussion.

Group identification and group consciousness are measured in multiple different manners, using different questions and different wordings (Czaja and Medenica, 2020). As an example, a measure of group identification asks respondents their feeling of connectedness towards their country of birth and/or whether they feel greater identification with their country of birth, country of residence or both (see Meeusen, Abts, and Meuleman, 2019). Additionally, measures of group identification can assess the extent to which pan-ethnicity – that is, the combination of multiple national groups into one single identity such as Latinx or Asian – is linked with political attitudes (Knoll, 2012).

Group consciousness is measured with a series of questions designed to tap into different aspects of the concept. Questions can assess the perception and experience of discrimination (Vega and Ortiz, 2018) and/or the importance and attachment towards the language spoken in the country of birth when different from the country of residence (Rouse, Wilkinson, and Garand, 2010). An additional measure of group consciousness is "linked fate" (McClain et al., 2009), which is defined as the extent to which individuals believe their future and experiences are linked with those of their fellow group members. While linked fate is a crucial concept in the study of racial identity, it has not been the object of many investigations of immigrant attitudes towards immigration. Interestingly, the reversed relationship has been studied where immigration levels and immigration policies have been found to influence foreign-born Latinx's levels of linked fate (Matby et al., 2020; Vargas, Sanchez, and Valdez, 2017).

For measuring group identification and group consciousness, political context matters (Czaja and Medenica, 2020). Individuals can have multiple identities and some might be more important than others depending on the context and everyday situations (McClain et al., 2009; Huddy, 2001). Furthermore, respondents can have different understandings of questions measuring group identity and group consciousness (Czaja and Medenica, 2020; Lee, 2008). This is especially concerning when respondents have to answer questions in a language other than their first language. To summarize the challenges in measuring group identification and group consciousness, Czaja and Medenica (2020) state that

> differences in the ways in which individuals understand the same question, differences in the ways that survey questions are worded, and the contexts in which these questions are administered complicate the measurement and comparison of group membership, identity, and consciousness across racial groups.
>
> *(p. 143)*

These three core concepts – group membership, group identification, and group consciousness – have not been equally investigated in the literature. The next section outlines how theories have developed around these concepts and the major empirical results associated.

THEORIES AND RESULTS

In this section, I first discuss the major findings associated with the group membership literature which constitutes the largest part of the literature. Second, I present an overview of the main theories explaining differences in attitudes among immigrants; these focus on economic competition between immigrants, group identification, and group consciousness.

Group membership

Early investigations of immigration status and immigration attitudes focused on whether immigrants held similar orientations to native-born individuals. A common finding in many established democracies is that immigrants have more favourable views of immigration than native-born individuals. For example, in an investigation of 18 West European democracies, Just and Anderson (2015) show that respondents from an immigrant background are less likely to agree that immigration has negative consequences for their country than native-born respondents. Social identity theory (Tajfel and Turner, 1986) stipulates that individuals distinguish between those that are part of their group (in-group) and those who are not (out-group) and will have more positive orientations towards those who they perceive to be part of their in-group. Consequently, immigrants view favourably other immigrants while native-born individuals are more likely to perceive immigrants negatively. Despite immigrants originating from different countries, they share similar experiences of immigration which can lead them to develop kinship and solidarity with each other (Just and Anderson, 2015). In turn, these positive feelings towards fellow immigrants can result in greater support for permissive immigration policies when compared to native-born attitudes.

A related branch of investigation focuses on acculturation and its impact on different immigrant generations' attitudes. Acculturation refers to "the process whereby immigrants assume the cultural values and norms of mainstream [U.S.] society" (Branton, 2007, p. 301). Early investigations in the United States found that newer generations of Mexican immigrants are more supportive of policies benefitting illegal immigrants (Polinard, Wrinkle, and de la Garza, 1984) and less supportive of restrictive immigration policies (Binder, Polinard, and Wrinkle, 1997) than older generations of Mexican immigrants. Similar findings have been reported by Sanchez (2006), Branton (2007), Knoll (2012), Rouse, Wilkinson, and Garand (2010), and Capers and Smith (2016) in the United States.

In Europe, van der Zwan, Bles, and Lubbers (2017) find that the longer immigrants have been in the host country, the more likely they are to perceive other immigrants as threats. The assimilation process explains these findings where the longer immigrants reside in a host country, the greater the opportunity these individuals have to come into contact with the host society norms, values, and culture. Consequently, their attitudes towards immigrants and immigration policies align more with native attitudes. The authors argue that the longer immigrants reside in a host country, the more distant are the memory and challenges of immigrating to a new country, which lessens the impact of in-group favouritism on support for immigration policies.

Similarly, Just and Anderson (2015) argue that the formal incorporation of immigrants through citizenship can be an expression of kinship with the host country. Acquisition of citizenship can also be a desire to acquire formal protection and material benefits generally reserved for citizens. Both motivations, Just and Anderson (2015) argue, lead naturalized immigrants to have more similar views of immigration to native-born individuals. They indeed find that immigrants with citizenship are more likely to agree that immigration produces negative consequences to their country and are less likely to agree with new arrivals of immigrants.

Deepening the investigation of the impact of citizenship acquisition on immigrant attitudes, Politi et al. (2020) argue that different naturalization motives can have a differential influence on preferences for restrictive or permissive immigration policies. They find that immigrants acquiring citizenship because of a desire to belong to the country of residency are more likely to believe that immigrants should adopt the host country's culture and values, leading them to favour restrictive immigration policy as a way of distancing themselves from less deserving immigrants. On the other hand, immigrants acquiring citizenship because of a desire to obtain legal rights and protection are more likely to be concerned by their underprivileged and different position from majority members in the host society. In turn, these immigrants are more inclined to support immigrants' preserving their cultural heritage and traditions, resulting in permissive immigration attitudes.

Providing nuance to these above findings, Vega and Ortiz (2018) show that cohorts play an important role in understanding the relationship between acculturation and immigration attitudes. Investigating Mexican immigrants in the United States, they identify two cohorts: those who came of age in the World War II era and those who did so after the Civil Rights movement. The first cohort grew up under an assimilation culture that required immigrants to renounce their ethnic attachment to become Americans while the second cohort was influenced by the Civil Rights discourse emphasizing the legitimacy of ethnic attachment and challenging race-based discrimination. Vega and Ortiz (2018) demonstrate that among Mexican Americans socialized under the World War II cohort, older generations of immigrants have more negative attitudes towards immigration than more recent immigrants. On the other hand, there are no significant generational differences among Mexican Americans of the Civil Rights cohort. For more on the role of age and cohort, see Chapter 4.

Economic competition between immigrants

The previous discussions of group membership emphasized under what circumstances individuals with an immigrant background are more likely to have positive views towards fellow immigrants and immigration policies than native-born individuals. There is an alternative line of investigation, at times called the "economic competition hypothesis," stipulating that self-interest instead of in-group favouritism drives immigrant attitudes (Rouse, Wilkinson, and Garand, 2010; Knoll, 2012). Some immigrants are economically vulnerable because they are more likely than native-born individuals to be in lower socioeconomic positions (Knoll, 2012). As such, a large influx of newcomers can be a threat to established immigrants by increasing competition for jobs, resulting in negative attitudes towards recent immigration (Scheepers, Gijsberts, and Coenders, 2002; van der Zwan, Bles, and Lubbers, 2017). Competition in the labour market is an important explanation for immigration attitudes for those (immigrants or natives) that are the most exposed to competition (see Chapter 14 this volume; Kunovich, 2013; Polavieja, 2016). When competition for jobs is between immigrant groups, established immigrants perceive newcomers in a negative light. This effect is more likely felt among established immigrants with a lower socioeconomic background.

Findings in the United States provide mixed support for this hypothesis. Hood, Morris, and Shirkey (1997) find that economic threat shapes immigrant attitudes in a similar manner as it does for native-born individuals. Rouse, Wilkinson, and Garand (2010) find no significant difference in immigration attitudes across levels of income among immigrants. Knoll (2012) finds a weakly significant relationship where higher income levels among immigrants are associated with greater negative views of immigration. But, there is no impact of negative evaluations of the economy on immigrant attitudes towards immigration, providing little support for the economic threat theory.

More consistent support occurs outside of the United States. In an investigation of 30 European countries, van der Zwan, Bles, and Lubbers (2017) demonstrate that unemployed immigrants are more likely to agree that immigration poses a threat to their host country than employed immigrants. In Switzerland, Strijbis and Polavieja (2018) observe that immigrants supported a popular initiative demanding limits and quotas on immigration in a similar proportion to native-born respondents. Established immigrants in Switzerland are more likely to be employed in jobs requiring lower levels of specific human capital – that is, occupations requiring lower skill specialization – exposing them to competition from newcomers.

Looking at the impact of the local economy on immigrant and native-born attitudes towards immigration policies, Kang and Look (2020) do not find support for the economic competition theory in Australia. They hypothesize that rising levels of economic inequality measured at the electoral district should signal that additional immigration will create increased competition for jobs. Consequently, immigrants should have less favourable immigration orientations than in districts where inequality is lower. However, immigrants are more supportive of increasing immigration, not less, when they reside in a district with higher economic inequality. Kang and Look (2020) suggest that inequality leads to increased nationalism and prejudice against minority groups. In this situation, established immigrants as well as newer immigrants are likely to be targeted by threats from native-born individuals. In turn, kinship and solidary between immigrants are activated by local economic inequality, leading immigrants to support increases in immigration levels.

Multiple group memberships

The intersections of group memberships are also investigated, as the diversity of origins and experiences with immigration among immigrants in Western countries influence attitudes towards fellow immigrants and immigration policies. In the United States, this research often looks at differences between immigrants from various Latin American countries. Branton (2007) finds that Cuban Americans and Puerto Ricans are more likely to favour decreasing immigration levels while Mexican Americans are less likely to agree that illegal immigration hurts the economy. Explanations for these findings refer to the different immigration pathways. While Cubans immigrated under provisions for political refugees and Puerto Ricans, as US citizens, can freely travel to the United States (Branton, 2007), Mexicans and Central Americans are more likely to have friends and family members that are recent immigrants (Knoll, 2012).

Less is known about how country of origin leads to differences among immigrants' attitudes towards immigration in other Western countries. A possible reason for this lack of research might be the difficulty of obtaining a large enough sample size of immigrants from each country of origin to be able to draw reliable conclusions. Thus, often, immigrants from multiple countries are studied as part of a larger group of immigrants or only some immigrants from specific countries are included (for example, Meeusen, Abts, and Meuleman [2019] only include Turkish and Moroccan Belgians in their study).

Immigrants are also divided by their race and their gender. Berg and Morley (2014) argue that racial minorities and women are less privileged in American society and have fewer resources. These group memberships should thus intersect with immigration status to influence immigration policy attitudes. For instance, Berg and Morley (2014) show that female immigrants when compared to male immigrants have more positive attitudes towards immigration. Due to their greater underprivileged position in society, women have a greater feeling of solidarity with fellow underprivileged groups such as immigrants. See Chapter 5 for more on gender.

Group identification and group consciousness

An important finding of the group membership literature is that not all immigrants have similar immigration attitudes. To further understand these differences, studies have turned to group identification and group consciousness. The psychological attachment to one's group and agreement with a set of ideological beliefs about one's group standing should influence whether immigrants support (or not) permissive immigration policies. Consequently, investigations look into the nature of group identification and the subsequent impact of identity in shaping immigration attitudes. This literature expects that individuals with an immigration background who strongly identify with the host nation have stronger negative views of newcomers and favour restrictive immigration policies. However, Sarrasin et al. (2018) find that while immigrants are less likely than native-born individuals to strongly identify with the host country, national identification has little impact on immigrants' orientations towards immigration policy.

Alternatively, immigrants can identify strongly with their country of origin or they can feel an equal attachment to both. Meeusen, Abts, and Meuleman (2019) argue that identifying more strongly with your country of origin than with your host country creates a sense of solidarity and kinship with other immigrants even if they are from different countries. Consequently, they find that Turkish and Moroccan Belgians who either identify primarily through their country of origin or who identify equally as Belgian and Turkish or Moroccan are less likely to support restrictive immigration policies than those who identify only as Belgians.

For immigrants, adopting more negative views of immigration and newcomers can be a way of affirming their belonging to their host country. This is more likely to occur among immigrants who would rather identify with a high-status group than with newcomers. In Switzerland, Strijbis and Polavieja (2018) show that immigrants who identify as a "Secondo" – a term commonly used in Swiss society for established second-generation immigrants – are more likely to support a popular initiative to adopt immigration quotas. Being a "Secondo" can be used to establish oneself as being part of the host country in-group while at the same time recognizing one's immigrant background.

An attempt at assessing immigrants' identification with other immigrants is also tested through the impact of pan-ethnicity on immigration attitudes. As explained above, pan-ethnicity refers to identification with a larger group composed of multiple different ethnicities that share a common geographical origin such as Hispanic, Latinx,[2] or Asian. However, looking at pan-ethnic identification among Latinx in the United States, Knoll (2012) finds that immigrants who identify as such are not more likely than other immigrants to disagree with the statement that immigrants are a burden. Vega and Ortiz (2018) similarly find that identifying as a Hispanic or Mexican is not significantly related to immigration attitudes. Alternatively, Park (2021) shows that respondents whose Asian American identity is extremely important are more likely to support granting legal rights to children who were brought illegally to the United States.

Finally, the impact of group consciousness on immigrants' attitudes towards fellow immigrants and immigration policies is studied to a much lesser extent than group membership and group identification. As mentioned above, group consciousness goes further than group identification to assess whether individuals perceive and experience discrimination and whether they feel their fate is linked with their fellow group members. Thus, the expectation is that immigrants with higher group consciousness have more positive attitudes towards immigrants and immigration policies. In the United States, however, Vega and Ortiz (2018) find no support for this expectation. On the other hand, Meeusen, Abts, and Meuleman (2019)'s findings of Turkish and Moroccan Belgians indicate that the impact of group consciousness on immigration orientations is more nuanced than originally stipulated. They argue that when immigrants experience unfair treatment specifically by government agencies or in daily life such as in restaurants or on public transport, it can reflect biases of the majority group, creating a sense of kinship and solidarity between immigrants. Consequently, unfair treatment by government agencies and in daily life leads immigrants to favour permissive immigration policies.

In sum, the current literature identifies multiple factors explaining differences in support for restrictive and permissive immigration policies among immigrants. Immigration generation, length of stay in the host country, acquisition of citizenship, economic competition, ties to host country and ties to country of origin, and experiences of discrimination play a significant role in shaping immigrant orientations towards immigration.

IMMIGRATION STATUS AND IMMIGRATION ATTITUDES IN ESTABLISHED DEMOCRACIES

I now turn to differences in attitudes between immigrants and native-born individuals in nine established democracies. I further assess whether second-generation immigrants have similar immigration attitudes to native-born across these countries. Figures 6.1 and 6.2 illustrate the distribution and average answers for whether respondents agree that immigrants are generally good for the economy of their country. Figure 6.1 shows that for most countries, foreign-born respondents have an average answer that is a lower value than the average answer for native-born respondents, indicating they are more likely to agree with the statement. Note that the US is excluded from that analysis as the survey did not ask if respondents were born or not in the country. The largest difference occurs in the Britain where the average answer for foreign-born respondents is 1.88 compared to 2.54 for native-born (on a 1 to 5 scale where 5 indicates strongly disagree). For Germany and Italy, foreign-born respondents have similar immigration attitudes to native-born (the average answer is 2.65 and 2.70, respectively, for Germany and 3.19 and 3.22, respectively, for Italy). While the distribution of answers for Germany indicates that both foreign-born and native-born respondents have either positive or neutral views of immigrants' impact on the economy, answers from Italy indicate a more negative opinion where 23% of native-born and nearly 17% of foreign-born respondents strongly disagree that immigrants are generally good for the economy.

Figure 6.2 illustrates differences in opinion between children of immigrants and respondents whose parents are born in the host country. This analysis also relies on eight countries because Australia did not ask the respondents whether their parents were foreign-born or not. For all eight countries considered, with the exception of Germany, the average answer for second-generation immigrants is significantly lower than the average answer for respondents with native-born parents. The largest difference occurs in the United States where the average answer for immigrants is 2.14 compared to 2.71 for native-born respondents. Canadians are the most supportive of immigration with 56% of second-generation immigrants and 42% of respondents with native-born parents strongly agreeing that immigrants are good for the economy. On the other hand, Italians have the most negative views of immigration with 10% of second-generation immigrants and 23% of respondents with native-born

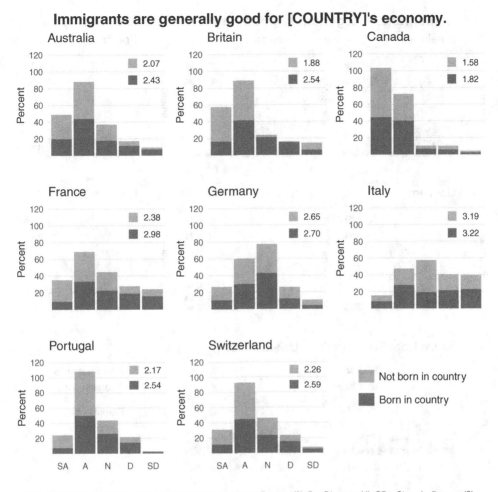

Immigrants are generally good for [COUNTRY]'s economy.

SA = Strongly agree (1); A = Agree (2); N = Neither agree nor disagree (3); D = Disagree (4); SD = Strongly disagree (5)

FIGURE 6.1 Attitudes about how immigrants are perceived to affect a country's economy, by immigration status (first-generation).

parents strongly disagreeing with the statement. Overall, Figure 6.2 indicates little acculturation of the second generation to the majority group, at least for this specific question.

Similar findings occur for whether respondents agree that a country's culture is threatened by immigration in Figures 6.3 and 6.4. Looking at first-generation immigrants, Figure 6.3 illustrates that, on average, immigrants are significantly more likely to disagree with the statement than native-born individuals, with the exception of Germany. The largest difference is in Britain (a score of 2.18 for immigrants and 2.81 for native-born) and Canadians have the most positive view of immigration (58% and 44%, respectively, strongly disagree that immigrants harm the country's culture). Figure 6.4 presents little evidence of acculturation in second-generation

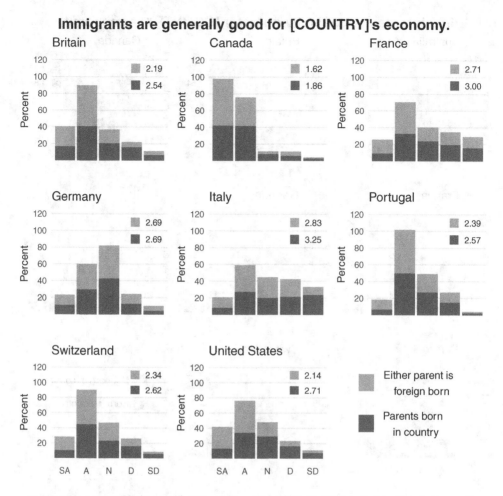

Immigrants are generally good for [COUNTRY]'s economy.

SA = Strongly agree (1); A = Agree (2); N = Neither agree nor disagree (3); D = Disagree (4); SD = Strongly disagree (5)

FIGURE 6.2 Attitudes about how immigrants are perceived to affect a country's economy, by immigration status (second-generation).

immigrants. The latter, with the exception of Germany and Italy, are less likely than respondents with native-born parents to agree that immigrants harm a country's culture. The largest difference is among French respondents where the average answer for second-generation respondents is 2.29 (on a 1–5 scale where 5 indicates strongly agree) compared to 2.80 for respondents with native-born parents. Italians and Swiss view immigration's impact on their country in a more negative light. For example, in Switzerland, 8% of second-generation immigrants and 16% of native-born respondents strongly agree that immigration hurts the country's culture.

The third question assessing immigration attitudes asks respondents whether immigrants increase crime rates. Figures 6.5 and 6.6 provide the distribution of

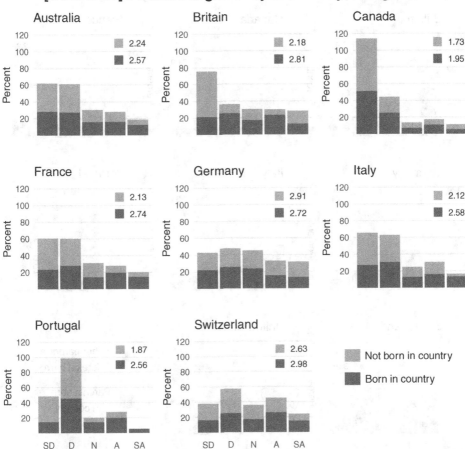

[COUNTRY]'s culture is generally harmed by immigrants.

SD = Strongly disagree (1); D = disagree (2); N = Neither agree nor disagree (3); A = Agree (4); SA = Strongly agree (5)

FIGURE 6.3 Attitudes about how immigrants are perceived to affect a country's culture, by immigration status (first-generation).

answers for native-born, first-, and second-generation immigrants. Figure 6.5 demonstrates that for all countries, with the exception of Italy, immigrants are significantly more likely than native-born to disagree with the statement that immigrants increase crime rates. The largest immigrant-native gap occurs for Britain where the average answer for immigrants is 2.41 compared to 2.94 (on a 1 to 5 scale where 5 indicates strongly agree) for native-born respondents. The highest agreement with this statement is in Germany where 20% of native-born and 27% of immigrants strongly agree that immigrants increase crime rates. Contrary to Figure 6.2 and Figure 6.4, Figure 6.6 indicates some acculturation of second-generation immigrants. For the Britain, Germany, Italy, and Portugal, second-generation immigrants are as

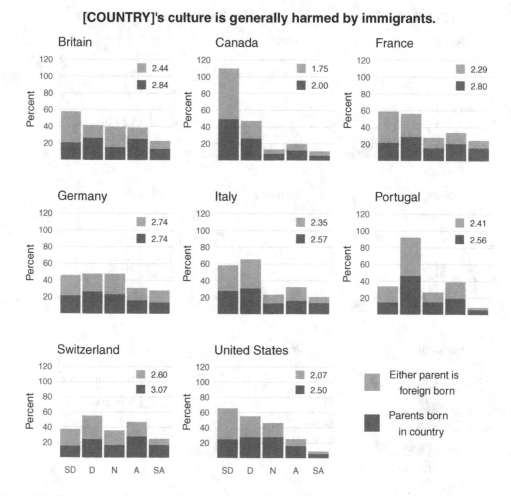

SD = Strongly disagree (1); D = disagree (2); N = Neither agree nor disagree (3); A = Agree (4); SA = Strongly agree (5)

FIGURE 6.4 Attitudes about how immigrants are perceived to affect a country's culture, by immigration status (second-generation).

likely as respondents with native-born parents to agree that immigrants increase crime rates. For example, the average answer for second-generation immigrants is 2.81 compared to 2.87 for Portuguese-born respondents. This result might indicate that acculturation to the majority opinion varies not only across the political context but also across the specific consequence of immigration under consideration.

Finally, an index of immigration orientations is obtained by combining the three questions discussed above. The differences in the distribution of answers on the index between native-born respondents and immigrants are illustrated in Figure 6.7 for first-generation immigrants and Figure 6.8 for second-generation immigrants. For all countries, with the exception of Germany in Figure 6.8, immigrants of either

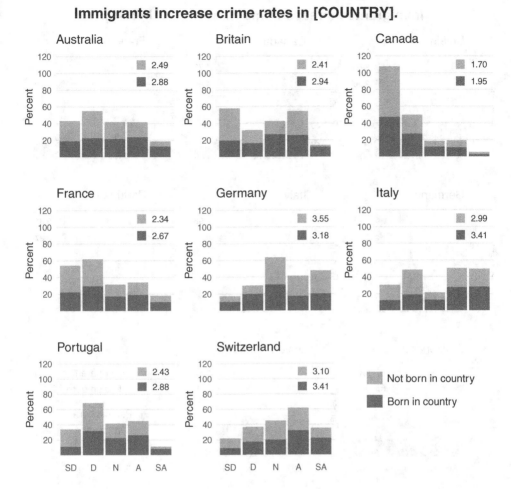

SD = Strongly disagree (1); D = disagree (2); N = Neither agree nor disagree (3); A = Agree (4); SA = Strongly agree (5)

FIGURE 6.5 Attitudes about how immigrants are perceived to affect a country's crime, by immigration status (first-generation).

the first or second generation are less likely to have negative attitudes towards immigration. The Britain, France, and Portugal have more distinct differences in their distribution while differences between immigrants and native-born are smaller in Australia and Canada.

The general trend emerging from these figures is that immigrants of either the first or second generation are more likely than native-born individuals to have favourable attitudes towards immigrants. This might indicate that group membership explanations emphasizing solidarity and kinship between immigrants are key to understanding immigrant attitudes in many established democracies. These feelings of solidarity and kinship further persist in second-generation immigrants, indicating

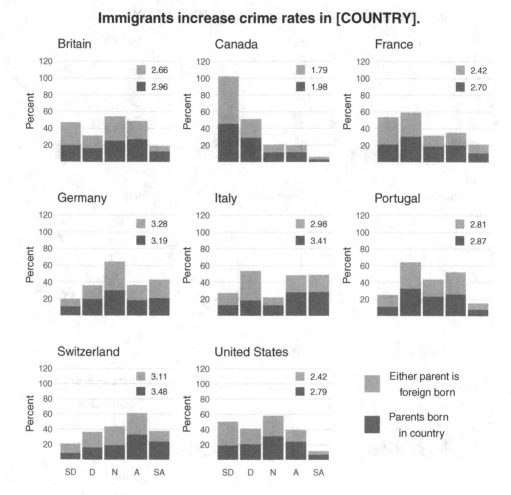

Immigrants increase crime rates in [COUNTRY].

SD = Strongly disagree (1); D = disagree (2); N = Neither agree nor disagree (3); A = Agree (4); SA = Strongly agree (5)

FIGURE 6.6 Attitudes about how immigrants are perceived to affect a country's crime, by immigration status (second-generation).

little acculturation to the majority-group opinions. Yet, Germany and Italy stand apart from other countries. We also observe differences in the perceived consequence of immigrants where second-generation immigrants have more similar opinions to native-born on whether immigrants increase crime rates. Solidarity and kinship with other migrants can act as boundaries that expand or retract depending on the political context (Vega and Ortiz, 2018). In their comparative analysis, van der Zwan, Bless, and Lubbers (2017) find that immigrants' attitudes towards immigration are influenced by the dominant public opinion of their host country. Consequently, it is possible that immigrant attitudes are more similar to native orientations when the political context emphasizes one aspect of immigration to a greater extent (economy vs. crime) and/or when the majority opinion is stronger and more unanimous.

Immigration index by respondent's country of birth

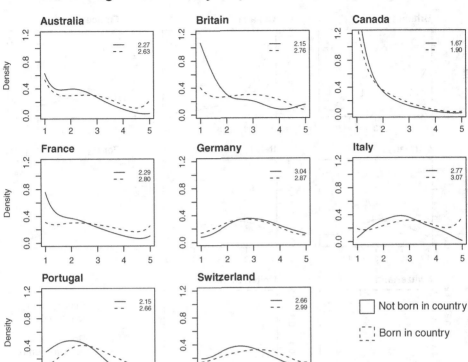

Values range from 1 to 5 with higher values indicating less favourable attitudes toward immigration.

FIGURE 6.7 Attitudes about how immigrants are perceived to affect a country's economy, culture, and crime, by immigration status (first-generation).

IMMIGRATION ATTITUDES IN AUSTRALIA

The previous section demonstrates that differences in immigration attitudes exist in multiple established democracies between native-born, first-generation, and second-generation immigrants. I next turn to a more in-depth analysis of Australian orientations towards immigrants, testing some of the explanations discussed in the literature. Immigration is a highly contentious topic in Australia; it is the object of multiple public debates (Markus, Jupp, and McDonald, 2009; Martinez i Coma and Smith, 2018) and influences vote choice (Carson, Dufresne, and Martin 2016). Over the years, immigration attitudes in Australia have been generally positive towards immigrants and immigration policies. Indeed, Markus (2014) argues that Australia is among the most receptive country to immigration among Western nations. Further, Dandy and Pe-Pua (2010) and Kang and Look (2020) find that Australians with an immigrant background are more favourable to increasing the number of immigrants

Immigration index by respondent's parents country of birth

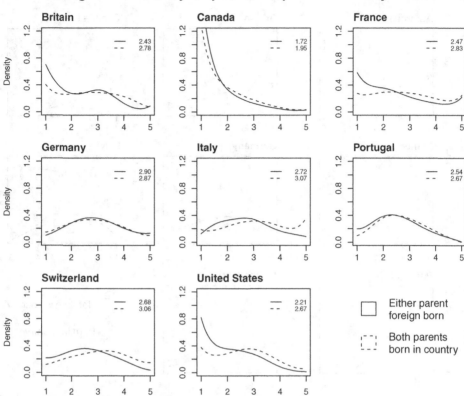

Values range from 1 to 5 with higher values indicating less favourable attitudes toward immigration.

FIGURE 6.8 Attitudes about how immigrants are perceived to affect a country's economy, culture, and crime (index), by immigration status (second-generation).

than native-born Australians. Kamp et al. (2018), in an investigation of Aboriginal and Torres Strait Islander people, show that Indigenous people have similar immigration attitudes than non-Indigenous Australians with the exception of immigration levels where the former is more likely than the latter to agree that immigration intakes are too high. Yet, there is some indication that support for immigration is declining, especially in light of the asylum seeker policy debates (McAllister, 2018). The issue became an important political concern in the 2000s following an increase in asylum seeker arrivals, especially by boat. The election of the Liberal Party in 2013 resulted in a "turning back the boat" policy where asylum seekers are prevented from landing in Australia by boat as well as a policy of processing and resettlement of asylum seekers offshore. According to McAllister (2018), in the mind of many Australians, the issues of asylum seekers and immigration are linked.

The Australian Election Study (AES; McAllister et al., 2019) allows an assessment of the impact of economic threat perceptions and some aspects of group consciousness on Australian attitudes towards immigration. I combine five questions (including two used in the previous analysis) into an index of immigration attitudes on a scale where "1" indicates positive attitudes towards immigration and "5" negative views of immigration. Questions ask whether (1) immigration numbers should be decreased; (2) immigrants increase crime rates; (3) immigrants are good for the economy; (4) immigrants take jobs away; and (5) immigrants make Australia more open. I present the results for three separate regression analyses. The first one includes all respondents, the second one only includes first-generation immigrants, and the third model includes second-generation immigrants. The full models with control variables are included in the Appendix. Figure 6.9 illustrates the regression coefficients and 95% confidence interval for the variables assessing the impact of economic threat perceptions and group consciousness on attitudes towards immigration.

Figure 6.9 shows, as expected, that first-generation immigrants are significantly less likely than native-born respondents to have negative views of immigrants (the confidence interval does not include zero), but there is no significant difference between second-generation immigrants and native-born respondents. Income level, whether respondents are in a better or worse financial situation than one year ago, employment status, job security, and education levels are used to assess whether socioeconomic situations influence immigration attitudes. Findings from Figure 6.9 provide support for the economic threat theory, but also demonstrate that there is little difference in the factors that influence first- and second-generation immigrants' attitudes as well as native-born Australians. For all respondents, an income level in the lower quartile is significantly associated with greater negative opinions of immigrants. Similarly, respondents whose financial situation has improved compared to one year ago are less likely to have negative immigration attitudes (the coefficient

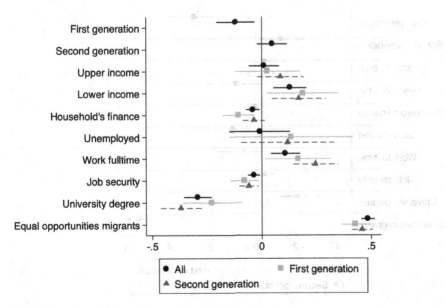

FIGURE 6.9 Immigration status and immigration attitudes.

is not significant for second-generation immigrants). Again, all respondents with job security are significantly less likely to have negative orientations. Finally, all respondents with a university degree regardless of their immigration status are significantly less likely to hold negative views of immigrants. Surprisingly, unemployed respondents are no more likely to hold negative orientations and respondents who work full time are significantly more likely to have negative attitudes. More on social class is found in Chapter 7.

The AES includes limited questions to test the impact of group identification and perceptions of discrimination. There is, however, one question asking whether equal opportunities for migrants have gone too far in Australia that resembles measures used to tap into group consciousness. Figure 6.9 shows that for native-born, first-, and second-generation immigrants, respondents who agree that equal opportunities have gone too far are more likely to hold negative immigration views.

Figure 6.10 tests whether the same factors contributing to immigration attitudes can help understand attitudes towards asylum seekers in Australia. I run the same three models as Figure 6.9 using a question asking respondents whether boats carrying asylum seekers should be turned back as the dependent variable. The full model is included in the Appendix; Figure 6.10 shows the main coefficients of interest and their respective confidence intervals.

Figure 6.10 indicates that first-generation immigrants are significantly more likely than native-born respondents to agree that asylum seekers' boats should be turned back while there is no significant difference between native-born and second-generation immigrants. Furthermore, we can observe in Figure 6.10 that none of the socioeconomic factors has a significant relationship with asylum seekers' attitudes.

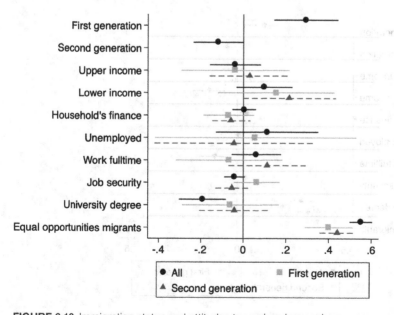

FIGURE 6.10 Immigration status and attitudes toward asylum seekers.

A notable exception occurs among all respondents where having a university degree significantly decreases the likelihood of agreeing with the policy. Equal opportunities for migrants, on the other hand, has a significant relationship with policy support as respondents agreeing that equal opportunities have gone too far are more likely to agree that boats should be turned back. Previous investigations about attitudes towards asylum seekers emphasize the role of emotions and beliefs about migrants (Hartley and Pedersen, 2015; Hartley, Anderson, and Pedersen, 2019). This might indicate that group identification and group consciousness – that is, how immigrants define and feel connected to their group – are more important than group membership in understanding orientations towards asylum seekers.

CONCLUSION

A growing literature focuses on exploring the role of immigration status in understanding attitudes towards immigrants and immigration policies in established democracies. This literature investigates three main concepts: group membership, group identification, and group consciousness. As demonstrated by the review of the literature and the empirical data presented in this chapter, group membership is studied the most. This does not mean that group identification and group consciousness are not crucial, but they might be more difficult to measure, making investigations of these concepts challenging when relying on existing surveys such as the AES. The CSES data also highlight the lack of comparative studies on immigrant status and immigration attitudes. Little is known as to how and why immigration status matters differently in different political contexts. Yet, the evidence presented here shows that differences between immigrants' and native-born individuals' attitudes vary across countries, but also across the type of questions asked, highlighting the role of political context. The discussion of the Australian case further demonstrates how immigrant attitudes vary depending on the type of policy under consideration. In sum, the impact of immigration status on immigration attitudes is nuanced.

SUMMARY POINTS

- The extant literature assesses three main theories to explain the differences in views between the immigrant and native-born populations: group membership, group identification, and group consciousness. Immigration generation, length of stay in the host country, acquisition of citizenship, economic competition, ties to host country and ties to country of origin, and experiences of discrimination are found to play a significant role in shaping immigrant orientations towards immigration.
- Examining data from nine Western democracies, we found that immigrants have more favourable views of immigration than the native-born population.
- The differences between immigrant and native-born populations vary across countries and types of questions, suggesting a role for political context.

NOTES

1 UN DESA Population Databases are available online at www.un.org/en/development/desa/population/publications/database/index.asp.
2 Hispanic refers to individuals who speak Spanish or are the descendant of Spanish-speaking parents or grandparents. Latinx indicates individuals who are from or are the descendants of individuals from Latin American countries.

SUGGESTED FURTHER READINGS

Branton, R., 2007. Latino attitudes toward various areas of public policy: The importance of acculturation. *Political Research Quarterly*, 60(2), 293–303.
Kang, W.C. and Look, E., 2020. Inequality and attitudes toward immigration: The native-immigrant gap in Australia. *Australian Journal of Political Science*, 55(3), 257–275.
McClain, P.D., Johnson Carew, J.D., Walton, E. Jr., and Watts, C.S., 2009. Group membership, group identity, and group consciousness: Measures of racial identity in American politics? *Annual Review of Political Science*, 12(1), 471–485.
Strijbis, O. and Polavieja, J., 2018. Immigrants against immigration: Competition, identity and immigrants' vote on free movement in Switzerland. *Electoral Studies*, 56, 150–157.

REFERENCES

Berg, J.A. and Morley, S., 2014. Intersectionality and the foreign-born: Explaining the variation in the immigration attitudes of immigrants. *Race, Gender & Class*, 21(3/4), 32–47.
Binder, N.E., Polinard, J.L., and Wrinkle, R.D., 1997. Mexican American and Anglo attitudes toward immigration reform: A view from the border. *Social Science Quarterly*, 78(2), 324–337.
Branton, R., 2007. Latino attitudes toward various areas of public policy: The importance of acculturation. *Political Research Quarterly*, 60(2), 293–303.
Capers, K.J. and Smith, C.W., 2016. Straddling identities: Identity cross-pressures on Black immigrants' policy preferences. *Politics, Groups, and Identities*, 4(3), 393–424.
Carson, A., Dufresne, Y., and Martin, A., 2016. Wedge politics: Mapping voter attitudes to asylum seekers using large-scale data during the Australian 2013 federal election campaign. *Policy & Internet*, 8(4), 478–498.
Czaja, E. and Medenica, V.E., 2020. Race, ethnicity, and public opinion. In: A.J. Berinsky, ed. *New directions in public opinion*. New York: Routledge, 137–158.
Dandy, J. and Pe-Pua, R., 2010. Attitudes to multiculturalism, immigration and cultural diversity: Comparison of dominant and non-dominant groups in three Australian states. *International Journal of Intercultural Relations*, 34(1), 34–46.
Hartley, L.K., Anderson, J.R., and Pedersen, A., 2019. Process in the community, detain offshore or 'turn back the boats'? Predicting Australian asylum-seeker policy support from false beliefs, prejudice and political ideology. *Journal of Refugee Studies*, 32(4), 562–582.
Hartley, L.K. and Pedersen, A., 2015. Asylum seekers and resettled refugees in Australia: Predicting social policy attitude from prejudice versus emotion. *Journal of Social and Political Psychology*, 3(1), 142–160.
Hood III, M.V., Morris, I.L., and Shirkey, K.A., 1997. ¡Quedate o Vente!: Uncovering the determinants of Hispanic public opinion toward immigration. *Political Research Quarterly*, 50(3), 627–647.
Huddy, L., 2001. From social to political identity: A critical examination of social identity theory. *Political Psychology*, 22(1), 127–156.

Just, A. and Anderson, C.J., 2015. Dual allegiances? Immigrants' attitudes toward immigration. *The Journal of Politics*, 77(1), 188–201.

Kamp, A., Dunn, K., Paradies, Y., and Blair, K., 2018. Aboriginal and Torres Strait Islander people's attitudes towards Australian multiculturalism, cultural diversity, 'race' and racism, 2015–16. *Australian Aboriginal Studies*, 2, 50–70.

Kang, W.C. and Look, E., 2020. Inequality and attitudes toward immigration: The native-immigrant gap in Australia. *Australian Journal of Political Science*, 55(3), 257–275.

Knoll, B.R., 2012. ¿Compañero o extranjero? Anti-immigrant nativism among Latino Americans. *Social Science Quarterly*, 93(4), 911–931.

Kunovich, R.M., 2013. Labor market competition and anti-immigrant sentiment: Occupations as contexts. *International Migration Review*, 47(3), 643–685.

Lee, T., 2008. Race, immigration, and the identity-to-politics link. *Annual Review of Political Science*, 11(1), 457–478.

Maltby, E., Rocha, R.R., Jones, B., and Vannette, D.L., 2020. Demographic context, mass deportation, and Latino linked fate. *Journal of Race, Ethnicity, and Politics*, 5(3), 509–536.

Markus, A., 2014. Attitudes to immigration and cultural diversity in Australia. *Journal of Sociology*, 50(1), 10–22.

Markus, A., Jupp, J., and McDonald, P., 2009. *Australia's immigration revolution*. Crows Nest, NSW: Allen & Unwin.

Martinez i Coma, F., Smith, R., 2018. Jobs, crime, proximity and boats: Explaining Australian public attitudes to immigrant numbers. *Australian Journal of Political Science*, 53(3), 271–289.

McAllister, I., 2018. National identity and attitudes towards immigration in Australia. *National Identities*, 20(2), 157–173.

McAllister, I., Bean, C., Gibson, R., Makkai, T., Sheppard, J., and Cameron, S., 2019. *Australian election study, 2019, ADA Dataverse.* doi: 10.26193/KMAMMW.

McClain, P.D., Johnson Carew, J.D., Walton, E. Jr., and Watts, C.S., 2009. Group membership, group identity, and group consciousness: Measures of racial identity in American politics? *Annual Review of Political Science*, 12(1), 471–485.

Meeusen, C., Abts, Koen, and Meuleman, B., 2019. Between solidarity and competitive threat? *International Journal of Intercultural Relations*, 71, 1–13.

Park, S., 2021. Identifying Asian American attitudes toward immigration: Testing theories of acculturation, group consciousness, and context effects. *Journal of Ethnic and Cultural Studies*, 8(1), 163–189.

Polavieja, J.G., 2016. Labour-market competition, recession and anti-immigrant sentiments in Europe: Occupational and environmental drivers of competitive threat. *Socio-Economic Review*, 14(3), 395–417.

Polinard, J.L., Wrinkle, R.D., and De La Garza, R., 1984. Attitudes of Mexican Americans toward irregular Mexican immigration. *International Migration Review*, 18(3), 782–799.

Politi, E., Chipeaux, M., Lorenzi-Cioldi, F., and Staerklé, C., 2020. More royalist than the king? Immigration policy attitudes among naturalized citizens. *Political Psychology*, 41(3), 607–625.

Rouse, S.M., Wilkinson, B.C., and Garand, J.C., 2010. Divided loyalties? Understanding variation in Latino attitudes toward immigration. *Social Science Quarterly*, 91(3), 856–882.

Sanchez, G.R., 2006. The role of group consciousness in Latino public opinion. *Political Research Quarterly*, 59(3), 435–446.

Sarrasin, Oriane, Green, E.G.T., Bolzman, C., Visintin, E.P., and Politi, E., 2018. Competition- and identity-based roots of anti-immigration prejudice among individuals with and without an immigrant background. *International Review of Social Psychology*, 31(1), 1–12.

Scheepers, P., Gijsberts, M., and Coenders, M., 2002. Ethnic exclusionism in European countries. Public opposition to civil rights for legal migrants as a response to perceived ethnic threat. *European Sociological Review*, 18(1), 17–34.

Schneider, S.L. and Heath, A.F., 2020. Ethnic and cultural diversity in Europe: Validating measures of ethnic and cultural background. *Journal of Ethnic and Migration Studies*, 46(3), 533–552.

Strijbis, O. and Polavieja, J., 2018. Immigrants against immigration: Competition, identity and immigrants' vote on free movement in Switzerland. *Electoral Studies*, 56, 150–157.

Tajfel, H. and Turner, J.C., 1986. The social identity theory of intergroup behavior. In: W.P. Austin and S. Worchel, eds. *Psychology of intergroup relations*. Chicago, IL: Nelson-Hall, 7–24.

van der Zwan, R., Bles, P., and Lubbers, M., 2017. Perceived migrant threat among migrants in Europe. *European Sociological Review*, 33(4), 518–533.

Vargas, E.D., Sanchez, G.R., and Valdez, J.A. Jr., 2017. Immigration policies and group identity: How immigrant laws affect linked fate among US Latino populations. *Journal of Race, Ethnicity, and Politics*, 2(1), 35–62.

Vega, I.I. and Ortiz, V., 2018. Mexican Americans and immigration attitudes: A cohort analysis of assimilation and group consciousness. *Social Problems*, 65(2), 137–153.

APPENDIX

TABLE 6.A1 Immigration status and immigration attitudes

	(1)	(2)	(3)
	All	First-generation	Second-generation
First-generation	−0.12**		
	(0.04)		
Second-generation	0.05		
	(0.03)		
Upper income	0.01	0.03	0.08
	(0.04)	(0.08)	(0.05)
Lower income	0.13***	0.19*	0.17**
	(0.04)	(0.08)	(0.06)
Household's finance compared to one year ago	−0.04*	−0.11**	−0.04
	(0.02)	(0.04)	(0.03)
Unemployed	−0.01	0.13	0.12
	(0.07)	(0.14)	(0.11)
Work full time	0.11**	0.16*	0.25***
	(0.03)	(0.08)	(0.05)
How easy would it be to find another job	−0.04**	−0.08*	−0.06**
	(0.01)	(0.03)	(0.02)
University degree	−0.29***	−0.23**	−0.37***
	(0.03)	(0.07)	(0.05)
Equal opportunities migrants (5 = gone too far)	0.48***	0.43***	0.46***
	(0.02)	(0.03)	(0.02)
Female	0.03	−0.02	0.04
	(0.03)	(0.07)	(0.05)
Age	−0.00	0.00	0.00
	(0.00)	(0.00)	(0.00)
Labor	0.04	0.14	0.03
	(0.04)	(0.08)	(0.06)
National	0.02	0.65**	0.16
	(0.09)	(0.24)	(0.18)
Greens	−0.23***	−0.03	−0.10
	(0.06)	(0.14)	(0.10)
Other	0.16***	0.20*	0.21***
	(0.04)	(0.08)	(0.06)
Left-right self-placement (0 = left, 10 = right)	0.07***	0.10***	0.08***
	(0.01)	(0.02)	(0.01)
Partner	−0.10**	−0.09	−0.17***
	(0.03)	(0.07)	(0.05)
Church attendance	−0.00	0.02	0.02
	(0.01)	(0.02)	(0.01)
Live in major city	−0.05^	0.06	0.05
	(0.03)	(0.07)	(0.05)
Constant	1.29***	1.19***	1.10***
	(0.12)	(0.27)	(0.18)
Observations	1,733	397	730

Notes: OLS coefficients with standard errors in parentheses.

Dependent variable is immigration index where 5 = more negative immigration attitudes.

^ $p < 0.10$, * $p < 0.05$, ** $p < 0.01$, *** $p < 0.001$.

TABLE 6.A2 Immigration status and attitudes toward asylum seekers

	(1)	(2)	(3)
	All	First-generation	Second-generation
First-generation	0.29***		
	(0.08)		
Second-generation	−0.12^		
	(0.06)		
Upper income	−0.04	−0.04	0.03
	(0.06)	(0.13)	(0.10)
Lower income	0.10	0.15	0.22^
	(0.07)	(0.14)	(0.11)
Household's finance compared to one year ago	0.00	−0.07	−0.06
	(0.03)	(0.06)	(0.05)
Unemployed	0.11	0.06	−0.04
	(0.12)	(0.24)	(0.19)
Work full time	0.06	−0.07	0.11
	(0.06)	(0.13)	(0.09)
How easy would it be to find another job	−0.04^	0.06	−0.05
	(0.02)	(0.05)	(0.04)
University degree	−0.19***	−0.06	−0.04
	(0.06)	(0.12)	(0.09)
Equal opportunities migrants (5 = gone too far)	0.55***	0.40***	0.44***
	(0.03)	(0.06)	(0.04)
Female	−0.25***	−0.58***	−0.40***
	(0.05)	(0.12)	(0.08)
Age	0.01***	0.01*	0.01***
	(0.00)	(0.00)	(0.00)
Labor	−0.35***	−0.20	−0.27*
	(0.07)	(0.14)	(0.11)
National	−0.21	0.09	−0.56^
	(0.16)	(0.40)	(0.32)
Greens	−0.45***	0.67**	−0.09
	(0.11)	(0.24)	(0.17)
Other	−0.12^	0.19	−0.10
	(0.07)	(0.14)	(0.11)
Left-right self-placement (0 = left, 10 = right)	0.09***	0.16***	0.15***
	(0.01)	(0.03)	(0.02)
Partner	−0.00	0.21^	0.07
	(0.06)	(0.12)	(0.09)
Church Attendance	0.04**	0.07*	0.05*
	(0.02)	(0.03)	(0.02)
Live in major city	−0.07	−0.06	−0.12
	(0.05)	(0.12)	(0.09)
Constant	1.24***	1.07*	1.26***
	(0.21)	(0.45)	(0.33)
Observations	1,731	397	729

Notes: OLS coefficients with standard errors in parentheses.

Dependent variable is agreement that all asylum seeker boats should be turned back (5 = strongly agree).

^ $p < 0.10$, * $p < 0.05$, ** $p < 0.01$, *** $p < 0.001$.

CHAPTER 7

Class and public opinion

··

Tyler Romualdi, John Kennedy, and Cameron D. Anderson

INTRODUCTION

An important aspect of political science has been the study of political difference. What are the structures of division and the eventual bases of competition for scarce resources in democratic societies? Historically, differences have centred on both intra- and inter-level conflict within a variety of group-level systems. For example, differences between church and state or between religions (Christian versus Muslim) and denominational variations within a religion (Catholic versus Protestant) outline well-known religious cleavages. Another salient difference in democratic politics and the subject of this chapter is socioeconomic status or class. During the political and economic upheavals of the industrial revolution in the 18th and 19th centuries, thinkers like Marx, Engels, and Schulz observed and documented the emerging structural differences between people and groups of various economic standing. Marx talked about the owners of production who had land, businesses, factories, and the political and economic power that these positions provided. By contrast, the working class consisted of people employed by the bourgeoisie to work the land or in businesses and factories. Marx observed and chronicled the impact of one's economic standing on one's opportunity to chart one's life course.

Since Marx, Engels, and Schulz, scholars in all subfields of political science (theory, comparative politics, international relations, etc.) have extended and contextualized one's understanding of class within the political milieu (examples include Lipset, 1959; Skocpol, 1979; Evans, 1999; Van der Waal et al., 2007). In this chapter, we consider how class influences public opinion in general and attitudes towards immigrants more specifically. We proceed by exploring first how the concept of class is defined and measured before considering various theoretical mechanisms of effect (how and why class affects public opinion). Following this discussion, we use education and income demographic variables to develop a multi-group class scheme. The

DOI: 10.4324/9781003121992-9

empirical literature is well-versed in various ways to operationalize "social class," an often complex and subjective concept to measure. We use a two-step approach that combines correspondence analysis and hierarchical clustering to compare public opinion on immigration across eight countries using the Comparative Study of Electoral Systems (CSES) dataset. The chapter concludes with a summary of the findings.

THE CONCEPT OF CLASS

Class is a complex social phenomenon that requires a detailed investigation of both individual and contextual factors to grasp how one's socioeconomic status impacts public opinion and feelings towards others. Cohen and colleagues (2017) argue that class is challenging to define, often complicated by variation in public perceptions and awareness of inequality and its effect on class structures. These issues underline what Becker (2021) calls the "indifference" and "ignorance" inequality perspectives. The former suggests that individuals are generally unconcerned about rising inequality levels, while the latter demonstrates that people are genuinely unaware of equity issues. Some scholars have pinned the problem on the public's ignorance, finding that laypersons often fail to recognize critical differences between social classes, let alone the level, direction, and impact of inequality gaps on themselves or other community members (Gimpelson and Triesman, 2018; Hauser and Norton, 2017). Others demonstrate that the public's over-generalization of their immediate reference group, ideology, media, and/or psychological effects drive misperceptions (Gimpelson and Triesman, 2018). While individuals often experience trouble identifying socioeconomic divisions, they have consistently become more conscious and supportive of marginalized groups when confronted with information about specific issues (MacDonald, 2020). Nevertheless, the conceptual muddiness coupled with widespread misperceptions of the social and economic hierarchy demonstrates the need to investigate further how material interests, access to opportunities, and individual attitudes stem from different class positions (Brooks and Svallfors, 2010).

Definitional debates

Scholars have attempted to define class structures by focusing on individual circumstances, the acceptance of social and economic hierarchy, and intergenerational linkages. Definitions rooted in the context of one's social realities build on Weberian ideas about life's chances to explain how outcomes vary across time and context. For example, the observable differences between individuals are often the result of differences in social relations and economic life driven by labour markets, annual income, educational attainment, and career success (Kraus et al., 2009; Kraus et al., 2017). Another line of scholarship has defined the term as part of people's acceptance of a social and economic hierarchy. Some emphasize that class describes different strata in society, which allow people to identify their equals as a relative measure of socioeconomic status and chances of moving up the social ladder (Chan and Goldthorpe, 2007; Kraus et al., 2009).

The literature also points to intergenerational ties when defining class. Rubin et al. (2014) claim that social class is best understood on a temporal dimension, as one's position in society is often static and remains that way across several generations. Jones and Vagle (2013) address this issue when defining classes in a path-dependent context, noting that social and economic status is difficult to change despite younger people's desire to avoid living the same material lives as their parents. These issues reinforce the challenges of accessing quality education, employment, and the networks needed to gain influence, often upholding existing class positions. While these definitions on their own do not provide a comprehensive understanding of class, they help orient our understanding to the intellectual challenges of considering class.

Theoretical perspectives

Scholars have leveraged labour, health psychology, and cultural frames to theoretically analyze how class influences individual attitudes. The labour perspective emerges from traditional analyses of class conflict discussed by Marx and Engels. Marx proposed that "class" provided a unified framework to understand social and institutional change, conflict, labour strikes, and the development of subjective beliefs about social reality (Wright, 2005). As research in this tradition has evolved, the emphasis has shifted from Marx's ideas and explanatory claims centred on historical materialism to discussing how the current capitalist system sustains uneven social relations between the working and ownership class in some form (Kraus et al., 2012).

From a psychological perspective, empirical evidence that the lived environment within which one operates shapes one's identities, behaviours, and beliefs about social mobility or feelings towards members of the outgroup often align with the theorized impact of the effects of class on opinions and attitudes (Newman et al., 2015; Manstead, 2018). Consequently, psychologists have found that social environments often create conditions where "lower-class individuals are more vulnerable to physical disease and psychological hardships than their upper-class counterparts" (Kraus et al., 2012, p. 547).

The cultural perspective considers the contextual effects of class. The approach emphasizes how class differences influence the values and priorities that shape people's manners, social etiquette, vocabulary or tone, attitudes, and general self-expression (Kraus et al., 2012). In a detailed assessment of class divisions between the rich and poor, Kraus and colleagues (2012) propose a fourth framework called the social cognitive approach, which combines structuralist ideas from the Marxist tradition with cultural perspectives. This perspective focuses on how class determinants like occupation, education, and wealth shape the social environment for upper and lower-class individuals and their feelings towards others.

Measurement

The definitional debates outlined earlier shed light on potential measurement issues, as different classes get evaluated on objective or subjective bases. Hunt and Ray (2012) note that these operational differences have forced scholars to grapple with determining the most effective measures to include in their work, as the choice often depends on "interactions between one's social, cultural, and economic backgrounds" (Rubin et al., 2014, p. 196). As a result, best practices for assessing disparities within and across classes are far from straightforward, and the tools deployed are often question- and context-dependent. While there is general disagreement about the most effective measures, most scholarly work acknowledges objective metrics like income, education level, and occupation (Hunt and Ray, 2012; Kraus et al., 2011). These measures are associated with material conditions that either enhance or limit opportunities for increased social mobility in the labour market, participation in social institutions, and the capacity to benefit from the economic system (Kraus et al., 2009). Objective assessments also provide a proxy measurement of human capital, lifestyle choices, and policy preferences (Hunt and Ray, 2012).

The subjective measures of various classes help one understand how individuals position themselves vis-à-vis the larger reference group, highlighting how class structure informs social and political beliefs, physical or mental health, and the motivation to improve one's situation. Some research has operationalized social and economic class using subjective socioeconomic status (SES) metrics, which require individuals to rank themselves in terms of their perceived standing across objective indicators of class like education, income, and occupational status (Kraus et al., 2011). As a result, SES measures provide a first-hand account of how people interpret their social and economic realities. For example, Cohen et al. (2017) found that some poor white Americans saw their class positions as lower than blacks and Latinxs, while blacks embraced a caste-like understanding of social class independent of their annual income, education, or wealth.

CLASS AND IMMIGRATION OPINION

Education

Turning from a more general treatment of the concept, we now explore different conceptualizations of class (specifically class vis-à-vis education, economic conditions, and labour market status) to outline how these versions of class influence opinions about immigration. We start with education.

Education is a critical proxy of one's class position and influences attitudes towards newcomers. Brooks and Svallfors (2010) note that one's academic background helps assess human capital, social status, and cognition. Theories of human capital, in particular, suggest that those with more education usually exhibit heightened consciousness and acceptance of others compared to people with less schooling (Rustenbach, 2010; Finseraas, Skorge, and Strøm, 2018). These ideas are nested within the broader observation that higher education is one of the leading aspects of a class identity associated with cosmopolitanism, political liberalism, and an appreciation for ethnic and cultural differences (Brenner and Fertig, 2006; Hainmueller and Hiscox, 2007).

Education and socialization

Several scholars have highlighted the role that education plays in the socialization process and its effect on public opinion. Some argue that the public education system and their modern curriculum condition future generations to adopt more sophisticated world views (Hainmueller and Hiscox, 2007; Haubert and Fussell, 2006). Hainmueller and Hopkins (2014) demonstrate that higher education increases the openness and flexibility of people's belief systems that, more often than not, leads to pro-immigration attitudes. Grigorieff and colleagues (2020), for instance, found that even among those holding strong anti-immigrant sentiments, exposure to objective information either changed their opinions or prompted individuals to at least acknowledge some of the benefits of immigrant inflows. Other studies demonstrate that increased knowledge has a tangible effect on how social and economic issues get discussed in the home, as parental education has a spillover effect on attitudes about various matters (Piopiunik, 2014; Dickson et al., 2016). Consequently, scholars have examined parental education to help predict the next generation's attitudes towards immigrants.

In Germany, Margaryan, Paul, and Siedler (2021) found that the likelihood of adult children developing concerns about immigration decreased by 27% for each additional year their mother spent in school. Two justifications have been developed to understand this effect. First, Esses et al. (2013) found a link between higher education and the importance of instilling pro-social values in children, including belief in equality, forgiveness, and altruism. Second, Weber (2020) argued that maternal education has a "character shaping" effect on families, as their academic backgrounds contributed to their activeness in raising their children to become good citizens. By contrast, Avdeenko and Siedler (2017) discovered that when children grew up in poorly educated households with parents who expressed deep concern about immigration, they often carried these fears into their adult life. In Scandinavian countries, like Finland, Mäkinen (2017) notes that when public education is low, the hostility and resentment towards immigrants consistently increases. Thus, providing further validation of the causal claim that "parents leave visible marks in the attitude formation process of their offspring" (Brenner and Fertig, 2006, p. 18). These results are generally consistent across the literature, confirming that the effect of parental education on their children's beliefs is relatively consistent with pro-immigrant sentiments, while less schooling often leads to more hostility (Brenner and Fertig, 2006; Sides and Citrin, 2007).

Another important layer of the debate about socialization is the impact of learning and social interactions while attending school. Post-secondary enrollment remains highly correlated with one's social and economic status. Those able to enrol in college or university are more likely to interact with various individuals through intergroup contact. According to Berg (2009), the core tenet of the group contact literature is that when members of the dominant group interact more regularly with racial or ethnic minorities, they develop more positive attitudes towards these individuals. Green, Fasel, and Sarrasin (2010) explains that the academic experience allows individuals to meet and form friendships with immigrants or international students, leading to more receptive views. Other research has also shown that frequent social contact through studying and forming bonds with newcomers decreases fears about competition for resources like well-paying jobs post-graduation because of a stronger belief in individual merit (Finseraas, Skorge, and Strøm, 2018).

Another feature of the literature on education and public opinion is the importance of academic institutions in shaping individual attitudes. Jackman and Muha (1984) developed the "education-as-liberator" paradigm, which assumes that the moral obligation to accept others improves with time spent in higher education. Scholars have consistently validated this liberalizing effect and its influence on critical thinking and social acceptance (Chandler and Tsai, 2001; Lancee and Sarrasin, 2015). They also acknowledge that the Western education system fosters ethnic, racial, and social tolerance producing "enlightened citizens" who are more inclined to favour liberal immigration policy agendas (Haimueller and Hiscox, 2007; Janus, 2010). As further evidence, d'Hombres and Nunziata (2016) point out that "time spent in education significantly affects values and the cognitive assessment of the role of immigration in host societies" (217). As a result, highly educated individuals are more likely to develop liberal, tolerant, and informed beliefs versus those barred from attending post-secondary school because of their relative social standing (Hello et al., 2006). That is not to say that well-educated people do not hold xenophobic or poorly informed opinions or that those unable to attend school never hold well-informed beliefs. However, the general takeaway is that the diffusion of progressive ideas coupled with regular interactions with newcomers or other racial and ethnic minorities at school helps foster more welcoming world views versus those unable to attend post-secondary school. We now turn to examine literature investigating how less-educated individuals often perceive immigrants.

Education and anti-immigrant attitudes

To what extent are opinions about immigrants driven by the educational attainment of one's family or their own education experience? Wilkes and colleagues (2008) found that people with university education are twice as likely to support immigration versus those who stopped studying after elementary school. Consequently, less-educated individuals have often preferred conservative social and economic policies and rally behind the populist rhetoric attached to some political parties (ibid). Breton (2015) found that several politicians have built successful election campaigns around the idea that immigration inflows threaten national identity by welcoming individuals who "disrespect the flag" to capture disaffected and less-educated voters. These findings were consistent with arguments raised by Harell and colleagues (2012), which determined that the link between public comprehension of immigration processes and racist attitudes is most evident when people perceive newcomers as racially, ethnically, and culturally different. The other well-established impact is that people with less education are susceptible to misinformation about immigrants and the immigration process itself (d'Hombres and Nunziata, 2016). While susceptibility to misinformation and support for conservative immigration policies receive frequent scholarly attention, other concerns have received consideration.

Scholars have devoted greater attention to discussing how educational differences can affect one's interpretation of immigration inflows on symbolic and cultural norms. Murray and Marx (2013) point out that perceived threats to morals, beliefs, identity, and communalism have become a rallying point for poorly educated individuals. These concerns constitute what Stephan et al. (1998) call "symbolic threats," where potential challenges to a society's social and cultural composition activate militant beliefs among natives. Perhaps the most documented impact of a poorly educated citizenry on immigration attitudes has focused on perceived threats to political culture. In the United States, a strong belief in Christian nationalism – the idea that America has a sacred purpose and God's favour – prompts some less-educated and religious individuals to believe that Latinx and non-white immigrants threaten its divine mission (Fussell, 2014). See Chapter 8 on religion and attitudes towards immigrants. Hostility also emanates from individual-level assessments of threats when people perceive immigrants as unwilling to speak or learn the dominant language, respect religious differences, or pay taxes (ibid). As a result, perceived cultural threats have led to higher blame assignment on immigrants for issues like crime and declining public trust, despite evidence disputing such claims (Rustenbach, 2010). The main point of emphasis is that perceived threats to dominant symbolic and cultural practices continue to activate anti-immigrant sentiments among less-educated individuals across Western democracies. Therefore, class, operationalized as individual or family educational attainment, impacts the development of immigration opinions.

ECONOMIC CONDITIONS

Economic conditions and perceptions of them are also central to the relationship between class and immigration opinion. Hopkins (2010) argues that one's sense of their finances and macro-economic conditions drive outlooks on newcomers and immigration policy. Three theoretical perspectives help assess the link between (perceptions of) economic conditions and the acceptance of immigrants. First, the egocentric or pocketbook theory has origins in the rational choice tradition, suggesting that individual evaluations of their economic context influence whether people see newcomers as an imminent threat or welcomed addition (Johnson and Sunil, 2015). These subjective economic evaluations are critical antecedents of people's opinions that shed light on immigration attitudes across various classes (Pettigrew et al., 2007). Second, the sociotropic economic threat argument centres on the idea that people consider the effect of immigration on the country as a whole during their assessments of the potential fiscal problems caused by rapid immigration inflows (Johnson and Sunil, 2015). Under both the pocketbook and sociotropic arguments, worse or worsening economic conditions correlate with lower support for immigrants and immigration. Lastly, the group conflict theory helps explain how relative economic standing affects attitudes, as hostility towards immigrants increases when natives, namely working-class individuals, perceive competition for resources like well-paying jobs or government benefits (Harell et al., 2012). Berg (2009) notes that individuals engage in group conflict during an economic recession when lower-class individuals can become increasingly hostile to immigrants as fears of job loss surface. These explanations provide a good starting point to contextualize how class and economic concerns affect public opinion on immigration.

Economic shocks and attitudes

The role of economic cycles and exogenous shocks has received significant scholarly attention in assessments of public attitudes about immigration across different classes. The consensus is that public support or hostility towards immigrants often depends on national and global economic conditions (Harell et al., 2012; Wilkes and Corrigall-Brown, 2011). Banting and Soroka (2020) found that Canadians' openness to immigration depended primarily on economic prosperity as people adjusted their beliefs and support based on the ebb and flow of the business cycle and its effect on their lives. Dancygier and colleagues (2013) also note that subjective evaluations of economic restructuring or exogenous shocks often negatively affect working-class individuals' opinions about immigration inflows. However, scholars continue to find that scepticism towards immigrants tends to dissipate during periods of growth regardless of one's social and economic standing and policy preferences (Meuleman, 2011; Chang and Kang, 2018). These findings demonstrate that attitudes towards immigrants are subject to economic change across all classes. Nonetheless, public opinion is the most variable among lower-class individuals, as economic shocks frequently impact people with more manual skills and jobs the hardest.

Potential costs

The other recurring discussion is the potential financial challenge that increased immigration poses to taxpayers and governments. The main argument is that national, sub-national, and local governments, in particular, are ill-equipped to shoulder the cost of integrating newcomers into society (Citrin et al., 1997). D'Hombres and Nunziata (2016) note that hostility towards immigrants can emerge when the public perceives newcomers as a tax burden, especially among those already struggling to get ahead. In other words, immigration can become a highly contentious issue when the public perceives immigrants as reliant on the welfare system without contributing to its financing, a belief most compatible with working-class individuals (Dustmann and Preston, 2007; Harell et al., 2012). Despite evidence that newcomers are more beneficial than burdensome to their host country, the perceived economic threat often triggers fear and anxiety about natives' advantage, access to health care, or other welfare provisions (Palmer, 1996; Citrin et al., 1997; Hjerm, 2009). Consequently, perceived economic concerns or adversity lend support to theories of group conflict and the idea that disadvantaged individuals "who feel economically threatened by immigrants favor a more restrictive immigration policy" (Meuleman, 2011, p. 307).

Class and the labour market

Lastly, labour market concerns are a critical component of public attitudes towards immigrants, as extensively discussed in Chapter 14. According to Berg (2009), the labour market perspective helps gauge how individuals adjust their feelings towards immigrants based on a perceived competition for economic resources. Kunovich (2013) summarizes this competition as a battle among native-born working-class individuals and newcomers for labour-intensive jobs. While the perceived consequences of immigration on labour market prospects have created hostility among people of all economic classes, the most extensive research has explored the impact of immigration inflows on job opportunities, wages, and public opposition among citizens already facing hardship (Scheve and Slaughter, 2001). The central argument is that native workers, especially those with poor labour skills, often oppose immigration because they fear losing their job or the prospect of being unable to improve their position in society as competition increases (Turner and Cross, 2015; Polavieja, 2016; Malhotra et al., 2013). In short, when key labour market indicators like unemployment rates peak, public polarization regarding immigration increases as lower-class individuals develop fears about future opportunities (Finseraas, Skorge, and Strøm, 2018). These findings run parallel to the theoretical expectations provided by group conflict and ethnic competition theories, which note that public hostility and perceived labour market competition often go hand-in-hand as the reality of an "immigrant" threat intensifies (Lancee and Sarrasin, 2015).

Despite the subjective basis of some public hostility towards immigrants, economists have found that immigration inflows can pose a labour problem that is likely to affect working-class individuals the hardest. The factor proportions theory outlines a scenario where the immigrant labour force is predominately less skilled than natives causing the bottom of the labour market to become saturated and highly competitive (Hainmueller and Hiscox, 2010). As a result, residents already facing economic hardship are likely to perceive low-skilled newcomers as the cause of downward pressure on their opportunities and wages (Dustmann and Preston, 2006; Bridges and Mateut, 2014; Edo, 2019). These claims have gained momentum as the increased visibility of newcomers flocking to low-wage jobs have heightened public hostility towards immigrants (Rustenbach, 2010). These developments have had a substantial effect on working-class natives and their ability to find meaningful employment, which is why some scholars have found that the public has an inherent preference for high-skilled immigrants irrespective of their class position (Hainmueller et al., 2015; Naumann et al., 2018). However, the effect of immigration inflow on the labour market is not exclusive to working-class people with modest skills and jobs. Lancee and Sarrasin (2015) found that increased job competition among natives and newcomers with vocational training fuelled anti-immigrant attitudes. Similarly, Borjas (2005) discovered that immigration-induced surpluses of people with doctorates could, in a given field, reduce the average annual earnings of the entire cohort by more than 3%, which has been a source of anti-immigrant sentiment among high-class individuals. Despite the evidence of increased immigration affecting the labour market potential of upper and middle-class individuals, the literature continues to point towards the reality that immigration inflows affect working-class natives' employment prospects the most.

EXAGGERATED PERCEPTIONS?

While the discussion of class and immigration attitudes is complicated some scholars argue that reducing this complexity to primarily labour market concerns is a possible exaggeration. For example, Dustmann and Glitz (2011) found that highly educated immigrants, on average, made 10% less than natives with the same level of education in Canada, France, and Portugal. Similarly, Dustmann and colleagues (2008) note that immigration only affects citizen wages if the skill distribution of newcomers disproportionately outweighs the existing workforce (either in terms of high or low skill). As further evidence, Edo (2019) added that increased immigration either had an insignificant or positive effect on average wages, so long as the labour supply remains balanced. Otherwise, the negative impact of immigration inflows on labour and earnings in the United Kingdom, for example, is likely to impact recent immigrants already working in the country the hardest, reinforcing struggles for newcomers attempting to integrate economically (Dustmann and Glitz, 2011). A final counterargument is that newcomers contribute to job creation through innovation. In the United States, high-skilled immigrants, especially those trained in the STEM disciplines, have developed high-growth firms and strengthened intellectual property and employment opportunities for high and low-skilled labourers globally (Hunt and Gauthier-Loiselle, 2010; Edo, 2019). These realities can impact the public's perception of newcomers and their ability to contribute and motivate natives to become more innovative (Edo, 2019). The key takeaway is that despite one's class position, public opinion about immigration can change as people get exposed to new evidence that newcomers improve their country.

In sum, conceptions of class remain contested in the literature, with the conventional understanding rooted in beliefs about chances in life, intergenerational ties, and the acceptance of social and economic hierarchy. These understandings have shaped the broader debate about measuring class differences, as scholars have engaged with objective and subjective measures of social standing. Educational backgrounds continue to be a significant marker of class differences, with those attending post-secondary school being more likely to develop warmer feelings towards newcomers through group contact. In the absence of academic experience, scholars continue to find evidence of xenophobic and misinformed beliefs. Second, changes in economic conditions elicit differences in opinions towards newcomers, as working-class individuals often engage in group conflict with newcomers during poor economic times. Lastly, the labour market literature provides examples of increased nativism as perceived job threats expand to different industries and occupations of varying skills. As a result, one's social and economic standing continues to serve as a critical barometer of immigration attitudes.

CLASS AND OPINION ABOUT IMMIGRATION

We now turn to explore the effects of class on immigration opinion in eight of the nine countries presented in Chapter 3.[1] Before considering the relationships of class with opinion, we need to outline our concept and operationalization of class. While the literature identifies several ways to subjectively identify and categorize a "social class" variable, given existing work on the topic, we elected to use indicators in combination to form our measure of class – education and income. Our measure of education is how much formal education a respondent received, which we recoded into three categories: "low" (up to high school completion), "medium" (some post-secondary schooling), and "high" (completion of university degree and beyond). Across the eight countries, 48% of respondents had "low" education, 34% had "medium" education levels, and 17% achieved a "high" education score.[2] Our measure of income represents the respondents' income levels in quintiles, which are referenced to the country of residence to allow for comparability across countries and so do not delineate a specific income amount in each category. We combined the second, third, and fourth quintiles into a middle-income category leaving the bottom and top quintiles to eliminate future issues with fewer observations across more categorizations. This resulted in a distribution of 19% in the low-income category, 62% in the middle-income category, and 20% in the high-income category.[3,4] The results in Figure 7.1 indicate that these preconceived variable pairings are appropriate and, ultimately, provide us with a 3 × 3 grouping schema where we can place respondents into designated "classes."

After understanding the relationship between our two major grouping variables, our process investigated how many class designations were needed to create and

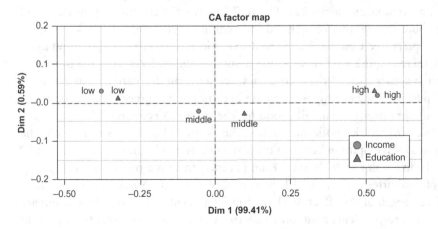

FIGURE 7.1 Income and education correspondence analysis.

TABLE 7.1 Hierarchical clustering with class assignment

| | | Income | | |
		Low	Med	High
Education	Low	Low (1)	Low (1)	Low-mid (2)
	Med	Low (1)	Low-mid (2)	High-mid (3)
	High	Low-mid (2)	High-mid (3)	High (4)

Note: class assignment denoted in parentheses ().

place respondents. Considering the number of classes was not pre-identified, we then conducted "agglomerative nesting" – a type of hierarchical clustering that groups similar cluster nodes into a new larger node or cluster.[5] Accordingly, we divided respondents into four class categories distributed on the mix of education and income as identified by our clustering approach, which we present in Table 7.1.

Figure 7.2 shows the breakdown of class positions for each of our eight countries. There are a few important points about these distributions. The high-class category is the smallest category for each country, exceeding 10% of respondents only in Portugal. The low-class category is the largest in six of the countries, which mainly reflects the incidence of a respondent being in either the low education or low-income category (or both) after demographic weighting was applied. Lastly, there is some important variation across countries in the distribution of respondents assigned to specific classes. In particular, Canada, the UK, Portugal, and Switzerland all exhibit a more even distribution across the class categories than France, Germany, Italy, and the US.[6]

We now consider the relationship of class position and opinion about immigration within each of the eight countries. For each figure, the higher values denote increased anti-immigrant sentiment. Figure 7.3 shows the relationship of class and responses about immigrants being good for a country's economy. As we know from previous chapters (see Chapter 3 and the distributions of immigration opinion more generally), there is quite a bit of variation across the cases. Exploring the impact of class position across each of these countries, we see a similar pattern – as respondents' class positions become higher, opinion becomes more agreeable with the assertion that immigrants are "generally good for the country's economy." However, the extent of this effect varies noticeably across the cases. In Portugal, for instance, the difference in average opinion between the lowest class and highest class is only 0.17 points on the five-point scale. In the UK and France, there is a relatively large gap, as average opinion differs by 1.18 and 1.00 points, respectively. So, despite some variations in the strength of the effect, we have consistent evidence across these countries that lower-class respondents hold more negative views about immigrants' impact on the economy than higher-class ones.

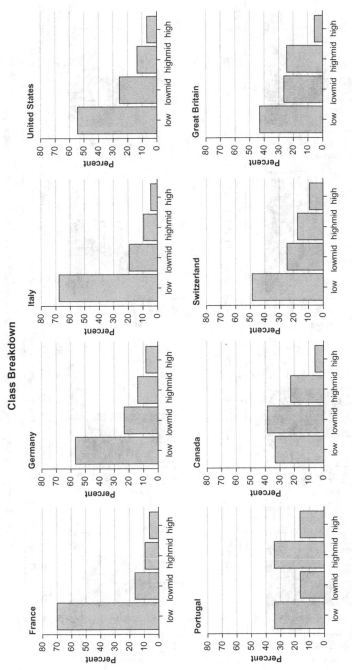

FIGURE 7.2 Class breakdown by country.

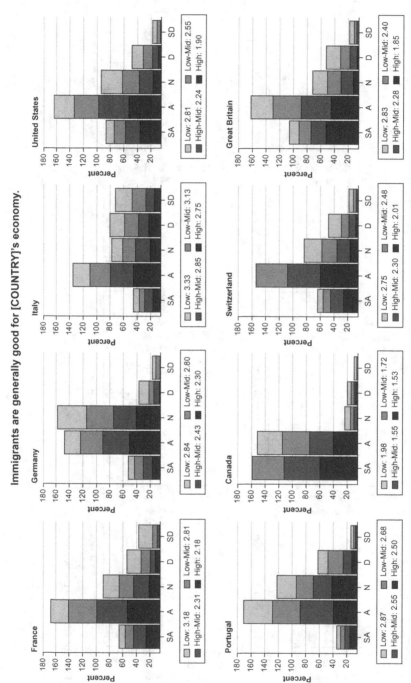

FIGURE 7.3 Attitudes about how immigrants are perceived to affect a country's economy, by class.

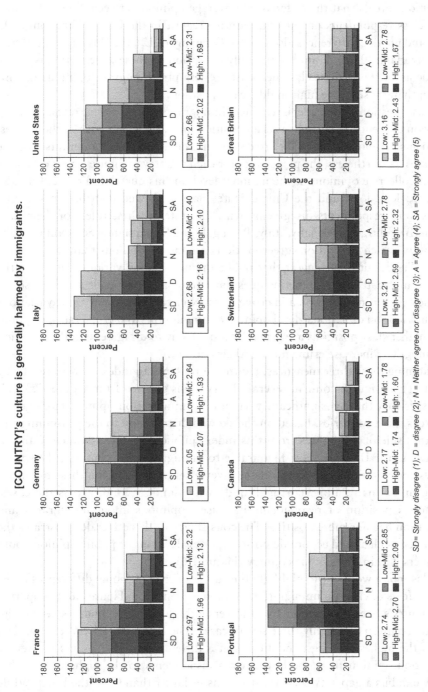

[COUNTRY]'s culture is generally harmed by immigrants.

France

Low: 2.97	Low-Mid: 2.32
High-Mid: 1.96	High: 2.13

Germany

Low: 3.05	Low-Mid: 2.64
High-Mid: 2.07	High: 1.93

Italy

Low: 2.68	Low-Mid: 2.40
High-Mid: 2.16	High: 2.10

United States

Low: 2.66	Low-Mid: 2.31
High-Mid: 2.02	High: 1.69

Portugal

Low: 2.74	Low-Mid: 2.85
High-Mid: 2.70	High: 2.09

Canada

Low: 2.17	Low-Mid: 1.78
High-Mid: 1.74	High: 1.60

Switzerland

Low: 3.21	Low-Mid: 2.78
High-Mid: 2.59	High: 2.32

Great Britain

Low: 3.16	Low-Mid: 2.78
High-Mid: 2.43	High: 1.67

SD= Strongly disagree (1); D = disagree (2); N = Neither agree nor disagree (3); A = Agree (4); SA = Strongly agree (5)

FIGURE 7.4 Attitudes about how immigrants are perceived to affect a country's culture, by class.

Figure 7.4 plots responses to the question of whether a "country's culture is generally harmed by immigrants" by country. We observe a similar relationship across each case – as class position improves, respondents are more likely to disagree with the statement that immigrants harm their country's culture. A closer look at the distribution reveals that the difference in average opinion between "low" class and "high" class respondents on this question is greatest in the United Kingdom (1.49 points) and notable differences also exist in Germany (1.12), the United States (0.97), and Switzerland (0.89). France is the only exception to these general trends where respondents in the highest class demonstrate less pro-immigrant opinions on this question than those in the high-middle class position.

The last question we consider is whether "immigrants increase crime rates." Bearing directly on the central question, as class position increases across each of these cases, respondents are more likely to disagree with the statement that immigrants increase crime rates. Nevertheless, the plot shapes for each country in Figure 7.5 reveals quite different collective opinions at the national level on this question. France, Canada, the United Kingdom, and the United States have a skewed distribution trending towards most respondents disagreeing with the statement regardless of their class position. By contrast, Germany, Italy, Portugal, and Switzerland each exhibit a distribution in which neutral or agree positions are more populous than the disagree options. The result may suggest that public opinion among various classes, as the literature insinuates, often remains question- and context-dependent, which seems to be the case for immigration and crime rates. Nonetheless, despite these variations in the distribution of national-level opinion on immigrants and crime rates, respondents in higher class positions are generally more likely to disagree with the assertion that immigrants increase crime rates in their country.

Combining these three measures, Figure 7.6 presents an index of these results by country. These figures confirm several observations gleaned from Figures 7.3–7.5. The first is that there is significant variation in immigration opinion more generally across these countries. Based on the skewed distribution to the pro-immigrant (left-hand) side of the figures from this index, public opinion in France, Canada, the UK, and the USA are most favourable to immigrants. By contrast, the spread of views across the scale reflects a more diverse set of opinions on these questions existing in Germany, Italy, Portugal, and Switzerland. Second, across the cases, as the class position of respondents increases, opinions about immigrants and immigration become more positive. The consistency of this effect demonstrates the importance of class and economic position for evaluations of public opinion about newcomers within one's home country (Figure 7.6).

The last point would be to highlight the nature of cross-national differences in the relative effects of class on immigration opinion evident from Figure 7.6. Comparing each country's average opinion for low versus high-class respondents reveals an interesting pattern of roughly three sets of cases. The first is the UK, where the class effect is the highest amongst these cases at a difference of 1.21 points in average immigration opinion from the lowest class respondents to the highest. No other country exhibits a gap between these two classes larger than 0.94 (the USA). While

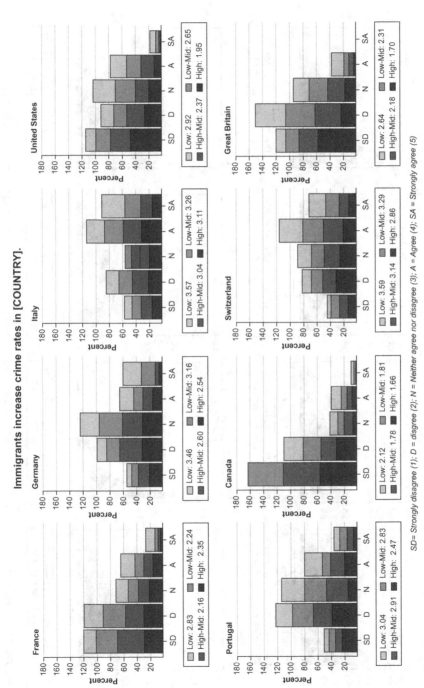

FIGURE 7.5 Attitudes about how immigrants are perceived to affect a country's crime, by class.

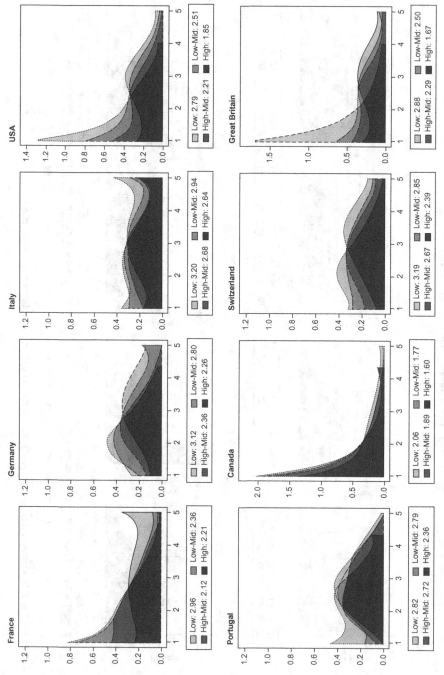

FIGURE 7.6 Attitudes about how immigrants are perceived to affect a country's economy, crime, and culture (index), by class.

work has denoted the end of class politics in the UK (e.g. Evans, 1999), it may be that vestiges of a historically pervasive class structure still influence aspects of British society. Alternatively, it may be that new socioeconomic cleavages borne out of economic and political challenges of the Brexit debates have served to differentiate citizens based on relative economic and educational positionings within British society.

On the flip side of the UK lie Canada and Portugal, where the differences in immigration opinion based on class are much smaller than in all other cases at 0.48 and 0.47 points, respectively. These two cases are at least 0.3 points lower in the highest versus lowest class difference than every other country. In the case of Canada, the smaller influences of class on opinion are consistent with a longer-term finding of relatively weak class effects within Canadian politics and public opinion more generally (Brodie and Jenson, 1988; Gidengil, 1989). Concerning Portugal, the lower effects of class differentiation on immigration opinion also conform with previous findings that the central factors in Portuguese politics focus on regime type and left-right ideology (e.g. Freire and Lobo, 2005; Gunther and Montero, 2001; Jalali, 2007).

CONCLUSION

This chapter has sought to consider the relationship of class and immigration opinion. We have examined definitional and measurement issues and explored the theoretical mechanisms underlying how one's socioeconomic position influences opinion about immigration. Despite some evident variation in the strength of the effect, our findings across these eight countries consistently point to a positive relationship between higher class position and pro-immigrant opinion. While these results do not allow us to determine the exact mechanisms through which class position serves to shape opinion, they confirm that class and immigration opinion correlates expectedly.

SUMMARY POINTS

- The chapter explored how the concept of class is defined and measured before considering various theoretical mechanisms of effect (how and why class affects public opinion) – paying particular attention to educational attainment, socialization, and personal economic condition.
- Class is an often complex and subjective concept to measure, and in this chapter, we used education and income variables to develop a multi-group class scheme.
- Despite some cross-national variation in the strength of the effect, findings consistently point to a positive relationship between higher class position and pro-immigrant opinions.

NOTES

1 Australia was excluded for lack of adequate social class measures.
2 We report percentages across these categories of education and income among those respondents for which we had both education and income information.
3 The "low-middle-high" approach was adopted to keep categorization consistency across all countries. We acknowledge that these are both perceived categorizations from the survey respondents and that there are contextual factors country-to-country that lack consideration when trying to aggregate data for comparative purposes. For example, "low" education (up to high school completion) in Country A could be the norm whereas it could be considered undereducated in Country B. This should be taken into consideration for each variable included in any models or indexes attempting to identify social class.
4 To understand if these categorizations match up, we used R's *FactoMineR* package to conduct a correspondence analysis that measures the relationships between these categorical variable pairings in a low-dimensional space (Husson et al., 2014).
5 Our initial process attempted use of a Latent Class Analysis (LCA) to determine respondents' individual position in each designated class. LCA is a type of finite mixture model or "model-based clustering" that attempts to identify unmeasured class membership among respondents using categorical variables. Considering the low number of parameters between these two variables, however, this approach provided unstable results and thus the more stable hierarchical clustering approach, which removes the probabilistic modelling component, was used.
6 We investigated the uneven class distribution of these latter four countries. With France, this distribution appears accurate considering the substantial country-level frequency in the low education category. For Germany, Italy, and the US, however, we identify potential issues with the weighting schemes for each country, particularly Italy where substantial weight is given to those who would be categorized as a "low" class respondent. This speaks to the difficulty in creating an accurate comparative measure of class using few parameters.

SUGGESTED FURTHER READINGS

Chandler, C.R. and Tsai, Y.M., 2001. Social factors influencing immigration attitudes: An analysis of data from the general social survey. *The Social Science Journal*, 38(2), 177–188.
Haubert, J. and Fussell, E., 2006. Explaining pro-immigrant sentiment in the US: Social class, cosmopolitanism, and perceptions of immigrants. *International Migration Review*, 40(3), 489–507.

REFERENCES

Avdeenko, A. and Siedler, T., 2017. Intergenerational correlations of extreme right-wing party preferences and attitudes toward immigration. *The Scandinavian Journal of Economics*, 119(3), 768–800.
Banting, K. and Soroka, S., 2020. A distinctive culture? The sources of public support for immigration in Canada, 1980–2019. *Canadian Journal of Political Science/Revue canadienne de science politique*, 53(4),821–838.
Becker, B., 2021. Temporal change in inequality perceptions and effects on political attitudes. *Political Research Exchange*, 3(1), 1–21.
Berg, J.A., 2009. White public opinion toward undocumented immigrants: Threat and interpersonal environment. *Sociological Perspectives*, 52(1), 39–58.
Borjas, G.J., 2005. The labor-market impact of high-skill immigration. *American Economic Review*, 95(2), 56–60.

Brenner, J. and Fertig, M., 2006. *Identifying the determinants of attitudes towards immigrants – A structural cross-country analysis, RWI Discussion Papers*, No. 47, Rheinisch-Westfälisches Institut für Wirtschaftsforschung (RWI), Essen.

Breton, C., 2015. Making national identity salient: Impact on attitudes toward immigration and multiculturalism. *Canadian Journal of Political Science/Revue canadienne de science politique*, 48(2), 357–381.

Bridges, S. and Mateut, S., 2014. Should they stay or should they go? Attitudes towards immigration in Europe. *Scottish Journal of Political Economy*, 61(4), 397–429.

Brodie, J. and Jenson, J., 1988. *Crisis, challenge and change: Party and class in Canada revisited*. Ottawa, ON: Carleton University Press.

Brooks, C. and Svallfors, S., 2010. Why does class matter? Policy attitudes, mechanisms, and the case of the Nordic countries. *Research in Social Stratification and Mobility*, 28(2), 199–213.

Chan, T.W. and Goldthorpe, J.H., 2007. Class and status: The conceptual distinction and its empirical relevance. *American Sociological Review*, 72(4), 512–532.

Chandler, C.R. and Tsai, Y.M., 2001. Social factors influencing immigration attitudes: An analysis of data from the general social survey. *The Social Science Journal*, 38(2), 177–188.

Chang, H.I. and Kang, W.C., 2018. Trust, economic development and attitudes toward immigration. *Canadian Journal of Political Science*, 51(2), 357–378.

Citrin, J., Green, D., Muste, C., and Wong, C., 1997. Public opinion toward immigration reform: The role of economic motivations. *Journal of Politics*, 59(3), 858–881.

Cohen, D., Shin, F., Liu, X., Ondish, P., and Kraus, M.W., 2017. Defining social class across time and between groups. *Personality and Social Psychology Bulletin*, 43(11), 1530–1545.

Dancygier, R.M. and Donnelly, M.J., 2013. Sectoral economies, economic contexts, and attitudes toward immigration. *The Journal of Politics*, 75(1), 17–35.

Dickson, M., Gregg, P., and Robinson, H., 2016. Early, late or never? When does parental education impact child outcomes? *The Economic Journal*, 126(596), 184–231.

d'Hombres, B. and Nunziata, L., 2016. Wish you were here? Quasi-experimental evidence on the effect of education on self-reported attitude toward immigrants. *European Economic Review*, 90, 201–224.

Dustmann, C. and Preston, I., 2006. Is immigration good or bad for the economy? Analysis of attitudinal responses. In: S. Polachek et al. *The economics of immigration and social diversity*. Oxford: Elsevier Limited.

Dustmann, C. and Preston, I., 2007. Racial and economic factors in attitudes to immigration. *The B.E. Journal of Economic Analysis & Policy*, 7(1).

Dustmann, C., Glitz, A., and Frattini, T., 2008. The labour market impact of immigration. *Oxford Review of Economic Policy*, 24(3), 477–494.

Dustmann, C. and Glitz, A., 2011. Migration and education. In: E. Hanushek et al. (Eds.), *Handbook of the economics of education*. Vol. 4. Amsterdam: Elsevier, 327–439.

Edo, A., 2019. The impact of immigration on the labor market. *Journal of Economic Surveys*, 33(3), 922–948.

Esses, V.M., Medianu, S., and Lawson, A.S., 2013. Uncertainty, threat, and the role of the media in promoting the dehumanization of immigrants and refugees. *Journal of Social Issues*, 69(3), 518–536.

Evans, G. ed., 1999. *The end of class politics?: class voting in comparative context*. Oxford: Oxford University Press.

Finseraas, H., Skorge, Ø.S., and Strøm, M., 2018. Does education affect immigration attitudes? Evidence from an education reform. *Electoral Studies*, 55, 131–135.

Freire, A. and Lobo, M.C., 2005. Economics, ideology and vote: Southern Europe, 1985–2000. *European Journal of Political Research*, 44(4), 493–518.

Fussell, E., 2014. Warmth of the welcome: Attitudes toward immigrants and immigration policy in the United States. *Annual Review of Sociology*, 40, 479–498.

Gidengil, E., 1989. Class and region in Canadian voting: A dependency interpretation. *Canadian Journal of Political Science*, 22(3), 563–587.

Gimpelson, V. and Treisman, D., 2018. Misperceiving inequality. *Economics & Politics*, 30(1), 27–54.

Green, E.G., Fasel, N., and Sarrasin, O., 2010. The more the merrier? The effects of type of cultural diversity on exclusionary immigration attitudes in Switzerland. *International Journal of Conflict and Violence*, 4(2), 177–190.

Grigorieff, A., Roth, C., and Ubfal, D., 2020. Does information change attitudes toward immigrants? *Demography*, 57(3), 1117–1143.

Gunther, R. and Montero, J.R., 2001. The anchors of partisanship: A comparative analysis of voting behaviour in four southern european democracies. In: P.N. Diamandouros and R. Gunther, eds. *Parties, politics and democracy in the New Southern Europe*. Baltimore, MD: Johns Hopkins University Press, pp. 83–152.

Hainmueller, J. and Hiscox, M.J., 2007. Educated preferences: Explaining attitudes toward immigration in Europe. *International Organization*, 61(2), 399–442.

Hainmueller, J. and Hiscox, M.J., 2010. Attitudes toward highly skilled and low-skilled immigration: Evidence from a survey experiment. *American Political Science Review*, 104(1), 61–84.

Hainmueller, J. and Hopkins, D.J., 2014. Public attitudes toward immigration. *Annual Review of Political Science*, 17, 225–249.

Hainmueller, J., Hiscox, M.J., and Margalit, Y., 2015. Do concerns about labor market competition shape attitudes toward immigration? New evidence. *Journal of International Economics*, 97(1), 193–207.

Harell, A., Soroka, S., Iyengar, S., and Valentino, N., 2012. The impact of economic and cultural cues on support for immigration in Canada and the United States. *Canadian Journal of Political Science/Revue canadienne de science politique*, 45(3), 499–530.

Haubert, J. and Fussell, E., 2006. Explaining pro-immigrant sentiment in the US: Social class, cosmopolitanism, and perceptions of immigrants. *International Migration Review*, 40(3), 489–507.

Hauser, O.P. and Norton, M.I., 2017. (Mis) perceptions of inequality. *Current Opinion in Psychology*, 18, 21–25.

Hello, E., Scheepers, P., and Sleegers, P., 2006. Why the more educated are less inclined to keep ethnic distance: An empirical test of four explanations. *Ethnic and Racial Studies*, 29(5), 959–985.

Hjerm, M., 2009. Anti-immigrant attitudes and cross-municipal variation in the proportion of immigrants. *Acta Sociologica*, 52(1), 47–62.

Hopkins, D.J., 2010. Politicized places: Explaining where and when immigrants provoke local opposition. *American Political Science Review*, 104(1), 40–60.

Hunt, J. and Gauthier-Loiselle, M., 2010. How much does immigration boost innovation? *American Economic Journal: Macroeconomics*, 2(2), 31–56.

Hunt, M.O. and Ray, R., 2012. Social class identification among Black Americans: Trends and determinants, 1974–2010. *American Behavioral Scientist*, 56(11), 1462–1480.

Husson, F., Josse, J., Le, S., and Mazet, J., 2014. FactoMineR: Multivariate exploratory data analysis and dating mining with R. Available from: http://cran.r-project.org/web/packages /FactoMineR/index.html

Jackman, M.R. and Muha, M.J., 1984. Education and intergroup attitudes: Moral enlightenment, superficial democratic commitment, or ideological refinement? *American Sociological Review*, 49(6), 751–769.

Jalali, C., 2007. The same old cleavage? Old cleavages and new values. In: A. Freire, M.C. Lobo, and P. Magalhaes, eds. *Portugal at the polls: In 2002*. Lanham: Lexington Books. pp. 49–74

Janus, A.L., 2010. The influence of social desirability pressures on expressed immigration attitudes. *Social Science Quarterly*, 91(4), 928–946.

Johnson, C. and Sunil, R., 2015. Did perception of the economy affect attitudes to immigration at the 2010 British general election? *Social Science Quarterly*, 96(5), 1214–1225.

Jones, S. and Vagle, M.D., 2013. Living contradictions and working for change: Toward a theory of social class–sensitive pedagogy. *Educational Researcher*, 42(3), 129–141.

Kraus, M.W., Piff, P.K., and Keltner, D., 2009. Social class, sense of control, and social explanation. *Journal of Personality and Social Psychology*, 97(6), 992–1004.

Kraus, M.W., Piff, P.K., and Keltner, D., 2011. Social class as culture: The convergence of resources and rank in the social realm. *Current Directions in Psychological Science*, 20(4), 246–250.

Kraus, M.W., Piff, P.K., Mendoza-Denton, R., Rheinschmidt, M.L., and Keltner, D., 2012. Social class, solipsism, and contextualism: How the rich are different from the poor. *Psychological Review*, 119(3), 546.

Kraus, M.W. et al., 2017. Signs of social class: The experience of economic inequality in everyday life. *Perspectives on Psychological Science*, 12(3), 422–435.

Kunovich, R., 2013. Labor market competition and anti-immigrant sentiment: Occupations as contexts. *The International Migration Review*, 47(3), 643–685.

Lancee, B. and Sarrasin, O., 2015. Educated preferences or selection effects? A longitudinal analysis of the impact of educational attainment on attitudes towards immigrants. *European Sociological Review*, 31(4), 490–501.

Lipset, S.M., 1959. Some social requisites of democracy: Economic development and political legitimacy. *American political science review*, 53(1), pp.69–105.

Macdonald, D., 2020. Class attitudes, political knowledge, and support for redistribution in an era of inequality. *Social Science Quarterly*, 101(2), 960–977.

Mäkinen, K., 2017. Struggles of citizenship and class: Anti-immigration activism in Finland. *The Sociological Review*, 65(2), 218–234.

Malhotra, N., Margalit, Y., and Mo, C.H., 2013. Economic explanations for opposition to immigration: Distinguishing between prevalence and conditional impact. *American Journal of Political Science*, 57(2), 391–410.

Manstead, A.S., 2018. The psychology of social class: How socioeconomic status impacts thought, feelings, and behaviour. *British Journal of Social Psychology*, 57(2), 267–291.

Margaryan, S., Paul, A., and Siedler, T., 2021. Does education affect attitudes towards immigration? Evidence from Germany. *Journal of Human Resources*, 56(2), 446–479.

Meuleman, B., 2011. Perceived economic threat and anti-immigration attitudes: Effects of immigrant group size and economic conditions revisited. In: E. Davidov et al. (Eds.), *Cross-Cultural Analysis: Methods and Applications*, London: Routledge, 218–310.

Murray, K.E. and Marx, D.M., 2013. Attitudes toward unauthorized immigrants, authorized immigrants, and refugees. *Cultural Diversity and Ethnic Minority Psychology*, 19(3), 332.

Naumann, E., Stoetzer, L., and Pietrantuono, G., 2018. Attitudes towards highly skilled and low-skilled immigration in Europe: A survey experiment in 15 European countries. *European Journal of Political Research*, 57(4), 1009–1030.

Newman, B.J., Johnston, C.D., and Lown, P.L., 2015. False consciousness or class awareness? Local income inequality, personal economic position, and belief in American meritocracy. *American Journal of Political Science*, 59(2), 326–340.

Nunziata, L., 2016. Wish you were here? Quasi-experimental evidence on the effect of education on self-reported attitude toward immigrants. *European Economic Review*, 90, 201–224.

Palmer, D., 1996. Determinants of Canadian attitudes towards immigration: More than just racism. *Canadian Journal of Behaviour Science*, 28, 180–192.

Pettigrew, T.F., Wagner, U., and Christ, O., 2007. Who opposes immigration? *Du Bois Review: Social Science Research on Race*, 4(1), 19–39.

Piopiunik, M., 2014. Intergenerational transmission of education and mediating channels: Evidence from a compulsory schooling reform in Germany. *The Scandinavian Journal of Economics*, 116(3), 878–907.

Polavieja, J.G., 2016. Labour-market competition, recession and anti-immigrant sentiments in Europe: Occupational and environmental drivers of competitive threat. *Socio-Economic Review*, 14(3), 395–417.

Rustenbach, E., 2010. Sources of negative attitudes toward immigrants in Europe: A multi-level analysis. *International Migration Review*, 44(1), 53–77.

Rubin, M., Denson, N., Kilpatrick, S., Matthews, K.E., Stehlik, T., and Zyngier, D., 2014. "I am working-class": Subjective self-definition as a missing measure of social class and socioeconomic status in higher education research. *Educational Researcher*, 43(4), 196–200.

Scheve, K. and Slaughter, M., 2001. Labor market competition and individual preferences over immigration policy. *Review of Economics and Statistics*, 83(1), 133–145.

Sides, J. and Citrin, J., 2007. European opinion about immigration: The role of identities, interests and information. *British Journal of Political Science*, 37(3), 477–504.

Stephan, W.G., Ybarra, O., Martnez, C.M., Schwarzwald, J., and Tur-Kaspa, M., 1998. Prejudice toward immigrants to Spain and Israel: An integrated threat theory analysis. *Journal of Cross-Cultural Psychology*, 29(4), 559–576.

Skocpol, T. 1979. States and social revolutions: A comparative analysis of France, Russia and China. Cambridge: Cambridge University Press.

Turner, T. and Cross, C., 2015. Do attitudes to immigrants change in hard times? Ireland in a European context. *European Societies*, 17(3), 372–395.

Van der Waal, J., Achterberg, P. and Houtman, D., 2007. Class is not dead—it has been buried alive: class voting and cultural voting in postwar western societies (1956–1990). *Politics & Society*, 35(3), 403–426.

Weber, H., 2020. The educational divide over feelings about ethnic minorities: Does more education really lead to less prejudice? *Journal of Ethnic and Migration Studies*, 48(1),228–247.

Wilkes, R., Guppy, N., and Farris, L., 2008. "No thanks, we're full": Individual characteristics, national context, and changing attitudes toward immigration. *International Migration Review*, 42(2), 302–329.

Wilkes, R. and Corrigall-Brown, C., 2011. Explaining time trends in public opinion: Attitudes towards immigration and immigrants. *International Journal of Comparative Sociology*, 52(1–2), 79–99.

Wright, E.O., ed., 2005. *Approaches to class analysis*. Cambridge: Cambridge University Press.

CHAPTER 8

Religion and public opinion

....

Paul A. Djupe

INTRODUCTION

One of the foundational teachings of most religions is to be charitable to strangers. Whether that involves the treatment of others (the "golden rule" – do unto others as you would have them do unto you) or commandments to contribute money to charitable endeavours (Islam's *zakat* or Buddhism's *Dana*), religions at their core are concerned with sociability. Nowhere are these commands put to a greater test than with immigration, where people are not just strangers passing through, but are asking to join the community. Immigrants are crossing the boundary from stranger to fellow citizen. This is a much more difficult proposition for many people and many religions. Even if religious teachings were clear, religious people do not reason in a vacuum filled only with holy teachings. This helps explain why religious adherents can be found on the side of nationalist opposition to immigration as well as on the side of inclusion and diversity (and everywhere in between). Instead, as with most things, religion has ambivalent effects on public matters conditioned on the national and social contexts and how we understand religion to work. Though the role that religion plays in reacting to the social environment is complex, a generation of thoughtful social science work has investigated how religion systematically influences immigration attitudes.

Scholars have approached religious influences on immigration attitudes mostly by thinking of religions as social groups, though they differ in what is meant by "social." One strand considers religion as a social interaction system, in which people are exposed to cues from other affiliates and leaders within the group. Another strand considers religious groups as identity groups in which communication is a secondary consideration, if necessary at all. These perspectives are not incompatible, of course, but serve to highlight the diverse ways in which we might conceptualize religion. Moreover, they lead to different predictions. The former is more flexible,

DOI: 10.4324/9781003121992-10

suggesting that the content of the cues provided in religious groups shape attitudes and those cues could either be pro- or anti-immigration. From the latter's perspective, making the ingroup identity salient often triggers greater dislike of (immigrant) outgroups.

While religion is generally a resource for immigrants (see, e.g. Alba et al., 2009; Cadge and Ecklund, 2007; Foner and Alba, 2008; Dana et al., 2017), it is easy to see how social difficulties may arise with the influx of people with different ethnicities, religions, and languages. Perhaps nowhere is this more apparent than in the contrasts between how immigrants have been received in Western Europe versus the United States (at least before the Trump administration). In Europe, Islam is overwhelmingly seen as a barrier to integration, whereas religious attachments are seen as benefits to social inclusion in the US (e.g. Foner and Alba, 2008). Of course, that can change along with national events such as "military adventures" (Haddad, 2018), like the US wars in Iraq and Afghanistan, that serve to politicize religious identity (see Calfano et al., 2016; Lajevardi, 2020).

In this chapter, I will first discuss the three primary approaches to religious influence on immigration attitudes – social identity, religiosity, and religious communication. Then the chapter transitions to a look at immigration attitudes for major religious groups across the nine countries studied in this volume, before pursuing a case study in the United States that enables us to see the variation in clergy engagement in the 2014 immigration debate – the last time immigration reform had a realistic chance of passage.

RELIGION AND IMMIGRATION ATTITUDES

These discussions beg the question of what religion is. Christian Smith's definition is not a bad one to start with, "Religion ... is best defined as a complex of culturally prescribed practices that are based on premises about the existence and nature of superhuman powers" (2017, p. 3). While he places emphasis on practices rather than beliefs, I am in favour of a more agnostic and subjective interpretation that allows for the importance of both for individuals. Religions are important to the extent that individuals follow them, which means that religion, in effect, is what individuals make of it. Religion can be as superficial as an identity, but as complex as rules that govern most social interactions and personal behaviour. Moreover, I would include as religious the groups doing the prescribing, which could be small groups, congregations, denominations, or nations. That is, groups are religious to the extent that they are affiliated with a religious identity that prescribes religious beliefs and behaviours and provides other relevant communication.

Owing to the complexity of what religion entails, prior research on religion and immigration attitudes is diverse, but can be captured by four rough groupings. Religion can be (1) considered an identity group, which is sufficient to draw boundaries with outsiders; (2) the way religious groups organize themselves has implications for how affiliates see outsiders; (3) the effects of religious affiliation depend upon the group's place in the social structure, perhaps forging bonds with national identities;

and (4) religious organizations may provide explicit political communication on immigration. These four conceptions of religious influence are explored below.

When we realize that religious faith is most often experienced with a homogeneous group of people strongly tied to a particular place, it would be no surprise that the default setting of people gathered together is to favour the ingroup. This dynamic is not exclusive to religion, but is expected from any group that assembles, even groups that are formed arbitrarily (Tajfel, 1970). That is, the very fact of forming a group creates an identity divide that drives the ingroup to dislike the outgroup even if it does not necessarily inspire a parallel amount of ingroup love (Brewer, 1999). See Chapters 6 and 11 for more on group identity.

While it may seem difficult to test this, it is possible to randomize group affiliation/identity to an extent. Participants can be reminded of their religious identity or some aspect of their religious affiliation, which is not always salient – this is called priming. And studies that have primed religious identity have found deleterious effects on attitudes towards outgroups (Ben-nun Bloom et al., 2019). For instance, priming the religious identity of Christians increases their racial prejudice (Johnson, Rowatt, and LeBouff, 2010; see also Lajevardi and Oskooii, 2018), and people have ethnic prejudices which drive their immigration attitudes, though depending on the type of threat they feel (Ben-nun Bloom, Arikan, and Lahav, 2015). Cultural threat is linked to immigrants with outgroup religions, while material (economic) threat is actually linked to greater opposition to *ingroup* religious immigrants who might be seen as more likely to be in competition with the study participant. This sort of economic threat is thought to explain why black Christians in the US do not have stronger pro-immigrant sentiment (Brown, 2010; Brown and Brown, 2017).

The social identity theory approach would also suggest that particular outgroups could elicit greater fear, threat, and opposition (Cowling and Anderson, 2019). Anderson and Antalíková (2014) document that certain groups are seen more negatively by Danish Christians, who respond more negatively to "Muslims" than "immigrants," while the reverse was true for Danish atheists. At the national level, this sort of flexibility is affirmed by Berkhout and Ruedin (2017), who show that religion varies as a frame for immigrants at the heart of public debate, and what cues are attached to groups are important in immigration debates more generally (Brader, Valentino, and Suhay, 2008).

Perhaps, though, priming different aspects of religion would yield different outcomes. When Ben-nun Bloom, Arikan, and Courtemanche (2015) did just this in a sample of Christians, Muslims, and Jews, they found that priming religious belief leads to more pro-immigrant sentiment when the immigrants were of the same religion, while religious behaviour priming leads to greater anti-immigrant sentiment when the immigrants do not share their religious faith. That helps to make sense of some conflicting findings in the literature and creates a more nuanced understanding of religion – it is not equivalent to the randomly assigned "minimal group."

Congregations are situated in particular communities with varying compositions of people and problems. Therefore, what affiliates need from their clergy and congregations may be quite different. There is a line of argument showing that clergy can become representatives to the community, in a political sense, when members have little other community leadership to rely on (Djupe and Gilbert, 2002; Djupe et al., 2016; Olson, 2000). If religious groups are often responsive to community needs, they also reflect and respond to the community social structure in other ways. Perhaps the most powerful representation of this is the identification of a religious group with the nation, such as Christian nationalism in the US or Hindu nationalism in India, though religious ties to ethnicity and cultures are widespread (e.g. Minkenberg, 2008; Storm, 2011).

For instance, American Christian nationalism, "a cultural framework … that idealizes and advocates a fusion of Christianity with American civic life" (Whitehead and Perry, 2020, p. 10), draws sharp normative boundaries around citizenship. Christian nationalists believe that the US is part of God's plan for the world and that the rights, responsibilities, and benefits conferred by the state are reserved for Christians (McDaniel, Noorudin, and Shortle, 2011; Dahab and Omori, 2018). Despite the fact that many immigrant source nations are majority Christian, Christian nationalists see immigrants as outsiders who would dilute the (white) Christian majority in the US (Whitehead and Perry, 2020, pp. 64–65; McDaniel et al., 2011). It almost goes without saying that Christian nationalists have much more restrictive views towards religious minorities, more generally, especially Muslims (Shortle and Gaddie, 2015).

Some researchers suggest that the nationalist variant of a religion is distinct from the true faith – for instance, Storm (2011) finds that worship attendance generally is linked to less threat perceived from immigrants, whereas religious identity predicts more threat (see also Whitehead and Perry, 2020; Daniels and von der Ruhr, 2005). A recent meta-analysis found a similar pattern in that religiously affiliated people had more negative attitudes towards immigrants, while religiosity had no cumulative effect (Deslandes and Anderson, 2019). By dint of the nature of samples, this means that religious *majorities* tend to have negative attitudes towards immigrants even if some religious organizations take more open and welcoming stands (see also Cowling and Anderson, 2019).

However, others see the nationalist project as linked tightly to religious faith, though religion has influence beyond its connection to the nation. That is, negative views of immigrants may not be restricted to those who tie their faith to the nation, and other studies have found that majority religiosity across European nations is linked to more negative views towards religious minorities (Scheepers, Gijsberts, and Hello, 2002), which often includes immigrants. So, it is particularly important to sort out why.

While that is powerful evidence about religion's baseline settings, it would be a mistake to think of religion in static terms, that it exists solely as an identity or set of beliefs inside the heads of affiliates or is determined simply by its place in the social structure. Religious groups are constantly in motion, navigating a more or less complex religious economy where people are circulating between religious organizations as well as dropping in and out of religious affiliations. As a result, religious organizations are faced with two perhaps competing questions: how to attract new members and how to retain current ones (Djupe and Neiheisel, 2019; Stark and Finke, 2000).

How clergy and congregations pursue their mix of inclusivity and exclusivity has implications for immigration and related attitudes. Djupe and Calfano (2013; see also Schaffer et al., 2015) show that they can be used effectively to prime people – greater exclusivity undermines and greater inclusivity augments political tolerance, support for immigrants, and cooperative foreign policy interventions. This evidence gathered across multiple studies of clergy and religious affiliates is important because it suggests that specific communication matters and that religious influence can change directions on a dime. From this perspective, there is no single expectation for the effects of religiosity. Of course, what this leaves out is the explicit *political* communication from religious sources.

> Protestant responses to immigration and immigration policies during US history have also been both inclusive and exclusive, driven at times by values of mercy and a broad-minded concept of justice, and frankly, sometimes by greed, insecurity, and/or prejudice, along with concerns with the rule of law.
>
> *(Melkonian-Hoover and Kellstedt, 2019, p. 14)*

The same could be said for Christian churches in EU countries, though recently it is more likely that Christian religious organizations play a role advocating for immigrants to the EU rather than opposing them (Foret and Permoser, 2015).

That is true in the US as well, perhaps most notably from the Evangelical Immigration Table (EIT); it is notable because, historically, evangelical identifiers have been less supportive of immigrants than other religious groups. The EIT is a pro-immigration reform organization with many notable evangelical signatories and at one point a considerable war chest that tried to whip up public support for reform. From one careful study of the opinion dynamics among evangelicals, the EIT was successful in boosting support in this crucial constituency in the US (Margolis, 2018a). We tend to think that national organizations are knit together with local congregations, but I found that a sample of clergy had almost no knowledge of the EIT when it was highly active with national news coverage (Djupe, 2017). At the same time, it is easy to find examples of prominent evangelicals providing full-throated support for Trump's anti-immigrant policies such as separating children from their parents (e.g. Boorstein and Zauzmer, 2018).

Christian churches are diverse in their engagement levels with and support of immigration. Fortunately, we have access to a number of studies that have looked at specific religious denominations/religious bodies in a number of contexts. For instance, the anti-immigration sentiment encouraged by the Greek Orthodox Church, the "guardian of national identity, inoculated people against the moderating attempts of Greek politicians" (Karyotis and Patrikios, 2010). But the Greek Orthodox Church is perhaps an exception among most religious bodies, especially in more pluralistic nations. There has been variation in how UK religious bodies took public stances on immigration, but the Church of England has been consistently supportive of immigrants; perhaps as a result, church-attending Anglicans were more supportive as well (Paterson, 2018). Recall that this flies against earlier evidence that religiosity had a consistent effect to undermine support for immigrants and supportive immigration policies (Scheepers et al., 2002), though that is not consistent with American evidence (Knoll, 2009). If religiosity is capturing exposure to supportive arguments, there is good evidence to validate that – Wallsten and Nteta (2016) randomly exposed affiliates to actual statements from denominational leaders in the US and generally found genial responses to it.

There are also good reasons to doubt a strong link between denominational, national-level elites, and what congregants hear in their congregations. Holman and Shockley (2017), for example, document the disjuncture between diocesan and parish-level communication about an election in Florida. And there is a raft of research that documents the diversity within religious bodies and sometimes antagonism between congregations and denominations, not unlike the states and the US government (for a review, see Djupe and Gilbert, 2009). In one study, clergy had little knowledge about the stances taken by denominational lobbying bodies (Djupe, Olson, and Gilbert, 2005).

While denominations send a signal of where member congregations might stand, there is often quite a lot of variability at the local level. So, instead, it is ideal to document what is communicated in congregations – the primary interface between religion and politics for members. In 2004 data, 17% of Christians reported hearing a sermon, lecture, or discussion on immigration (Nteta and Wallsten, 2012). Brown et al. (2017) break down this figure in 2004–2008 data and find much higher numbers among Latinxs (37%) compared to whites (13%) and blacks (14%). This is effectively consistent with evidence from 2016–2018, during which time a maximum of 18% of Christians in 2016 heard their clergy discuss immigration, declining to 10% by 2018 (Djupe, 2021). More recent data of mine from just before the 2020 elections show about the same results – only 10% of whites, 13% of African Americans, and 23% of Latinxs indicated they heard "immigration, dreamers, or DACA" discussed by clergy in the past year (among those who attend worship services).

The low numbers may reflect a lack of salience of the issue across the nation. In 2011, Alabama passed a strict anti-immigration measure that made national headlines. When Wickersham (2013) surveyed clergy to gauge their response in the aftermath, she found that 39% had given a sermon related to immigration in the past year, which accompanied a great deal of public action by religious organizations in the state.

Are these cues effectual in persuading congregants to adopt similar immigration attitudes? This is far less clear. Several papers link respondent reports of hearing a sermon with more pro-immigrant views (Brown, 2010; Brown et al., 2017; Nteta and Wallsten, 2012), but none have reports of the content of the sermon. There is good reason to doubt the association as congregants tend to downplay clergy speech when they disagree with it (Djupe and Gilbert, 2009). Moreover, when asked, clergy report quite diverse argument repertoires that could sustain a vast array of immigration attitudes as Djupe et al. document (2015).

Alternative theory: politics drives religion

It would be wrong to assume that religious actors are the only ones active on questions of immigration or almost any other issue for that matter. We need to remain open to the argument that the division we see among religious groups is a function of some other force, such as political parties or mass media. See, for example, Chapter 10 on ideology, Chapter 11 on partisanship, and Chapter 16 on media. A growing literature in the United States has found politics driving religious attachments. For instance, people decide whether to return to church in part based on their political ideology (Margolis, 2018b), and the extreme politics of the Christian Right has served to drive up the percentage of people identifying as religious nones (e.g. Hout and Fischer, 2002; Djupe, Neiheisel, and Conger, 2018). There is a strong possibility of this here, that national conditions of citizenship shape the politics of religious groups (Wald, 2015), or more specifically that national social and political environments give strong shape to the immigration debate and views towards religious minorities (e.g. Berkhout and Ruedin, 2017; Lajevardi, 2020). One recent piece finds that immigration attitudes were strong enough in the Netherlands to shape defection from religious parties (Otjes, 2020); could they be strong enough to induce congregational change too?

In light of this discussion, it might be useful to consider Wald, Owen, and Hill's (1988, p. 532) requirements for a "contextual effect" from religious groups: there must be some political communication about the issue, and people must be able to observe each other in order to bring their behaviour in line with others in the group. Clearly, people may respond differently based on their identity or beliefs, but inferences about religious influence will only grow stronger if we can identify a plausible communication link between religious actors, members, and/or identifiers (Djupe and Calfano, 2013). A good place to start is whether Western democracies still have a religious basis for reacting to political questions about immigration.

In what follows, I will provide an overview of religion in the nine Western democracies covered in Part 2 of this volume and related data before examining how religion is linked to immigration attitudes in these countries. To connect with the discussion above, I will then show some evidence of clergy engagement at the height of the US immigration debate in 2014, which highlights the variability of religious perspectives on immigration.

RELIGIOUS IDENTITY IN WESTERN DEMOCRACIES

It is a truism that religion has been in decline in Europe and the United States for some time. The rate of decline is uneven, leaving considerable division among religious groups, and likely exacerbating polarization in politics (Gaskins, Golder, and Siegel, 2013). Complicating historic divisions between Catholics and Protestants, both groups now have to contend with a growing non-religious population as well as growing numbers of non-Christian religious groups, especially, but not exclusively, Islam through immigration. In many ways, however, the numbers of religious non-Christians are more symbolic than apparent – their numbers tend to remain small.

Figure 8.1 shows the distribution of religion across the Western democracies studied in this book. I've collapsed the specific denominations into broader "religious traditions" to make comparison easier. Each has a majority of Christian identifiers except the United States (though I believe this number is too high – most other survey efforts put the US figure around 30% non-religious). Around a quarter of the total sample is non-religious, though Portugal, Italy, and France have very small numbers of non-religious identifiers.

Only one country has a majority of Protestants (UK), while several are majority Catholic (Portugal, Italy, and France). The others are pluralistic – Canada, for instance, has a plurality of Protestants, which only amounts to 35%. High pluralism holds out the potential that groups recognize and respect their minority status and benefit from interactions with a diverse array of people, all of which could expand their political tolerance. However, these national statistics sometimes hide potential

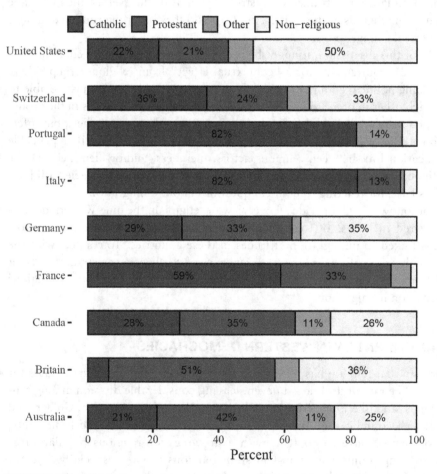

FIGURE 8.1 The distribution of religious groups across Western democracies.

problems: sub-national provinces in Canada are not as pluralistic as the country – Quebec, for instance, has roughly 75% identifying as Catholic.

This is not to say that religious behaviour is necessarily high across the religious-identifying population – it's almost universally not. Using the subset of five countries in the CSES wave 5 (because they use the same worship attendance measure), only Protestants in the US and Catholics in Italy have a majority attending worship services at least once a month. On the other side of the spectrum, *only 10%* of France's Catholic majority attends at least monthly. In Germany, non-Christians stand out as the most pious – roughly 40% attend worship services monthly or more often; the next closest group is Catholics, among whom just under 30% attend regularly. This disjuncture between identity and behaviour reinforces the notion discussed above that there are different dimensions of religion that are more or less independent from each other. There are no easy assumptions about how religion "works" on public opinion.

LINKS BETWEEN RELIGIOUS IDENTITY AND IMMIGRATION ATTITUDES

Can we find links between religious identity groups and immigration attitudes? I'll start with the index combining the three attitudes about culture, crime, and the economy before examining each component. Figure 8.2 shows the distribution of the immigration index for each religious grouping by country. It is notable that almost every country-religion group has a pro-immigration set of opinions (a score less than 3 out of 5 on the scale), on average. Only Italian Catholics and French and Swiss Protestants take stances leaning anti-immigrant, though their fellow Christians are not far behind them. It is also notable that all religious groups vary in their support across countries – there is not one single Protestant or Catholic position.

Some countries are quite unified in their attitudes. Canada is a great example – Canadians are very supportive of immigrants with only a small minority of anti-immigrant sentiment. As suggested above, Canadian Catholics are somewhat less supportive of immigrants, which begs the question of whether a nation's pluralism encourages acceptance of diverse others. Building on this notion, the United States is also quite unified in its immigration attitudes, and Protestants, who are highly concentrated in less plural states in the South and Midwest, are the least supportive. But this idea inevitably runs into snags or at least qualifications – Switzerland and Germany are quite pluralistic, but their religious groups are divided. I suspect that sub-national concentrations of religious groups (e.g. Catholics in the south of Germany) may factor into these group averages. Another way to look at Germany and Switzerland is that they are "united in their disunity" – the distributions look the same for each group despite group averages near the middle of the scale.

In no country are the non-religious less supportive of immigrants than Christians, which makes it clear that Christianity can be linked to more exclusive orientations. Exactly why that is the case is not clear and is worth exploring in greater detail. In most cases (6/9), the non-religious are less supportive than "other" religious people

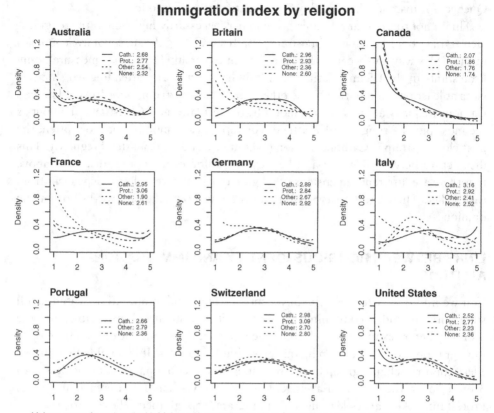

Immigration index by religion

Values range from 1 to 5 with higher values indicating less favourable attitudes toward immigration.

FIGURE 8.2 Attitudes about how immigrants are perceived to affect a country's economy, culture, and crime (index), by major religious group.

(other refers to any religious group that is non-Christian). So, the remaining three nations where the non-religious are more supportive are interesting. Portugal is an example. One possible reason why "religious other" support is not stronger is that the sources of immigration to Portugal are often not religious others. Muslims remain a very small proportion of the Portuguese population and former Portuguese colonies, such as Brazil, are some of the major sources of mainly Christian immigrants. Note, too, that there is essentially *no* strongly anti-immigrant sentiment in Portugal in these data.

The individual items addressing perceptions of immigrants' effect on crime rates, the culture, and the economy tend to track the overall index, of course, though most show at least one out of step with the others (see Figures 8.3–8.5). Typically, nations tended to disagree that immigrants hurt the economy and agree that immigrants would adversely affect the culture and crime rates. It is not too surprising to find religious majorities (i.e. Christians) more likely than religious minorities to perceive a cultural threat by immigrants – the UK is a good example of this pattern. But

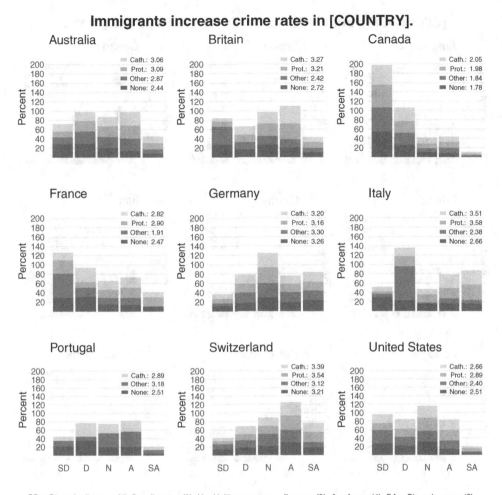

FIGURE 8.3 Attitudes about how immigrants are perceived to affect a country's crime, by major religious group.

that's not true everywhere. Italians are less concerned about immigrants' effects on the culture and more so by crime fears and the economic effects of immigration. Italian Catholics are clearly divided on these questions, which is also reflected in their ambivalent view of the Pope (e.g. Barigazzi, 2018), who is quite liberal on immigration policy. Germany and Switzerland are good examples of having symmetrically distributed opinions about all three dimensions – each option is chosen by a proportional amount of each religious group.

While there are some groups that have opinions opposed to the majority, religious groups tend to follow country-specific patterns. This suggests that the national context is critical to consider in order to understand the distribution of religious group opinions. While the national distribution may reflect the input of religion

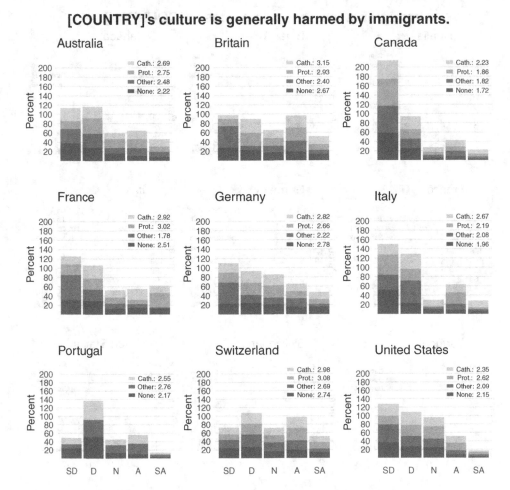

[COUNTRY]'s culture is generally harmed by immigrants.

SD = Strongly disagree (1); D = disagree (2); N = Neither agree nor disagree (3); A = Agree (4); SA = Strongly agree (5)

FIGURE 8.4 Attitudes about how immigrants are perceived to affect a country's culture, by major religious group.

– highlighting cultural tensions, for instance – it is much more likely that religious groups are reacting to the political, social, and economic environments as well as national dialogue on the issues associated with immigration. This is to be expected. While religions have been at the root of some social movements, most often they simply do not have the resources to lead the charge.

COMPLEXITIES OF RELIGIOUS ENGAGEMENT IN THE US

We have an opportunity to explore the mechanisms behind religious influence in the United States with survey data specifically geared to capture the engagement of

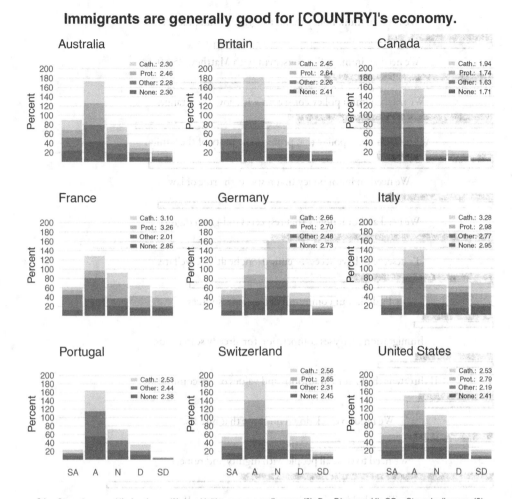

FIGURE 8.5 Attitudes about how immigrants are perceived to affect a country's economy, by major religious group.

religious actors in the immigration debate. These data were gathered from clergy in 2014,[1] when there seemed like a real possibility for immigration reform to pass. While reform did not pass, we get a report from these data of what clergy in a sample of Protestant denominations were saying and doing about immigration and why.

Figure 8.6 shows the extent to which this clergy sample agrees with various immigration policy arguments as well as whether they claimed to have mentioned that argument in public discussion (the statements are abbreviated for the figure – the full text is available in the Appendix). They tend to be correlated, such that agreement with an argument is linked to mentioning it, but far from perfectly. Indeed, about one in every four arguments mentioned was one with which the clergy disagreed.

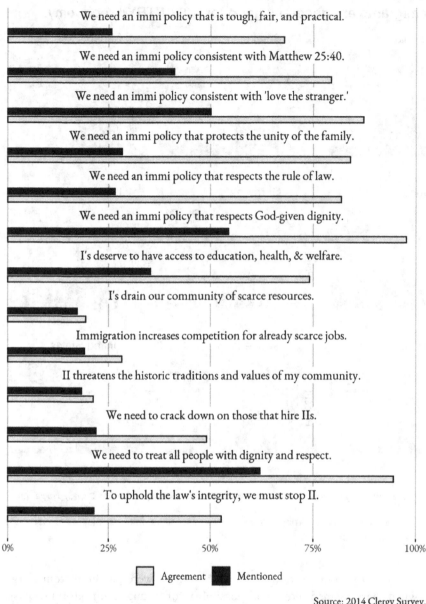

We need an immi policy that is tough, fair, and practical.

We need an immi policy consistent with Matthew 25:40.

We need an immi policy consistent with 'love the stranger.'

We need an immi policy that protects the unity of the family.

We need an immi policy that respects the rule of law.

We need an immi policy that respects God-given dignity.

I's deserve to have access to education, health, & welfare.

I's drain our community of scarce resources.

Immigration increases competition for already scarce jobs.

II threatens the historic traditions and values of my community.

We need to crack down on those that hire IIs.

We need to treat all people with dignity and respect.

To uphold the law's integrity, we must stop II.

0%   25%   50%   75%   100%

☐ Agreement ■ Mentioned

Source: 2014 Clergy Survey.
Note: I=Immigrants, II=Illegal immigration.

FIGURE 8.6 A clergy sample's opinions and communication on immigration in 2014.

And some of the broadest gaps between agreement and mentions are on arguments with which most sample clergy agreed. Because it conformed to the talking points of reformers at the time, one important example is the top one: that we need an immigration policy that is tough, fair, and practical. About two-thirds agreed with that statement, while only a quarter said they mentioned it. The only arguments that garnered mention by a majority of the sample were broad principles: that policy needs to treat people with respect, respect their God-given dignity, and "love the stranger." Those are useful baseline conditions for any contentious policy debate, and remarkable in some ways given the outsized harsh rhetoric in the debate, but they may not have moved the policy needle one way or another.

In addition, there was little agreement with some of the more conservative talking points in 2014, that immigrants drain resources, disrupt historic traditions, and take jobs from Americans. If these data are representative of Protestant clergy (admittedly a big if), then it is hard to sustain a finding of religious influence that generated the anti-immigrant opinion distribution among Protestants in 2014. There were simply too few people hearing a connection of their faith and immigration policy, especially the conservative approach.

Immigration did not go away as a political issue, but arguably was even more salient in the Trump years (2015–2020) given his demonization of immigrants on the campaign trail and harsh policies towards them while in office. Yet, only small minorities of religious identifiers indicated that they heard their clergy address immigration. Only about 15% of Christians so indicated in 2016, which fell to 10% or less in 2018 (see Djupe, 2021). Since the Trump administration's family separation policy was released in 2018, this is a startlingly low number (see also Boorstein and Zauzmer, 2018).

Speech is not the only way in which clergy could engage the immigration debate. Figure 8.7 helps provide some additional context by showing the rather small numbers engaging the debate in other ways. The most common is speaking out in the congregation, but less than 30% reported doing so; this also tells us that the arguments mentioned (see Figure 8.6) were not necessarily made to the full congregation. A fifth contacted a public official with their views, but very few made their views known in very public ways – only 4% attended a public rally, surely in part because they simply did not live near one. In total, 45% of this sample did at least one thing on this list and 1% did all five. That's a high rate of engagement relative to the general populace, but I think it's fair to claim that the probability of the public hearing or seeing any kind of religious witness on immigration policy was low.

Even so, religious engagement in the immigration debate may follow some of the classic fault lines described earlier in the chapter. Recall that one of the primary functions of religion is boundary management as religious groups help define what is pure and impure, whether to reach out to new people or keep the world at bay. The clergy survey contained measures to make indexes of exclusive and inclusive values – normative commands to reinforce the ingroup or expand membership to new people as discussed above.[2] I expect that exclusivity would be linked to beliefs that immigration does harm to the community in various ways, while inclusivity would be linked to the opposite as well as to the action taken to make immigration reform a reality.

While there are many reasons, some idiosyncratic, why clergy engage in action on public policy, there is evidence to suggest that it follows the contours of inclusivity and exclusivity. For instance, more exclusivity is linked to the agreement that "Illegal immigration threatens the historic traditions and values of my community" ($r = 0.32$, $p < 0.01$) as well as that "Immigration increases competition for already scarce jobs" ($r = 0.23$, $p < 0.01$). Those valuing exclusivity are also less likely to agree that "Regardless of how people immigrated, we need to treat all people with

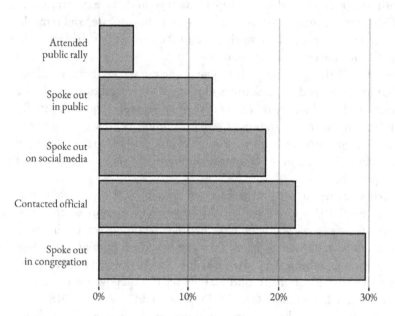

FIGURE 8.7 Clergy engagement with the immigration debate in 2014.

Source: 2014 Clergy Survey.

dignity and respect" ($r = -0.12$, $p < 0.05$). While exclusivity is not correlated with taking action (an index of the items in Figure 8.7), inclusivity is – the most inclusive are 25 percentage points more likely to engage in at least one of those activities than the least inclusive.

That is, there is good evidence across a wide range of measures that the core dimensions of inclusivity and exclusivity that together define the range of religious approaches help to structure public policy engagement by religious elites. This falls in line with a variety of experimental and observational studies of clergy and average members that prime these values to assess their effects (see Djupe and Calfano, 2013). Priming can be thought of as akin to a sermon that attempts to put certain ideas, values, or beliefs front and centre in an individual's decision making. Put another way, even if clergy are not engaging with the immigration debate directly, the fact that their public presentations generally are marked by inclusivity and exclusivity suggests they can have policy effects.

CONCLUSION

Religions are fundamentally concerned with presenting worldviews that bear on whether to welcome or fear outsiders. Some place emphasis on being welcoming and open, while others draw close and adopt rules that keep others at a distance. These orientations bear on many areas of public policy that divide identity groups. Of course, religions are complex, so there are many other aspects of them that help to shape attitudes towards immigration. Some become interlinked with national and racial identity – such as Christian nationalists in the United States (Perry and Whitehead, 2019) and Hindu nationalism in India (Bhatt, 2020). But that is not all. Many religious institutions have international ties, which helps to facilitate immigration among religious affiliates (and others).

But we also need to consider that religions and religious people are often not in the driver's seat and instead are reactive to the political, economic, and social contexts. The country-level overview of immigration attitudes for broad religious groupings in this chapter is highly suggestive that there are no default levels of support for religions. Christians are not necessarily more or less open to immigration than others. Instead, majority status has a strong influence on immigration attitudes, which is far less important in highly pluralistic countries. It is easier to establish a strong tether between religion, ethnicity, and national identity in homogeneous countries, such that immigration that crosses those bonds can become threatening, especially to the dominant group.

Exactly how that resistance to immigration manifests may depend on country conditions and specific religious engagements. That is, there is no lock on religious groups being more concerned with culture and tradition by dint of the cultural space they occupy. Religious groups may be more concerned with the (perceived) economic effects of immigrants in one country and crime in another. Though religious groups may reflect the state of the discourse in the country, it may in fact be the case that religious organizations (clergy, denominations) are actively working against it. There is little to suggest from the evidence shown here that religious organizations have been driving anti-immigrant sentiment in the US, even though devout evangelical Protestants tend to have much more anti-immigrant attitudes than others. Such are the complexities of studying religion in politics.

SUMMARY POINTS

- Prior research on religion and immigration attitudes is diverse but can be captured by four rough groupings: (1) religion can be considered an identity group, which is sufficient to draw boundaries with outsiders; (2) the way religious groups organize themselves has implications for how affiliates see outsiders; (3) the effects of religious affiliation depend upon the group's place in the social structure, perhaps forging bonds with national identities; and (4) religious organizations may provide explicit political communication on immigration.
- Cross-national comparison of religious groups suggests there is no single Protestant or Catholic view and that the national context for the immigration debate is important to consider.
- The non-religious are almost always more supportive of immigration than Christians.
- While religious majorities tend to identify with the state and are wary of immigration, some religious leaders take counter-cultural stands to be more inclusive of immigrants or at least establish ethical baselines for public discourse. What emerges is a view of religion as responsive to national and local interests.

NOTES

1 These data from clergy result from a survey conducted via the internet through the Qualtrics platform, after clergy were invited by email to participate. Addresses were culled from publicly-available parish and denominational websites that listed this individual-level contact information. PCUSA clergy contact information were provided to the authors from the denomination's in-house research office. For the largest denominations in our study – the UMC and SBC – we relied on a commercially generated email list from the vendor Exact Data, which maintains current congregational lists for a variety of US denominations. Each of the culling methods has drawbacks from the standpoint of representativeness, although it is not possible to determine exact sampling biases a priori. In each denominational case, we endeavoured to use the total population of clergy with listed email addresses, which is a subset of the total clergy population in each denomination. In February 2014, we emailed 16,740 survey invitations. Given missing data, we received somewhere between 375–411 valid responses depending on the question. We obtained responses from United Methodist, Southern Baptist Convention, Reformed Church in America, Presbyterian Church (USA), and Greek Orthodox clergy, religious groups chosen in part by convenience and primarily because they covered a wide range of the Christian religious spectrum. This is clearly not a random sample of clergy, nor are the denominations/traditions present necessarily representative of the American religious population. What is useful about the sample, despite its limitations, is that appropriate questions were asked to gauge communication and involvement in the immigration debate.

2 The exclusive values are captured by agreement with these statements: "It is important to shop as much as possible at stores owned by people of our faith" and "It is important to keep company with other people of our faith." The inclusive value statements included: "It is important to 'love the stranger as yourself'" and "It is important to invite others to our house of worship even if it begins to change as a result." Note that these are not necessarily in opposition – it is possible to want to vigorously recruit new members while retaining high barriers to leaving.

SUGGESTED FURTHER READINGS

Ben-Nun Bloom, P., Arikan, G., and Courtemanche, M., 2015. Religious social identity, religious belief, and anti-immigration sentiment. *American Political Science Review*, 109(2), 203–221.

Lajevardi, N., 2020. *Outsiders at home: the politics of American Islamophobia.* Cambridge: Cambridge University Press.

Leon McDaniel, E., Nooruddin, I., and Faith Shortle, A., 2011. Divine boundaries: How religion shapes citizens' attitudes toward immigrants. *American Politics Research*, 39(1), 205–233.

Storm, I., 2011. Christian nations? Ethnic Christianity and anti-immigration attitudes in four Western European countries. *Nordic Journal of Religion and Society*, 24(1), 75–96.

REFERENCES

Alba, R. and Foner, N., 2014. Comparing immigrant integration in North America and Western Europe: How much do the grand narratives tell us? *International Migration Review*, 48(S1), 263–291.

Alba, R., Raboteau, A.J., and DeWind, J., eds., 2009. *Immigration and religion in America: Comparative and historical perspectives.* New York: NYU Press.

Anderson, J.R. and Antalíková, R., 2014. Framing (implicitly) matters: The role of religion in attitudes toward immigrants and Muslims in Denmark. *Scandinavian Journal of Psychology*, 55(6), 593–600.

Barigazzi, J., 2018. Italy's catholics flock to the right. Available from: https://www.politico.eu/article/italy-catholic-church-problem-attracted-by-matteo-salvini/ Accessed 1/7/21.

Ben-Nun Bloom, P., Arikan, G., and Courtemanche, M., 2015. Religious social identity, religious belief, and anti-immigration sentiment. *American Political Science Review*, 109(2), 203–221.

Ben-Nun Bloom, P., Arikan, G., and Lahav, G., 2015. The effect of perceived cultural and material threats on ethnic preferences in immigration attitudes. *Ethnic and Racial Studies*, 38(10), 1760–1778.

Ben-Nun Bloom, P., Vishkin, A., Ben-Nun, P., Korenman, M., and Tamir, M., 2019. Religion and anti-immigration sentiments in context: Field studies in Jerusalem. *The International Journal for the Psychology of Religion*, 29(2), 77–93.

Berkhout, J. and Ruedin, D., 2017. Why religion? Immigrant groups as objects of political claims on immigration and civic integration in Western Europe, 1995–2009. *Acta Politica*, 52(2), 156–178.

Bhatt, C., 2020. *Hindu nationalism: Origins, ideologies and modern myths*. New York: Routledge.

Boorstein, M. and Zauzmer, J., 2018. Why many white evangelicals are not protesting family separations on the U.S. border. *Washington Post*. Available from: https://www.washingtonpost.com/news/acts-of-faith/wp/2018/06/18/why-many-white-evangelical-christians-are-not-protesting-family-separations-on-the-u-s-border/ [Accessed 1 July 2021].

Brader, T., Valentino, N.A., and Suhay, E., 2008. What triggers public opposition to immigration? Anxiety, group cues, and immigration threat. *American Journal of Political Science*, 52(4), 959–978.

Brewer, M.B., 1999. The psychology of prejudice: Ingroup love or outgroup hate? *Journal of Social Issues*, 55(3), 429–444.

Brown, R.K., 2010. Religion, economic concerns, and African American immigration attitudes. *Review of Religious Research*, 52(2), 146–158.

Brown, R.K. and Brown, R.E., 2017. Race, religion, & immigration policy attitudes. *Race and Social Problems*, 9(1), 4–18.

Brown, R.K., Kaiser, A. Kaiser, Rusch, L., and Brown, R.E., 2017. Immigrant-conscious congregations: Race, ethnicity, and the rejection of anti-immigrant frames. *Politics and Religion*, 10(4), 887–905.

Cadge, W. and Howard Ecklund, E.H., 2007. Immigration and religion. *Annual Review of Sociology*, 33(1), 359–379.

Calfano, B.R., Djupe, P.A., Cox, D., and Jones, R.P., 2016. Muslim mistrust: The resilience of negative public attitudes after complimentary information. *Journal of Media and Religion*, 15(1), 29–42.

Cowling, M.M. and Anderson, J.R., 2019. The role of Christianity and Islam in explaining prejudice against asylum seekers: Evidence from Malaysia. *The International Journal for the Psychology of Religion*, 29(2), 108–127.

Dahab, R. and Omori, M., 2018. Homegrown foreigners: How Christian nationalism and nativist attitudes impact Muslim civil liberties. *Ethnic and Racial Studies*, 42(29), 1–20.

Dana, K., Wilcox-Archuleta, B., and Barreto, M., 2017. The political incorporation of Muslims in the United States: The mobilizing role of religiosity in Islam. *Journal of Race, Ethnicity, and Politics*, 2(2), 170–200.

Daniels, J.P. and von der Ruhr, M., 2005. God and the global economy: Religion and attitudes toward trade and immigration in the United States. *Socio-Economic Review*, 3(3), 467–489.

Deslandes, C. and Anderson, J.R., 2019. Religion and prejudice toward immigrants and refugees: A meta-analytic review. *The International Journal for the Psychology of Religion*, 29(2), 128–145.

Djupe, P.A., 2017. What is religious influence? Perspectives on the legacy of the evangelical immigration table. Available from: https://religioninpublic.blog/2017/01/26/what_is_religious_influence/ [Accessed 1 July 2021].

Djupe, P.A., 2021. Cues for the pews - Political messaging in American congregations and the decline of religious influence. In: B.R. Calfano, ed. *Exploring the public effects of religious communication on politics*. Ann Arbor, MI: University of Michigan.

Djupe, P.A., Burge, R.P., and Calfano, B.R., 2016. The delegational pulpit? Clergy identifying as congregational political representatives. *Representation*, 52(1), 43–69.

Djupe, P.A. and Calfano, B.R., 2013. *God talk: Experimenting with the religious causes of public opinion*. Philadelphia, PA: Temple University Press.

Djupe, P.A. and Gilbert, C.P., 2002. *The prophetic pulpit: Clergy, churches, and communities in American politics*. Lanham, MD: Rowman & Littlefield.

Djupe, P.A. and Gilbert, C.P., 2009. *The political influence of churches*. New York: Cambridge University Press.

Djupe, P.A. and Neiheisel, J.R., 2019. Political mobilization in American congregations: A test of the religious economies perspective. *Politics & Religion*, 12(1), 123–152.

Djupe, P.A., Neiheisel, J.R., and Conger, K.H., 2018. Are the politics of the Christian right linked to state rates of the non-religious? The importance of salient controversy. *Political Research Quarterly*, 71(4), 910–922.

Djupe, P.A., Neiheisel, J.R., and Olson, L.R., 2015. Carriers of the creed: The effects of urging tolerance on persuasion. In: P.A. Djupe, ed. *Religion and political tolerance in America: Advances in the state of the art*. Philadelphia: Temple University Press, pp. 183–199

Djupe, P.A., Olson, L.R., and Gilbert, C.P., 2005. Sources of clergy support for denominational lobbying in Washington. *Review of Religious Research*, 47(1), 86–99.

Foner, N. and Alba, R., 2008. Immigrant religion in the US and Western Europe: Bridge or barrier to inclusion? *International Migration Review*, 42(2), 360–392.

Foret, F. and Mourão Permoser, J.M., 2015. Between faith, expertise and advocacy: The role of religion in European Union policy-making on immigration. *Journal of European Public Policy*, 22(8), 1089–1108.

Gaskins, B., Golder, M., and Siegel, D.A., 2013. Religious participation, social conservatism, and human development. *Journal of Politics*, 75(4), 1125–1141.

Haddad, Y.Y., 2018. The politics of inclusion: American Muslims and the price of citizenship. In: M. Bozorgmehr and P. Kasinitz (eds.), *Growing up Muslim in Europe and the United States*. New York: Routledge, 105–120.

Holman, M.R. and Shockley, K., 2017. Messages from above: Conflict and convergence of messages to the catholic voter from the catholic church hierarchy. *Politics & Religion*, 10(4), 840–861.

Hout, M. and Fischer, C.S., 2002. Why more Americans have no religious preference: Politics and generations. *American Sociological Review*, 67(2), 165–190.

Johnson, M.K., Rowatt, W.C., and LaBouff, J., 2010. Priming Christian religious concepts increases racial prejudice. *Social Psychological and Personality Science*, 1(2), 119–126.

Karyotis, G. and Patrikios, S., 2010. Religion, securitization and anti-immigration attitudes: The case of Greece. *Journal of Peace Research*, 47(1), 43–57.

Knoll, B.R., 2009. And who is my neighbor? Religion and immigration policy attitudes. *Journal for the Scientific Study of Religion*, 48(2), 313–331.

Lajevardi, N., 2020. *Outsiders at home: The politics of American Islamophobia*. Cambridge: Cambridge University Press.

Lajevardi, N. and Oskooii, K.A.R., 2018. Old-fashioned racism, contemporary Islamophobia, and the isolation of Muslim Americans in the age of trump. *Journal of Race, Ethnicity, and Politics*, 3(1), 112–152.

Margolis, M.F., 2018a. How far does social group influence reach? Identities, elites, and immigration attitudes. *Journal of Politics*, 80(3), 772–785.

Margolis, M., 2018b. *From politics to the pews: How partisanship and the political environment shape religious identity*. Chicago, IL: University of Chicago Press.

McDaniel, E., Nooruddin, I., and Faith Shortle, A., 2011. Divine boundaries: How religion shapes citizens' attitudes toward immigrants. *American Politics Research*, 39(1), 205–233.

Melkonian-Hoover, R.M. and Kellstedt, L.A., 2019. *Evangelicals and immigration: Fault lines among the faithful*. Cham, Switzerland: Palgrave Macmillan.

Minkenberg, M., 2008. Religious legacies, churches, and the shaping of immigration policies in the age of religious diversity. *Politics and Religion*, 1(3), 349–383.

Mooney, M., 2006. The catholic bishops conferences of the United States and France: Engaging immigration as a public issue. *American Behavioral Scientist*, 49(11), 1455–1470.

Nteta, T.M. and Wallsten, K.J., 2012. Preaching to the choir? Religious leaders and American opinion on immigration reform. *Social Science Quarterly*, 93(4), 891–910.

O'Connell, G., 2019. Pope Francis reminds Christians that migrants and refugees should be welcomed around the world. Available from: https://www.americamagazine.org/faith/2019/09/29/pope-francis-reminds-christians-migrants-and-refugees-should-be-welcomed-around.

Olson, L.R., 2000. *Filled with spirit and power: Protestant clergy in politics*. New York: State University of New York Press.

Otjes, S. and de Wardt, M.V., 2020.journal Distance, dissatisfaction or a Deficit in attention: why do citizens vote for new parties?. *Journal of Elections, Public Opinion and Parties*, pp.1–22.

Otjes, S., 2021. Between eradicate all false religion and love the stranger as yourself: How immigration attitudes divide voters of religious parties. *Politics and Religion*, 14(1), 106–131. doi: 10.1017/S1755048319000518.

Paterson, I., 2018. Any room at the inn? The impact of religious elite discourse on immigration attitudes in the United Kingdom. *British Journal of Politics and International Relations*, 20(3), 594–612.

Perry, S.L., Whitehead, A.L. and Davis, J.T., 2019. God's country in black and blue: How Christian nationalism shapes Americans' views about police (mis) treatment of blacks. *Sociology of Race and Ethnicity*, 5(1), 130–146.

Schaffer, J., Sokhey, A.E., and Djupe, P.A., 2015. The religious economy of political tolerance. In: P.A. Djupe, ed. *Religion and political tolerance in America: Advances in the state of the art*. Philadelphia, PA: Temple University Press, 151–164.

Scheepers, P., Gijsberts, M., and Hello, E., 2002. Religiosity and prejudice against ethnic movements in Europe: Cross-national tests on a controversial relationship. *Review of Religious Research*, 43(3), 242–265.

Shortle, A.F. and Gaddie, R.K., 2015. Religious nationalism and perceptions of Muslims and Islam. *Politics and Religion*, 8(3), 435–457.

Smith, C., 2017. *Religion: What it is, how it works, and why it matters*. Princeton, NJ: Princeton University Press.

Stark, R. and Finke, R., 2000. *Acts of faith: Explaining the human side of religion*. Berkeley, CA: University of California Press.

Storm, I., 2011. Christian nations? Ethnic Christianity and anti-immigration attitudes in four Western European countries. *Nordic Journal of Religion and Society*, 24(1), 75–96.

Tajfel, H., 1970. Experiments in intergroup discrimination. *Scientific American*, 223(5), 96–102.

Wald, K.D., 2015. The choosing people: Interpreting the puzzling politics of American Jewry. *Politics and Religion*, 8(1), 4–35.

Wald, K.D., Owen, D.E., and Hill, S.S., 1988. Churches as political communities. *American Political Science Review*, 82(2), 531–548.

Wallsten, K. and Nteta, T.M., 2016. For you were strangers in the land of Egypt: Clergy, religiosity, and public opinion toward immigration reform in the United States. *Politics and Religion*, 9(3), 566–604.

Whitehead, A.L. and Perry, S.L., 2020. *Taking America back for god: Christian nationalism in the United States*. New York: Oxford University Press.

Wickersham, M.E., 2013. Parables and politics: Clergy attitudes toward illegal immigration in Alabama. *Hispanic Journal of Behavioral Sciences*, 35(3), 336–353.

APPENDIX

The full text of the statements displayed in Figure 8.6 from the clergy survey follows here. The question text read, "In the following set of questions, we would like to know the shape of public arguments around immigration in America. Specifically, we'd like to ask if you have MENTIONED each argument in public discussion (or something like it – please be generous to our wording) and if you AGREE with each argument (generally speaking)." Each asked for a yes or no response.

To uphold the law's integrity, we must work harder to stop illegal immigration.

Regardless of how people immigrated, we need to treat all people with dignity and respect.

We need to crack down on individuals and businesses that hire illegal immigrants.

Illegal immigration threatens the historic traditions and values of my community.

Immigration increases competition for already scarce jobs.

Immigrants drain our community of scarce resources.

Immigrants deserve to have access to education, health care, and welfare just like any other American.

We need an immigration policy that respects the God-given dignity of every person.

We need an immigration policy that respects the rule of law.

We need an immigration policy that protects the unity of the family.

We need an immigration policy consistent with the principle that we love the stranger as ourselves.

We need an immigration policy consistent with Matthew 25:40, in which "whatever you did for one of the least of these brothers and sisters of mine, you did for me."

We need an immigration policy that is tough, fair, and practical.

CHAPTER 9

Personality and public opinion

....

Kathrin Ackermann and Jan Eckardt

INTRODUCTION

Over the past 15 years, we have seen a growing interest of political scientists in the role of personality for political attitudes and behaviour (Gerber et al., 2011; Mondak, 2010). This development goes along with a general increase in the interest in the psychological roots of politics that complement socio-structural and institutional explanations. Following psychological approaches to personality, it is understood as a multidimensional concept. One of these dimensions is personality traits, which are psychological dispositions that structure an individual's thinking and acting in everyday life. Most often, these traits are conceptualized using the Big Five model of personality.

In this chapter, we will present an overview of the literature on personality and public opinion and, in particular, about attitudes towards immigration. We will discuss the conceptualization and measurement of personality as well as theoretical arguments and empirical findings regarding the link between personality traits and political attitudes. In addition, we present original evidence on the relationship between personality traits and attitudes towards immigration in four Western democracies (Canada, France, Germany, and the US). We conclude by pointing to promising avenues for future research.

PERSONALITY TRAITS IN PUBLIC OPINION RESEARCH

According to Caprara and Vecchione (2013, p. 24), we can understand personality as a "dynamic system of psychological structures and processes that mediates the relationship between the individual and the environment and accounts for what a person is and may become." Within psychology, different approaches to personality exist. A very popular and influential approach is trait theory. It understands

DOI: 10.4324/9781003121992-11

personality traits as stable patterns of thought and behaviour that build the core of human personality (Allport, 1931, 1937). Stability and consistency over time and situations distinguish traits from other individual characteristics like habits, values, or attitudes (Olver and Mooradian, 2003, Roccas et al., 2002). There are multiple ways to further conceptualize these traits and make them measurable in empirical research. One of the standard models in personality psychology is the Big Five model of personality (John et al., 2008). It has also become the model of personality, which is most often used in political science and social sciences more generally. Thus, we will focus on this conceptualization of personality traits.

Conceptualizing personality traits

The Big Five model of personality relies on the so-called lexical approach, which assumes that relevant differences in personality are reflected in our everyday language (for a detailed review of the approach, see John et al., 1988 or McCrae and John, 1992). Starting with early works in the first half of the 20th century, psychologists have extracted lists of words, mostly adjectives like sociable or aggressive, that describe human behaviour and have the potential to distinguish the behaviour of one person from another. They have tried to detect clusters and patterns in these lists of words to describe the dimensionality of human personality. Multiple scholars concluded that five higher-level factors can be extracted: openness to experience (earlier name: culture), conscientiousness, extraversion, agreeableness, and neuroticism (or its counterpart: emotional stability) (see Digman, 1990 for an overview). The factor structure has been confirmed in later studies and researchers started to develop survey instruments that allow us to measure the five traits (Goldberg, 1981, 1990, 1992; McCrae and Costa, 1985; Saucier, 1994). During this period, the label of the "Big Five" has been attributed to the model because of its substantive breadth (Goldberg, 1981).

To grasp the substance of the Big Five or the Five-Factor Model of Personality (both terms are used in the literature), Costa and McCrae's (1992) Revised NEO Personality Inventory (NEO-PI-R) is useful in different respects. The NEO-PI-R is a questionnaire to capture the Big Five by measuring six conceptually derived facets per trait. These facets can be understood as sub-dimensions of the five higher-order traits and describe the substance of the traits. Table 9.1 illustrates the Big Five by providing short definitions as well as the names of the associated facets according to the NEO-PI-R (Costa and McCrae, 1992). Individuals scoring high on openness to experience tend to be imaginative, intelligent, experience rich and deep emotions, seek to make new experiences, and are open to new ideas and values. Conscientious individuals are likely to be orderly, hard-working, persevering, ambitious, and dutiful. Extraversion describes how an individual interacts with others and behaves in public. Extraverts are social, outgoing, active, energetic and assertive, and excitement-seeking. Agreeable individuals are likely to desire harmonious social interactions and be soft-hearted and generous. Finally, people high in neuroticism tend to be more prone to experience negative emotions like anger, nervousness, and discontent.

TABLE 9.1 The Big Five model of personality

Trait	Short definition	Facets
Openness to experience	"Describes the breadth, depth, originality, and complexity of an individual's mental and experiential life." (John et al., 2008, p. 138)	Fantasy Aesthetics Feelings Actions Ideas Values
Conscientiousness	"Describes socially prescribed impulse control that facilitates task- and goal oriented behavior." (John et al., 2008, p. 138)	Competence Order Dutifulness Achievement striving Self-discipline Deliberation
Extraversion	"Implies an energetic approach toward the social and material world." (John et al., 2008, p. 138)	Warmth Gregariousness Assertiveness Activity Excitement seeking Positive emotions
Agreeableness	"Contrasts a prosocial and communal orientation toward others with antagonism." (John et al., 2008, p. 138)	Trust Straightforwardness Altruism Compliance Modesty Tender-mindedness
Neuroticism	"Contrasts emotional stability and even-temperedness with negative emotionality." (John et al., 2008, p. 138)	Anxiety Angry hostility Depression Self-consciousness Impulsiveness Vulnerability

Source: Ackermann (2017), based on John et al. (2008).

The described structure of personality has been validated using different methods as well as peer and observer ratings (Goldberg, 1990; McCrae and Costa, 1987). Concerning intrapersonal stability, personality traits are understood as "relatively stable" (McCrae and Costa, 2008, p. 167) over the life course but they might well be affected by processes of maturation and life experiences (Bleidorn et al., 2009; Specht et al., 2011) (see also Chapter 4 in this volume on the relationship of personality and life course). Considering the universality of the concept, studies have shown that the structure of the Big Five model of personality persists across different countries and cultures (McCrae et al., 2005; McCrae and Costa, 1997; Schmitt et al., 2007), although the prevalence of single traits differs across countries (Allik and McCrae, 2004).

Measuring personality traits

The growing interest in personality traits as an explanatory variable in political science research is closely related to methodological developments regarding the measurement of personality. Short measures of larger personality questionnaires have been developed and made the inclusion in large-scale population surveys possible (John et al., 2008). Two of the most widely used measures are presented in Table 9.2: the Ten-Item Personality Inventory (TIPI) (Gosling et al., 2003) as well as a short version of the Big Five Inventory (BFI) proposed by Rammstedt and John (2007).[1] The downside of short measures is that they are not able to capture every facet of each trait. That makes facet-level analyses impossible. Moreover, the relationship between personality traits and political ideology has been shown to be stronger and more consistent when larger batteries are used to measure the Big Five (Bakker and Lelkes, 2018). Yet, the great advantage is that they can easily be implemented into public opinion surveys. Moreover, established short measures, like the TIPI or the BFI-10, have been proven to be valid and reliable measures of the Big Five (Gosling et al., 2003; Rammstedt and John, 2007). To construct scales capturing the Big Five personality traits, political scientists have used different strategies. Some estimate exploratory factor analyses and work with the factor scores (e.g. Ackermann and Ackermann, 2015); others construct simple additive indices (e.g. Dinesen et al., 2016). It is important to keep in mind that factor scores are weighted sums of the items that do not use the same metric as the original items.

LINKING PERSONALITY TRAITS AND PUBLIC OPINION

Building on McCrae and Costa (2008), who have developed a theoretical framework (Five-Factor Theory) that links the Big Five personality traits to potential antecedents and consequences, we can expect that personality traits will shape characteristic adaptations and behavioural patterns. Characteristic adaptations are understood as a concrete manifestation of personality traits in terms of habits, attitudes, skills, roles, and relationships. Thus, political attitudes would be labelled as characteristic adaptations in this framework. They are more volatile than personality traits and not only influenced by personality traits but also by external factors. On a very abstract level, we can assume that psychological desires are rooted in personality traits and that concrete attitudes function to fulfil these desires.

To dig deeper into the literature on personality traits and political attitudes, *ideological orientations* as a broad generic term for attitudes provide a good starting point. The most clear-cut theoretical expectations have been developed for openness to experience and conscientiousness. Individuals scoring high on openness to experience are expected to embrace liberal and progressive political ideas because they are willing to engage with new approaches and question existing values and political concepts. This preference for novelty, variety, and intense experience is best catered to by liberal political attitudes (Roets et al., 2014). Thus, open-minded individuals are expected to hold liberal or left-wing political orientations. Meanwhile, conscientiousness is related to

TABLE 9.2 Examples of short measures of the Big Five personality traits

Ten-Item Personality Inventory (TIPI) (Gosling et al., 2003)

Survey question:

Here are a number of personality traits that may or may not apply to you. Please write a number next to each statement to indicate the extent to which you agree or disagree with that statement. You should rate the extent to which the pair of traits applies to you, even if one characteristic applies more strongly than the other.

I see myself as:

1. _____ Extraverted, enthusiastic.
2. _____ Critical, quarrelsome.
3. _____ Dependable, self-disciplined.
4. _____ Anxious, easily upset.
5. _____ Open to new experiences, complex.
6. _____ Reserved, quiet.
7. _____ Sympathetic, warm.
8. _____ Disorganized, careless.
9. _____ Calm, emotionally stable.
10. _____ Conventional, uncreative.

Disagree strongly (1)
Disagree moderately (2)
Disagree a little (3)
Neither agree nor disagree (4)
Agree a little (5)
Agree moderately (6)
Agree strongly (7)

Scale construction:

Openness to experiences:
5, 10 (reverse)
Conscientiousness:
3, 8 (reverse)
Extraversion:
1, 6 (reverse)
Agreeableness:
2 (reverse), 7
Emotional stability:
4 (reverse), 9

Big Five Inventory (BFI-10) (Rammstedt and John, 2007)

Survey question:

How well do the following statements describe your personality? I see myself as someone who…

…is reserved (A)
…is generally trusting (B)
…tends to be lazy (C)
…is relaxed, handles stress well (D)
…has few artistic interests (E)
…is outgoing, sociable (F)
…tends to find fault with others (G)
…does a thorough job (H)
…gets nervous easily (I)
…has an active imagination (J)

Disagree strongly (1)
Disagree a little (2)
Neither agree nor disagree (3)
Agree a little (4)
Agree strongly (5)

Scale construction:

Openness to experiences:
E (reverse), J
Conscientiousness:
C (reverse), H
Extraversion:
A (reverse), F
Agreeableness:
B, G (reverse)
Emotional stability:
D, I (reverse)

traditional values and adherence to rules and norms. Jost et al. (2003) argue that conservatism is assumed to be a function of the need to manage fear and uncertainty and to satisfy a desire for orderliness that is related to conscientiousness (Stenner, 2005). Hence, we expect individuals scoring high on conscientiousness to hold conservative or right-wing political orientations. These expectations are confirmed in empirical research: Openness has consistently been linked to a preference for liberalism and an arguably less strong, but nonetheless clear connection between conscientiousness and conservatism has been found by a variety of studies (e.g. Carney et al., 2008; Hirsh et al., 2010; Jost et al., 2007; Van Hiel et al., 2000).[2] While studies have failed to show a clear association for extraversion, agreeableness, and neuroticism with political ideology, there are instances in which sub-facets of these traits could be linked to conservatism or liberalism. For instance, Hirsh et al. (2010) find that two of agreeableness's sub-facets, namely compassion and politeness, are associated with higher and lower levels of liberalism, respectively.

Next to general ideological orientations, research has been further concerned with domain-specific political attitudes and their relationship with personality traits. One popular example is *economic attitudes*, mostly understood as preferences for liberal economic policies with low levels of state regulation versus preferences for conservative economic policies. The theoretical argumentation relates closely to the general lines of reasoning regarding ideological orientations. Gerber et al. (2010) and Fatke (2017) theorize conscientiousness to be associated with economic conservatism because they assume that conscientious individuals' rule- and norm-adhering nature as well as their impulse control are likely to cause them to be in favour of traditional, i.e. conservative, economic norms and practices. Mirroring findings for ideology, Gerber et al. (2010) expect open individuals' attraction to the complex and unconventional to make them more likely to support liberal economic and social policies. Also, Fatke (2017) proposes that these individuals might prefer economic systems with less state intervention for that very reason. In addition, Gerber et al. (2010) expect agreeable individuals to be in favour of liberal economic policies, as they might consider them a means to help those in need because of their prosocial and altruistic character. They also argue for a negative relationship between emotional stability and liberal economic preferences. As a mechanism, they assume that individuals scoring low on emotional stability prefer economic policies that create safety nets and protect them from market risks (Gerber et al., 2010). While there again are no clear expectations regarding extraversion, Schoen and Schumann (2007), in reference to Caprara et al. (1999), hypothesize a possible connection between extraversion and a preference for conservative economic policies.

Empirical findings regarding the relationship between personality and economic attitudes largely confirm these theoretical expectations. Reflecting the results for ideology, openness to experience is found to be associated with economic liberalism in several studies (Bakker, 2017; Gerber et al., 2010; Jost et al., 2009). Conscientiousness seems to act as an even stronger correlate of economic conservatism across a wider range of geographic contexts (Bakker, 2017; Fatke, 2017; Gerber et al., 2010; Jost et al., 2009; McCann, 2014). In addition, the link between emotional stability and economic liberalism is also well-documented in the literature (Bakker, 2017; Fatke, 2017; Gerber et al., 2010; McCann, 2014). In line with theoretical expectations, multiple studies also find an association between agreeableness and economic liberalism (Bakker, 2017; Gerber et al., 2010, Van Hiel and Mervielde, 2004). Extraversion seems to be the weakest correlate of this set of political attitudes, as only Gerber et al. (2010) find indications for a connection with economic conservatism.

In addition to associations between economic attitudes and personality, researchers have also attempted to link personality traits with *attitudes on environmental policy* and *environmental protection* in general. To begin with, Hirsh (2010) and Milfont and Sibley (2012) assume openness to experience and agreeableness to be related to pro-environmental attitudes because the traits foster values such as benevolence and universalism. Moreover, Pavalache-Ilie and Cazan (2018) and Milfont and Sibley (2012) also expect conscientious individuals to be more likely to engage in pro-environmental behaviour. In addition, Gifford and Nilsson (2014) link pro-environmental attitudes to higher levels of neuroticism because neurotic individuals tend to worry about many aspects of life, including environmental issues. Milfont and Sibley (2012) put forward a related argument, assuming that individuals scoring high on neuroticism are concerned with the conservation of resources and therefore in favour of environmental protection.

Turning to the empirical findings, openness to experience seems to be the most consistent correlate of pro-environmental attitudes. Studies can confirm the positive link between openness to experience and pro-environmentalism for a variety of countries (Brick and Lewis, 2016; Hirsh and Dolderman, 2007; Hirsh, 2010; Markowitz et al., 2012; McConochie, 2011; Milfont and Sibley, 2012; Milfont et al., 2015; Pavalache-Ilie and Cazan, 2018). Connections for other traits seem less clear: Agreeableness is also associated with pro-environmental attitudes by multiple studies, but to a lesser degree than openness to experience (Brick and Lewis, 2016; Hirsh and Dolderman, 2007; Hirsh, 2010; McConochie, 2011; Milfont and Sibley, 2012; Milfont et al., 2015; Pavalache-Ilie and Cazan, 2018). The connection between neuroticism and pro-environmental attitudes is ambivalent, however, and the results are inconsistent (Brick and Lewis, 2016; Hirsh, 2010; McConochie, 2011; Milfont and Sibley, 2012; Milfont et al., 2015). In accordance with theoretical expectations, conscientiousness is positively related to pro-environmental attitudes in many studies (Brick and Lewis, 2016; Hirsh, 2010; Milfont and Sibley, 2012; Milfont et al., 2015; Pavalche-Ilie and Cazan, 2018). Just like for economic attitudes, extraversion again does not seem to be a relevant correlate of pro-environmental attitudes, as the trait could not be related to pro-environmental attitudes by any of the studies discussed here.

Personality traits and attitudes towards immigration

Finally, we turn to the main subject of this volume: attitudes towards immigration. This policy dimension has gained increasing salience in Western societies in recent years. Thus, it is important to study its antecedents from a broad and comprehensive perspective. We will add to this by focusing on its psychological roots in terms of personality traits.

In their influential study, Gallego and Pardos-Prado (2014) outline an especially detailed set of theoretical expectations. The authors propose that individuals high on agreeableness should be likely to hold pro-immigration attitudes due to their "caring and kind orientation towards other people in general" (Gallego and Pardos-Prado, 2014, p. 82). In addition, avoidance of intergroup conflict is commonly associated with the trait. A positive relationship between openness to experience and pro-immigration attitudes is assumed as well, as open-minded individuals have been found to have higher levels of tolerance and tend to value diversity (Freitag and Rapp, 2015). Additionally, open people's attentiveness to information disconfirming stereotypes might relate to a reduction in prejudice and anti-immigrant sentiment. Due to their interest in different cultures, open-minded individuals are also thought to be more likely to befriend immigrants, which should add to their pro-immigration sentiments. Similarly, Ackermann and Ackermann (2015) connect openness to experience to pro-immigration attitudes because of the trait's general connection to more liberal values. When it comes to neuroticism, theoretical expectations regarding the relationship with immigration attitudes are tied to concepts of threat. Ackermann and Ackermann (2015) predict neurotic persons to be opposed to equal opportunities for immigrants due to their tendency to see immigrants as a threat (see Marcus et al., 1995). This is partly supported by Dinesen et al. (2016, p. 58), who, despite not postulating a definite relationship between neuroticism and attitudes towards immigration, consider "the uneasy and anxious nature" of neurotic individuals to be a potential factor in shaping neurotic individuals' perception of immigrants as a threat. Gallego and Pardos-Prado (2014, p. 83) also follow this line of argumentation and tie neuroticism to a "higher salience of personal threats and the propensity to react to them." Concerning conscientiousness, Ackermann and Ackermann (2015), Dinesen et al. (2016), and Ziller and Berning (2021) argue that the desire for order associated with the trait might cause opposition towards immigration. Since immigration can change the status quo and the pre-existing societal order, conscientious people might oppose immigration based on their psychological needs. Finally, the connection between extraversion and immigration attitudes is only rarely discussed, as the trait does not seem to hold implications for migration attitudes at first glance. An exception is the study by Ackermann and Ackermann (2015) who argue that the sociability of extraverts might increase the propensity for intercultural contact and, thus, positive attitudes towards foreigners and immigration.

Empirically, and contrary to their theoretical expectations, Gallego and Pardos-Prado (2014) do not find a connection between openness to experience and pro-immigration attitudes in a Dutch sample. In addition, conscientiousness and extraversion are also not significantly related to pro-immigration attitudes in their analysis. In line with their expectations, agreeableness correlates positively with pro-immigration attitudes, while neuroticism is connected with slightly more negative immigration attitudes. In a comparable study, Ackermann and Ackermann (2015) report slightly differing results for a Swiss sample. They find individuals high in openness to experience and agreeableness to be more likely to hold pro-immigration attitudes, whereas conscientiousness acts as a strong correlate of anti-immigration attitudes. When taking the moderating role of perceived levels of ethnic diversity in participants' neighbourhoods into account, the negative relationship vanishes. Conscientiousness is no longer negatively related to pro-immigration attitudes for people living in neighbourhoods with high perceived ethnic diversity. Studying the Swiss case as well, Freitag and Rapp (2015) find immigrant rejection to be connected to extraversion, whereas agreeableness is associated with lower levels of immigrant rejection. At the same time, openness to experience acts as a significant correlate of granting immigrants the right to vote, whereas extraversion is negatively related to pro-immigration attitudes. Using a Danish sample, Dinesen et al. (2016) identify positive relationships between openness to experience and agreeableness and pro-immigration attitudes, while conscientiousness is negatively correlated with pro-immigration attitudes to a slightly weaker degree. When accounting for perceived cultural and economic threats as potential mechanisms, only economic threat seems to mediate the link between conscientiousness and immigrant attitudes (Dinesen et al., 2016). This implies that the negative attitudes towards immigration that conscientious individuals hold are not rooted in a rejection of other cultures, but fear of economic competition. As part of a cross-country analysis using both Danish and Canadian data, Danckert et al. (2017) find that open-minded individuals are more likely to develop pro-immigration attitudes when engaging in personal interethnic encounters and when exposed to ethnic diversity in the neighbourhood. In another cross-country study, Vecchione et al. (2012) observe positive relationships between openness to experience and agreeableness and pro-immigration attitudes in Italy, Spain, and Germany. Neuroticism is relatively weakly negatively associated, but only for the Spanish and Italian samples. After controlling for personal values, such as social justice, equality, and security, the authors find only weak direct relationships between agreeableness, openness to experience, and pro-immigration attitudes. In a German study investigating relationships between the Big Five and attitudes regarding minority rights for various groups, Ziller and Berning (2021) find positive relationships between openness to experience and agreeableness and the will to grant immigrants a variety of political and social rights, whereas the opposite relations are observed for conscientiousness and extraversion. Further, they show that various political attitudes mediate these relationships. Specifically, internal political efficacy (perceived competency to take part in politics), external political efficacy (perceived responsiveness of the political elite), and group-specific attitudes towards migrants mediate the described links between personality traits and attitudes towards immigration. In a Swedish study, Akrami et al. (2011) report openness to experience and agreeableness to be negatively related to immigrant prejudice. Finally, in the only study covering Eastern Europe discussed here, Matić et al. (2018) find that among Croatian students openness to experience is positively and extraversion is negatively linked to pro-immigration attitudes. Meanwhile, the remaining traits are only indirectly linked to these attitudes via right-wing authoritarianism and social-dominance orientation.

Based on this literature review, four main takeaway messages can be identified. First, it seems that there is indeed a link between personality and immigration attitudes, even if associations for some traits remain ambivalent. It is fair to say, however, that openness to experience is consistently positively related to pro-immigration attitudes across multiple studies (Ackermann and Ackermann, 2015; Danckert et al., 2017; Dinesen et al., 2016; Freitag and Rapp, 2015; Matić et al., 2018; Vecchione et al., 2012; Ziller and Berning, 2021). Second, pro-immigration attitudes seem to be almost as clearly connected to agreeableness (Ackermann and Ackermann, 2015; Akrami et al., 2011; Dinesen et al., 2016; Gallego and Pardos-Prado, 2014; Matić et al., 2018; Vecchione et al., 2012; Ziller and Berning, 2021). Third, the relationships for the remaining traits are less consistent and often indirect. While more conscientious individuals do seem to hold more negative attitudes towards immigration, this relationship seems to be largely indirect and context-dependent (Ackermann and Ackermann, 2015; Dinesen et al., 2016; Matić et al., 2018; Ziller and Berning, 2021). The same holds for neuroticism, which is a rather weak correlate of negative immigration attitudes (Gallego and Pardos-Prado, 2014; Vecchione et al., 2012; Ziller and Berning, 2021). Finally, extraversion seems to be associated with negative immigration attitudes to a moderate degree in the studies by Freitag and Rapp (2015), Matić et al. (2018), and Ziller and Berning (2021). In sum, openness to experience and agreeableness are positively related to pro-immigration attitudes in a consistent manner, while the relationships between conscientiousness, extraversion, and neuroticism (or emotional stability) and immigration attitudes are inconsistent across the reviewed studies.

PERSONALITY TRAITS AND ATTITUDES TOWARDS IMMIGRATION – EMPIRICAL EVIDENCE FROM FOUR COUNTRIES

Building on the review of the existing literature, the empirical analysis will examine the patterns of relationships between personality traits and attitudes towards immigration in four of the nine Western democracies examined in this part of the book. Unfortunately, a measure of the Big Five personality traits is not one of the standard measures included in Module 5 of the Comparative Study of Electoral Systems (CSES) data. Fortunately, however, four of the CSES-countries have included measures of the Big Five personality traits in their longer, country-specific questionnaire. They are: Canada (2019), France (2017), Germany (2017), and the US (2016).[3] Since most of the studies on personality and immigration attitudes are single-country studies, our analysis will provide important new insights into the generalizability of the findings across different countries.

To begin, Figure 9.1 illustrates the distribution of the Big Five personality traits for the four countries. Two issues related to measurement have to be considered. First, we have discussed different ways of constructing personality scales earlier in this chapter. In these analyses, we follow the approach of building an additive index for

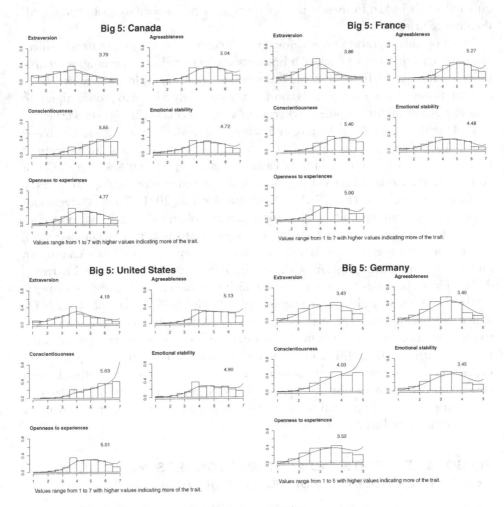

FIGURE 9.1 Distribution of personality traits in four countries.

Note: Own calculations based on Stephenson et al. (2020); Gougou and Sauger (2017); ANES (2017) and GLES (2019). The scale used in the German study is a 5-point scale, while a 7-point scale was used in the remaining countries.

each trait. The scores are kept as metric variables because the understanding of personality traits is a gradual one in the literature, i.e. a person is agreeable to a greater or lesser extent. Second, the measurement instruments included in the surveys differ across countries. Canada, France, and the US use the TIPI, while Germany makes use of the BFI-10 (see Table 9.2). This somewhat impairs the comparability across countries because the measures also operate with different scales. Despite the limited comparability, Figure 9.1 shows that the distributions are rather similar across the four countries. There are no huge differences in the personality profiles.

In the next step, we consider the relationship between the Big Five personality traits and attitudes towards immigration using linear regression models. The results are shown graphically using coefficient plots. These graphs illustrate the regression coefficient and the 95% confidence interval. A coefficient is significant if the confidence interval does not cross 0 on the y-axis. In what follows, we will only interpret statistically significant relationships.

Figure 9.2 illustrates the link between the Big Five personality traits and attitudes regarding migration-related crime rates. We find a consistent pattern regarding openness to experience, which is in all countries negatively related to anti-immigration attitudes with regard to crime rates. This is very much in line with previous research. For the other traits, the findings are inconsistent. Extraversion is positively related to anti-immigration attitudes in Canada and Germany; agreeableness is negatively related to anti-immigration attitudes in Canada and the US; and, conscientiousness is positively related to anti-immigration attitudes in Germany and the US. Emotional stability is only negatively related to anti-immigration attitudes in the US. Overall, the findings are in line with theoretical considerations and confirm earlier findings

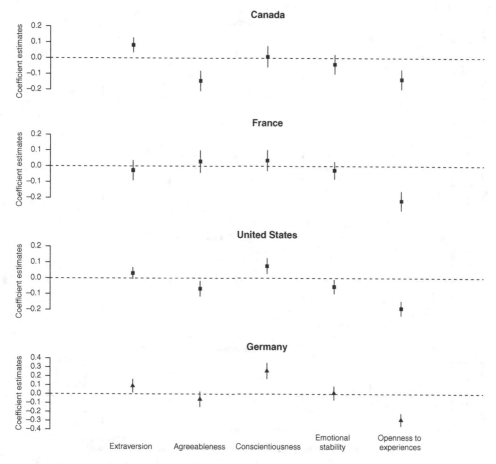

FIGURE 9.2 Attitudes about how immigrants are perceived to affect a country's crime, by personality traits.

in the literature. Yet, only the relationship between openness to experience and attitudes towards migration-related crime rates seems to be generalizable across the four
countries.

Analyzing the link between personality traits and attitudes towards migration as
a cultural threat, we find a quite similar picture (Figure 9.3). Openness to experience is consistently negatively related to the perception of migration as a cultural
threat. Meanwhile, the findings regarding the remaining four traits are less clear-cut.
Again, extraversion is positively related to anti-immigration attitudes in Canada and
Germany, whereas agreeableness is negatively related to anti-immigration attitudes
in Canada and the US. Conscientiousness is positively related to anti-immigration
attitudes only in Germany and emotional stability is negatively related to anti-immigration attitudes in France. Thus, the results very much resemble the former findings
for crime rates.

Considering attitudes towards the economic effects of immigration, openness to
experience is again the only personality trait that is systematically related to this

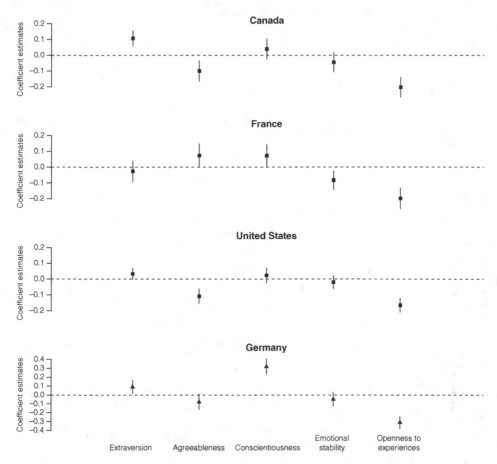

FIGURE 9.3 Attitudes about how immigrants are perceived to affect a country's culture, by personality traits.

attitude across all four countries (Figure 9.4). The relationship is negative, as we would expect based on both theory and the literature. Agreeableness is positively linked to anti-immigrant sentiments based on economic consideration in France and negatively in Canada. Conscientiousness is also positively related to anti-immigration attitudes in all countries except for the US. Finally, emotional stability is negatively related to anti-immigration attitudes in all countries except for Germany. There is no significant relationship for extraversion in any of the countries.

In a final step, we combine the immigration items and create a general index. Higher values on the index indicate negative attitudes towards immigration (Figure 9.5). In essence, the results echo the former findings. The only consistent relationship can be found for openness to experience and the relationship is negative. This is very much in line with existing evidence in the literature. It indicates that this finding indeed seems to be generalizable: open-minded persons are less likely to hold anti-immigration

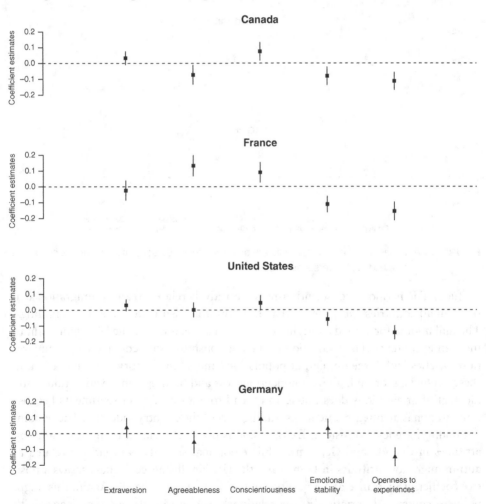

FIGURE 9.4 Attitudes about how immigrants are perceived to affect a country's economy, by personality traits.

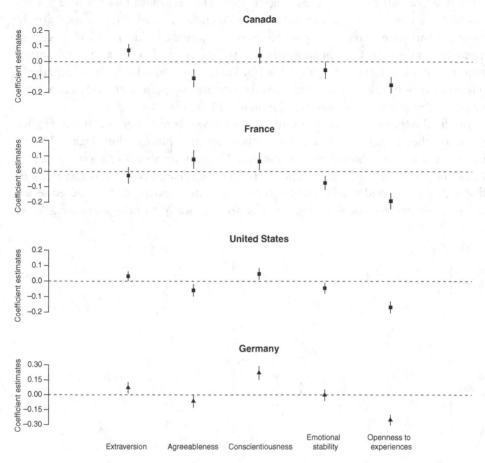

FIGURE 9.5 Attitudes about how immigrants are perceived to affect a country's economy, crime and culture (index), by personality traits.

attitudes. Furthermore, conscientiousness is positively related to anti-immigration attitudes in all countries except for Canada. Again, this also matches previous findings. The null finding for Canada and the relatively weak relation for the US might point to interesting context-related variation in the relationships. Both countries are immigration societies with large immigrant populations and a long history of immigration. In these contexts, scoring high in conscientiousness and holding conservative values and ideological orientations does not seem to lead to anti-immigrant sentiments because immigration is an integral and longstanding part of the country's identity. The remaining findings are less consistent. Extraversion is positively related to anti-immigration attitudes in Canada and Germany, while emotional stability is negatively related to anti-immigration attitudes in France and the US. Finally, agreeableness shows a positive coefficient in France and a negative one in Canada and the US. Again, this might point to contextual variation in the relationships due to different experiences with migration in the countries.

CONCLUSION

This chapter has introduced the Big Five personality traits as a relevant correlate of political attitudes. We have outlined the conceptual foundations of the Big Five model of personality and introduced two of the most prevalent short measures, the TIPI and the BFI-10. In the main section of the chapter, we have discussed how personality traits relate to ideological orientation and domain-specific political attitudes. A special focus is on immigration attitudes that have often been the subject of research on personality and politics. The literature review has revealed openness to experience and agreeableness as consistent correlates of pro-immigration attitudes. The links between the remaining personality traits, conscientiousness, extraversion, and neuroticism (or its counterpart emotional stability), and attitudes towards immigration are less consistent across multiple studies conducted in different countries. Finally, we have complemented the literature review with original analyses on the relationship between personality traits and anti-immigration attitudes in Canada, France, Germany, and the US. The empirical findings largely corroborate existing evidence in the literature. Openness to experience is most consistently linked to anti-immigration attitudes. Thus, open-minded individuals take a more positive stance on immigration issues, as expected theoretically. Furthermore, conscientiousness is – with some exceptions – positively linked to anti-immigration attitudes, while emotional stability seems to be negatively related. The findings for agreeableness and extraversion are rather inconsistent. Yet, this may point to the relevance of contextual factors in the study of personality and politics (Ackermann, 2017). It is highly likely that contextual factors, such as ethnic diversity or the immigration history of a country, activate or deactivate single relationships between personality traits and attitudes towards immigration. Thus, it is important to study personality and political attitudes from a comparative perspective to examine these complex effects more thoroughly.

In light of that, we can formulate several directions for future research on personality and public opinion. First, there is a need for comparative data collection endeavours and studies to gain knowledge on the generalizability of findings and the role of contextual effects. Second, breaking down scores for personality traits to the facet level, if possible, would help in understanding the more fine-grained mechanisms that link personality and political attitudes. Third, the focus should widen when it comes to the conceptualization of personality and personality traits. The Big Five model of personality is a highly established and useful conceptual model to study personality and politics from a general perspective. Yet, it might be fruitful to go beyond this model and examine the role of more specific personality models, such as the Dark Triad. The Dark Triad comprises three malevolent personality traits, narcissism, Machiavellianism, and psychopathy. Recent research shows that these traits also matter in the political sphere, for instance as correlates of political orientation (Hatemi and Fazekas, 2018). Finally, it would be useful to contrast the relationships of personality traits and political attitudes with other correlates of public opinion, e.g. the other factors discussed in this textbook. This could inform us about the relative importance of personality traits, in particular, compared to more volatile and changeable factors.

SUMMARY POINTS

- Political scientists are increasingly interested in the psychological roots of public opinion and political behaviour and, in particular, the relationship between personality and public opinion.
- In this chapter, we introduced the conceptualization and measurement of personality and discussed the theoretical arguments and empirical findings regarding the link between personality traits and political attitudes.
- Our empirical analysis of Canada, France, Germany, and the US largely corroborate existing evidence in the literature: (1) openness to experience is consistently negatively linked to anti-immigration attitudes; (2) conscientiousness is – with some exceptions – positively linked to anti-immigration attitudes; and (3) emotional stability seems to be negatively related.
- Interestingly, the patterns differ across the four countries, suggesting that contextual factors matter in the study of personality and politics, as the countries considered differ in terms of ethnic diversity or their immigration histories.

NOTES

1 Note that there is also a short version of the BFI comprising 15 items, which was originally developed for the German Socioeconomic Panel (G-SOEP) (Gerlitz and Schupp, 2005).
2 It has to be noted that recent experimental research shows that the associations between personality traits and political preferences do not imply a clear causal direction. Causal influence seems to be reciprocal, as ideological primes are able to affect self-reported personality scores (Bakker et al., 2021).
3 Canada: Stephenson et al. (2020); France: Gougou and Sauger (2017); US: ANES (2017); Germany: GLES (2019).

SUGGESTED FURTHER READINGS

Danckert, B., Dinesen, P.T., Klemmensen, R., Nørgaard, A.S., Stolle, D., and Sønderskov, K.M., 2017. With an open mind: Openness to experience moderates the effect of interethnic encounters on support for immigration. *European Sociological Review*, 33(5), 721–733.
Gallego, A. and Pardos-Prado, S., 2014. The Big Five personality traits and attitudes towards immigrants. *Journal of Ethnic and Migration Studies*, 40(1), 79–99.
Gerber, A.S., Huber, G.A., Doherty, D., and Dowling, C.M., 2011. The Big Five personality traits in the political arena. *Annual Review of Political Science*, 14, 265–287.
Mondak, J.J., 2010. *Personality and the foundations of political behavior*. Cambridge: Cambridge University Press.

REFERENCES

Ackermann, K. and Ackermann, M., 2015. The Big Five in context: Personality, diversity and attitudes toward equal opportunities for immigrants in Switzerland. *Swiss Political Science Review*, 21(3), 396–418.

Ackermann, K., 2017. Personality and politics in context – The interaction of personality traits and contextual factors in shaping political behavior and attitudes. Available from: http://biblio.unibe.ch/download/eldiss/17ackermann_k.pdf [Accessed 30 June 2021].

Akrami, N., Ekehammar, B., and Bergh, R., 2011. Generalized prejudice: Common and specific components. *Psychological Science*, 22(1), 57–59.

Allik, J. and McCrae, R.R., 2004. Toward a geography of personality traits: Patterns of profiles across 36 cultures. *Journal of Cross-Cultural Psychology*, 35(1), 13–28.

Allport, G.W., 1931. What is a trait of personality? *Journal of Abnormal and Social Psychology*, 25(4), 368–372.

Allport, G.W., 1937. *Personality: A psychological interpretation*. New York: Henry Holt and Company.

ANES., 2017. *American National Election Studies (ANES) 2016 time series study*. Inter-University Consortium for Political and Social Research [Distributor]. Available from: https://doi.org/10.3886/ICPSR36824.v2

Bakker, B.N., 2017. Personality traits, income, and economic ideology: Personality and economic ideology. *Political Psychology*, 38(6), 1025–1041.

Bakker, B.N. and Lelkes, Y., 2018. Selling ourselves short? How abbreviated measures of personality change the way we think about personality and politics. *The Journal of Politics*, 80(4), 1311–1325.

Bakker, B.N., Lelkes, Y., and Malka, A., 2021. Reconsidering the link between self-reported personality traits and political preferences. *American Political Science Review*, 115(4), 1482–1498.

Bleidorn, W., Kandler, C., Riemann, R., Angleitner, A., and Spinath, F.M., 2009. Patterns and sources of adult personality development: Growth curve analyses of the NEO PI-R scales in a longitudinal twin study. *Journal of Personality and Social Psychology*, 97(1), 142–155.

Brick, C. and Lewis, G.J., 2016. Unearthing the "green" personality: Core traits predict environmentally friendly behavior. *Environment and Behavior*, 48(5), 635–658.

Caprara, G.V., Barbaranelli, C., and Zimbardo, P.G., 1999. Personality profiles and political parties. *Political Psychology*, 20(1), 175–197.

Caprara, G.V. and Vecchione, M., 2013. Personality approaches to political behavior. In: L. Huddy, D.O. Sears, and J.S. Levy, eds. *The Oxford handbook of political psychology*. Oxford: Oxford University Press, 23–58.

Carney, D.R., Jost, J.T., Gosling, S.D., and Potter, J., 2008. The secret lives of liberals and conservatives: Personality profiles, interaction styles, and the things they leave behind: liberals and conservatives. *Political Psychology*, 29(6), 807–840.

Costa, P.T. and McCrae, R.R., 1992. *Revised NEO personality inventory (NEO-PI-R) and NEO five-factor inventory (NEO-FFI): Professional manual*. Odessa: Psychological Assessment Resources, Inc.

Danckert, B., Dinesen, P.T., Klemmensen, R., Nørgaard, A.S., Stolle, D., and Sønderskov, K.M., 2017. With an open mind: Openness to experience moderates the effect of interethnic encounters on support for immigration. *European Sociological Review*, 33(5), 721–733.

Digman, J.M., 1990. Personality structure: Emergence of the five-factor model. *Annual Reviews Psychology*, 41, 417–440.

Dinesen, P.T., Klemmensen, R., and Nørgaard, A.S., 2016. Attitudes toward immigration: the role of personal predispositions: Personality and immigration attitudes. *Political Psychology*, 37(1), 55–72.

Fatke, M., 2017. Personality traits and political ideology: A first global assessment: personality traits and political ideology. *Political Psychology*, 38(5), 881–899.

Freitag, M. and Rapp, C., 2015. The personal foundations of political tolerance towards immigrants. *Journal of Ethnic and Migration Studies*, 41(3), 351–373.

Gallego, A. and Pardos-Prado, S., 2014. The Big Five personality traits and attitudes towards immigrants. *Journal of Ethnic and Migration Studies*, 40(1), 79–99.

Gerber, A.S., Huber, G.A., Doherty, D., Dowling, C.M., and Ha, S.E., 2010. Personality and political attitudes: Relationships across issue domains and political contexts. *American Political Science Review*, 104(1), 111–133.

Gerber, A.S., Huber, G.A., Doherty, D., and Dowling, C.M., 2011. The Big Five personality traits in the political arena. *Annual Review of Political Science*, 14, 265–287.

Gerlitz, J.-Y. and Schupp, J., 2005. Zur Erhebung der Big-Five-basierten persoenlichkeitsmerkmale im SOEP. In DIW Research Notes 4. Available from: http://www.diw.de/documents/publikationen/73/diw_01.c.43490.de/rn4.pdf [Accessed 30 June 2021].

Gifford, R. and Nilsson, A., 2014. Personal and social factors that influence pro-environmental concern and behaviour: A review. *International Journal of Psychology*, 49(3), 141–157.

GLES., 2019. Nachwahl-Querschnitt (GLES 2017). GESIS Datenarchiv, Köln. ZA6801 Datenfile Version 4.0.1. Available from: https://doi.org/10.4232/1.13235

Goldberg, L.R., 1981. Language and individual differences the search for universals in personality lexicons. In: L. Wheeler, ed. *Review of personality and social psychology*. Thousand Oaks: Sage, 141–165.

Goldberg, L.R., 1990. An alternative "description of personality": The big-five factor structure. *Journal of Personality and Social Psychology*, 59(6), 1216–1229.

Goldberg, L.R., 1992. The development of markers for the big-five factor structure. *Psychological Assessment*, 4(1), 26–42.

Gosling, S.D., Rentfrow, P.J., and Swann, W.B., 2003. A very brief measure of the big-five personality domains. *Journal of Research in Personality*, 37(6), 504–528.

Gougou, F. and Sauger, N., 2017. The 2017 French election study (FES 2017): A post-electoral crosssectional survey. *French Politics* 15(3), 360–370.

Hatemi, P.K. and Fazekas, Z., 2018. Narcissism and political orientations. *American Journal of Political Science*, 62(4), 873–888.

Hiel, A.V. and Mervielde, I., 2004. Openness to experience and boundaries in the mind: Relationships with cultural and economic conservative beliefs. *Journal of Personality*, 72(4), 659–686.

Hirsh, J.B. and Dolderman, D., 2007. Personality predictors of consumerism and environmentalism: A preliminary study. *Personality and Individual Differences*, 43(6), 1583–1593.

Hirsh, J.B., 2010. Personality and environmental concern. *Journal of Environmental Psychology*, 30(2), 245–248.

Hirsh, J.B., DeYoung, C.G., Xu, X., and Peterson, J.B., 2010. Compassionate liberals and polite conservatives: Associations of agreeableness with political ideology and moral values. *Personality and Social Psychology Bulletin*, 36(5), 655–664.

John, O.P., Angleitner, A., and Ostendorf, F., 1988. The lexical approach to personality: A historical review of trait taxonomic research. *European Journal of Personality*, 2(3), 171–203.

John, O.P., Naumann, L.P., and Soto, C.J., 2008. Paradigm shift to the integrative Big Five trait taxonomy. History, measurement, and conceptual issues. In: O.P. John, R.W. Robins, and L.A. Pervin, eds. *Handbook of personality*. New York: Guilford Press, 114–158.

Jost, J.T., Glaser, J., Kruglanski, A.W., and Sulloway, F.J., 2003. Political conservatism as motivated social cognition. *Psychological Bulletin*, 129(3), 339–375.

Jost, J.T., Napier, J.L., Thorisdottir, H., Gosling, S.D., Palfai, T.P., and Ostafin, B., 2007. Are needs to manage uncertainty and threat associated with political conservatism or ideological extremity? *Personality and Social Psychology Bulletin*, 33(7), 989–1007.

Jost, J.T., West, T.V., and Gosling, S.D., 2009. Personality and ideology as determinants of candidate preferences and "obama conversion" in the 2008 presidential election. *Du Bois Review: Social Science Research on Race*, 6(1), 103–124.

Marcus, G.E., Sullivan, J.L., Theiss-Morse, E., and Wood, S.L., 1995. Individual differences – The influence of personality. In: G.E. Marcus, ed. *With malice toward some: How people make civil liberties judgments.* Cambridge: Cambridge University Press, 160–178.

Markowitz, E.M., Goldberg, L.R., Ashton, M.C., and Lee, K., 2012. Profiling the "pro-environmental individual": A personality perspective: Personality and pro-environmental action. *Journal of Personality,* 80(1), 81–111.

Matić, J., Bratko, D., and Löw, A., 2018. Personality and ideological bases of anti-immigrant prejudice among Croatian youth. *Journal of Ethnic and Migration Studies,* 45(13), 2387–2406.

McCann, S.J.H., 2014. Big Five personality differences and political, social, and economic conservatism: An American state-level analysis. In: P.J. Rentfrow, ed. *Geographical psychology: Exploring the interaction of environment and behavior.* Washington D.C.: American Psychological Association, 139–160.

McConochie, W.A., 2011. Psychological correlates of pro-environmental attitudes. *Ecopsychology,* 3(2), 115–123.

McCrae, R.R. and Costa, P.T., 1985. Updating Norman's "adequacy taxonomy": Intelligence and personality dimensions in natural language and in questionnaires. *Journal of Personality and Social Psychology,* 49(3), 710–721.

McCrae, R.R. and Costa, P.T., 1987. Validation of the five-factor model of personality across instruments and observers. *Journal of Personality and Social Psychology,* 52(1), 81–90.

McCrae, R.R. and John, O.P., 1992. An introduction to the five-factor model and its applications. *Journal of Personality,* 60(2), 175–215.

McCrae, R.R. and Costa, P.T., 1997. Personality trait structure as a human universal. *American Psychologist,* 52(5), 509–516.

McCrae, R.R., Terracciano, A., Khoury, B., Nansubuga, F., Knežević, G., Djuric Jocic, D., Ahn, H., Ahn, C., De Fruyt, F., Gülgöz, S., Ruch, W., Arif Ghayur, M., Avia, M.D., Sánchez-Bernardos, M.L., Rossier, J., Dahourou, D., Fischer, R., Shakespeare-Finch, J., Yik, M., ... Camart, N., 2005. Universal features of personality traits from the observer's perspective: Data from 50 cultures. *Journal of Personality and Social Psychology,* 88(3), 547–561.

McCrae, R.R. and Costa, P.T., 2008. The five-factor theory of personality. In: O.P. John, R.W. Robins, and L.A. Pervin, eds. *Handbook of personality.* New York: The Guilford Press, 159–181.

Milfont, T.L. and Sibley, C.G., 2012. The Big Five personality traits and environmental engagement: Associations at the individual and societal level. *Journal of Environmental Psychology,* 32(2), 187–195.

Milfont, T.L., Milojev, P., and Sibley, C.G., 2015. Socio-structural and psychological foundations of climate change beliefs. *New Zealand Journal of Psychology,* 44(1), 17–30.

Mondak, J.J., 2010. *Personality and the foundations of political behavior.* Cambridge: Cambridge University Press.

Olver, J.J. and Mooradian, T.A., 2003. Personality traits and personal values: A conceptual and empirical integration. *Personality and Individual Differences,* 35(1), 109–125.

Pavalache-Ilie, M. and Cazan, A.-M., 2018. Personality correlates of pro-environmental attitudes. *International Journal of Environmental Health Research,* 28(1), 71–78.

Rammstedt, B. and John, O.P., 2007. Measuring personality in one minute or less: A 10-item short version of the Big Five inventory in English and German. *Journal of Research in Personality,* 41(1), 203–212.

Roccas, S., Sagiv, L., Schwartz, S.H., and Knafo, A., 2002. The Big Five personality factors and personal values. *Personality and Social Psychology Bulletin,* 28(6), 789–801.

Roets, A., Cornelis, I., and Van Hiel, A., 2014. Openness as a predictor of political orientation and conventional and unconventional political activism in Western and Eastern Europe. *Journal of Personality Assessment,* 96(1), 53–63.

Saucier, G., 1994. Mini-markers: A brief version of goldberg's unipolar big-five markers. *Journal of Personality Assessment*, 63(3), 506–516.

Schmitt, D.P., Allik, J., McCrae, R.R., Benet-Martínez, V., Alcalay, L., Ault, L., Austers, I., Bennett, K.L., Bianchi, G., Boholst, F., Borg Cunen, M.A., Braeckman, J., Brainerd, E.G., Caral, L.G.A., Caron, G., Martina Casullo, M., Cunningham, M., Daibo, I., De Backer, C., ... Sharan, M.B., 2007. The geographic distribution of Big Five personality traits: Patterns and profiles of human self-description across 56 nations. *Journal of Cross-Cultural Psychology*, 38(2), 173–212.

Schoen, H. and Schumann, S., 2007. Personality traits, partisan attitudes, and voting behavior. Evidence from Germany. *Political Psychology*, 28(4), 471–498.

Specht, J., Egloff, B., and Schmukle, S.C., 2011. Stability and change of personality across the life course: The impact of age and major life events on mean-level and rank-order stability of the Big Five. *Journal of Personality and Social Psychology*, 101(4), 862–882.

Stenner, K., 2005. *The authoritarian dynamic*. Cambridge: Cambridge University Press.

Stephenson, L.B., Harell, A., Rubenson, D., and Loewen, P.J., 2020. 2019 Canadian election study – Online survey, Harvard Dataverse, V1. Available from: https://doi.org/10.7910/DVN/DUS88V

Van Hiel, A., Kossowska, M., and Mervielde, I., 2000. The relationship between openness to experience and political ideology. *Personality and Individual Differences*, 28(4), 741–751.

Vecchione, M., Caprara, G., Schoen, H., Castro, J.L.G., and Schwartz, S.H., 2012. The role of personal values and basic traits in perceptions of the consequences of immigration: A three-nation study: Values, traits, and perceptions of immigration. *British Journal of Psychology*, 103(3), 359–377.

Ziller, C. and Berning, C.C., 2021. Personality traits and public support of minority rights. *Journal of Ethnic and Migration Studies*, 47(3), 723–740.

CHAPTER 10

Ideology and public opinion

....

Philippe Chassé and Éric Bélanger

INTRODUCTION

First introduced during the French Revolution to differentiate members of the National Assembly who opposed the Bourbon monarchy (and sat on the left of the president) from members who supported King Louis XVI (and sat on the right of the president), the terms "left" and "right" are now widely used to describe the ideological positions of citizens and political actors (Benoit and Laver, 2006). Although they are sometimes replaced by the terms "liberal" and "conservative" – most notably in the United States – these ideological labels are prevalent in the Western world and, to a lesser extent, in other regions of the world as well (Geser, 2008). The pervasiveness of the left–right dichotomy in political debates has even led some scholars to describe this concept aptly as "the core currency of political exchange" around the world (Noël and Thérien, 2008).

In this chapter, we examine the extent to which the left–right divide shapes the views of citizens about the (perceived) impact of immigrants on their society. Do individuals who identify themselves with the ideological left have attitudes vis-à-vis immigration that are persistently different from those held by individuals who locate themselves closer to the right of the ideological spectrum? Do citizens who position themselves near the centre of the ideological divide have views on the immigration issue that steadily fall in between those who situate themselves on the left or right? And to what extent are these patterns consistent across Western nations? We answer these questions via an analysis of the left–right scale in the nine Western democracies presented in Chapter 3. We first discuss the meaning and measurement of the left–right ideological spectrum in public opinion. We then consider the theoretical reasons why this ideological cleavage may structure the public's attitudes towards immigration. Finally, we take a close look at the cross-national evidence offered by our data, with a brief consideration of the Canadian and French cases as arguably

DOI: 10.4324/9781003121992-12

the least and most representative, respectively, of the general relationship between left–right ideology and attitudes towards immigration.

THE LEFT–RIGHT SCALE AND ITS MEANING

Political scientists usually acknowledge that the left–right scale has at least two dimensions: one that is economic and another that is cultural (Hooghe et al., 2002; Kriesi et al., 2006, 2008). The economic dimension encompasses the traditional class cleavage and taps greater versus lesser state intervention in the redistribution of resources. In this first dimension, the left is associated with pro-state views and the right with pro-market views. The cultural dimension, on the other hand, structures issues that pertain to cultural liberalism, immigration, and in Western Europe, European integration. In this second dimension, the left is associated with a more "progressive" discourse and the right with a more "traditional" discourse.

The two-dimensionality of the ideological positions of citizens and political actors has led some scholars to argue that the relationship between issue preferences and the left–right scale is not linear, as this would entail an almost perfect correlation between people's attitudes towards economic and cultural issues. Using data from 28 West European countries, Lachat (2018) has for instance shown that economic issue preferences have a stronger impact on ideology among left-wing voters, but that cultural issue preferences have a stronger impact among right-wing voters. This means that, in general, far-left and centre-left voters tend to share similar views on cultural issues, but not on economic issues, and that centre-right and far-right voters tend to share similar views on economic issues, but not on cultural issues.

Most of the time, political scientists measure citizens' left–right orientation using either a ten- or an 11-point scale (Kroh, 2007). Some also use seven- and 101-point scales, but this practice is much less common in the literature. The main difference between the ten- and the 11-point scale is that the latter includes a midpoint, whereas the first forces respondents to indicate whether they side on the left or on the right. The main argument against the inclusion of a midpoint is that it might lead respondents who do not know where to place themselves on the left–right scale to choose the neutral value instead of reporting their absence of attitude (see Inglehart and Klingemann, 1976), so that the midpoint would be more akin to an ideological "swamp" (Deutsch et al., 1966). Indeed, van der Eijk and Niemöller (1984) have noted that the proportion of nonresponses increases when researchers do not allow respondents to select the midpoint. Other scholars have nonetheless underlined the importance of providing a true centre, as some citizens might truly identify as neither left-leaning nor right-leaning. More recently, Kroh (2007) attempted to determine which scale generates the highest quality data. His results indicate that both scales perform equally well in terms of reliability, but that the 11-point scale produces the highest validity left–right data. He therefore concludes that researchers should avoid using the ten-point scale.

Even though many have criticized the left–right scale for being vague and – in some contexts – meaningless, this abstract dimension arguably fulfils its main objective, which is to allow citizens to "orient themselves in a complex political world" (Fuchs and Klingemann, 1990, p. 203). In Western countries, a vast majority of people are both able and willing to define themselves in left–right terms (Bréchon, 2006). And this trend is far from reversing. Whereas some 80% of European voters could place themselves on the left–right scale in the 1970s, around 90% can do so now (Mair, 2007). There are however non-negligible variations across countries. As reported by Mair (2007), the proportion of citizens who are unwilling or unable to place themselves on a left–right scale is especially low in Nordic countries like Norway (2.2%), Finland (4.6%), and Sweden (4.9%), but is higher in Eastern Europe (mean of 22.8%) and Portugal (34.1%).

CITIZENS' PLACEMENT ON THE LEFT–RIGHT SCALE AND ATTITUDES TOWARDS IMMIGRATION

In most Western European and North American countries, self-reported political ideology is usually considered a good predictor of attitudes towards immigration. Whereas individuals on the left are typically favourable to immigration, individuals on the right tend to support more restrictive policies (Chandler and Tsai, 2001; Sides and Citrin, 2007; Vrânceanu and Lachat, 2021; Wilkes et al., 2008). People who identify as right-leaning are also more likely than people who identify as left-leaning to hold negative views of immigrants (Semyonov et al., 2006, 2008; Sides and Citrin, 2007; Wilkes et al., 2007) and to oppose multiculturalism (Citrin et al., 2001). Centrists, on the other hand, tend to have attitudes that fall between those of left-wing citizens and right-wing voters: on average, they are less tolerant towards immigration than the first, but hold more positive views than the second (Espenshade and Hempstead, 1996). The effect of political ideology on attitudes towards immigration is statistically significant across studies, even when controlling for a wide array of individual characteristics, like age, gender, education, and income. It is also statistically significant when taking into account respondents' party identification (Citrin et al., 1997).

Interestingly, Semyonov et al. (2006) have found that between the late 1980s and the early 2000s, the impact of political ideology on anti-foreigner attitudes has increased in Western Europe. Their results show that the gap in attitudes between individuals on the left and individuals on the right has widened sharply after 1988, and that since then, right-wing ideology is even more closely related to negative views of immigrants. Using the same dataset, but different model specifications, Wilkes et al. (2007, p. 836) have for their part found that "higher levels of support for extreme right-wing parties at the country level increase the association between political orientation and anti-foreigner sentiment at the individual level." Such findings suggest that the right is not a monolithic block, and that individuals who vote for extreme-right parties are considerably more critical of immigration than individuals who vote for mainstream right-wing parties. They also suggest that extreme-right parties can have a non-negligible influence on citizens' perception of immigrants. It is indeed likely that by presenting immigration as a cultural threat and by blaming newcomers for various economic and societal problems, these political organizations create a social climate that is more conducive to anti-immigrant attitudes (see Semyonov et al., 2006).

Even though many studies have demonstrated that political ideology and attitudes towards immigration are intertwined, very few scholars have investigated the causal mechanisms that underlie the relationship between these variables. As Pardos-Prado (2011) mentions, citizens' self-placement on the left–right scale is often considered strictly as a control variable in the literature. In fact, some studies do not even take political ideology into consideration in their statistical models. In the following three subsections, we explore different reasons that can potentially explain why citizens' self-reported political ideology is a good predictor of their opinion on immigration. We begin by noting that the basic personal values that motivate self-placement on the left–right scale also influence people's attitudes towards immigration. Then, we draw attention to the fact that ideological labels are one of the main cognitive shortcuts that citizens use to reach opinions about immigration. This entails that left-wing, centrist, and right-wing political actors can have an influence on the way citizens perceive immigration. Finally, we consider the possibility that scholars overestimate the extent to which individuals on the left are favourable to immigration by highlighting that social desirability pressures sometimes lead these citizens to conceal their real attitudes regarding sensitive issues.

Personal values, the left–right scale, and attitudes towards immigration

According to Inglehart and Klingemann (1976), personal values are one of the major components of citizens' self-placement on the left–right scale. Values are "general and basic beliefs" that influence the attitudes and opinions of a person (Davidov and Meuleman, 2012, p. 760). They are trans-situational, which means that they do not change from one context to another, and can be ordered by relative importance (Schwartz, 1992, 1994). Values differ from attitudes in that they are more abstract and limited in number. Usually, the political left is associated with cosmopolitan values, and the political right with conservative values. Research shows that West European and North American citizens share a similar understanding of the terms "left" and "right." For instance, Fuchs and Klingemann (1990) have observed that in the Netherlands, West Germany, and the United States, people associate general societal values such as equality and solidarity with the left, and individualism and freedom with the right. In these countries, the political left is perceived as progressive, and the political right is deemed to maintain the system in place.

Recently, some studies (Caprara et al., 2017; Piurko et al., 2011) have aimed to determine whether basic personal values motivate citizens' self-placement on the left–right scale. Their results indicate that values have a strong explanatory power in most countries (with the notable exception of post-communist countries). Using Schwartz's (1992) circular model of values,[1] they show that the two basic values associated with self-transcendence – universalism and benevolence – are good predictors of left-wing identification and that the two basic values associated with conservation – tradition and conformity – are good predictors of right-wing identification (Caprara et al., 2017; Piurko et al., 2011). The motivational goals of universalism are defined as the "understanding, appreciation, tolerance, and protection for the welfare of all people and for nature," and those of benevolence as the "preservation and enhancement of the welfare of people with whom one is in frequent personal contact." On the other hand, the motivational goals of tradition are defined as the "respect, commitment and acceptance of the customs and ideas that traditional culture or religion provide the self," and those of conformity as the "restraint of actions, inclinations, and impulses likely to upset or harm others and violate social expectations or norms" (Piurko et al., 2011, p. 539).

Perhaps unsurprisingly given their motivational goals, the same four basic personal values also have an impact on citizens' attitudes towards immigration. In two different studies, Davidov and his colleagues (2012, 2008) have found that individuals scoring high on self-transcendence values tend to support allowing more immigrants into their country, and that individuals scoring high on conservative values tend to oppose doing so. Their results further indicate that people who score high on universalism and benevolence are more likely than others to reject conditions for accepting newcomers. It is therefore likely that one of the reasons why citizens on the left are generally more favourable to immigration than citizens on the right is that people who identify as left-leaning score higher on self-transcendence values than others. Nevertheless, basic personal values do not fully explain the attitudinal difference between left-wing and right-wing citizens. Even when taking into consideration the values to which individuals adhere, self-placement on the left–right scale still has a statistically significant – albeit less important – effect on attitudes towards immigration (Davidov and Meuleman, 2012; Davidov et al., 2008). It is possible that such is the case because ideological labels are not only repositories for personal values, but also cognitive shortcuts that people can use to reach opinions about political issues they are not familiar with.

Ideological labels as cognitive shortcuts

The cost of acquiring political information is high, and citizens have little incentive to gather knowledge on every political issue (Downs, 1957). Yet, even with incomplete information, they can make sense of politics using heuristics, or cognitive shortcuts (Popkin, 1991). Heuristics help people organize their opinion and simplify their political choices; they allow citizens to make decisions that mirror those they would have made under conditions of "full information" without engaging in rigorous rational computation (Lau and Redlawsk, 1997, p. 586; Sniderman et al., 1991). For instance, citizens may rely on the positions of well-known interest groups to determine whether they agree with a given public policy (Lupia, 1994). They may also use statements made by political actors they trust as cues on where to stand on a variety of issues (Carmines and Kuklinski, 1990; Mondak, 1993). Even though some scholars have pointed out that heuristics are not infallible, and that they sometimes lead citizens astray (Lau and Redlawsk, 2001; Pétry and Duval, 2017; Somin, 2006), evidence shows that most people rely on cognitive shortcuts when making political choices (Lau and Redlawsk, 2006; Lupia and McCubbins, 1998).

Political ideology is one of the main heuristics that citizens use when it comes to adopting issue positions (Lau and Redlawsk, 2001; Popkin, 1991; Sniderman et al., 1991). This is especially true for issues on which there is no consensus, and that political parties frame on the left–right axis, such as the role of the government in the economy or welfare. Citizens who identify as left-leaning, as centrist, or as right-leaning can use these ideological labels to reach opinions about topics or policies they know little about. By knowing where left-wing, centrist, or right-wing political actors (parties, candidates, organizations, etc.) stand on a given issue, they can determine what their own position should be without doing extensive research. In Western Europe and in North America, the ideological labels of political parties provide a "consistent indicator" of their stance on immigration: in general, left-wing parties adopt a more "positive/expansive" position and use moral-universal arguments, whereas right-wing parties adopt a more restrictive position and use nationalistic arguments (Carvalho and Ruedin, 2020, p. 381; Helbling, 2014). Therefore, even if they do not know much about immigration policies, citizens who are able to place themselves on the left–right scale can follow the cues provided by political actors to establish whether they are favourable to immigration or not. They can also follow the same cues to determine whether immigrants have a positive impact on the economy or on the culture of their country. It should be noted, however, that despite the fact heuristics allow people to make sense of politics without engaging in rigorous rational calculation, citizens still need a certain degree of political awareness to know what the positions of the various political actors of their country are (Sides and Citrin, 2007). If they are ignorant of where left-wing, centrist, and right-wing actors typically stand on immigration, they can hardly use political ideology as a cognitive shortcut.

Some studies nonetheless suggest that citizens do not always rely on ideological labels to make up their minds. Weber and Saris (2015) note that people tend to use political ideology as a cognitive shortcut when they consider that the issue at stake is not of major concern. When they think that a certain topic or policy is important, they are more likely to invest time and resources to form their opinion. They might, for example, read newspaper articles or seek information online. Therefore, the effect of left–right identification on issue preferences can vary greatly from one person to another (Weber and Saris, 2015). One could indeed expect people to give greater importance to issues that have direct and tangible consequences on their daily lives than to issues that have little to no impact on them (Citrin and Green, 1990). The effect of ideology also varies from one issue to another. A vast body of literature (e.g., Carmines and Kuklinski, 1990; Lupia, 1994) demonstrates that citizens are particularly likely to use cognitive shortcuts when evaluating what Carmines and Stimson (1980) call "hard issues," or issues which are "means-oriented, technical, and unfamiliar" to them (Gilens and Murakawa, 2002, p. 19).

More particularly, Pardos-Prado (2011) attempted to determine under which conditions citizens rely on political ideology to form their opinion about immigration.

Using data from 22 European countries, he found that self-placements on the left–right scale help people to organize, frame, constrain, and articulate their attitudes towards immigration "especially when the experience of direct competition for scarce resources with migrants is weaker" (Pardos-Prado, 2011, p. 1010). Indeed, because they generally compete for the same jobs, houses, and public services as newcomers, individuals who are in a situation of socioeconomic vulnerability tend to perceive immigrants as a threat and, accordingly, to consider that immigration is a salient issue. They pay more attention to the debates surrounding immigration policies and do not have to rely too much on ideological labels to determine what their position is (Pardos-Prado, 2011). Conversely, individuals who are not in a situation of socioeconomic vulnerability do not necessarily view immigrants as competitors. They are less inclined to be concerned about immigration and have fewer incentives to closely follow the debates surrounding immigration policies. Therefore, political ideology tends to play a more important role in the formation of their attitudes towards immigration.

The role of social desirability pressures

Although they do not directly challenge the conventional wisdom that ideology is a good predictor of attitudes towards immigration, some studies suggest that scholars might overestimate the extent to which individuals on the left are willing to accept more newcomers. In fact, Gilens et al. (1998, p. 179) argue that left-wing voters sometimes hide opinions that "would present [them] in a light that they themselves would find unflattering." They are, for instance, reluctant to admit that they oppose affirmative action because they do not want to appear indifferent to racial inequalities (Gilens et al., 1998). To assess whether social desirability pressures exert an influence on self-reported attitudes towards immigration, Janus (2010) conducted a list experiment in the United States. Participants were randomly assigned to two groups and had to indicate *how many* statements they agreed with from a list of either three or four statements. The first group received three non-controversial statements, whereas the second group received an additional statement about cutting off immigration to the United States. The attitudes towards immigration of the first group were measured subsequently using a direct question.

By calculating the difference between the two groups, Janus (2010) was able to obtain an unobtrusive estimate of respondents' support for restrictive immigration policies. His findings indicate that people who identify as "liberals" (or as left-leaning) are far more likely than people who identify as "conservatives" (or as right-leaning) to conceal that they favour more restrictions on immigration. Indeed, while support for cutting off immigration is low among liberals who responded to the direct question (26%), more than two thirds (71%) of liberals whose attitudes were measured unobtrusively support immigration restrictions. On the other hand, the difference between conservative respondents from the first group and conservative respondents from the second group is not statistically significant (Janus, 2010). What citizens believe to be appropriate – or socially desirable – positions on immigration therefore seems to vary depending on where people place themselves on the left–right scale. Consequently, it is possible that the results of the studies that use direct questions to measure respondents' attitudes towards immigration also partly reflect the different ideological pressures that people face when answering surveys.

DATA AND RESULTS

To study the relationship between political ideology and attitudes towards immigration, we use the CSES data presented in Chapter 3 for all nine Western democracies (Australia, the United Kingdom, Canada, France, Germany, Italy, Portugal, Switzerland, and the United States). All CSES respondents were asked to place themselves on an 11-point left–right scale, where 0 means "the left" and 10 means "the right." Most respondents were able to locate themselves on the scale, with only 7.6%, on average, who answered "don't know" to this question.

To present our results in a more intuitive manner, we grouped respondents into three categories: those who placed themselves between 0 and 3 were labelled as "left leaning," those who placed themselves between 4 and 6 were labelled as "centrists," and those who placed themselves between 7 and 10 were labelled as "right leaning." As Figure 10.1 shows, a plurality of respondents identifies as centrist in all nine countries of our sample. In the figure, the mean ideological score is displayed in the upper right corner of each country's respective distribution panel. On average, German respondents are the most left-leaning (average of 4.27), and American respondents are the most right-leaning (average of 5.80). Figure 10.1 also reveals that an important number of Italian respondents placed themselves at one of the two ends of the left–right scale. This might reflect the growing polarization recently found in that country, with more Italians inclined to locate themselves to the right of the ideological spectrum (see Dassonneville, 2021).

We use the same three indicators to measure respondents' attitudes towards immigration, namely (1) their perception of the effect that immigrants have on crime rates; (2) their opinion on the impact that immigrants have on culture; and (3) their stance on immigrants' contribution to the economy. Again, lower values (1 or 2) indicate that respondents have positive or somewhat positive views of immigrants, whereas higher values (4 or 5) indicate that respondents have somewhat negative or negative views of immigrants. A mid-value (3) means that respondents neither have positive nor negative views of immigrants.

As could be expected, our results denote a clear relationship between self-reported political ideology and attitudes towards immigration. Figure 10.2 shows the national distributions of respondents' perception of the effect that immigrants have on crime rates per ideological label. The bars indicate the percentage of left-leaning, centrist, and right-leaning respondents that selected each answer option. This is the reason why they go above 100%. They do *not* indicate how each answer option is distributed between the three groups. In each country of our sample, individuals on the left are less likely than individuals on the right to believe that immigrants increase crime rates. The proportion of right-leaning citizens who associate newcomers with

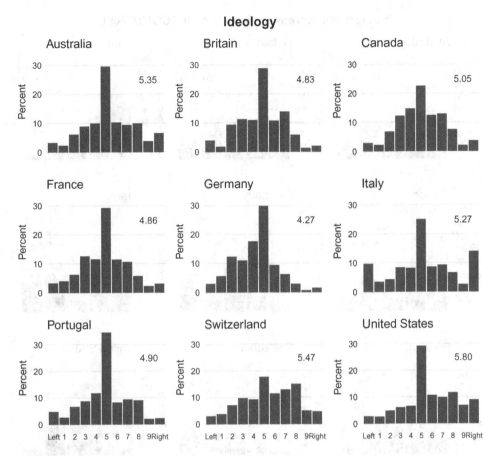

FIGURE 10.1 Distribution of ideology.

criminality is higher in continental European countries like Italy, Switzerland, and Germany, and lower in North American and Oceanic countries like Canada, the United States, and Australia. It is also relatively lower in Portugal, the country with the smallest proportion of foreign-born citizens in our sample (United Nations, Department of Economic and Social Affairs, 2019). On average, respondents who identify as centrists have attitudes that fall between those of respondents who lean left and those of respondents who lean right.[2]

As Figures 10.3 and 10.4 show, political ideology is also strongly linked to citizens' views on the impact that immigrants have on culture and the economy. In all the countries of our sample except Portugal (and the UK as it pertains to the question on immigrants' contribution to the economy), right-leaning respondents are more likely than left-leaning and centrist respondents to believe that culture is harmed by newcomers and that immigrants have a negative impact on the economy. This indicates that the relationship between self-placement on the left–right scale and attitudes towards immigration does not change from one indicator to

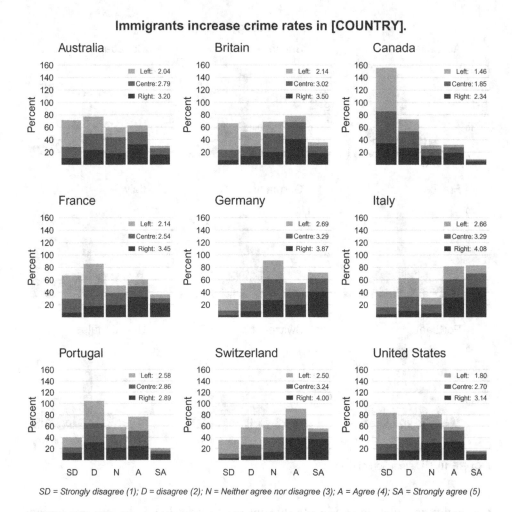

FIGURE 10.2 Attitudes about how immigrants are perceived to affect a country's crime, by ideology.

another. Yet, regardless of their political ideology, respondents are more likely to believe immigrants increase crime rates than to perceive them as a cultural or as an economic threat. The sole exceptions are in France, where respondents hold more negative views towards immigrants' impact on the national culture and the economy than towards their impact on crime rates, and the United States, where left-leaning respondents show less enthusiasm about newcomers' contribution to the economy than they do on the other two indicators (crime and culture).

There are two reasons that might explain why left-leaning, centrist, and right-leaning Portuguese respondents tend to have generally similar attitudes towards immigrants. First, an important proportion of Portuguese citizens are unable or unwilling to define themselves in left–right terms (Mair, 2007). For instance, 13.9%

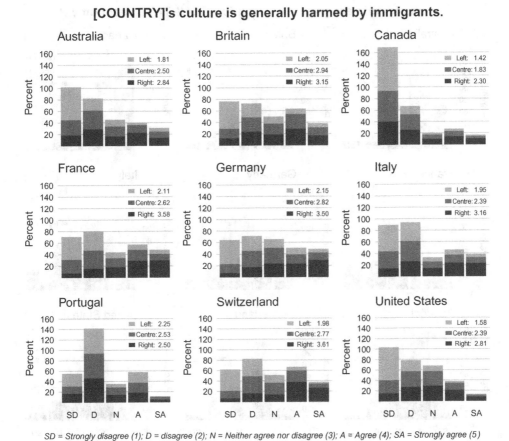

[COUNTRY]'s culture is generally harmed by immigrants.

SD = Strongly disagree (1); D = disagree (2); N = Neither agree nor disagree (3); A = Agree (4); SA = Strongly agree (5)

FIGURE 10.3 Attitudes about how immigrants are perceived to affect a country's culture, by ideology.

of the Portuguese sample of the CSES fail to locate themselves on the left-to-right opinion scale, whereas that proportion is only 6.8%, on average, in the other eight countries examined. This suggests that the terms "left" and "right" do not have a clear meaning in Portugal, and that, therefore, they are not necessarily associated with clear policy preferences or attitudes in this country. Second, the issue of immigration is not as salient in Portugal as it is elsewhere in Western Europe. Even though the proportion of foreign-born citizens doubled in the early 2000s, left- and right-wing Portuguese mainstream political parties have not attached great importance to this topic over the course of the last two decades: most indeed have adopted a positive approach towards immigration (Carvalho and Duarte, 2020).

Finally, Figure 10.5 illustrates the country-specific distribution of an immigration index that combines answers to all three of the indicators examined so far. The figure broadly confirms the ideological patterns previously discussed. It also allows highlighting more clearly the extent to which the ideological distribution of

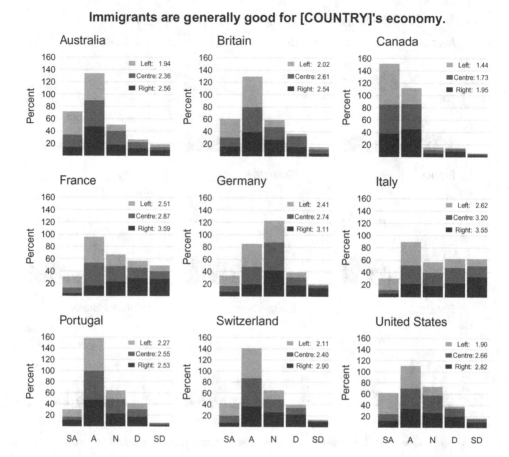

FIGURE 10.4 Attitudes about how immigrants are perceived to affect a country's economy, by ideology.

immigration views in Canada represents a peculiar case due to its strong skewness towards positive attitudes across all its ideological spectrum, while the distribution observed in France represents a more typical case where each of the left, centre, and right hold relatively distinct views about the immigration issue. We briefly discuss each of these two cases in the remainder of this section.

Canada: an outlier?

In Canada, like in all the other countries of our sample except Portugal, individuals on the right (average of 2.20) are more likely to hold negative views of immigrants than individuals on the left (average of 1.44) and centrists (average of 1.80).[3] Yet, whatever their self-placement on the left–right scale, Canadian citizens tend to have a good opinion of newcomers. As Figure 10.5 shows, the vast majority of Canadian

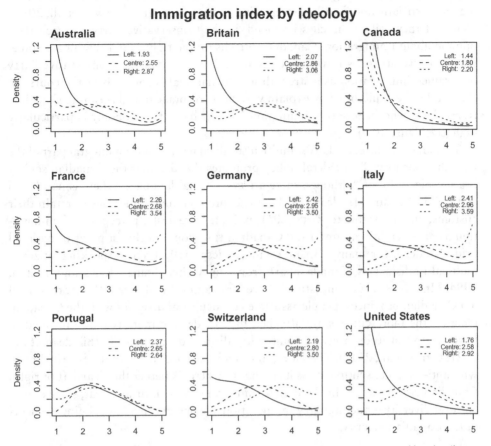

Immigration index by ideology

Values range from 1 to 5 with higher values indicating less favourable attitudes toward immigration.

FIGURE 10.5 Attitudes about how immigrants are perceived to affect a country's economy, crime and culture (index), by ideology.

respondents believe that immigrants contribute positively to the economy, do not increase crime rates, and do not harm the culture of their country. There are two reasons that could potentially explain why even Canadian citizens who identify as right-leaning are generally favourable to immigration.

First, although Canada annually welcomes more newcomers per capita than the United States and most Western European countries (United Nations, Department of Economic and Social Affairs, 2019), immigration is rarely a subject of contention in Canadian federal elections. All major federal political parties endorse pro-immigration policies, and most Canadian immigration critics do not qualify as anti-foreigners by international standards (Hiebert, 2016; Reitz, 2011). While in power from 2006 to 2015, the Conservative Party – the main right-wing political party in Canada – maintained high immigration numbers and emphasized the benefits of immigration for the economy.[4] It also attempted to gain support among new Canadians, most notably by adopting a more positive stance on multiculturalism and by reaching out to socially and fiscally conservative immigrant voters (Marwah et al., 2013). Hence, if they follow the cues provided by the Conservative Party to reach their opinion about immigration, Canadian citizens on the right are likely to have somewhat positive attitudes towards newcomers. The fact that the Conservative Party has framed immigration as a strength for the national economy over the course of the last decade could possibly explain why the percentage of right-leaning Canadian respondents who believe that immigrants do not harm the economy is particularly high (see Figure 10.4).

Second, since the early 1970s, multiculturalism has become an integral part of the Canadian identity. This federal policy promotes the idea that the Canadian society is a mosaic and that "although there are two official languages, there is no official culture" in Canada (Trudeau, 1971). It encourages ethnic minorities to retain their customs, and according to Reitz (2011, p. 7), it "[creates] a perception of immigration as an essential feature of the Canadian tradition and thus a point of national pride." Indeed, for many Canadian citizens (especially English-speaking citizens), multiculturalism sets Canada apart from the United States (Reitz and Breton, 1994).[5] In recent years, some studies have for example highlighted the fact that in all ten Canadian provinces, people associate ethnocultural diversity with the Canadian identity: the more citizens are attached to Canada, the more they are inclined to have positive attitudes towards multiculturalism and immigration (Bilodeau et al., 2021; Citrin et al., 2012). Therefore, in Canada, patriotism is not necessarily linked with anti-foreigner sentiments as it can be elsewhere. Whether they lean left or right, Canadian citizens are unlikely to view immigrants as a cultural threat, since ethnocultural diversity – and arguably immigration – is one of the main defining elements of the Canadian identity.

France: a more typical case study

To some extent, France is a more typical, or conventional, case than Canada. The relationship between French citizens' self-placement on the left–right scale and attitudes towards immigration is linear: respondents who lean left tend to hold more positive views of immigrants (average of 2.26), and respondents who lean right tend to hold more negative views of immigrants (average of 3.54). Respondents who identify as centrists fall in between (average of 2.68), but their attitudes are slightly more similar to those of left-wing voters.[6] Nevertheless, French citizens are more critical of immigration than Canadian citizens. They are notably far less likely than the latter to believe that immigrants have a positive impact on the economy (see Figure 10.4). This result is not particularly surprising since immigration is a more controversial issue in France – and in Western Europe more generally – than in Canada (see Helbling, 2014; Reitz, 2011). The trends we find in France are similar to those we find elsewhere in Europe, especially in Germany, Italy, and Switzerland.

Unlike in Canada, where no major federal political party holds an anti-immigrant discourse, there is no consensus on immigration among political parties in France.

Over the course of the last few years, the *Rassemblement national* (which was known as the *Front national* until 2018), a party that pushes strong anti-foreigner messages, has become a credible contender in French politics (Lewis-Beck et al., 2012; Perrineau, 2016). While the integration of newcomers was already a salient issue in France in the early 1980s, the recent rise in popularity of this extreme-right political party has led mainstream right-wing parties to revise their stance on immigration. For instance, Haegel (2011) has found that during his presidential term, Nicolas Sarkozy (UMP–centre right) adopted more critical positions on immigration than his predecessor, Jacques Chirac (also from the UMP). In his political speeches, Sarkozy advocated widening the possibilities of forfeiture of French nationality by people of foreign origin, and drew links between insecurity and immigration – a rhetoric that raised criticism among many moderate right-wing political actors (Haegel, 2011; 2012; Martin, 2010).

The electoral performances of the *Rassemblement national* also had an influence on the discourse of left-wing political actors. Even though François Hollande (*Parti socialiste*–centre left) criticized Sarkozy for "promoting the division of the French people," he also started to use a more restrictive tone on immigration during his presidential term (Carvalho, 2019, p. 7). This corresponds to what Meguid (2005, 2008) calls "accommodative strategies": instead of opposing the positions of anti-immigration political actors, mainstream parties adapt their political platforms in order to retain the support of citizens who would otherwise vote for these niche parties. In doing so, their goal is to undermine the issue ownership of their more radical competitors by "challenging the exclusivity of the niche [parties'] policy stance" (Meguid, 2005, p. 349). Yet, it should be noted that despite this shift in the discourse of France's mainstream political actors, ideological labels still provide a consistent indicator of the positions of the major French political parties on immigration: left-wing parties have a more positive stance, whereas right-wing parties have a more negative stance.

CONCLUSION

For more than two centuries, left–right ideology has played a central role in terms of structuring political debates in the Western world and beyond, and it continues to do so today. As such, it has come to be linked to, and to subsume, a host of more specific political issues, not only in the party discourse but also in the public's opinion formation process. From the standpoint of citizens, the concepts of "left" and "right" have proven to be useful referents: they allow individuals to better orient themselves by simplifying a complex political world. Much like partisanship, left–right ideology has thus become an "anchor" variable of political choice, that is, a deep-seated political orientation that informs an individual's issue attitudes and that summarizes them (Laponce, 1970; Inglehart and Klingemann, 1976; Inglehart, 1984; Fuchs and Klingemann, 1990).

In this chapter, we have shown that such is indeed the case when it comes to attitudes towards immigration. We have seen that citizens positioning themselves to the left of the ideological scale tend to display more favourable views towards immigrants' impact on the crime rates, the culture, and the economy of the host society, whereas those positioning themselves to the right hold less favourable attitudes, which most likely makes them supportive of more restrictive immigration policies. For their part, people locating themselves near the centre of the left–right scale typically present attitudes vis-à-vis immigrants that are somewhere in between these two poles. We have also seen that this relationship between left–right ideology and immigration attitudes is observable across several Western democracies, although some countries in our sample display peculiar patterns. For instance, Canadians hold disproportionately positive views about immigrants that are widely shared across the ideological divide, while the Portuguese do not seem to identify with the left–right cleavage as much as citizens in other countries. As some research has shown that left–right ideological identification and attitudes towards immigrants have become more strongly linked over time (De Vries et al., 2013), this relationship is unlikely to vanish any time soon.

SUMMARY POINTS

- For more than two centuries, left–right ideology has played a central role in terms of structuring political debates in the Western world and beyond.
- For citizens, the concepts of "left" and "right" are useful referents, as they allow individuals to better orient themselves and form opinions by simplifying a complex political world.
- Our empirical analysis suggests that citizens positioning themselves to the left of the ideological scale tend to display more favourable views towards immigrants, whereas those positioning themselves to the right hold less favourable attitudes and those locating themselves near the centre of the scale typically present attitudes vis-à-vis immigrants that are somewhere in between these two poles.
- The chapter also shows that this relationship between left–right ideology and immigration attitudes is observable across the nine Western democracies examined in this volume, although some countries in the sample display peculiar patterns. For instance, Canadians hold disproportionately positive views about immigrants that are widely shared across the ideological divide, while the Portuguese do not seem to identify with the left–right cleavage as much as citizens in the other countries.

NOTES

1 The ten basic values identified in Schwartz's (1992) circular model are (1) power; (2) achievement; (3) hedonism; (4) stimulation; (5) self-direction; (6) universalism; (7) benevolence; (8) tradition; (9) conformity, and (10) security.
2 Note, however, that the difference between the average answer of right-leaning Portuguese respondents and the average answer of centrist Portuguese respondents is not statistically significant.

3 The difference between Canadian respondents who lean left and Canadian respondents who lean right or identify as centrists is statistically significant (p < 0.05). The same is true for the difference between Canadian respondents who identify as centrists and Canadian respondents who lean right.

4 Nevertheless, it should be noted that during the same period, the Conservative Party also adopted policies that make Canadian citizenship "harder to get, and easier to lose" to appeal to a certain part of its electorate (Marwah et al., 2013, p. 95).

5 In Quebec, the only Canadian province in which the majority of the population is of French-Canadian descent, multiculturalism has been received with less enthusiasm. Many Quebecers indeed believe that this federal policy undermines their culture and their claim to a special status within Canada (Bloemraad, 2012). Consequently, the Quebec government promotes the concept of interculturalism, which is somewhat similar to multiculturalism, but puts greater emphasis on French language integration and on the importance of shared values (see Bouchard, 2011, 2012).

6 The difference between French respondents who lean left and French respondents who lean right or identify as centrists is statistically significant (p < 0.05). The same is true for the difference between French respondents who identify as centrists and French respondents who lean right.

SUGGESTED FURTHER READINGS

Lachat, R., 2018. Which way from left to right? On the relation between voters' issue preferences and left–right orientation in West European democracies. *International Political Science Review*, 39(4), 419–435. Available from: https://doi.org/10.1177/0192512117692644

Pardos-Prado, S., 2011. Framing attitudes towards immigrants in Europe: When competition does not matter. *Journal of Ethnic and Migration Studies*, 37(7), 999–1015. Available from: https://doi.org/10.1080/1369183X.2011.572421

Semyonov, M., Raijman, R., and Gorodzeisky, A., 2006. The rise of anti-foreigner sentiment in European societies, 1988–2000. *American Sociological Review*, 71(3), 426–449. Available from: https://doi.org/10.1177/000312240607100304

Weber, W. and Saris, W.E., 2015. The relationship between issues and an individual's left–right orientation. *Acta Politica*, 50(2), 193–213. Available from: https://doi.org/10.1057/ap.2014.5

REFERENCES

Benoit, K. and Laver, M., 2006. *Party policy in modern democracies*. New York: Routledge.

Bilodeau, A., Gagnon, A., White, S.E., Turgeon, L., and Henderson, A., 2021. Attitudes toward ethnocultural diversity in multilevel political communities: Comparing the effect of national and subnational attachments in Canada. *Publius: The Journal of Federalism*, 51(1), 27–53. Available from: https://doi.org/10.1093/publius/pjaa020

Bloemraad, I., 2012. *Understanding 'Canadian exceptionalism' in immigration and pluralism policy*. Washington, DC: Migration Policy Institute.

Bouchard, G., 2011. Qu'est-ce que l'interculturalisme?/What is interculturalism? *McGill Law Journal*, 56(2), 395–468. Available from: https://doi.org/10.7202/1002371ar

Bouchard, G., 2012. *L'Interculturalisme. Un point de vue québécois*. Montréal: Les Éditions du Boréal.

Bréchon, P., 2006. Valeurs de gauche, valeurs de droite et identités religieuses en Europe. *Revue française de sociologie*, 47(4), 725–753. Available from: https://doi.org/10.3917/rfs.474.0725

Caprara, G.V., Vecchione, M., Schwartz, S.H., Schoen, H., Bain, P.G., Silvester, J., Cieciuch, J., Pavlopoulos, V., Bianchi, G., Kirmanoglu, H., Baslevent, C., Mamali, C., Manzi, J.,

Katayama, M., Posnova, T., Tabernero, C., Torres, C., Verkasalo, M., Lönnqvist, J.-E., and Caprara, M.G., 2017. Basic values, ideological self-placement, and voting: A cross-cultural study. *Cross-Cultural Research*, 51(4), 388–411. Available from: https://doi.org/10.1177/1069397117712194

Carmines, E.G. and Stimson, J.A., 1980. The two faces of issue voting. *American Political Science Review*, 74(1), 78–91. Available from: https://doi.org/10.2307/1955648

Carmines, E.G. and Kuklinski, J.H., 1990. Incentives, opportunities, and the logic of public opinion in American political representation. In: J.A. Ferejohn and J.H. Kuklinski, eds. *Information and democratic processes*. Champaign: University of Illinois Press, 240–268.

Carvalho, J., 2019. The Front National's influence on immigration during president François Hollande's term. Do they make a difference? In: B. Biard, L. Bernhard, and H. Betz, eds. *Do they make a difference? The policy influence of radical right populist parties in Western Europe*. London: ECPR Press, pp. 30–45.

Carvalho, J. and Duarte, M.C., 2020. The politicization of immigration in Portugal between 1995 and 2014: A European exception? *Journal of Common Market Studies*, 58(6), 1469–1487. Available from: https://doi.org/10.1111/jcms.13048

Carvalho, J. and Ruedin, D., 2020. The positions mainstream left parties adopt on immigration: A cross-cutting cleavage? *Party Politics*, 26(4), 379–389. Available from: https://doi.org/10.1177/1354068818780533

Ceobanu, A.M. and Escandell, X., 2010. Comparative analyses of public attitudes toward immigrants and immigration using multinational survey data: A review of theories and research. *Annual Review of Sociology*, 36, 309–328. Available from: https://doi.org/10.1146/annurev.soc.012809.102651

Chandler, C.R. and Tsai, Y.M., 2001. Social factors influencing immigration attitudes: An analysis of data from the General Social Survey. *Social Science Journal*, 38(2), 177–188. Available from: https://doi.org/10.1016/S0362-3319(01)00106-9

Citrin, J. and Green, D.P., 1990. The self-interest motive in American public opinion. *Research in Micropolitics*, 3(1), 1–28.

Citrin, J., Green, D.P., Muste, C., and Wong, C., 1997. Public opinion toward immigration reform: The role of economic motivations. *Journal of Politics*, 59(3), 858–881. Available from: https://doi.org/10.2307/2998640

Citrin, J., Sears, D.O., Muste, C., and Wong, C., 2001. Multiculturalism in American public opinion. *British Journal of Political Science*, 31(2), 247–275.

Citrin, J., Johnston, R., and Wright, M., 2012. Do patriotism and multiculturalism collide? Competing perspectives from Canada and the United States. *Canadian Journal of Political Science*, 45(3), 531–552. Available from: https://doi.org/10.1017/S0008423912000704

Dassonneville, R., 2021. Change and continuity in the ideological gender gap: A longitudinal analysis of left-right self-placement in OECD countries. *European Journal of Political Research*, 60(1), 225–238. Available from: https://doi.org/10.1111/1475-6765.12384

Davidov, E., Meuleman, B., Billiet, J., and Schmidt, P., 2008. Values and support for immigration: A cross-country comparison. *European Sociological Review*, 24(5), 583–599. Available from: https://doi.org/10.1093/esr/jcn020

Davidov, E. and Meuleman, B., 2012. Explaining attitudes towards immigration policies in European countries: The role of human values. *Journal of Ethnic and Migration Studies*, 38(5), 757–775. Available from: https://doi.org/10.1080/1369183X.2012.667985

Deutsch, E., Lindon, D., and Weill, P., 1966. *Les familles politiques aujourd'hui en France*. Paris: Les Éditions de Minuit.

De Vries, C.E., Hakhverdian, A., and Lancee, B., 2013. The dynamics of voters' left/right identification: The role of economic and cultural attitudes. *Political Science Research and Methods*, 1(2), 223–238. Available from: https://doi.org/10.1017/psrm.2013.4

Downs, A., 1957. *An economic theory of democracy*. New York: Harper.

Espenshade, T.J. and Hempstead, K., 1996. Contemporary American attitudes toward U.S. immigration. *International Migration Review*, 30(2), 535–570. Available from: https://doi.org/10.1177/019791839603000207

Fuchs, D. and Klingemann, H.D., 1990. The left–right schema. In: M.K. Jennings and J.W. van Deth, eds. *Continuities in political action: A longitudinal study of political orientations in three Western democracies*. New York: Walter de Gruyter, 203–234.

Geser, H., 2008. The limits of ideological globalization. Current patterns of "left and right" in different geographical regions. *Sociology in Switzerland: World Society and International Relations*, Working Paper 5, University of Zurich.

Gilens, M., Sniderman, P.M., and Kuklinski, J.H., 1998. Affirmative action and the politics of realignment. *British Journal of Political Science*, 28(1), 159–183.

Gilens, M. and Murakawa, N., 2002. Elite cues and political decision-making. *Research in Micropolitics*, 6(1), 15–49.

Haegel, F., 2011. Nicolas Sarkozy a-t-il radicalisé la droite française? Changements idéologiques et étiquetages politiques. *French Politics, Culture & Society*, 29(3), 62–77. Available from: https://doi.org/10.3167/fpcs.2011.290305

Haegel, F., 2012. *Les droites en fusion: Transformations de l'UMP*. Paris: Presses de Sciences Po.

Helbling, M., 2014. Framing immigration in Western Europe. *Journal of Ethnic and Migration Studies*, 40(1), 21–41. Available from: https://doi.org/10.1080/1369183X.2013.830888

Hiebert, D., 2016. *What's so special about Canada? Understanding the resilience of immigration and multiculturalism*. Washington, DC: Migration Policy Institute.

Hooghe, L., Marks, G., and Wilson, C.J., 2002. Does left/right structure party positions on European integration? *Comparative Political Studies*, 35(8), 965–989. Available from: https://doi.org/10.1177/001041402236310

Inglehart, R. and Klingemann, H.D., 1976. Party identification, ideological preference and the left–right dimension among Western mass publics. In: I. Bulge, I. Crewe, and D. Farlie, eds. *Party identification and beyond: Representations of voting and party competition*. London: Wiley, 243–273.

Inglehart, R., 1984. The changing structure of political cleavages in Western society. In: R.J. Dalton, S.C. Flanagan, and P.A. Beck, eds. *Electoral change in advanced industrial societies: Realignment or dealignment?*. Princeton: Princeton University Press, 25–69.

Janus, A.L., 2010. The influence of social desirability pressures on expressed immigration attitudes. *Social Science Quarterly*, 91(4), 928–946. Available from: https://doi.org/10.1111/j.1540-6237.2010.00742.x

Kriesi, H., Grande, E., Lachat, R., Dolezal, M., Bornschier, S., and Frey, T., 2006. Globalization and the transformation of the national political space: Six European countries compared. *European Journal of Political Research*, 45(6), 921–956. Available from: https://doi.org/10.1111/j.1475-6765.2006.00644.x

Kriesi, H., Grande, E., Lachat, R., Dolezal, M., Bornschier, S., and Frey, T., 2008. *West European politics in the age of globalization*. Cambridge University Press. Available from: https://doi.org/10.1017/CBO9780511790720

Kroh, M., 2007. Measuring left–right political orientation: The choice of response format. *Public Opinion Quarterly*, 71(2), 204–220. Available from: https://doi.org/10.1093/poq/nfm009

Lachat, R., 2018. Which way from left to right? On the relation between voters' issue preferences and left–right orientation in West European democracies. *International Political Science Review*, 39(4), 419–435. Available from: https://doi.org/10.1177/0192512117692644

Laponce, J.A., 1970. Note on the use of the left-right dimension. *Comparative Political Studies*, 2(4), 481–502.

Lau, R.R. and Redlawsk, D.P., 1997. Voting correctly. *American Political Science Review*, 91(3), 585–598. Available from: https://doi.org/10.2307/2952076

Lau, R.R. and Redlawsk, D.P., 2001. Advantages and disadvantages of cognitive heuristics in political decision making. *American Journal of Political Science*, 45(4), 951–971. Available from: https://doi.org/10.2307/2669334

Lau, R.R. and Redlawsk, D.P., 2006. *How voters decide: Information processing in election campaigns*. Cambridge: Cambridge University Press.

Lewis-Beck, M.S., Nadeau, R. and Bélanger, É., 2012. *French presidential elections*. New York: Palgrave Macmillan.

Lupia, A., 1994. Shortcuts versus encyclopedias: Information and voting behavior in California insurance reform elections. *American Political Science Review*, 88(1), 63–76. Available from: https://doi.org/10.2307/2944882

Lupia, A. and McCubbins, M.D., 1998. *The democratic dilemma: Can citizens learn what they need to know?*. Cambridge: Cambridge University Press.

Mair, P., 2007. Left–right orientations. In: R. Dalton and H. Klingemann, eds. *The Oxford handbook of political behavior*. Oxford University Press, 206–222. Available from: https://doi.org/10.1093/oxfordhb/9780199270125.003.0011

Martin, P., 2010. L'immigration, un piège pour la droite? *Commentaire*, 132(4), 1027–1035. Available from: https://doi.org/10.3917/comm.132.1027

Marwah, I., Triadafilopoulos, T., and White, S.E., 2013. Immigration, citizenship, and Canada's new conservative party. In: J.H. Farney and D. Rayside, eds. *Conservatism in Canada*. Toronto: University of Toronto Press, 95–119.

Meguid, B.M., 2005. Competition between unequals: The role of mainstream party strategy in niche party success. *American Political Science Review*, 99(3), 347–359. Available from: https://doi.org/10.1017/S0003055405051701

Meguid, B.M., 2008. *Party competition between unequals*. Cambridge: Cambridge University Press.

Mondak, J.J., 1993. Source cues and policy approval: The cognitive dynamics of public support for the Reagan agenda. *American Journal of Political Science*, 37(1), 186–212. Available from: https://doi.org/10.2307/2111529

Noël, A. and Thérien, J.-P., 2008. *Left and right in global politics*. Cambridge: Cambridge University Press.

Pardos-Prado, S., 2011. Framing attitudes towards immigrants in Europe: When competition does not matter. *Journal of Ethnic and Migration Studies*, 37(7), 999–1015. Available from: https://doi.org/10.1080/1369183X.2011.572421

Perrineau, P., 2016. Montée en puissance et recompositions de l'électorat frontiste. *Pouvoirs*, 157(2), 63–73. Available from: https://doi.org/10.3917/pouv.157.0063

Pétry, F. and Duval, D., 2017. When heuristics go bad: Citizens' misevaluations of campaign pledge fulfilment. *Electoral Studies*, 50, 116–127. Available from: https://doi.org/10.1016/j.electstud.2017.09.010

Piurko, Y., Schwartz, S.H., and Davidov, E., 2011. Basic personal values and the meaning of left-right political orientations in 20 countries. *Political Psychology*, 32(4), 537–561. Available from: https://doi.org/10.1111/j.1467-9221.2011.00828.x

Popkin, S.L., 1991. *The reasoning voter: Communication and persuasion in presidential campaigns*. Chicago: University of Chicago Press.

Reitz, J.G. and Breton, R., 1994. *The illusion of difference: Realities of ethnicity in Canada and the United States*. Toronto: CD Howe Institute.

Reitz, J.G., 2011. *Pro-immigration Canada: Social and economic roots of popular views*. Institute for Research on Public Policy. Available from: https://on-irpp.org/2y960Rv

Schwartz, S.H., 1992. Universals in the content and structure of values: Theoretical advances and empirical tests in 20 countries. *Advances in Experimental Social Psychology*, 25, 1–65.

Schwartz, S.H., 1994. Are there universal aspects in the content and structure of values? *Journal of Social Issues*, 50(4), 19–45. Available from: https://doi.org/10.1111/j.1540-4560.1994.tb01196.x

Semyonov, M., Raijman, R., and Gorodzeisky, A., 2006. The rise of anti-foreigner sentiment in European societies, 1988–2000. *American Sociological Review*, 71(3), 426–449. Available from: https://doi.org/10.1177/000312240607100304

Semyonov, M., Raijman, R., and Gorodzeisky, A., 2008. Foreigners' impact on European societies: Public views and perceptions in a cross-national comparative perspective. *International Journal of Comparative Sociology*, 49(1), 5–29. Available from: https://doi .org/10.1177/0020715207088585

Sides, J. and Citrin, J., 2007. European opinion about immigration: The role of identities, interests and information. *British Journal of Political Science*, 37(3), 477–504. Available from: https://doi.org/10.1017/S0007123407000257

Sniderman, P.M., Brody, R.A., and Tetlock, P.E., 1991. *Reasoning and choice: Explorations in political psychology*. Cambridge: Cambridge University Press.

Somin, I., 2006. Knowledge about ignorance: New directions in the study of political information. *Critical Review*, 18(1–3), 255–278. Available from: https://doi.org/10.1080 /08913810608443660

Trudeau, P., 1971. *Debates at the House of Commons*. 8 October 1971.

United Nations, Department of Economic and Social Affairs, 2019. *International migration 2019: Report (ST/ESA/SER.A/438)*.

Van der Eijk, C. and Niemöller, B., 1984. Theoretical and methodological considerations in the use of left–right scales. Paper presented to the ECPR Joint Sessions, Salzburg.

Vrânceanu, A. and Lachat, R., 2021. Do parties influence public opinion on immigration? Evidence from Europe. *Journal of Elections, Public Opinion and Parties*, 31(1), 1–21. Available from: https://doi.org/10.1080/17457289.2018.1554665

Weber, W. and Saris, W.E., 2015. The relationship between issues and an individual's left–right orientation. *Acta Politica*, 50(2), 193–213. Available from: https://doi.org/10.1057/ ap.2014.5

Wilkes, R., Guppy, N., and Farris, L., 2007. Right-wing parties and anti-foreigner sentiment in Europe. *American Sociological Review*, 72(5), 831–840. Available from: https://doi.org /10.1177/000312240707200509

Wilkes, R., Guppy, N., and Farris, L., 2008. "No thanks, we're full": Individual characteristics, national context, and changing attitudes toward immigration. *International Migration Review*, 42(2), 302–329. Available from: https://doi.org/10.1111/j.1747-7379.2008 .00126.x

CHAPTER 11

Partisanship and public opinion

······································

Laura B. Stephenson

INTRODUCTION

When it comes to understanding why people hold the opinions they do, we often think about a number of factors: where someone lives, how old they are, their economic situation, and many other individual- and contextual-level determinants, as illustrated in the chapters from Parts 2 and 3. All of these can shape what a person thinks is the right policy for a political issue that will benefit them, either by improving their own personal situation or by corresponding to their view of a just society. We might expect someone with low income, for example, to be in favour of more social services because they are more likely to need them. Similarly, we might expect that immigrants would be more supportive of generous immigration policies that would help others like themselves.

There is another factor, the topic of this chapter, that also needs to be considered when thinking about policy opinions: partisanship. This might seem strange. Why would which party a person supports affect how they benefit from specific policy initiatives? Unlike knowing someone's socioeconomic status, it is not obvious how party support is related to what kinds of policies will improve someone's daily life. But in fact, because political parties tend to represent a bundle of issue-positions that make up party platforms and programmes, knowing which party a person supports can tell us quite a lot about their opinions. For example, being a supporter of a conservative party has been associated with preferences for less immigration (Gravelle, 2018).

This chapter explores the relationship between partisanship and public opinion. First, I define partisanship and discuss its measurement. Second, I discuss the mechanisms of the relationship between partisanship and public opinion. Finally, I delve into comparative data to demonstrate how public opinion on immigration is related

DOI: 10.4324/9781003121992-13

to partisanship before showing some interesting variation related to the intensity of party support and measurement in the Canadian case.

DEFINING PARTISANSHIP

What is partisanship? One must start by understanding what the term means and where it comes from. Partisanship is also known as "party identification." The concept is most famously described in *The American Voter* (Campbell et al., 1960), an early investigation into voting behaviour with survey data. The authors found that one of the most important factors that influenced vote choice was the party that someone identified with. This might seem obvious, but the key finding of Campbell et al. is that partisanship colours evaluations of candidates, policies, and government performance. In their view, party identification is a long-standing, psychological attachment to a party that has additional, indirect effects on vote choice through other factors that affect voting. Partisanship has been called the "unmoved mover" (Johnston, 2006) because it is expected to be a stable identification that affects other, more temporary opinions and attitudes that people hold.

Although influential, not all researchers agree with this description of party identification. One of the most different is Fiorina's (1981) concept of a "running tally." In this formulation, party identification is a rational summary measure of the positive and negative evaluations of a party held by a voter. The biggest difference from the Campbell et al. perspective is that a running tally of evaluations is expected to change as more information is gathered, so voters should be constantly gathering new inputs and updating their evaluations. While many researchers agree that party identification is not static (Whiteley, 1988; Lupu, 2013), it is generally understood to be "sticky," or slow to change.

More in line with the psychological conceptualization of party identification, several scholars prioritize the emotional aspects of partisanship. Greene (1999) argues that partisanship is a social identity, and like any other social identity, it creates an "us vs. them" dynamic that enforces loyalty to a party. Recently, scholars like Huddy, Mason, and Aarøe (2015) and Iyengar and Westwood (2015) have focused on the expressive or affective component of partisanship, demonstrating that one's partisanship can lead to negative feelings towards out-groups. This is related to what we know about social identities from work by Tajfel (1974) and Tajfel and Turner (1979). Identifying with one group is often strengthened by opposing an out-group. Importantly, this can occur even in the absence of issue polarization – out-parties do not need to support a hated policy position for a partisan to dislike them.

Huddy et al. (2018) suggest a useful categorization: that the various views of partisanship can be categorized as either instrumental or expressive. The instrumental category aligns with the idea of a running tally that adjusts with additional information. The expressive category, on the other hand, integrates the ideas of psychological attachments, social identities, and affective orientations. Green, Palmquist, and Schickler (2002) titled their book *Partisan Hearts and Minds* to emphasize their view that partisanship was much more than just a rational calculation, subject to change with new information. Expressive forms of partisanship are more akin to sports team loyalties – full of emotion and loyalty (even during losing streaks!). This view of partisanship fits well with the way that Campbell et al. (1960) understood partisanship as colouring other evaluations, similar to a pair of "rose-coloured glasses."

Thinking of partisanship as an expressive identity highlights that supporting one party entails a rejection of others. Using the sports team analogy, supporting one team usually means disliking their rivals. Recent work by Iyengar and Westwood (2015) documents how partisanship leads to negative out-party attitudes in the two-party American system. They find that partisanship's impact is stronger than that of racial identity (a significant social cleavage) and note "that hostile feelings for the opposing party are ingrained and automatic in [partisan] voters' minds" (p. 691).

Relating partisanship to negative feelings towards out-groups is not, however, a new idea. In fact, negative attitudes were part of *The American Voter* view of party identification (Maggiotto and Piereson, 1977). In Wattenberg's view (1982, p. 31), "[i]f partisanship represents a long-term force that is resistant to short-term trends favoring a particular party, then it should involve some sense of rejection of the other major party in order to insulate partisans from shifts to the opposition." Rose and Mishler (1998) actually identify different types of partisanship based upon whether it includes positive and/or negative attitudes. It is possible, in their view, even to hold a partisanship that is only negative (rejection of a specific party). This is similar to the argumentation put forward by Wattenberg (1982), who went so far as to say that partisanship cannot be fully understood without looking at attitudes towards political alternatives. Negative partisanship has been documented in many countries (Anderson, McGregor, and Stephenson, 2021), including the United States (Abramowitz and Webster, 2016), post-Communist countries (Rose and Mishler, 1998), Canada (McGregor et al., 2015; Caruana et al., 2015); and Brazil (Samuels and Zucco, 2018).

While partisanship has been found to be a significant political factor around the world (although with some disagreement about whether it is always separate from vote choice; see Thomassen, 1976), there is variation that should be recognized. Importantly, the concept was first developed in a two-party system (the US) where supporting one party naturally means not supporting the other, in a zero-sum fashion. In multi-party systems, however, this one-for-one exchange does not hold. If partisanship is an instrumental, rational attachment then this means little, as one still prefers the party closest to them on the issues. If we think of the other, identity-based, affective variant (which is more and more common in recent research) then there is another implication. If affective partisanship implies both affinity for one party (and its related issue-positions and candidates) as well as a negative affinity for the other party (and its related issue-positions and candidates), then a multi-party system might complicate things. However, Huddy, Bankert, and Davies (2018) have demonstrated that expressive partisanship exists even in multi-party systems where there are multiple out-groups.

MEASURING PARTISANSHIP

Party identification is measured somewhat differently around the world. In the United States, where the measure originated, survey respondents are asked "Generally speaking, do you usually think of yourself as [a Democrat, a Republican/a Republican, a Democrat], an Independent, or what?"[1] Those who choose a party are then asked about intensity: "Would you call yourself a strong [Democrat/Republican] or a not very strong [Democratic/Republican]?" Those who answer Independent, no preference, other or don't know are asked a follow-up question about thinking of themselves as "closer" to the Republican Party or to the Democratic Party. American researchers use these questions to construct a seven-point scale ranging from very strong Democrat to very strong Republican, with indicators for leaning, weak, and strong partisans.

While the exact phrasing of the question changes slightly from country to country, asking about party identification, separate from voting and as a general attitude, is common. Blais et al. (2001) show that how the question is asked has implications for measuring partisanship in the United Kingdom, Canada, and the US. They note three similarities across the usual measures used in each country – each includes some allusion to thinking of oneself as a partisan, references a time period outside of the present, and follows up with a question to assess intensity. There are also differences, most prominently whether there is an explicit option for non-partisanship. Blais et al. compare the native measures to a common one that was fielded in each country as part of the Comparative Study of Electoral Systems (CSES). The common measure is asked in three parts: first about holding a party preference, then about which party, then about strength. In the recent Module 5 of the CSES, the exact wording was: "Do you usually think of yourself as close to any particular party?"; "Which party do you feel closest to?"; and "Do you feel very close to this party, somewhat close, or not very close?"[2] Blais and his colleagues find that there is a significant difference in the number of individuals identified as a partisan using each measure in Canada and the United Kingdom, but a much smaller difference in the United States. This suggests that voters did not interpret the questions in the same way in each country. Nonetheless, they find that strong party identification is related to party evaluations, leader evaluations, and vote choice in all cases.

Figure 11.1 demonstrates the distribution of partisanship strength using the CSES measure across the countries studied in this volume. Note that the modal category in most countries is identifying as "somewhat close" to a political party. In Switzerland, for example, 39% of respondents identify that way, while in Canada and Britain a majority (56% in each case) do. In Portugal, a majority indicate they do not feel close to any party, but the United States is the opposite – no respondents identified as non-partisans. This is a curious result and can be compared to other measures of partisanship. The American National Election Study (ANES) also asks respondents about party identification but uses the "Generally speaking" formulation. That data shows 12% of respondents identifying as Independents in 2020 (which is not an option in the CSES question).[3] This small comparison demonstrates how question wording can make a difference for how many people are identified as partisans.

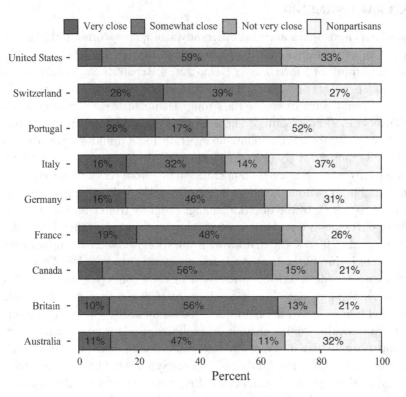

FIGURE 11.1 Distribution of partisanship strength, by country.

Recently, researchers have suggested other ways of measuring partisanship that focus more on its affective components. The US-style measure has been criticized for mixing two different concepts together – a general political attitude (support for a party) and an identity ("do you usually think of yourself as") (Greene, 2002). Greene and others have used variations of the Identification with a Psychological Group Scale (IDPG) developed by Mael and Tetrick (1992) to assess the degree to which someone holds a partisan social identity. Questions ask about feeling criticized when the party is criticized and happy when it is praised, for example, as well as referring to it as "my party." Huddy et al. (2015) used questions similar to those used for national identity, such as "How well does the term [Democrat/ Republican] describe you?" In a comparative study of four nations, Bankert, Huddy, and Rosema (2017) adapted the IDPG scale, adding some new items, to create another version of an expressive partisanship battery.

WHAT DOES PARTY IDENTIFICATION DO AND HOW DOES THAT RELATE TO PUBLIC OPINION?

Party identification can act as a shortcut for many of the decisions that voters need to make. Imagine going into a voting booth and not having had time to read about each of the candidates on the ballot. How would you decide? Without knowing specifics, it would be easy for a voter to default to vote for the candidate affiliated with the party they usually supported. In this way, partisanship can act as a heuristic, or shortcut, that people use to help them make sense of something ambiguous, just like ideology as discussed in the precedent chapter. When full information is not available to help voters form opinions about a candidate, for example, they can infer from their party label whether the candidate is likely to stand for something they would agree with, reasoning that a co-partisan is more likely to hold similar beliefs than an out-partisan. Along these lines, research has shown that partisanship can influence evaluations of candidates (Weisberg and Rusk, 1970; Lavine and Gschwend, 2007).

Similarly, party labels can guide how citizens understand complex political issues. Knowing which party supports which issues can help citizens understand which types of attitudes are "appropriate" for them, in the sense of being consistent with their other values. In this way, party labels can act as "cues" for individuals about what their own opinions should be. The influence of party cues on public opinion has been demonstrated in many different country contexts, from the United States (for example, Kam, 2005) to Canada (Merolla et al., 2008) to Russia (Brader and Tucker, 2009) to Denmark (Slothuus and Bisgaard, 2021), and especially on issues that are more difficult to assess (Nicholson and Hansford, 2014).

In some cases, the links between partisanship and attitudes can be due to motivated reasoning. This type of reasoning occurs when someone's biases push them to arrive at a specific outcome that is consistent with existing beliefs (Kunda, 1990; Slothuus and de Vreese, 2010; Taber and Lodge, 2006). This can come about in two ways – by seeking out information that is in line with stances (confirmation bias) and discounting or ignoring information that is contradictory (disconfirmation bias) (Taber and Lodge, 2006). Partisans can even be motivated to evaluate information in ways that allow them to maintain or bolster their partisan leanings, such as responsibility attributions (Tilly and Hobolt, 2011) and perceptions of the economy (Jones, 2020). Even whether information is considered when forming opinions can be influenced by partisanship (Zaller, 1992). However, Bolsen, Druckman, and Cook (2014) show that the influence of party cues can be partially mitigated when people are motivated to form "accurate" opinions.

Partisanship is therefore an important consideration in understanding public opinion because parties structure how people understand the political world. Party identification is a psychological connection with a party that can be internalized as part of one's identity and shape their vote choices, but its reach is so much more than that – it provides a structure for other political views. Leeper and Slothuus (2014) have proposed a "partisan conflict-predisposition model" to better understand opinion formation. They argue that parties structure the choices available to voters as well as provide information about how the choices relate to citizens' own predispositions. For example, when the options available for a particular policy area are linked to the ideas put forward by the parties, then those options become the political choices available to voters. If parties all agree on an issue, then there is unlikely to be any differences among supporters of different parties. If parties disagree, however, then a predisposition to support a party can translate into support for that party's policy position.

Polling information consistently demonstrates that partisanship and public opinion are related. Take support for environmental policies, for example – supporters of right-wing parties tend to be much less supportive than Green Party supporters. Similarly, those who support liberal parties typically support liberal policies, and vice versa. That there is a relationship, however, does not tell us anything about which affects which – does partisanship affect public opinion or public opinion affect partisanship? Research on party cues suggests that partisanship is a driver of public opinion, but while there is considerable evidence that that is true, it is important to recognize that the relationship between partisanship and public opinion flows both ways. On the one hand, clear party stances structure political issues for voters and can sway the opinions of their supporters; people act to confirm their identity as partisans by establishing consistency between their partisanship and their views. On the other hand, public opinion also plays a role in influencing party stances (Soroka and Wlezien, 2009) as well as leading voters to support whichever party shares their views. After all, citizens align themselves with a party (adopt a party identification) when that party is seen as best representing their interests. This is very much in line with the running tally or instrumental view of partisanship (Fiorina, 1981).

In practical terms, the link between partisanship and public opinion, regardless of causal direction, means that if you know that someone supports a conservative party, for example, you may be able to infer that they are in favour of lower taxes and a weaker social safety net. Someone who supports a more progressive party is likely to be in favour of socially progressive policies, such as increasing services to serve the disadvantaged. To the extent that public policies can be aligned on a political spectrum, it is therefore possible to translate partisan support into likely public opinion. Partisanship can be both an indicator of public opinion as well as a driver of public opinion.

For the purpose of this chapter, whether public opinion or partisanship comes first is not important. My focus is on understanding the relationship between the two concepts and whether it varies across countries, with the strength of partisanship or measurement. In the remainder of this chapter, I concentrate specifically on public opinion about immigration. As with the other chapters in Part 2, I use three separate and one combined measure of public opinion, drawing upon the following attitudes: whether immigrants are good for the economy, whether immigrants harm a country's culture, and whether immigrants increase crime rates.

PARTISANSHIP AND PUBLIC OPINION ON IMMIGRATION

Because there are many different parties in each country, I have summarized partisan identification into general ideological stances – left, centre, and right. Given that immigration tends to divide people with more conservative views (who are less open to accepting people into their country) from those with more liberal views, this helps us to understand whether immigration opinion aligns with partisanship in each country. Table 11.A1 in the Appendix shows how the parties in each country fit into this categorization.

To begin our look at the link between party identification and public opinion about immigration, we turn to Figures 11.2–11.4. These figures show the relationship between party identification and three measures of public opinion for the nine Western democracies under study in Part 2 of the book. Quite clearly, there is variation in how supportive different partisans are of immigration. Figure 11.2 shows the mean opinion scores for whether immigrants increase crime rates for partisans of each ideological position. In each country, we see that the mean response for partisans on the left is lower (more ideologically liberal) on the five-point scale (1–5) than the mean of partisans on the right (more ideologically conservative). In most cases, the distance is over 1.0 points on the scale – for example, from 2.16 to 3.30 (1.14 points) in Australia, or from 2.66 to 3.92 (1.26 points) in Switzerland.

Visually, the results for the United States most clearly demonstrate what we might expect – that supporters of the right-wing party (Republicans) are more likely to agree that immigrants increase crime rates, while left-wing supporters (Democrats) are more likely to disagree. This division is also visible in France and Italy. However, the spread between left-wing and right-wing in Italy is far greater – 2.29 points – and

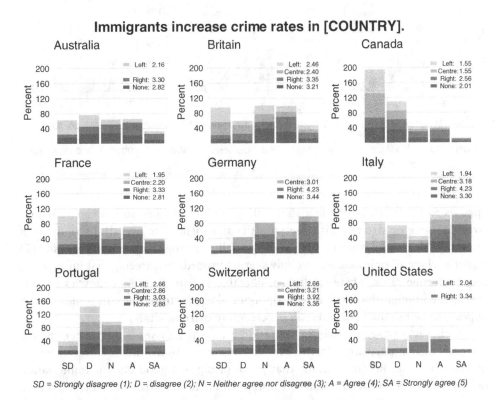

Immigrants increase crime rates in [COUNTRY].

SD = Strongly disagree (1); D = disagree (2); N = Neither agree nor disagree (3); A = Agree (4); SA = Strongly agree (5)

FIGURE 11.2 Attitudes about how immigrants are perceived to affect a country's crime, by party identification.

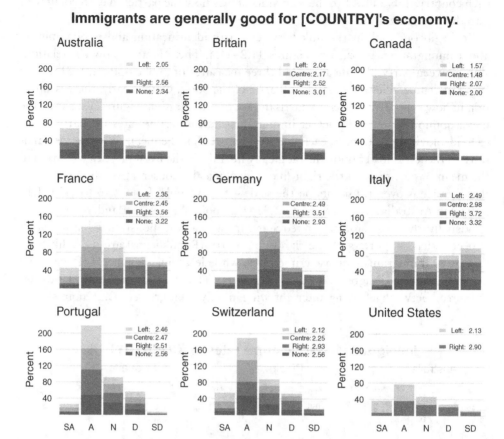

FIGURE 11.3 Attitudes about how immigrants are perceived to affect a country's economy, by party identification.

appears to be driven by the fact that Italians are more likely to indicate that they strongly agree or strongly disagree with the statement. The overall distribution of opinion in that country is bimodal, and especially striking compared to the results in Canada where all opinions are strongly skewed towards disagreeing that immigrants increase crime rates. There is also considerable variation across countries in how clearly the immigration issue divides opinions along partisan lines. In some cases, it appears to be minimal (Canada); in others, more extreme (Italy).

Another way to see whether immigration is a partisan issue is by considering the opinions of non-partisans. To the extent that non-partisans hold neutral views on an issue, it could be an indicator that partisanship is a good cue for immigration opinions. We see this most clearly in Britain where non-partisans are most likely to indicate they neither agree nor disagree that immigrants increase crime rates. A similar pattern exists in Australia, and in Portugal we see that non-partisans are more likely to avoid either extreme response. Contrast this with the pattern in Canada and in Switzerland, where there seems to be an overall positive (Canada) and negative (Switzerland) view of immigrants and crime. In those countries, knowing the type of party that someone supports would be less helpful for understanding attitudes on immigration.

Figure 11.3 shows the relationship between party identification and opinions about whether immigrants are good for the country's economy. Note that the horizontal scale labels are reversed here, so that more liberal responses (in this case, agreement) are still to the left on the graph. The results here do not follow the same pattern as the immigration and crime question. Whereas in Figure 11.2 the United States showed the clearest contrast between party supporters, in Figure 11.3 we see that supporters of both parties in that country are more likely to agree that immigrants are good for the economy. Republicans were more likely to agree that immigrants increased crime rates, but they do not have an equally negative view of

[COUNTRY]'s culture is generally harmed by immigrants.

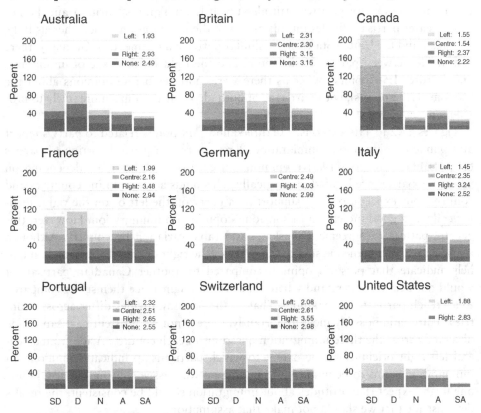

SD = Strongly disagree (1); D = disagree (2); N = Neither agree nor disagree (3); A = Agree (4); SA = Strongly agree (5)

FIGURE 11.4 Attitudes about how immigrants are perceived to affect a country's culture, by party identification.

immigrants when it comes to the economy. The views of Democrats, however, are more consistently positive.

We see similar between-measure variation in other countries as well. Take Italy, for example. The difference between the means of left-wing and right-wing supporters is largest in Figure 11.2 but is considerably smaller (1.23 points) in Figure 11.3. Looking at Switzerland, we see that there is overall agreement that immigrants are good for the economy, but there was more partisan variation in views about immigrants and crime. Indeed, while the left and right positions of partisans are consistent across Figures 11.2 and 11.3, the distance on the five-point scale between supporters of left-wing and right-wing parties is smaller in each country for attitudes about immigrants and the economy compared to immigrants and crime. This suggests less partisan division on this aspect of public opinion regarding immigration.

Figure 11.4 shows opinions about immigrants and their impact on a country's culture. Once again, left-wing partisans express more liberal attitudes and right-wing partisans express more conservative attitudes, across all nine countries. However, we also see many countries where the clarity of the partisan opinion divide is not replicated from the other questions about immigrants (except Canada, which has consistent cross-party positive attitudes towards immigrants). Britain and France show clearer partisan divides on this aspect of the immigration issue, whereas Italy, Portugal, and the United States show similar partisan agreement. In Germany, there is a divide between parties of the centre and the right on the issue of immigrants and culture (1.54 points), whereas there were more temperate opinions about the economy (1.02 points), with partisans of both ideological groups more likely to provide centrist views.

Figures 11.2 to 11.4 demonstrate three important points related to party support and public opinion about immigration. First, there is a general sorting of parties towards liberal or conservative opinions on each of the questions, depending on where the parties are located ideologically. This holds across all nine countries and confirms our expectation that supporting a party on the left or on the right, ideologically, is a good indication of someone's opinion on immigration. However, this general pattern of agreement masks considerable variation by country. Although knowing whether someone supports a party of the right or the left in Canada might help indicate that person's opinion compared to another Canadian partisan, it would not help to understand where that person might place themselves compared to a French partisan, for example. That is, the partisan divides differ across countries. Third, and possibly most importantly, there is not a consistent partisan divide observed across the three immigration questions in each country. Aside from a general left-right orientation, the extent to which partisanship indicates opinions on immigration seems to be nuanced depending on what issue is being queried. While one might expect that attitudes about immigration should be consistent, the results demonstrate that we should not make that assumption.

This brings us to Figure 11.5, which shows results for a summary index of immigration attitudes (averaging across all three issues). The lines in these figures show the overall trend of left-wing, centrist, right-wing, and non-partisan individuals in

Immigration index by party identification

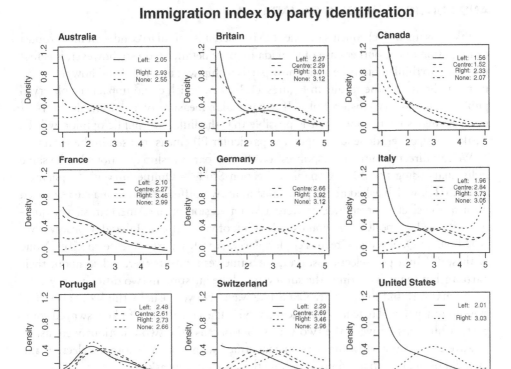

Values range from 1 to 5 with higher values indicating less favourable attitudes toward immigration.

FIGURE 11.5 Attitudes about how immigrants are perceived to affect a country's economy, crime and culture (index), by party identification.

each country. In five countries (Australia, Britain, Canada, Italy, and the United States), knowing whether someone supports a party of the left is a good indicator of their views on immigration, demonstrated by the clear bias towards more liberal views. However, knowing that someone supports a right-wing party will only be a good indication of public opinion in Germany, Italy, and, to a lesser degree, France. Only in Italy and France do we see strong upward spikes in attitudes towards the extremes of the immigration opinion scale among partisans of opposite sides of the ideological spectrum. This suggests that immigration is a consistently divisive issue for partisans in those countries only. Finally, Canada most clearly stands out as an outlier with cross-partisan support for immigration. In this country, knowing a person's party identification will do little to help understand their public opinion, at least from a comparative perspective. When it comes to understanding public opinion about immigration, then, party identification is a somewhat (but not perfectly, and not everywhere) useful indicator. Party identification can be a proxy for opinions, but only when there is partisan disagreement.

A CLOSER LOOK: PARTISAN STRENGTH
AND PUBLIC OPINION IN CANADA

To take this (tentative) conclusion one step further, it is useful to conduct a more robust examination of the outlier case of Canada in more detail. To do so, however, it is first necessary to think a bit more about how partisanship was measured and how measurement might impact the results in Figures 11.3–11.5, which could impact the observed public opinion–partisanship links. If a particular measure of partisanship over- or underestimates party support, it is possible that the link with public opinion will be weaker or stronger, depending upon the particular PID measure used in the survey.

We can directly compare responses to different partisanship questions by the same individuals using the 2019 Canadian Election Study – Online Survey[4] (Stephenson et al., 2021), which asked about partisanship in two different ways. In a survey asked prior to the election, respondents were asked a version of the American survey question – "In federal politics, do you usually think of yourself as a: Liberal, Conservative, N.D.P., Bloc Québécois, Green, People's Party, Another party (please specify), None of these?"[5] In a post-election survey, the same respondents were asked about their partisanship again. This time, the survey asked the question in two different ways, the traditional way and then a more CSES-like way: "Do you usually think of yourself as close to any particular federal political party?" The election itself likely swayed some party affiliations between the two waves, but because the two questions were asked in wave 2 we can see how many people identified with a party before the election and then did or did not after, comparing how the question was asked.

Table 11.1 shows the proportion of people who indicated they were a partisan in wave 1 of the survey and how many indicated the same partisanship in wave 2, with the two separate measures. For simplicity only the three largest national parties and non-partisans are shown.

The diagonal entries show that about 80% of partisans retained their allegiance to the major parties when asked the traditional question in wave 2. However, with the CSES measure the rate falls to between 53 and 61%. The number of non-partisans who retain non-partisanship in wave 2 is also relatively low using the traditional question, compared to party loyalty, while it is higher in the CSES comparison. Clearly, fewer people indicate they are a partisan with the CSES measure than with the traditional measure.

TABLE 11.1 Comparing measures of party identification

Wave 1	Traditional measure				CSES measure			
	LPC	CPC	NDP	Non-partisan	LPC	CPC	NDP	Non-partisan
LPC	82%	2%	5%	6%	57%	1%	9%	30%
CPC	5%	82%	2%	6%	3%	61%	2%	31%
NDP	7%	5%	78%	5%	4%	3%	53%	35%
Non-partisan	12%	10%	7%	61%	5%	5%	6%	80%

This is also evident in the proportion of non-partisans identified with each question. Almost 17% did not identify with a party when asked the traditional question prior to the election, and after the election that number fell slightly to 15%. However, with the CSES measure the proportion of non-partisans jumps to 41%. Further, 33% of people who indicated they identified with a party in wave 1 of the survey did not indicate they were "close to" a party in wave 2 (only 6% of partisans indicated no party affiliation in wave 2 with the traditional measure). The sharp increase in non-partisans using the CSES "closer to" wording confirms the findings of Blais et al. (2001) and suggests that measurement is really an important consideration when looking at partisanship and public opinion. More people would be classified as partisans using the traditional measure than the "closer to" measure, which could lead to a dilution in the coherence of attitudes in the group.

How does measurement affect the results for the relationship between public opinion on immigration and partisanship? In Figures 11.2–11.5 we looked at partisans identified by the CSES question, undifferentiated by strength. But, in addition to how it was measured, how strongly someone identifies with a party (as shown in Figure 11.1) could have an impact on how closely their attitudes link to their partisanship. Figure 11.6 digs deeper into this, looking at immigration attitudes (using the immigration index) amongst Canadian partisans of the three major parties in the 2019 Canadian Election Study, differentiated by both the way that the party identification question was asked and reported strength. Figure 11.6 shows the mean immigration index values for strong and weak partisans identified by the traditional question in wave 1 of the survey (prior to the election; CPS), by the traditional question in

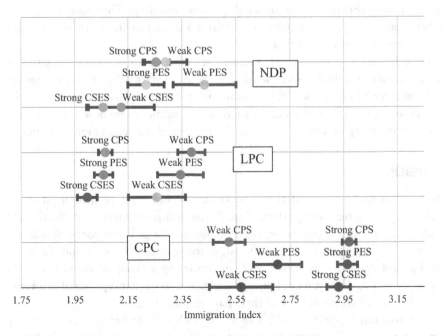

FIGURE 11.6 Canadian immigration attitudes, by party identification measure and strength.

wave 2 (after the election; PES), and by the "closer to" question in wave 2 (CSES; the error bars show the linearized standard error of the estimated means).

Figure 11.6 provides insight into three aspects of public opinion and partisanship: strength, differentiation, and measurement. First, weak partisans have more moderate views than strong partisans. Across the three major Canadian parties, weak identifiers have more centrist attitudes about immigration than strong identifiers. The link between public opinion and partisanship is also less clear for weak partisans – a weak Conservative is not very different from a weak Liberal or weak NDP on the immigration index. The story is much different for strong partisans. Especially comparing Liberals and Conservatives, strong identifiers from different parties hold very different attitudes about immigration.

Second, we see that there is actually variation if we compare strong partisans, contrary to the overall similarity across Canadian partisans shown in Figures 11.2–11.5. In those figures, the differences between the party on the left (NDP) and the centre (Liberals) is almost imperceptible. In Figure 11.6, however, we see that strong Liberals are actually more liberal on the issue of immigration than strong NDP supporters. This complicates the basic pattern shown earlier, as the relationship between immigration attitudes and ideology is not as linear as expected.

Finally, looking at the data this way also clarifies the importance of measurement. The data in Figures 11.2–11.5 are drawn from estimates using the CSES partisanship question. In Figure 11.6, we see that which measure of partisanship is used has little impact on the positions of Liberal and Conservative identifiers, both weak and strong, but it has more consequences for NDP supporters. NDP partisans identified by the CSES measure are much further to the left in their attitudes than NDP partisans identified through the traditional question-wording. Therefore, the linear pattern between ideology and immigration attitudes shown earlier could be partially due to how partisanship was measured.

This more in-depth look at the Canadian data adds an important caveat to the tentative conclusion reached above. While for the most part partisan identification is a good indicator of one's opinion on immigration compared to other partisans in their own country, it is not universal. It can also be conditional on how partisans are identified, the intensity of identification, and the proximity of campaign activities.

CONCLUSION

This chapter has tackled one of the most common, but perhaps also most complex, factors in public opinion: partisanship. Partisanship, or party identification, is commonly understood as a psychological attachment to a political party. While the nature of the concept has long been debated, a growing consensus is that the most influential aspect of partisanship is affective, similar to a group identity. Partisans not only support a specific political party, but they also evaluate political information, candidates, and issues in light of their partisan leaning.

The party that one supports can be a signal of one's opinions as well as a factor in shaping those opinions. This chicken-and-egg issue does not detract from the fact that, in most cases, knowing a person's party identification means knowing their opinion on political issues. The results in this chapter for the issue of immigration generally support this position. Across nine Western democracies, there is general agreement that partisans of left-wing parties hold more liberal attitudes while partisans of right-wing parties hold more conservative attitudes. However, there is important variation. First, the degree of party polarization on the issue of immigration varies considerably across countries. Second, the partisanship–public opinion relationship varies with the specific aspect of immigration (economy, culture, or crime) being considered. Third, as shown with a closer look at Canadian data, the partisanship–opinion relationship varies with the strength of one's partisan identification. Weaker partisans tend to have less polarized attitudes, at least in Canada where there is very little distinction among different partisans to begin with. Finally, how one measures party identification has implications for the relationships observed. While the overall pattern of partisan differences on an issue may hold, the extent of the differences can vary.

SUMMARY POINTS

- Partisanship, or party identification, is commonly understood as a psychological attachment to a political party. While the nature of the concept has long been debated, a growing consensus is that the most influential aspect of partisanship is affective, similar to a group identity.
- Partisans not only support a specific political party, but they also evaluate political information, candidates, and issues in light of their partisan leaning. Because political parties tend to represent a bundle of issue-positions that make up party platforms and programmes, knowing which party a person supports can tell us quite a lot about their opinions.
- By examining nine Western democracies, we found that those who identify with parties on the left are generally more favourable to immigrants than those that identify with parties on the right. There are, however, some interesting country differences.

NOTES

1 The order of presentation of the parties is randomized.
2 There is also a follow-up question for those who do not indicate closeness right away, "Do you feel yourself a little closer to one of the political parties than the others?"
3 This result can be found at https://electionstudies.org/resources/anes-guide/top-tables/?id=22.
4 The 2019 Canadian Election Study was conducted in two different modes, telephone (probability sample) and online (non-probability sample). The telephone data is included in the CSES dataset, but it contains fewer questions than the online data. For the purpose of expounding upon measurement issues, partisanship and public opinion, Table 11.1 and Figure 11.5 use the online dataset (Stephenson et al. 2020).
5 The question also included a "Don't know/ Prefer not to answer" option.

SUGGESTED FURTHER READINGS

Blais, A., Gidengil, E., Nadeau, R., and Nevitte, N., 2001. Measuring party identification: Britain, Canada, and the United States. *Political Behavior*, 23(1), 5–22.

Gravelle, T.B., 2018. Partisanship, local context, group threat, and Canadian attitudes towards immigration and refugee policy. *Migration Studies*, 6(3), 448–467.

Johnston, R., 2006. Party identification: Unmoved mover or sum of preferences? *Annual Review of Political Science*, 9(1), 329–351.

Slothuus, R., and Bisgaard, M., 2021. How political parties shape public opinion in the real world. *American Journal of Political Science*, 65(4), 896–911.

REFERENCES

Abramowitz, A.I. and Webster, S., 2016. The rise of negative partisanship and the nationalization of U.S. elections in the 21st century. *Electoral Studies*, 41, 12–22.

Anderson, C.A., McGregor, R.M., and Stephenson, L.B., 2021. Us vs. them: Do the rules of the game encourage negative partisanship? *European Journal of Political Research.* Available from: https://doi.org/10.1111/1475-6765.12485

Bankert, A., Huddy, L., and Rosema, M., 2017. Measuring partisanship as a social identity in multi-party systems. *Political Behavior*, 39, 103–132.

Blais, A., Gidengil, E., Nadeau, R., and Nevitte, N., 2001. Measuring party identification: Britain, Canada, and the United States. *Political Behavior*, 23(1), 5–22.

Bolsen, T., Druckman, J.N., and Cook, F.L., 2014. The influence of partisan motivated reasoning on public opinion. *Political Behavior*, 36: 235–262.

Brader, T.A. and Tucker, J.A., 2009. What's left behind when the party's over: Survey experiments on the effects of partisan cues in Putin's Russia. *Politics & Policy*, 37, 843–868.

Campbell, A., Converse, P.E., Miller, W.E., and Stokes, D.E., 1960. *The American Voter.* New York: John Wiley & Sons, Inc.

Caruana, N.J., McGregor, R.M., and Stephenson, L.B., 2015. The power of the dark side: Negative partisanship and political behaviour in Canada. *Canadian Journal of Political Science*, 48(4), 771–789.

Fiorina, M.P., 1981. *Retrospective voting in American national elections.* New Haven, CT: Yale University Press.

Gravelle, T.B., 2018. Partisanship, local context, group threat, and Canadian attitudes towards immigration and refugee policy. *Migration Studies*, 6(3), 448–467.

Green, D., Palmquist, B., and Schickler, E., 2002. *Partisan hearts and minds: Political parties and the social identities of voters.* New Haven, CT: Yale University Press.

Greene, S., 2002. The social-psychological measurement of partisanship. *Political Behavior*, 24(3), 171–197.

Greene, S., 1999. Understanding party identification: A social identity approach. *Political Psychology*, 20(2), 393–403.

Huddy, L., Bankert, A., and Davies, C., 2018. Expressive versus instrumental partisanship in multiparty European systems. *Political Psychology*, 39, 173–199. https://doi.org/10.1111/pops.12482

Huddy, L., Mason, L., and Aarøe, L., 2015. Expressive partisanship: Campaign involvement, political emotion, and partisan identity. *American Political Science Review*, 109(1), 1–17.

Iyengar, S. and Westwood, S.J., 2015. Fear and loathing across party lines: New evidence on group polarization. *American Journal of Political Science*, 59(3), 690–707.

Johnston, R., 2006. Party identification: Unmoved mover or sum of preferences? *Annual Review of Political Science*, 9(1), 329–351.

Jones, P.E., 2020. Partisanship, political awareness, and retrospective evaluations, 1956–2016. *Political Behavior*, 42, 1295–1317.

Kam, C.D., 2005. Who toes the party line? Cues, values, and individual differences. *Political Behavior*, 27(2), 163–182.

Kunda, Z., 1990. The case for motivated reasoning. *Psychological Bulletin*, 108(3), 480–498.

Lavine, H. and Gschwend, T., 2007. Issues, party and character: The moderating role of ideological thinking on candidate evaluation. *British Journal of Political Science*, 37(1), 139–163.

Leeper, T.J. and Slothuus, R., 2014. Political parties, motivated reasoning, and public opinion formation. *Political Psychology*, 35(Supplement 1), 129–156.

Lupu, N., 2013. Party brands and partisanship: Theory with evidence from a survey experiment in Argentina. *American Journal of Political Science*, 57(1), 49–64.

Mael, F.A. and Tetrick, L.E., 1992. Identifying organizational identification. *Educational and Psychological Measurement*, 52(4), 813–824.

Maggiotto, M.A. and Pieresen, J.E., 1977. Partisan identification and electoral choice: The hostility hypothesis. *American Journal of Political Science*, 21(4), 745–767.

McGregor, R.M., Caruana, N.J., and Stephenson, L.B., 2015. Negative partisanship in a multi-party system: The case of Canada. *Journal of Elections, Public Opinion and Parties*, 25(3), 300–316.

Merolla, J.L., Stephenson, L.B., and Zechmeister, E.J., 2008. Can Canadians take a hint? The (in)effectiveness of party labels as information shortcuts in Canada. *Canadian Journal of Political Science*, 41(3), 673–696.

Nicholson, S. and Hansford, T., 2014. Partisans in robes: Party cues and public acceptance of supreme court decisions. *American Journal of Political Science*, 58(3), 620–636.

Rose, R. and Mishler, W., 1998. Negative and positive party identification in post-communist countries. *Electoral Studies*, 17(2), 217–234.

Samuels, D.J. and Zucco, C., 2018. *Partisans, antipartisans, and nonpartisans: Voting behavior in Brazil.* New York: Cambridge University Press.

Slothuus, R. and Bisgaard, M., 2021. How Political Parties Shape Public Opinion in the Real World. *American Journal of Political Science* 65(4), 896–911.

Slothuus, R. and de Vreese, C.H., 2010. Political parties, motivated reasoning, and issue framing effects. *The Journal of Politics*, 72(3), 630–645.

Soroka, S.N. and Wlezien, C., 2009. *Degrees of democracy.* New York: Cambridge University Press.

Stephenson, L.B., Harell, A., Rubenson, D., and Loewen, P.J., 2020. 2019 Canadian election study – Online survey. Harvard Dataverse, V1. Available from: https://doi.org/10.7910/DVN/DUS88V

Stephenson, L.B., Harell, A., Rubenson, D., and Loewen, P.L., 2021. Measuring preferences and behaviours in the 2019 Canadian election study. *Canadian Journal of Political Science*, 54(1), 118–124.

Taber, C.S. and Lodge, M., 2006. Motivated skepticism in the evaluation of political beliefs. *American Journal of Political Science*, 50(3), 755–769.

Tajfel, H., 1974. Social identity and intergroup behaviour. *Social Science Information/Sur les Sciences Sociales*, 13(2), 65–93.

Tajfel, H. and Turner, J.C., 1979. An integrative theory of intergroup conflict. In: W.G. Austin and S. Worchel, eds. *The social psychology of intergroup relations*. Monterey, CA: Brooks/Cole, pp. 33–47.

Thomassen, J., 1976. Party identification as a cross-national concept: Its meaning in the Netherlands. In: I. Budge, I. Crewe, and D. Farlie, eds. *Party identification and beyond: Representations of voting and party competition.* London: John Wiley & Sons, 63–79.

Tilly, J. and Hobolt, S.B., 2011. Is the government to blame? An experimental test of how partisanship shapes perceptions of performance and responsibility. *The Journal of Politics*, 73(2), 316–330.

Wattenberg, M.P., 1982. Party identification and party images: A comparison of Britain, Canada, Australia, and the United States. *Comparative Politics*, 15(1), 23–40.

Weisberg, H.F. and Rusk, J.G., 1970. Dimensions of candidate evaluation. *The American Political Science Review*, 64(4), 1167–1185.

Whiteley, P.F., 1988. The causal relationships between issues, candidate evaluations, party identification, and vote choice--the view from "rolling thunder". *The Journal of Politics*, 50(4), 961–984.

Zaller, J.R., 1992. *The nature and origins of mass opinion*. New York: Cambridge University Press.

APPENDIX

TABLE 11.A1 Ideological classification of parties, by country

	Left	Centre	Right
Australia	Australian Labor Party Australian Greens		Liberal Party National Party of Australia United Australia Party One Nation Party
Britain	Green Party SNP Plaid Cymru	Labour Liberal Democrats	Conservatives UKIP
Canada	New Democratic Party Bloc Québécois Green Party	Liberal Party	Conservative Party People's Party
France	Indomitable France	The Republic Onwards! Socialist Party	National Front The Republicans France Arise

Germany	Left Party	Christian Democratic
		    Union of Germany
		Social Democratic Party
		    of Germany
		Free Democratic Party
		Alliance 90/The Greens
			Alternative for Germany

Italy	Free and Equal	Five Star Movement Democratic Party	League Go Italy Brothers of Italy
Portugal	Left Bloc Unitary Democratic Coalition	Socialist Party People-Animals-Nature Social Democratic Party	Alliance People's Party Chega

Switzerland	Social Democratic
	    Party
	Green Party
		Christian Democratic
		    People's Party
		Green Liberal Party
			Swiss People's Party
			Liberal Radical Party

US	Democratic Party Greens		Republican Party Libertarian

PART 3

Context and complexity in determinants of public opinion

Building off the groundwork established in Part 2 exploring the individual-level determinants of public opinion about immigration, the chapters contained in Part 3 deepen our understanding of public opinion by highlighting the additional influence of context and attitudinal complexity on public opinion about immigration and related issues. In a variety of countries, the chapters in Part 3 address the influence on public opinion about immigration of partisan polarization, locally experienced immigrant diversity, labour market vulnerability, linguistic cleavage, media coverage, and racial attitudes. Opening Part 3, Chapter 12 explores the effects of partisan and ideological polarization in Brazil and considers the possibility that respondents on the left and right process information about immigration in different ways. The next chapter (13) shifts the empirical terrain to Japan. This chapter assesses the effects of the presence of foreign workers at the local level (prefecture) and how group conflict theory between immigrant and native-born Japanese influences public opinion about immigrants and immigration in Japan. Chapter 14 is broadly comparative – looking at 18 countries from Europe – and considers whether and when labour market vulnerability can influence opinion on immigration in these states. Language as a political cleavage serves as the focus of Chapter 15. In particular, this chapter explores the extent to which linguistic diversity in Belgium and Canada has any noticeable effect on opinion about immigration. The literature on public opinion is replete with references to the effects of popular media on public opinion and this topic is the focus of Chapter 16. This chapter considers the relationship of media and public opinion on immigration and to a lesser extent the environment and economic globalization in the case of Canada. The last chapter of this part (17) emphasizes the important influence of underlying racial attitudes on opinion about immigration in Canada and the United States. Taken together, the chapters in this part of the volume add depth to our theoretical understanding of the factors driving opinion about immigration. Beyond deepening our theoretical understanding, these chapters are united in their use of sophisticated statistical analyses to consider these relationships.

DOI: 10.4324/9781003121992-14

CHAPTER 12

Immigration and public opinion in Brazil

Taking stock of new waves of migration and polarization

....

Ryan Lloyd and Amâncio Jorge de Oliveira

INTRODUCTION

Migration is one of the most sensitive aspects of regional integration and globalization. This is because the reception of migrants in destination countries represents, in its most direct form, the sharing of public goods between the local population and the migrants. A good part of the anti-integrationist discourses and narratives refer to the risks of integration in terms of losses of jobs and competition for public services (Jaret, 1999; Fussell, 2014).

Two phenomena tend to make the discussion about migration even more sensitive in terms of public opinion. The first refers is the COVID-19 pandemic and its effects, from the point of view of global public health and the mobility of people. The risks associated with flows of migration can provide support more and more support for protectionist government measures (see Benton et al., 2021). The second phenomenon has to do with the political polarization that has become a focus in many countries around the world and is currently growing systematically in Latin America (Singer, 2016; Ellner, 2013; Grigera, 2017; Bruhn and Greene, 2007), as one can observe in the most recent electoral results within the region. As polarization grows, it increases the political sensitivity of migration (Castilla and Sørensen, 2019).

Despite its growing importance, there has been little investment from the Latin American literature in studying the relationship between partisan electoral/political competition and migration. Even though more than 5.5 million Venezuelans have fled the country, primarily to other countries on the region, little is understood about the political positioning of voters in Latin America around migration questions. The literature has made advances in this area, as will be shown in this chapter, in the field of public opinion about how partisan politics affects support for regional integration (Onuki, Mouron, and Urdinez, 2016). But this has not quite extended to the field of migration, which is odd given the topic's popularity in North America and Western

DOI: 10.4324/9781003121992-15

Europe and the size of the Venezuelan diaspora.[1] Venezuelan migration to Brazil, more specifically to the northern region, is important because it is the first wave of immigration after re-democratization (post-military dictatorship) involving the massive displacement of populations. This migration is also important because it is the result of political conflicts generated by the Maduro regime, a representative of leftist populism from the left. This allows us to see if this type of migration, within such an explicitly political Context, has generated an anti-immigrant sentiment among Brazilian voters from certain segments of the ideological spectrum.

This chapter seeks to make an original contribution by specifically addressing the topic of political partisanship and its relation to public opinion regarding migration. It looks to do so in two ways. First, it seeks to determine if support for migration is affected by political partisanship in Brazil (see Chapters 10 and 11 for more on the role of political ideology and partisanship, respectively). Second, it assesses whether Brazilians who identify with the left and the right process information about migration in different ways. In other words, this chapter examines Brazil – a case study from an important area of the world that is rarely studied regarding migration – in order to understand how the opinions of those on the political left and right are affected by new information about migration.

This study draws on original survey experiment data to examine political polarization and migration attitudes. We look to see if Brazilians hold more negative opinions of public policies that either favour or are endorsed by given immigrant communities. We also examine the partisan dimension of migration attitudes, in particular whether the support for migration is lower among those who voted in 2018 for far-right President Jair Bolsonaro (PSL) or among those who voted for his opponent, Fernando Haddad from the centre-left Worker's Party (PT). Finally, we also look to see if this perception varies in accordance with the origin of the migrant, and if European migrants are seen differently than Venezuelan or Haitian migrants, particularly by Bolsonaro and Haddad supporters.

MIGRATION, REGIONAL INTEGRATION, AND PUBLIC OPINION

The literature is rather assertive about the relationship between political ideology and regional integration. It is rather less so, however, when it comes to political ideology and migration, at least in Latin America. Milner and Kubota, for example, find evidence in the U.S. that voters on the left are more likely to support regional integration processes than those on the right (Milner and Kubota, 2005). Similar findings were found in empirical studies that used Brazil and Argentina as case studies (Mouron and Onuki, 2015). Survey experiments using priming found that, in both cases, those who identified with the left had a higher baseline level of support for integration than those on the right. This support was also significantly more resilient among respondents from the left than for those on the right. Specifically, when pressed to respond after receiving a negative piece of information about the South American trade bloc Mercosul (specifically, that Mercosul membership entailed less freedom to establish bilateral treaties), support for integration declined more significantly for respondents from the right than for those from the left. The left therefore held positions about regional integration that were a priori more resilient than those of the right (Onuki, 2015).

Until recently, few studies have shown a connection in Latin America between anti-immigration attitudes and a fear of competition in the labour market (as discussed further in Chapter 14). Meseguer and Maldonado (2015) use surveys similar to those used in this chapter to understand the reasons why a portion of Mexicans consider there to be too many immigrants in the country. They test two hypotheses in particular. The first is of a material nature, related to the risk of competition for jobs through the entrance into the job market of immigrants with similar professional skills. The second is of a social nature, related to the perception of public security risks due to immigrants' origins, depending on whether they are coming from the United States or Central America. They do not find evidence for the former hypothesis, but they do for the latter.

More recently, however, this has begun to change. Acosta Arcarazo and Freier noted that, behind an official liberal discourse in Latin America that is welcoming of migrants, regimes in places such Argentina, Brazil, and Ecuador have begun to follow a "populist liberalism," increasingly discouraging immigration from the Global South (Arcarazo and Freier, 2015). Meseguer and Kemmerling (2018) use OECD data about migration in non-member countries to test hypotheses related to the distributive costs and political economy of factor endowment. Using a comparison of natives' abilities in relation to migrants' as a predictive factor of anti-immigrant sentiment, they find that anti-immigrant sentiment has emerged in Latin America, but more in relation to taxes than to a fear of competition for jobs.

No one has found a real correlation between political stances and support for migration in Brazil, but that is partially because few have tried. That said, one other possible explanation behind the lack of a correlation between political partisanship and support for migration in the Brazilian case could be the timing of opinion polls. Despite large-scale immigration from Europe and Asia in the late 19th and early mid-20th century, Brazil has not been a country of destination for large-scale influxes of migration since the 1970s and 80s – until the last few years, that is (Wejsa and Lesser, 2018). Moreover, while some level of polarization has always existed in Brazil, partisan social sorting has only recently begun to have an effect on national-level politics (Borges and Vidigal, 2018; Samuels and Zucco, 2018; Layton et al., 2021). As a result, the topic of migration would presumably not have been politically sensitive enough to generate polarization along partisan lines in Brazil for the majority of the post–re-democratization era.

More recently, however, Brazil has begun to experience the two conditions necessary for a partisan polarization on migration. On the one hand, there have been large influxes of migration from Haiti and Venezuela in particular, leading to pressure on public services in certain locations (Azeredo Alves and Jarochinski Silva, 2018; Jarochinski and Carlos, 2018; Sampaio and Jarochinski Silva, 2018). On the other hand, a political polarization has also emerged, in particular from parties and coalitions on the right, despite its absence since the re-democratization of Brazil in the 1990s. Could this, then, have led to a polarization on migration?

Before jumping to conclusions, however, we should also recognize another possibility. The other possibility that could explain a lack of correlations in observational data is the phenomenon is social desirability bias–whether these opinions are consciously hidden or not–which could play out in different ways on these two topics. The existing values of a given social group can affect how a participant responds to a survey, while the pressure for a respondent to adhere to a given standard is not as heavy in the case of integration as it is in the case of migration (Janus, 2010; Knoll, 2013). It is more costly, from a moral point of view, to be opposed to immigration, especially for more vulnerable populations, than it is to be opposed to regional integration. For more on social desirability, see the discussion in Chapter 10.

The empirical test of the relationship between political partisanship and support for immigration depends, in the last instance, on overcoming a social desirability bias through specific techniques. In short, respondents could believe that certain points of view regarding immigration would not be considered socially acceptable, which could cause them to hide these views when asked directly about them. Instead, the use of certain other techniques can more accurately gauge the prevalence of certain attitudes towards immigration within a population without requiring a direct response about one's attitude. These techniques include survey experiments using endorsements, vignettes, framing, priming, and lists, all of which experimentally alter aspects of questions in order to parse out the causal factors behind certain attitudinal elements (Rosenfeld, Imai, and Shapiro, 2016; Blair and Imai, 2012).

This chapter's contribution is to provide results from survey experiments about the increasingly sensitive topic of migration in the largest country of a region that is rarely studied regarding this topic. In addition to showing us more about the extent to which immigration is accepted in general within Brazil, these empirical data try to capture the support for immigration when taking the immigrant's country of origin into consideration. The assumption regarding this is that natives tend to be more likely to welcome migrants from developed countries, believing that they are more likely to bring investment and generate business in the region, than they are to welcome migrants from less-developed countries (Hainmueller and Hopkins, 2014). This is because natives can sometimes fear competition for public services and jobs. This can lead to a demonization of migrants, creating a link between this form of immigration and threats to security and public safety.

HYPOTHESES

Given the growing political literature on migration attitudes in Latin America, we also expect to find some sort of preference for policies that support non-foreigners as opposed to those who support foreigners. This should especially be the case when social desirability bias is minimized, as would be the case with endorsement experiments. As such, our first hypothesis is that:

H1: Brazilian respondents should rate lower any social policies that favour, or are endorsed by, foreigners in comparison to those endorsed by non-foreigners.

Next, we expect opinions about immigration to be expressed in different forms depending on the country of origin of the immigrant in question. The foreign policy of the centre-left Workers' Party (PT) governments (particularly Lula) during the 2000s was marked, both in discourse and practice, by a south–south realignment. Rodrigues et al. (2019) show that Brazil's linkages with countries in the Global South increased significantly during those years, particularly in comparison to its links with countries from the Global North. In other words, there was an emphasis on south–south relations during leftist, progressive governments in Brazil. The emergence of centre-right (Michel Temer) and far-right governments (Jair Bolsonaro) altered this official discourse in favour of north–south relations (Rodrigues, Urdinez, and Oliveira, 2019).

We expect to see that the actions and discourses of relevant actors (parties, leaders, and government figures) in the political sphere will have repercussions on public opinion. These repercussions might not necessarily be causal, strictly speaking, but there should presumably be some sort of correlation. This correlation has been the object of hypothesis tests related to other topics, such as regional integration and international alliances, as was the case of the BRICS (Brazil, Russia, India, China, and South Africa), a group of emerging economies (see Oliveira and Onuki, 2018). In both cases, respondents from the right and centre-right were more likely to support alliances with the developed Global North in detriment to special south–south relations.

In this chapter, we test whether attitudes about migration follow cues from political leaders and conform to expectations of political polarization, like other issues in the field of public opinion. Respondents who supported Bolsonaro should be more likely to support Global North–focused migration and policies, while those who supported his 2018 opponent, the PT's Fernando Haddad, should be more likely to support migration and policies oriented towards the south–south axis.

Consequently, our second and third hypotheses are as follows:

H2: Immigrants from the Global North will be viewed more favourably by respondents who voted for Jair Bolsonaro in 2018 than those from the Global South.
H3: Immigrants from the Global South will be viewed more favourably by respondents who voted for Fernando Haddad in 2018 than those from the Global North.

DATA AND METHODS

The data for this analysis come from a survey conducted in 2019 by the Institute of International Relations at the University of São Paulo within a network led by the Center of Economic Research of Teaching (CIDE) in Mexico. The survey had a nationally representative sample of 2000 adult Brazilians.

With this dataset, we conducted two endorsement experiments (we also conducted a third, related experiment, which we detail in Appendix 12B). We used the following vignettes, experimentally altering who was endorsing the policy in question in order to determine respondents' opinions of certain immigrant groups.

English translations of the vignettes follow, with the original wording in Portuguese included as footnotes.

1. *[publichealth] Imagine that a bill being discussed in Congress seeks to increase public resources for SUS (the Brazilian public health care system). The project would penalize states and municipalities that deny access to SUS for people without up-to-date documentation. {Subject} in your state would support a bill of this type. How would you feel about the project?*[2]
2. *[publichousing] Imagine a bill being discussed in the City Council that would authorize the construction of public housing in your neighbourhood. {Subject} in your state would support a bill of this type and would move to your neighbourhood. How do you feel about the project?*[3]

The set of possible values for the subject of the experiments were {People in general; Northeastern Brazilians; Germans; Haitians; Venezuelans}. The possible responses to this question were totally disagree (1), partially disagree (2), partially agree (3), strongly agree (4), and don't know (missing).

Our main independent variable was the treatment condition of the experiment. We reported these results in two different ways: first, we reported the results, disaggregating for every possible value; second, we aggregated responses by whether the endorsement was by a non-foreigner (Northeastern Brazilians and "people in general") or by a foreigner (Germans, Haitians, and Venezuelans). This allowed us to determine the extent of any bias against foreigners as a whole by using chi-squared tests.

We then looked at how the treatment effect varied by political subgroup in order to gauge the effect of political polarization on the migration issue. We divided our respondents by two dummy variables: one indicated whether the respondent had voted for far-right presidential candidate (and eventual victor) Jair Bolsonaro in the 2018 election (*bolsonaro*) while the other indicated whether the respondent had voted for centre-left presidential candidate Fernando Haddad in the 2018 election (*haddad*). We also used chi-squared tests for these analyses.

Finally, we conducted an ordered logistic regression to measure the heterogeneity of these treatment effects. In addition to the independent variables cited above, we included a number of covariates. First, we included an ideology variable (*ideology*) along which respondents placed themselves on a 1–100 scale, with higher numbers indicating more conservative ideologies. We also included variables measuring the household income (*income*) and sex (*sex*) of the respondent, as well as a political knowledge variable (*political knowledge*) that was an index of the percentage of three political knowledge questions that the respondent answered correctly.[4] The results of this model are presented in Appendix 12B.

DESCRIPTIVE STATISTICS

To get a more general baseline idea of respondents' opinions regarding migration, we started by asking respondents directly how they felt about it. We first asked them for their general opinions on people from a selection of nationalities. As one can see from Figure 12.1, respondents had slightly higher opinions for German immigrants (and foreigners living in Brazil in general) than they did for Haitians or Venezuelans.[5]

We then analyzed our respondents' support for laws that would make immigration to Brazil easier. While not a direct analogue for the questions we ask later within an experimental framework, it also serves as a useful source of comparison by showing further baseline levels of support under direct questioning. The generally favourable impression of foreigners from Figure 12.1 translates into a more ambiguous evaluation of laws that would make immigration to Brazil easier, with support almost evenly split, as Figure 12.2 shows.

As shown in Figure 12.2, we also compare the baseline levels of support between respondents who voted for Bolsonaro and those who did not, as well as between those who voted for Haddad and those who did not. One-sample proportion tests showed that these proportions were significantly different for Bolsonaro supporters than for those who did not vote for him; having voted for Bolsonaro made respondents significantly less likely to support these laws, with almost 6% fewer Bolsonaro supporters supporting them. Meanwhile, Haddad voters were not significantly different from the rest of the sample with respect to their support for laws that would make immigration to Brazil easier.

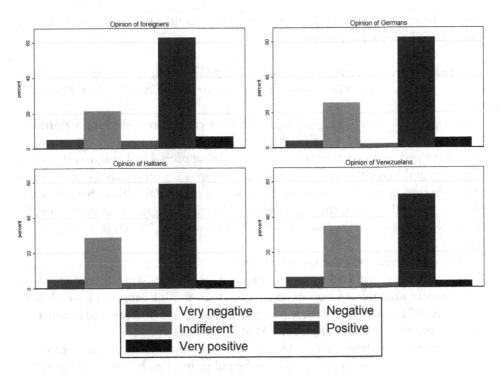

FIGURE 12.1 Opinions of different nationalities.

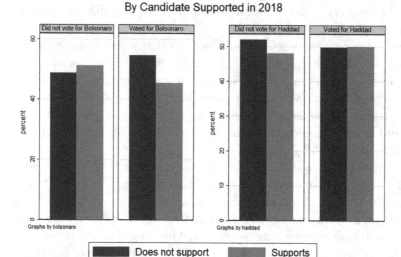

FIGURE 12.2 Support for laws making immigration to Brazil easier, by votes for Bolsonaro and Haddad.

RESULTS

As can be seen in the following, the two endorsement experiments tell a coherent story. Recall our first hypothesis:

H1: Brazilian respondents should rate social policies that favour, or are endorsed by, foreigners lower than those that favour, or are endorsed by non-foreigners.

This hypothesis found clear backing, with both experiments showing significantly higher support for policies that were endorsed by non-foreigners (Northeastern Brazilians and people in general) than for those supported by foreigners (Germans, Haitians, and Venezuelans). For instance, as Figure 12.3 shows, the endorsement of non-foreigners does make the bill significantly more popular, although not to such a degree as the bill about technical schools. When non-foreigners endorse the bill, 3% fewer respondents totally disagree with the bill, whereas 7% more strongly agree, for instance.[6]

Among different types of endorsers, there are significant differences in support, but the pattern is not as clear-cut, as Figure 12.4 shows. Northeastern Brazilians' endorsement increases support by even more than that of people in general, while Venezuelans' endorsement is the least popular among respondents, and is noticeably less popular than that of German and Haitian immigrants.

As Figure 12.5 shows, the endorsement of foreigners decreases the percentage of respondents who strongly agree with the public housing bill by more than 25%,

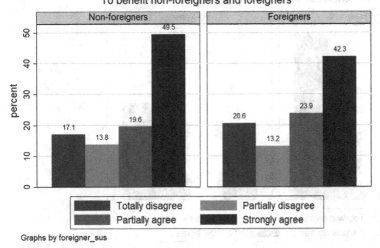

FIGURE 12.3 Support for increasing public health care resources, by origin of endorser.

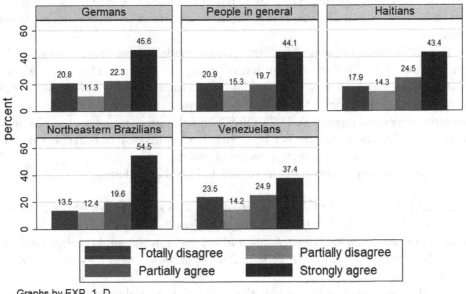

FIGURE 12.4 Support for increasing public health care resources, by national origin of endorser.

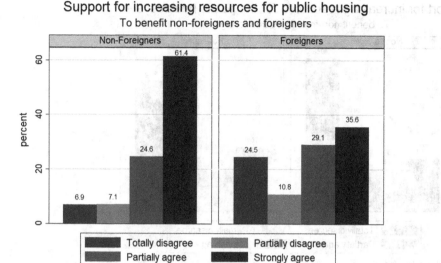

FIGURE 12.5 Support for increasing public housing, by origin of endorser.

while simultaneously increasing the percentage who totally disagree by almost fourfold. The endorsement of foreigners, in other words, significantly harms support for the public housing bill in comparison to the endorsement of non-foreigners. It is worth noting, however, that the effect of foreigners' endorsements is not uniform.

Indeed, in this case, more of a distinction is made by respondents between the endorsements of different nationalities. As Figure 12.6 shows, Haitians' endorsements are seen as more positive than those of Germans or Venezuelans, yet not as positive as those of people in general or Northeasterners. More specifically, Haitian endorsements garner more than 15% more "strongly agree" responses than German and Venezuelan endorsements, but 10% fewer than Northeastern Brazilian endorsements, and 20% fewer than that of people in general.

Turning now our attention to our second and third hypotheses:

H2: *Immigrants from the Global North will be seen more favourably by respondents who voted for Jair Bolsonaro in 2018 than those from the Global South.*
H3: *Immigrants from the Global South will be seen more favourably by respondents who voted for Fernando Haddad in 2018 than those from the Global North.*

Curiously, our second and third hypotheses found more ambiguous results. On the one hand, a series of chi-squared tests showed that Bolsonaro voters were clearly different from non-Bolsonaro voters when it came to our first experiment on public health care, as Table 12.1 shows. Bolsonaro voters made clear distinctions between migrants from the Global North and South, while non-Bolsonaro voters did not.

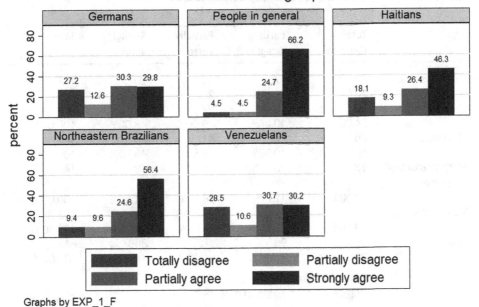

Graphs by EXP_1_F

FIGURE 12.6 Support for increasing public housing, by national origin of endorser.

Furthermore, they clearly favoured German migrants more than non-Bolsonaro voters in both experiments, while the endorsement of Haitian migrants decreased Bolsonaro voters' support. Venezuelan migrants' support, however, seemed to make no difference.

On the other hand, the public housing experiment did not have particularly heterogeneous effects, as Table 12.2 demonstrates. Both Bolsonaro and non-Bolsonaro voters made distinctions between migrants from the Global North and South, even if Bolsonaro voters reacted more favourably to the endorsement of German migrants and reacted more negatively to the endorsements of Venezuelan and Haitian migrants. Still, these results were not as clear-cut as one might have been expected.

Voting for Haddad in 2018 produced even more ambiguous results. Haddad voters were less likely to support bills endorsed by Germans and Venezuelans, but more likely to support bills endorsed by Haitians and Northeastern Brazilians than non-Haddad voters. Endorsements from different nationalities made almost-significant differences in support among non-Haddad voters, but began to make significant differences for Haddad voters. However, the differences between these two groups of voters seem to be subtler than the differences between Bolsonaro voters and non-Bolsonaro voters.

On the one hand, Table 12.3 shows that Haddad voters had more favourable reactions to Haitian migrants' endorsements and less favourable reactions to German

TABLE 12.1 Treatment effect, public health care bill, by 2018 vote (Bolsonaro)

Nationality of endorser	Support for public health care				
	Did not vote for Bolsonaro				
	Chi-sq: 16.32, P-value: 0.177				
	Totally disagree	**Partially disagree**	**Partially agree**	**Strongly agree**	**Total**
Germans	44	27	40	80	191
	23.04%	14.14%	20.94%	41.88%	100.00%
People in general	36	15	27	72	150
	24.00%	10.00%	18.00%	48.00%	100.00%
Haitians	36	20	41	85	182
	19.78%	10.99%	22.53%	46.70%	100.00%
Northeastern Brazilians	23	16	26	78	143
	16.08%	11.19%	18.18%	54.55%	100.00%
Venezuelans	41	21	38	53	153
	26.80%	13.73%	24.84%	34.64%	100.00%
Total	180	99	172	368	819
	21.98%	12.09%	21.00%	44.93%	100.00%
	Voted for Bolsonaro				
	Chi-sq: 23.72, P-value: 0.022				
Germans	25	12	29	62	128
	19.53%	9.38%	22.66%	48.44%	100.00%
People in general	25	25	30	49	129
	19.38%	19.38%	23.26%	37.98%	100.00%
Haitians	24	28	39	55	146
	16.44%	19.18%	26.71%	37.67%	100.00%
Northeastern Brazilians	15	17	33	74	139
	10.79%	12.23%	23.74%	53.24%	100.00%
Venezuelans	35	23	40	50	148
	23.65%	15.54 %	27.03%	33.78%	100.00%
Total	124	105	171	290	690
	17.97%	15.22%	24.78%	42.03%	100.00%

migrants' reactions than non-Haddad voters for the public health care bill. This was as expected – what was not expected, however, was that Haddad voters had considerably less favourable reactions to Venezuelan migrants' endorsements than non-Haddad voters.

On the other hand, as Table 12.4 shows, the public housing bill had different results. Chi-squared tests showed that both Haddad and non-Haddad voters made distinctions between the endorsements of different nationalities, not just Haddad voters. In addition, Haitian and Venezuelan migrant endorsements increased support for the public housing bill among Haddad voters (as expected), but the endorsement of German migrants made no difference, which did not follow our prior expectations.

TABLE 12.2 Treatment effect, public housing bill, by 2018 vote (Bolsonaro)

Nationality of endorser	Support for public housing *Did not vote for Bolsonaro* Chi-sq: 105.49, P-value: < 0.01				
	Totally disagree	**Partially disagree**	**Partially agree**	**Strongly agree**	**Total**
Germans	48	27	56	50	181
	26.52%	14.92%	30.94%	27.62%	100.00%
People in general	6	4	33	106	149
	4.03%	2.68%	22.15%	71.14%	100.00%
Haitians	27	15	44	79	165
	16.36%	9.09%	26.67%	47.88%	100.00%
Northeastern Brazilians	14	13	41	92	160
	8.75%	8.13%	25.62%	57.50%	100.00%
Venezuelans	45	11	56	54	166
	27.11%	6.63%	33.73%	32.53%	100.00%
Total	140	70	230	381	821
	17.05%	8.53%	28.01%	46.41%	100.00%
	Voted for Bolsonaro Chi-sq: 83.66, P-value: < 0.01				
Germans	36	14	31	41	122
	29.51%	11.48%	25.41%	33.61%	100.00%
People in general	7	8	41	99	155
	4.52%	5.16%	26.45%	63.87%	100.00%
Haitians	27	14	46	62	149
	18.12%	9.40%	30.87%	41.61%	100.00%
Northeastern Brazilians	12	16	28	69	125
	9.60%	12.80%	22.40%	55.20%	100.00%
Venezuelans	44	19	41	35	139
	31.65%	13.67%	29.50%	25.18%	100.00%
Total	126	71	187	306	690
	18.26%	10.29%	27.10%	44.35%	100.00%

In short, these results defy easy categorization and would be worth further investigation in the future.

DISCUSSION

Our results show a pattern that is different from those traditionally shown in Brazilian surveys. Before, the most consistent evidence has always pointed to a conclusion that migration was a topic of low-medium political salience for Brazilian public opinion. As a consequence, it had limited influence on national-level partisan politics. Furthermore,

TABLE 12.3 Treatment effect, public health care bill, by 2018 vote (Haddad)

Nationality of endorser	Support for public health care *Did not vote for Haddad* Chi-sq: 20.89, P-value: 0.052				
	Totally disagree	**Partially disagree**	**Partially agree**	**Strongly agree**	**Total**
Germans	47	25	48	104	224
	20.98%	11.16%	21.43%	46.43%	100.00%
People in general	41	28	44	83	196
	20.92%	14.29%	22.45%	42.35%	100.00%
Haitians	41	40	64	100	245
	16.73%	16.33%	26.12%	40.82%	100.00%
Northeastern Brazilians	23	30	49	106	208
	11.06%	14.42%	23.56%	50.96%	100.00%
Venezuelans	51	34	55	79	219
	23.29%	15.53%	25.11%	36.07%	100.00%
Total	203	157	260	472	1092
	18.59%	14.38%	23.81%	43.22%	100.00%
	Voted for Haddad Chi-sq: 22.75, P-value: 0.03				
Germans	22	14	21	38	95
	23.16%	14.74%	22.11%	40.00%	100.00%
People in general	20	12	13	38	83
	24.10%	14.46%	15.66%	45.78%	100.00%
Haitians	19	8	15	40	83
	22.89%	9.64%	19.28%	48.19%	100.00%
Northeastern Brazilians	15	3	10	46	74
	20.27%	4.05%	13.51%	62.16%	100.00%
Venezuelans	25	10	23	24	82
	30.49%	12.20%	28.05%	29.27%	100.00%
Total	101	47	83	186	417
	24.22%	11.27%	19.90%	44.60%	100.00%

the federal design of the Brazilian state had ensured that public opinion had never played a major role with respect to regional integration and migration.

More recently, however, this is beginning to change, and our survey has detected this. Firstly, the support for certain public policies declines when foreigners, not Brazilians, are the main beneficiaries. Second, one's political leanings are correlated with one's responses to questions about migration. In some circumstances, right-leaning Brazilians support policies that favour migration from the Global North, while left-leaning Brazilians support policies that favour migration from the Global South.

Our interpretation is that this new reality is a response to two phenomena. The first is that migration flows have now reached a sufficient size to have generated

TABLE 12.4 Treatment effect, public housing bill, by 2018 vote (Haddad)

Nationality of endorser	Support for public housing				
	Did not vote for Haddad Chi-sq: 100.93, P-value: < 0.01				
	Totally disagree	**Partially disagree**	**Partially agree**	**Strongly agree**	**Total**
Germans	57	26	65	64	212
	26.89%	12.26%	30.66%	30.19%	100.00%
People in general	10	12	61	143	226
	4.42%	5.31%	26.99%	63.27%	100.00%
Haitians	41	22	64	97	224
	18.30%	9.82%	28.57%	43.30%	100.00%
Northeastern Brazilians	19	25	44	116	204
	9.31%	12.25%	21.57%	56.86%	100.00%
Venezuelans	68	23	73	61	225
	30.22%	10.22%	32.44%	27.11%	100.00%
Total	195	108	307	481	1,091
	17.87%	9.90%	28.14%	44.09%	100.00%
	Voted for Haddad Chi-sq: 69.91, P-value: < 0.01				
Germans	27	15	22	27	91
	29.67%	16.48%	24.18%	29.67%	100.00%
People in general	3	0	13	62	78
	3.85%	0.00%	16.67%	79.49%	100.00%
Haitians	13	7	26	44	90
	14.44%	7.78%	28.89%	48.89%	100.00%
Northeastern Brazilians	7	4	25	45	81
	8.64%	4.94%	30.86%	55.56%	100.00%
Venezuelans	21	7	24	28	80
	26.25%	8.75%	30.00%	35.00%	100.00%
Total	71	33	110	206	420
	16.90%	7.86%	26.19%	49.05%	100.00%

distributive costs in terms of public policies. Even though immigration is not new to Brazil, the presence of immigrants had not been of a sufficient scale to affect the supply of public services in redistributive terms since at least World War II. In some regions, this is now changing.

The second phenomenon is a growing political polarization in Brazil. Until recently, political competition typically took place between two big political coalitions: a centre-left and a centre-right. There was not, however, the degree of affective polarization and partisan sorting typical of countries like the United States. The emergence of *bolsonarismo* has inserted an atypical political polarization into the national Brazilian context. While we do not find consistent experimental evidence of polarization affecting attitudes towards immigration, it is quite possible that immigration will become the object of more intense partisan political disputes as Bolsonaro continues to leave his imprint on Brazilian politics. In other words, these results are very much a product of 2019, a time in which partisan sorting is increasing, but still in a nascent stage. Conducting a subsequent survey with the same questions in five years time might reveal a country that is much more organized along partisan lines, both socially and politically.

These empirical results also shine light on the relationship between public opinion and migration, as moderated by migrants' nationalities. Our results did not reveal evidence that the level of economic development of a migrant's country of origin uniformly affected respondents' likelihood of supporting certain public policies. Furthermore, we did not find significant uniform differences between migrants from high-income countries in the Global North and those from low-income countries in the South, nor did we find differences between migrants from countries in economically vulnerable situations. What we did find was a bias in favour of Brazilians when compared to foreigners.

These ambiguous results show that this topic deserves further investigation in the future. Future studies should look to separate and explain the effects of these two phenomena on attitudes towards migration in Brazil. Since 2019, with the COVID-19 pandemic, immigration to Brazil might have decreased from its peak, but the same cannot be said for affective political polarization. Keeping a close watch on how these twin dynamics have affected attitudes towards migration in Brazil should be on researchers' and practitioners' agendas for years to come.

SUMMARY POINTS

- In this chapter, we explored the extent to which support for migration is affected by political partisanship.
- By looking at Brazil, a common destination for migration in recent years and a country with growing partisan polarization, we examined the partisan dimension of migration attitudes, and whether support for migration is lower among those who voted in 2018 for far-right President Jair Bolsonaro or those who voted for his opponent, the centre-left Fernando Haddad.
- Our results showed a consistent bias privileging Brazilians over foreigners. We also found cautious experimental support suggesting that one's political leanings are correlated with responses to questions about migration. In some circumstances, right-leaning Brazilians support policies that favour migration from the Global North, while left-leaning Brazilians support policies that favour migration from the Global South.

NOTES

1 5.6 million Venezuelans have left Venezuela, according to the UN High Commissioner for Refugees on 5 June 2021; see https://data2.unhcr.org/en/situations/platform.
2 *Imagine que um projeto de lei em discussão no Congresso pretenda aumentar os recursos públicos para o SUS. O projeto penalizaria Estados e municípios que negassem acesso ao SUS para pessoas sem documentação em dia. {Subject} morando no seu Estado apoiariam um projeto desse tipo. Como você se sentiria em relação a isso?*
3 *Imagine um projeto de lei em discussão na Câmara de Vereadores que autorizasse a construção de moradia popular no seu bairro. {Subject} morando no seu Estado apoiariam esse projeto e se mudariam para o seu bairro. Como você se sente em relação a isso?*
4 *Qual o significado de ONU* (What does UN stand for)? *Qual o significado de MRE* (What does MRE [Ministry of Foreign Relations] stand for)? *Qual o significado de BRICS* (What does BRICS stand for)? "Don't know" was counted as an incorrect answer.
5 Additional basic descriptive statistics are included in Appendix 12A.
6 It is interesting to note that partisan difference made little difference here; voting for Haddad did not affect the treatment effect. Non-foreigners' endorsements were significantly more well-evaluated than that of foreigners.
7 *Imagine que um projeto de lei em discussão no Congresso tenha como objetivo aumentar os recursos públicos para escolas técnicas. Isso deve ajudar {subject} morando no seu Estado a encontrarem emprego com mais facilidade. Como você se sente em relação ao projeto?*

FURTHER READINGS

Arcarazo, D.A. and Freier, L.F., 2015. Turning the immigration policy paradox upside down? Populist liberalism and discursive gaps in south America. *International Migration Review*, 49(3), 659–696.

Hainmueller, J. and Hopkins, D.J., 2014. Public attitudes toward immigration. *Annual Review of Political Science*, 17(1), 225–249.

Layton, M.L., Smith, A.E., Moseley, M.W., and Cohen, M.J., 2021. Demographic polarization and the rise of the far right: Brazil's 2018 presidential election. *Research & Politics*, 8(1): 2053168021990204.

Rodrigues, P., Urdinez, F., and de Oliveira, A., 2019. Measuring international engagement: Systemic and domestic factors in Brazilian foreign policy from 1998 to 2014. *Foreign Policy Analysis*, 15(3), 370–391.

REFERENCES

Arcarazo, D.A. and Freier, L.F., 2015. Turning the immigration policy paradox upside down? Populist liberalism and discursive gaps in south America. *International Migration Review*, 49(3), 659–696.

Azeredo Alves, L. and Silva, J.C.J., 2018. A Migração Internacional enquanto tema político entre os anos de 2010–2017 no Brasil Revista del CESLA. *International Latin American Studies Review*, 22, 203–226.

Benton, M., Batalova, J., Davidoff-Gore, S., and Schmidt, T., 2021. COVID-19 and the state of global mobility in 2020. Migration Policy Institute. Available from: https://www.migrationpolicy.org/research/covid-19-state-global-mobility-2020.

Blair, G. and Imai, K., 2012. Statistical analysis of list experiments. *Political Analysis*, 20(1), 47–77.

Borges, A. and Vidigal, R., 2018. Do lulismo ao antipetismo? Polarização, partidarismo e voto nas eleições presidenciais brasileiras. *Opinião Pública*, 24(1), 53–89.

Bruhn, K. and Greene, K.F., 2007. Elite polarization meets mass moderation in Mexico's 2006 elections. *PS: Political Science and Politics*, 40(1), 33–38.

Castilla, C. and Sørensen, N.N., 2019. Venezuelans flee accelerating collapse: Latin Americas EVOLVING MIGRATION CRISIS. Available from: https://www.jstor.org/stable/resrep21353. Danish Institute for International Studies [Accessed 30 June 2021].

Ellner, S., 2013. Introduction: Latin America's Radical Left in power: Complexities and challenges in the twenty-first century. *Latin American Perspectives*, 40(3), 5–25.

Fussell, E., 2014. Warmth of the welcome: Attitudes toward immigrants and immigration policy. *Annual Review of Sociology*, 40, 479–498.

Grigera, J., 2017. Populism in Latin America: Old and new populisms in Argentina and Brazil. *International Political Science Review* / Revue internationale de science politique 38(4), 441–455.

Hainmueller, J. and Hopkins, D.J., 2014. Public attitudes toward immigration. *Annual Review of Political Science*, 17(1), 225–249.

Janus, A.L., 2010. The influence of social desirability pressures on expressed immigration attitudes. *Social Science Quarterly*, 91(4), 928–946.

Jaret, C., 1999. Troubled by newcomers: Anti-immigrant attitudes and action during two eras of mass immigration to the United States. *Journal of American Ethnic History*, 18(3), 9–39.

Jarochinski, S. and Carlos, J., 2018. Uma política Migratória Reativa e Inadequada – A migração venezuelana para o Brasil e a Resolução N°. 126 do Conselho Nacional de Imigração (CNIg). In: Núcleo de Estudos de População Elza Berquó – Nepo/Unicamp (Ed.), *Migrações sul-sul*. Campinas, SP: Núcleo de Estudos de População Elza Berquó – Nepo/Unicamp, 637–650.

Knoll, B.R., 2013. Implicit nativist attitudes, social desirability, and immigration policy preferences. *International Migration Review*, 47(1), 132–165.

Layton, M.L., Smith, A.E., Moseley, M.W., and Cohen, M.J., 2021. Demographic polarization and the rise of the Far right: Brazil's 2018 presidential election. *Research & Politics*, 8(1): 2053168021990204.

Meseguer, C. and Kemmerling, A., 2018. What do you fear? Anti-immigrant sentiment in Latin America. *International Migration Review*, 52(1), 236–272.

Meseguer, C. and Maldonado, G., 2015. Las actitudes hacia los inmigrantes en México: Explicaciones económicas y sociales. *Foro Internacional* 55(3), 772–804.

Milner, H.V. and Kubota, K., 2005. Why the move to free trade? Democracy and trade policy in the developing countries on JSTOR. *International Organization*, 59(1), 107–143.

Mouron, F. and Onuki, J., 2015. Brasil es un líder en América del Sur? El papel brasileño a través del concepto de liderazgo situacional. Revista de Estudos Internacionais, 3, 9–26.

Oliveira, A.J. de, and Onuki, J., 2018. Balance of power and international trade: The perception of the Brazilian public opinion about China and BRICS. In: *The coordination of BRICS development strategies towards shared prosperity*. World Scientific. Available from: https://www.worldscientific.com/doi/abs/10.1142/9789811201004_0010. 109–119 [Accessed 3July2021].

Onuki, J., 2020. Opinião Pública e integração regional na Argentina e Brasil. Working Paper. Caeni.

Onuki, J., Mouron, F., and Urdinez, F., 2016. Latin American perceptions of regional identity and leadership in comparative perspective. *Contexto Internacional*, 38(1), 433–465.

Rodrigues, P., Urdinez, F., and de Oliveira, A., 2019. Measuring international engagement: Systemic and domestic factors in Brazilian foreign policy from 1998 to 2014. *Foreign Policy Analysis*, 15(3), 370–391.

Rosenfeld, B., Imai, K., Shapiro, J.N., 2016. An empirical validation study of popular survey methodologies for sensitive questions. *American Journal of Political Science*, 60(3), 783–802.

Sampaio, C. and Silva, J.C.J., 2018. Complexidade X Singularidade-a necessidade de outras soluções duradoras. In: Núcleo de Estudos de População Elza Berquó–Nepo/Unicamp, (Ed.), *Migrações Venezuelanas*. Campinas, SP: Núcleo de Estudos de População Elza Berquó–Nepo/Unicamp, 391–394.

Samuels, D. and Zucco, C., 2018. *Partisans, antipartisans, and nonpartisans: Voting behavior in Brazil*. Cambridge: Cambridge University Press.

Singer, M., 2016. Elite polarization and the electoral impact of left-right placements: Evidence from Latin America, 1995–2009. *Latin American Research Review*, 51(2), 174–194.

Wejsa, S. and Lesser, J., 2018. Migration in brazil: The making of a multicultural society. *The Online Journal of Migration Policy Institute*. https://www.migrationpolicy.org/article/migration-brazil-making-multicultural-society

APPENDIX 12A: BASIC DESCRIPTIVE STATISTICS

Here in Table 12.A1, we provide some basic descriptive statistics of our dataset. One can see that our sample trends to the right, with Bolsonaro having received more support in the 2018 election than Haddad within our sample, and an average ideology score of 59 out of 100 (higher scores indicating more conservative ideological self-placement). It is also worth noting that the political knowledge questions also were not answered with a high rate of success. We did count "don't know" responses as incorrect answers, but even so, an average rate of 11% correct answers for all three questions showed that knowledge of our international relations questions was not particularly high.

TABLE 12.A1 Descriptive statistics, all variables

Variables	(1) N	(2) Mean	(3) Sd	(4) Min	(5) Max
Year of birth	1,849	1,979	16.18	1,926	2,003
Age	1,849	39.36	16.17	16	92
Bolsonaro	1,547	0.46	0.5	0	1
Haddad	1,547	0.27	0.45	0	1
Ideology	1,519	59.71	33.23	0	100
Support for technical schools	1,805	3.375	0.910	1	4
Support for public health care	1,802	2.929	1.163	1	4
Support for public housing	1,805	3.007	1.122	1	4
Sex	1,849	1.475	0.503	1	3
Race	1,826	5.533	2.546	1	8
Household income	1,659	2,786	2,982	0	40,008
Political knowledge	1,826	0.112	0.1848	0	1

APPENDIX 12B: ADDITIONAL EXPERIMENTAL RESULTS

As mentioned earlier, we also conducted a third, related vignette experiment that did not have an endorsement element, but shared other similar factors to the two endorsement experiments. The prompt follows below, along with the original Portuguese wording of the question.

3. *[technicalschools] Imagine that a bill being discussed in Congress has the objective of increasing public resources for technical schools. This should help {subject} living in your state find jobs more easily. How do you feel about the project?*[7]

As can be seen here, the vignette experiment corroborates the story of a preference for policies supporting non-foreigners (Northeastern Brazilians and people in general) over those supporting foreigners (Germans, Haitians, and Venezuelans). Figure 12.A1, for instance, shows that when technical schools supposedly help non-foreigners, they garner significantly more support than when they supposedly help foreigners find jobs.

The number of respondents who strongly agree with the bill, for instance, decreases by more than 25% as the main benefactor becomes foreigners.

However, the type of foreigner does not make a very big difference regarding the level of support respondents gave bills. Figure 12.A2 does not show strong effects on the number of respondents who strongly agree with it when the nationality of the beneficiary or endorser changes.

It is, however, worth noting that when a bill helps German and Venezuelan immigrants, it increases the number of respondents who totally disagree with the bill.

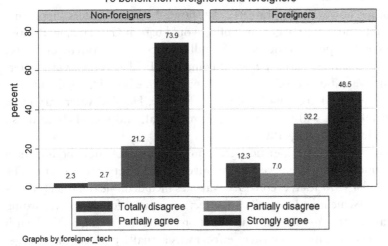

FIGURE 12.A1 Support for increasing technical schools, by origin of beneficiary.

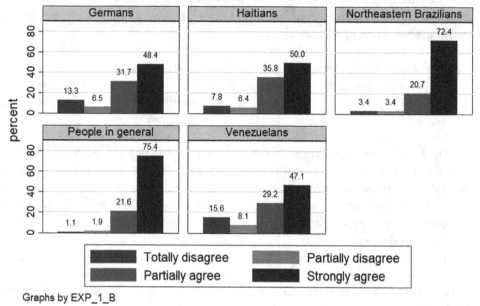

Graphs by EXP_1_B

FIGURE 12.A2 Support for increasing technical schools, by national origin of beneficiary.

In terms of finding treatment effects that are heterogeneous across political loyalties, this third experiment makes little difference. As Table 12.A2 shows, respondents have different opinions about the technical schools bill, regardless of the nationality that the vignette said would benefit.

It is worth noting, however, that Table 12.A4 shows Bolsonaro voters supporting policies considerably more often when the policy would benefit Germans, while non-Bolsonaro voters will support Venezuelan-friendly policies more often. Likewise, Table 12.A3 shows a similar pattern when it comes to Haddad voters, with differences between the evaluation of technical school bills. While both Haddad and non-Haddad voters evaluate different nationalities differently, Haddad voters are more likely to support bills that will help out people in general, and less likely to do so when it will help Haitians specifically.

We also conducted an ordered logistic regression on all three of our experiments in order to include a more comprehensive analysis involving a variety of covariates. The results in Table 12.A4 show that, even with covariates included, the treatment of foreigner support/endorsement had a significant effect on support for the bill regarding public housing, although it did not have an effect on the bill regarding public health care). However, one of the most persistent effects was actually political knowledge, which had a significant positive effect on both endorsement experiments.

TABLE 12.A2 Treatment effect, technical schools by 2018 vote (Bolsonaro)

Nationality of endorser	Support for technical schools				
	Did not vote for Bolsonaro				
	Chi-sq: 79.84, P-value: < 0.01				
	Totally disagree	**Partially disagree**	**Partially agree**	**Strongly agree**	**Total**
Germans	18	11	51	61	141
	12.77%	7.80%	36.17%	43.26%	100.00%
People in general	2	5	36	134	177
	1.13%	2.82%	20.34%	75.71%	100.00%
Haitians	11	10	62	74	157
	7.01%	6.37%	39.49%	47.13%	100.00%
Northeastern Brazilians	9	6	38	136	189
	4.76%	3.17%	20.11%	71.96%	100.00%
Venezuelans	25	10	45	79	159
	15.72%	6.29%	28.30%	49.69%	100.00%
Total	65	42	232	484	823
	18.59%	14.38%	23.81%	43.22%	100.00%
	Voted for Bolsonaro				
	Chi-sq: 61.55 P-value: < 0.01				
Germans	19	8	41	87	155
	12.26%	5.16%	26.45%	56.13%	100.00%
People in general	2	2	28	96	128
	1.56%	1.56%	21.88%	75.00%	100.00%
Haitians	15	8	43	69	135
	11.11%	5.93%	31.85%	51.11%	100.00%
Northeastern Brazilians	3	7	29	104	143
	2.10%	4.90%	20.28%	72.73%	100.00%
Venezuelans	19	15	44	53	131
	14.50%	11.45%	33.59%	40.46%	100.00%
Total	58	40	185	409	692
	24.22%	11.27%	19.90%	44.60%	100.00%

Quite surprisingly, when covariates are accounted for in an ordered logit regression, a vote for President Bolsonaro or Fernando Haddad in 2018 did not have an effect on any of the three experiments. Foreign origin, however, still is a significant explanatory factor for all three experiments, while more political knowledge improves opinions of bills for the public health and public housing endorsement experiments.

TABLE 12.A3 Treatment effect, technical schools by 2018 vote (Haddad)

Nationality of endorser	Support for technical schools *Did not vote for Haddad* Chi-sq: 82.83, P-value: < 0.01				
	Totally disagree	Partially disagree	Partially agree	Strongly agree	Total
Germans	30	13	73	117	233
	12.88%	5.58%	31.33%	50.21%	100.00%
People in general	3	4	47	153	207
	1.45%	1.93%	22.71%	73.91%	100.00%
Haitians	19	11	70	108	208
	9.13%	5.29%	33.65%	51.92%	100.00%
Northeastern Brazilians	10	10	48	172	240
	4.17%	4.17%	20.00%	71.67%	100.00%
Venezuelans	31	22	64	99	216
	14.35%	10.19%	29.63%	45.83%	100.00%
Total	93	60	302	649	1,104
	8.42%	5.43%	27.36%	58.79%	100.00%
	Voted for Haddad Chi-sq: 56.02, P-value: < 0.01				
Germans	7	6	19	31	63
	11.11%	9.52%	30.16%	49.21%	100.00%
People in general	1	3	17	77	98
	1.02%	3.06%	17.35%	78.57%	100.00%
Haitians	7	7	35	35	84
	8.33%	8.33%	41.67%	41.67%	100.00%
Northeastern Brazilians	2	3	19	68	92
	2.17%	3.26%	20.65%	73.91%	100.00%
Venezuelans	13	3	25	33	74
	17.57%	4.05%	33.78%	44.59%	100.00%
Total	101	47	83	186	417
	7.30%	5.35%	27.98%	59.37%	100.00%

TABLE 12.A4 Ordered logistic regressions, support for policies benefiting foreigners

	Public health care		Public housing		Technical schools	
	Coef. (std. error)	Z-value	Coef. (std. error)	Z-value	Coef. (std. error)	Z-value
Beneficiary: foreign origin	−0.32 (0.11)	−2.81**	−1.16 (0.12)	−9.66***	−1.15 (0.13)	−9.13***
Bolsonaro	−0.11 (0.14)	−0.79	−0.05 (0.14)	−0.34	−0.12 (0.15)	−0.79
Haddad	−0.09 (0.15)	−0.62	0.11 (0.16)	0.74	−0.1 (0.17)	−0.58
Ideology	< 0.001 (0.002)	−0.05	−0.003 (0.002)	−1.55	0.002 (0.002)	1.16
Income	< 0.001 (< 0.001)	0.09	< 0.001 (< 0.001)	0.64	< 0.001 (< 0.001)	−0.1
Sex	0.16 (0.11)	1.43	−0.02 (0.11)	−0.18	−0.18 (0.12)	−1.53
Political knowledge	0.77 (0.3)	2.57**	0.63 (0.3)	2.08**	0.26 (0.32)	0.8

CHAPTER 13

The inflow of immigrants and natives' attitudes towards immigration in Japan

....

Tetsuya Matsubayashi and Masateru Yamatani

INTRODUCTION

Studies of inter-ethnic relations in Western Europe and North America argue that a greater presence of immigrants in society increases natives' hostile attitudes towards them, leading to support for a more restrictive immigration policy. This relationship, known as the group conflict (or threat) hypothesis (Key, 1949; Blumer, 1958; Blalock, 1967), is primarily attributable to the perception of the emotional and economic threats posed by immigrants (Hainmueller and Hopkins, 2014). On the one hand, the greater presence of ethnic minorities triggers inter-group conflicts because members of the majority are frustrated by the anticipated threat of undermining the country's cultural homogeneity (Sniderman et al., 2004). On the other hand, aggression against new minorities can be explained more rationally: competition over scarce political and economic resources, such as job opportunities and welfare benefits (Facchini and Mayda, 2009; Mayda, 2006; Scheve and Slaughter, 2001). See Chapter 14 for more on this line of argument.

This chapter extends the group conflict hypothesis to Japan and examines whether the recent inflow of foreign workers in local areas is associated with natives' attitudes towards both them and immigration policy. Japan has long been known as an ethnically and linguistically homogeneous society, but the country has been experiencing a rapid change in the number of foreign workers and immigrants since the early 1990s. As shown in detail later, the number of registered foreign workers in Japan has approximately tripled from 1.08 million in 1990 to 2.93 million in 2019 (Immigration Service Agency of Japan, 2020). As of 2019, 2.32% of the residents of Japan were foreign-born. As Japanese society is rapidly ageing and will continue to do so over the next several decades, it is almost inevitable that the government will further ease restrictions on immigration and invite more workers to immigrate from other countries.

DOI: 10.4324/9781003121992-16

Japan offers an interesting case to test the group conflict hypothesis for two reasons. First, until recently the size of the immigrant population, including long-term residents with Chinese or Korean backgrounds, was small and had changed little for several decades. This allows us to examine how the first exposure to an out-group population in close proximity as a result of the rapid inflow of foreign workers affected natives' views of them and immigration policy. This situation can be contrasted with countries in North America and Western Europe, where immigrant populations have been sizable and growing over the last several decades.

Second, Japanese society has recently seen a backlash against non-Japanese citizens. A number of hate crime incidents, especially hate speech demonstrations against Koreans, have been organized by radical groups (Center for Human Rights Education and Training, 2016). Between 2012 and 2015, there were 1,152 confirmed cases of demonstrations, mostly against Koreans and Korean Japanese.[1] Quantitative studies addressing explicit racism and nativism in Japan are scarce, possibly due to a lack of data. However, Higuchi's (2020) qualitative analysis indicates that these nativist movements are likely to derive from historical revisionism and escalated territorial conflicts with South Korea and China (see Igarashi, 2018). Accordingly, it is of great importance to understand whether hostile attitudes towards out-group members are widespread, even among the general public in Japan, and whether the recent increase in foreign workers is indeed part of the reasons for the negative attitudes and backlash.

Our study differs in several respects from previous works showing that Japanese natives in areas with larger foreign residents show more negative attitudes towards them (e.g. Green, 2017; Mazumi, 2015; Nagayoshi, 2009; Nakazawa, 2007; Nukaga, 2006). First, we assess whether native citizens in areas with an increasing number of foreign workers accurately perceive this change. This is crucial because the number of foreign workers is increasing but remains small in many parts of Japan, and their presence may not be visible to many natives. In addition, natives have been reported to misperceive the prevalence of other groups (e.g. Citrin and Sides, 2008; Wong, 2007). Second, we measure the numbers of foreign workers in municipalities, in contrast to previous studies that typically used prefectures as geographical units. The use of population data for municipalities, political and administrative subunits of prefectures, allows us to measure the number of foreign workers in close proximity and thus better estimate local residents' potential daily exposure to their presence. Third, building on previous research, we assess the possible mechanisms (e.g. perceived cultural or economic threats) underlying the relationship between the presence of foreign workers in local areas and natives' attitudes towards them.

The next section summarizes the theoretical foundation and empirical evidence for the group conflict hypothesis. The third section describes the immigration policy of Japan, historical changes in the immigrant population in the last three decades, immigrants' geographical distribution, and the country of origin. The fourth section describes how Japanese citizens view foreign workers and their influence on society. Using survey data collected in early 2018, we examine the share of respondents who perceive the changing number of foreign workers in their local area, whether they are willing to accept more foreign workers in their area, and whether they perceive foreign workers and immigrants as generating beneficial or adverse influences on the economy, culture, and crime. In this part of the analysis, we combine our survey data with the Comparative Study of Electoral System (CSES) Module 5 for cross-national comparison (the same data as used in Part 2 of the book).

The fifth section examines whether the number of immigrants in local areas is correlated with the natives' views of foreign workers. Our regression analyses show that the respondents accurately perceive the larger presence of foreign workers in their municipality and that they are less supportive of accepting more immigrants when residing in areas with more foreign workers. However, we find no strong support for the hypothesis that the presence of foreign workers increases respondents' fear of economic and cultural threats.

THE GROUP CONFLICT HYPOTHESIS

The group conflict hypothesis was originally developed by Key (1949), Blumer (1958), and Blalock (1967) to understand the relationship between whites and blacks in American society. They argued that a dominant racial group (i.e. whites) in society becomes more hostile to a minority group (i.e. blacks) as the size of the minority group in close proximity increases. Hostility by the dominant group may manifest itself in numerous ways, such as prejudice, less tolerant policy views, party support, and violence (Giles and Hertz, 1994; Glaser, 2003; Olzak, 1992; Oliver, 2010; Taylor, 1998; Welch et al., 2001). The dominant group shows stronger hostility because the greater presence of the minority group threatens the economic, political, and cultural privileges enjoyed by members of the dominant group.

The logic behind the group conflict hypothesis in explaining the reactions of natives to the inflow of immigrants in the destination society posits that numerically dominant natives will show more hostile attitudes towards incoming immigrants and refugees because they perceive that their economic interests, political power, and cultural values are threatened by the greater presence of non-natives in close proximity. Natives' hostile reactions are manifested as prejudice (e.g. Quillian, 1995), support for more restrictive immigration policies (Hopkins, 2010; Newman et al., 2012), support for radical parties (e.g. Golder, 2003; Swank and Betz, 2003), and violent actions (e.g. Braun and Koopmans, 2010; Piatkowska and Lantz, 2021; Green et al., 1998). Negative reactions to immigrants may be stronger when immigration is a salient policy agenda (Hopkins, 2010), the economic situation worsens (e.g. Quillian, 1995), immigrants gain electoral power (Dancygier, 2010), or there is a combination of these conditions.

The hypothesized negative reactions of natives to immigrants have been empirically confirmed in many parts of the world. For example, Quillian (1995) and Schneider (2008) show that the size of the immigrant population is positively correlated with the perceived threat in European countries. Hopkins (2010) shows that native-born citizens in the United States show more hostile attitudes towards immigrants when they reside in areas with more immigrants and immigration is a salient policy agenda, while Dancygier (2010) and Hopkins (2011) offer similar evidence using data from the United Kingdom. Hangartner et al. (2019) focused on the refugee crisis as a result of the Syrian conflict in the 2010s, showing that native Greeks on islands receiving more refugees show hostility towards them and support more restrictive refugee and immigration policies.

The mechanisms underlying these relationships are more likely to be cultural threats. Immigrants' country of origin influences natives' attitudes in both the United States and European countries (e.g. Hainmueller and Hangartner, 2013; Dustmann and Pretson, 2007; Brader and Suhay, 2008). Language fluency per se receives limited support but serves as a cue that conveys prospects for adhering to norms and fitting in society (Hopkins, 2014; Sniderman et al., 2004; Hainmueller and Hopkins, 2015). The socioeconomic attributes of immigrants are not irrelevant, yet the fact that both high- and low-skilled natives prefer more skilled and educated immigrants provides less support for the labour market competition theory (e.g. Hainmueller and Hiscox, 2010; Hainmueller and Hopkins, 2015).

THE INFLOW OF IMMIGRANTS INTO JAPAN

Figure 13.1 illustrates that the percentage of foreign residents in Japan has increased rapidly, with a notable surge since 2013. The number of foreign residents was 1.08 million in 1990 and had risen to 2.93 million in 2019 (Immigration Service Agency of Japan, 2020). About 60% are temporary workers, and their recent increase has contributed to the overall growth of the foreign population (Ministry of Health, Labour, and Welfare, 2018). While the specific status granted varies over time, the inflow of immigrants in Japan is predominantly a result of government policies to supplement the workforce.

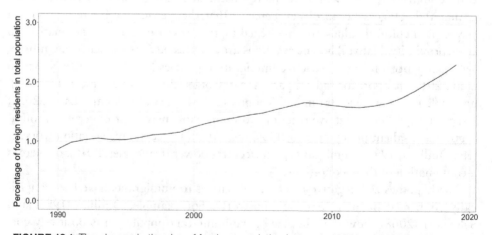

FIGURE 13.1 The change in the size of foreign population between 1990 and 2019 in Japan.

Source: Statistics of Foreign Nationals by Immigration Services Agency of Japan and Population Estimates by the Statistics Bureau of Japan.

As of 2020, there were 29 legal statuses of residences with different periods of stay. The number of those with permanent residency has increased from about 145,000 in 2000 to 793,000 in 2019, and they accounted for the largest share of foreign residents (27%) in 2019 (Ministry of Justice, 2019). This increase can be partly attributed to the revision of the Immigration Control and Refugee Recognition Act in the 1990s, which aimed to alleviate the labour shortage under the bubble economy in the late 1980s and the early 1990s. This policy led to an inflow of Japanese descendants abroad, mainly from Brazil and Peru (Ministry of Health, Labour, and Welfare, 2002). Upon recording a stay of ten consecutive years, immigrants are entitled to permanent residency.

The sharp rise in foreign residents since 2013 is explained by the greater presence of short-term workers and students, who make up the second and third-greatest proportions of foreign residents. The Japanese government supposedly has taken a very cautious stance towards inviting foreign workers without professional skills. The government is concerned about the possibility of greater competition over the same jobs with native elderly, higher unemployment rates during economic downturns, and greater government expenditures for social services. In the face of the declining working population, however, various industries have manifested a growing demand for less-skilled labour, which has led the government to accept many de facto manual workers through the Technical Intern Training Programme (Gino Jisshu Seido in Japanese). The programme is designed to aid developing countries by transferring skills and knowledge, and allows invited workers to serve as trainees, typically in the manufacturing, construction, and retail industries, for up to five years in Japan. Furthermore, foreign students from Vietnam, China, and Nepal are also viewed as a source of inexpensive labour (Mochizuki, 2019). About 70–80% of them work part-time jobs, mainly in the food-service industry. In short, the recent increase in foreign residents is attributable to the government policy to address labour shortages, especially in industries that require fewer skills.

Next, we assess the geographical distribution of the foreign population across Japan. Figure 13.2 shows a significant regional variation in the numbers of foreign workers and students. As of 2019, 4.3% of the total population in Tokyo had a foreign background. Of the total foreign population, 20.2% resided in Tokyo. This is followed by Aichi and Osaka Prefectures with 9.6% and 8.7%, respectively. In Tokyo and Osaka, more than half of them are permanent residents, students, or highly skilled professionals. In contrast, more short-term workers (i.e. trainees in the Technical Intern Training Programme) live in Aichi, where manufacturing industries play a major economic role. Importantly, during the last decade, the increase in the foreign population has not been concentrated in Tokyo, Aichi, and Osaka. Hokkaido in the north and prefectures in Kyushu in the southern region of Japan are experiencing more rapid increases; for instance, the size of the foreign population has roughly doubled in Hokkaido, Kagoshima, and Okinawa.

Most immigrants originate from a few countries. Table 13.1 summarizes the number of foreign residents by country of origin. Those with Chinese backgrounds accounted for 27.7% of the total foreign population in Japan as of 2019. The sizes of

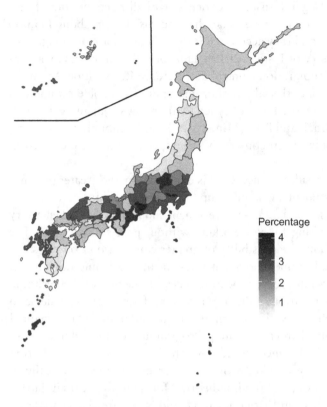

FIGURE 13.2 The geographical variation in the size of foreign population across Japan.

Source: Trend of Foreign Residents by Prefecture by Immigration Service Agency of Japan, and Population Estimates by the Statistics Bureau of Japan.

TABLE 13.1 Top five countries of origin of foreign population in Japan

	2015	2016	2017	2018	2019	Percentage as of 2019
Total	2,232,189	2,382,822	2,561,848	2,731,093	2,933,137	100.0
China	665,847	695,522	730,890	764,720	813,675	27.7
South Korea	457,772	453,096	450,663	449,634	446,364	15.2
Vietnam	146,956	199,990	262,405	330,835	411,968	14.0
Philippines	229,595	243,662	260,553	271,289	282,798	9.6
Brazil	173,437	180,923	191,362	201,865	211,677	7.2

Source: *Trend of Foreign Residents by Nationality and Region* by Immigration Service Agency of Japan.

Chinese, Filipino, and Brazilian residential populations have shown a steady growth of about 20% over the past five years, while the size of the Vietnamese resident population has nearly tripled due to a surge in the number of trainees and students. On the other hand, the number of those with a Korean background declined slightly. About 30–50% of Chinese, South Korean, Filipino, and Brazilian nationals are entitled to permanent residency. Foreign residents from the five countries in Table 13.1 account for 73.9% of the total foreign population in Japan.

NATIVES' ATTITUDES TOWARDS IMMIGRATION

How do Japanese citizens view immigrants and foreign workers? We answer this question using data from a nationally representative survey conducted in January and February 2018 to assess political opinion and behaviour in the general election in October 2017. The survey relied on a two-stage stratified random sampling method targeting the entire population and selected a total of approximately 3,000 respondents. The number of respondents who agreed to participate in a face-to-face interview was 1,544. For those who did not participate in the face-to-face interview, 144 respondents later answered the shorter version of the questionnaire by mail. The total response rate was 56.3%. Our analysis reported below excludes a small number of respondents who were born outside Japan. This survey was designed as part of the Comparative Study of Electoral Systems (CSES) Module 5.

We used two groups of survey questions to measure native respondents' attitudes towards immigrants and immigration. The first group included two questions about respondents' perceptions of and support for the increasing numbers of immigrants in local areas. More specifically, the first question asked, "Over the past five years, has the number of foreign residents living in the same area as you increased?" The response was scored on a three-point scale of increased, no change, and decreased. The second question asked, "Would you agree with or oppose increasing the number of foreign residents living near you?" Responses were measured on a four-point scale ranging from agree, somewhat agree, and somewhat oppose to oppose.

Figure 13.3 reports the distribution of the responses to the first group of survey questions. The left panel shows that about 60% of the respondents recognized no change in the size of the immigrant population in local areas, while 40% reported that it has increased. Importantly, virtually none reported that the number of immigrants had decreased. This result indicates that native-born people in many areas of Japan accurately perceive the rapidly increasing size of immigrants. The right panel of Figure 13.3 reports the percentage of respondents who agree or disagree with accepting more immigrants in their areas. Natives' views on this issue are balanced; approximately half of respondents agreed with accepting more immigrants in local areas, while the other half disagreed. About 80% of respondents chose somewhat agree and somewhat disagree, implying that they have only a weak position on this issue.

The second group of questions (also used in Chapters 3–11 of this volume) asked respondents about the potential consequences of accepting immigrants. The respondents reported whether they agreed or disagreed that "immigrants are generally good for Japan's economy"; "Japan's culture is generally harmed by immigrants"; and "immigrants increase crime rates in Japan." The response items included strongly disagree, somewhat disagree, neither agree nor disagree, somewhat agree, and strongly disagree. These three questions were also included in the CSES Module 5;

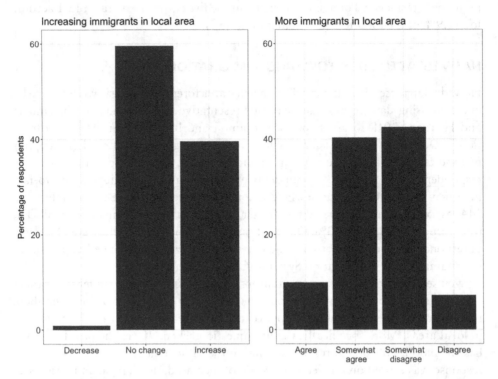

FIGURE 13.3 Natives' views on immigrants in Japan.

Source: CSES Japan data.

thus, the responses in Japan can be compared with those from 20 other countries and regions, including some covered in Part 2 of the book. They are Austria, Australia, Brazil, Chile, France, Germany, Greece, Hong Kong, Hungary, Iceland, Ireland, Italy, Lithuania, Montenegro, New Zealand, Norway, South Korea, Taiwan, Turkey, and the United States.[2]

Figure 13.4 reports the distribution of the responses to the second group of survey questions. The graphs report the percentage of respondents who strongly disagreed or disagreed with the statement that immigrants are good for the economy (left panel), the percentage of respondents who strongly agree or agree with the statement that culture is harmed by immigrants (middle panel), and the percentage of respondents who strongly agree or agree with the statement that immigrants increase crime rates (right panel). These percentages denote the share of respondents who have a negative view of immigrants and immigration. The left and middle panels suggest that less than 20% of respondents disagreed that immigrants are good for the economy and agreed that Japanese culture is harmed by immigrants. This means that only a limited segment of the population is concerned about the economic and cultural changes caused by immigrants. The right panel suggests that the respondents were more concerned about crime; about 35% of respondents agreed that immigrants increase crime.

Notably, a cross-national comparison indicates that Japanese respondents show less negative views of the threats posed by immigrants among the countries included

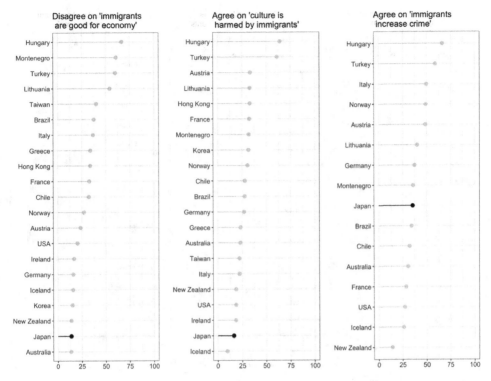

FIGURE 13.4 Natives' views of immigrants as economic, cultural, and security threats in Japan and other countries.

Source: CSES Japan data and CSES Module 5 data.

in our data. In particular, we focus on three neighbouring regions, Hong Kong, Korea, and Taiwan, for comparison. More respondents in Taiwan and Hong Kong than in Japan disagreed that immigrants are good for the economy, while more respondents in these three regions agreed that culture is harmed by immigrants. These differences are interesting because the number of immigrants is comparable between Korea, Taiwan, and Japan.

The patterns in Figure 13.4 do not necessarily mean that Japanese citizens are positive and optimistic about the greater presence of immigrants in society. Given the small size of immigrants in Japan, it is likely that a sizable number of respondents have never considered the economic and cultural influences of immigrants on society and thus have developed no strong opinion. To check this possibility, we calculated the percentage of respondents who neither agree nor disagree with each of the three statements, which allows us to assess the extent to which respondents take a neutral position. Figure 13.5 shows that more than a quarter of the respondents chose a neutral position on each of the three statements. Compared to the other countries, the percentage of respondents with a neutral position is the highest among Japanese respondents, which implies that many Japanese citizens have never considered or are ambivalent about the potential consequences of accepting more immigrants. A

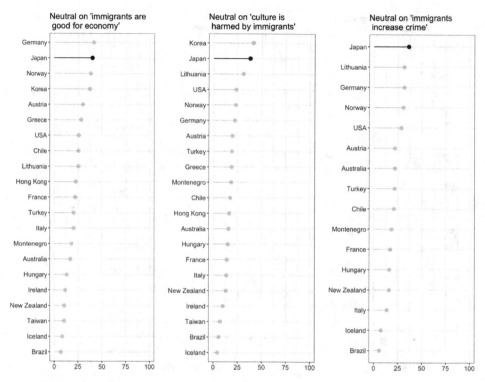

FIGURE 13.5 Ambivalence on economic, cultural, and security threats in Japan and other countries.

Source: CSES Japan data and CSES Module 5 data.

similar pattern is present in Korea, where the size of immigration is similar to that in Japan.

THE INFLOW OF IMMIGRANTS INTO LOCAL AREAS AND NATIVES' ATTITUDES TOWARDS THEM

Next, we investigate whether the inflow of immigrants in local areas is associated with natives' attitudes towards them. Our regression analysis used responses to the five questions in the previous section as an outcome variable. We used a three-point scale of 1 (decrease), 2 (no change), and 3 (increase) regarding the perceived increase in the number of immigrants in local areas. For the question of whether the respondents were willing to accept more immigrants in local areas, we assigned the values of 1 to 4 to each response item (i.e. agree, somewhat agree, somewhat disagree, and disagree), so that larger values denote more negative attitudes towards the increasing size of immigrants. For the potential consequences of accepting immigrants, we used a five-point scale (i.e. strongly disagree, disagree, neither agree nor disagree, agree, and strongly agree). For the statement "immigrants are good for the economy," we assign 1 to strongly agree and 5 to strongly disagree, so that the higher values denote more negative attitudes. For the statements "culture is harmed by immigrants" and "immigrants increase crime," we assign 1 to strongly disagree and 5 to strongly agree, so that the higher values denote more negative attitudes.

Our primary explanatory variable in our regression model is the number of immigrants in the municipality where the respondent resided at the time of the survey. Using data from the Basic Resident Registers, we computed the percentage of foreign residents in the municipalities where the respondents resided in 2017. Our data include 220 municipalities with eight respondents in each municipality, on average. Since many municipalities, apart from major cities, had had only a very limited number of foreign residents until recent years, their number in 2017 can be interpreted as a rough measure of the increase. Foreign residents are required to register in their municipality of residence when staying in Japan for more than three months. Figure 13.6 displays the distribution of the percentage of immigrants in the 220 municipalities in our data. The mean is 1.63, with a minimum of 0.07 and a maximum of 7.53. The variation in the number of immigrants in the municipality allowed us to examine the hypothesis that the respondents showed more negative attitudes as the number of immigrants in the local area increased.

Our regression model controls for several socioeconomic characteristics of municipalities, including population size, per capita income, the percentage of people above 65 years old, college graduates, and the working population in the agricultural, manufacturing, and service sectors. Population size and per capita income were transformed into natural logs.[3] The data for these variables were obtained from the system of social and demographic statistics compiled by the Statistics Bureau of Japan.

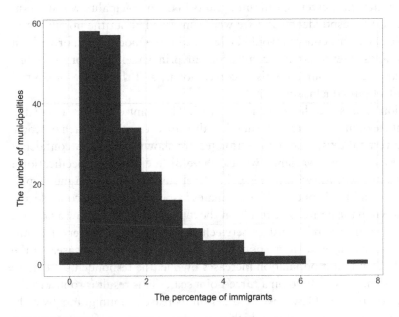

FIGURE 13.6 The size of immigrants in municipalities.

Source: The Basic Resident Registers by Statistic Bureau of Japan.

Furthermore, the regression model also controls for respondents' gender, age, household income, education, marital status, and homeownership. Gender equalled one if the respondent is female and zero otherwise. Age was classified into three categories: young, aged below 40 years; middle-aged, between 41 and 64 years; and senior, aged above 65 years. The youngest group was used as the baseline. Household income was measured in three categories: low, middle, and high, ranging from 2 to 4 million yen, 4 to 8 million yen, and 8 million yen and above. The baseline category was set as the low-income group. We also created an indicator variable that equalled one if the respondent reported no income and zero otherwise, in order to minimize the size of missing observations. College education was equal to one if the respondent graduated from a college or higher institution of education, and zero otherwise. Marital status was equal to one if married and zero otherwise. Homeownership was equal to one if the respondent owned a house and zero otherwise.

As mentioned previously, the respondents answered the survey questions either through in-person interviews or by mail questionnaire. The in-person and mail questionnaires were designed in a similar manner. We created an indicator variable that equalled one if interviewed in person and zero if by mail to consider whether the responses to the questions on immigrants differ between the less anonymous (i.e. in-person interview) and more anonymous modes (i.e. mail questionnaire).

Using these variables, we estimated the linear regression models using three different specifications. The first model included only the percentage of foreign workers as an explanatory variable, while the second model included the percentage of foreign workers and individual-level controls. The third model added municipality-level controls to the second model. We compared the estimation results of these three specifications because the percentage of immigrants in the municipality was not randomly assigned to the respondents, and we were concerned about the possibility of omitted variable bias. This concern would be lessened if the models with or without the control variables showed similar results for our primary explanatory variable. This is important because our analysis is correlational, and the choice of control variables can affect our conclusion.

The estimation results are shown in Figure 13.7. The point estimates associated with the percentage of immigrants in the municipality are presented for each outcome variable on the vertical axis. The point estimates are shown with 95% confidence intervals.[4] For each outcome variable, we use three different model specifications: models without any controls, with municipality-level controls, and with municipality-level and individual-level controls. The estimates associated with the control variables are not shown in the figure. The results at the top of Figure 13.7 show a positive and statistically significant relationship between the increasing number of immigrants in the municipality and the respondent's perception of the increase. As the percentage of the immigrant population increases by one, the respondents are more likely to report an increase of 0.06 on a three-point scale. This result is robust to the inclusion of the control variables. If we consider an increase of immigrants by eight percentage points in the municipality, which is the maximum size of immigrants in our sample, then the coefficient for the model with two sets of controls indicates that

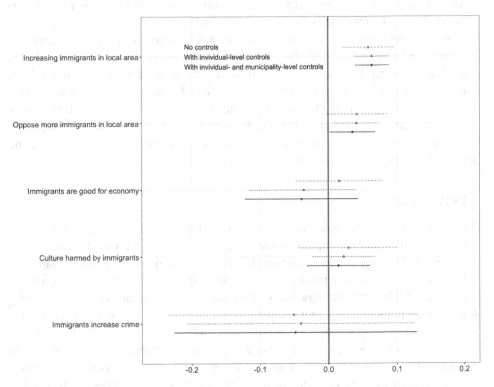

FIGURE 13.7 The percentage of foreign workers in municipalities and negative attitudes towards immigrants among natives.

Source: CSES Japan data.

this increase in foreign population alters the perception by 0.5, half of the change from decreased to no change, or from no change to increased, holding the other variables constant. These results confirm that natives tend to accurately recognize the increase in immigrants in their areas.

Next, the estimation results at the second top of Figure 13.7 show a positive relationship between the percentage of immigrants and the willingness to accept more immigrants. The estimate for the model without any controls is marginally statistically insignificant at the conventional level, but when the individual-level or both the individual and municipality-level controls are included, the 95% confidence intervals do not include zero. The estimate from the model with both sets of controls indicates that the respondents are more likely to oppose increasing the number of foreign residents nearby by about 0.04 on a four-point scale as the percentage of the immigrant population increases by one. The influence of the increasing immigrant population is statistically significant, but substantively small.

Turning to the estimation results for the questions on the economic, cultural, and crime threats imposed by immigrants in Figure 13.7, none of the coefficients is statistically significant, regardless of the specification. The group threat hypothesis predicts that a greater presence of immigrants in the local area would be associated with more negative attitudes and perceived threats. The confidence intervals are particularly large when we focus on the potential increase in crime.

Overall, our regression analyses indicate that Japanese respondents accurately perceive the increasing size of the population of foreign nationals in the local area and show stronger opposition to this increase when faced with a greater inflow. However, the mechanisms that drive such negative attitudes remain unclear because of the lack of strong support for economic and cultural threats. As in Western Europe and North America, the group conflict hypothesis seems to be applicable to Japan with the greater presence of immigrants in recent years, but economic, cultural, and public safety concerns do not seem to be at play.

DISCUSSION

This chapter applies the group conflict hypothesis to Japan, where the size of the immigrant population has been rapidly increasing in recent years. Our analysis using survey data collected in early 2018 reveals that the majority of native-born people in Japan do not show strong negative attitudes towards immigrants and immigration. When residing in areas with more immigrants, people tend to accurately perceive the increasing size of immigrants and oppose it but perceive no economic, cultural, or safety threats.

Some of these results are consistent with the previous literature focusing on Japan and other nations, yet it remains unclear why the greater presence of foreign residents induces natives' opposition to immigration in local areas if the economic and cultural threats are not a powerful explanation. The consensus on the need to address the ageing and declining labour population in Japan may attenuate the negative reactions to the greater presence of immigrants. As mentioned previously, the Technical Training Internship Programme was established primarily to address the labour demands of industries experiencing labour shortages. Foreign workers may pose a limited threat to native-born citizens because they are unlikely to compete for job opportunities with natives.

Limited interactions between immigrants and native-born may also account for the lack of perceived threats. Anecdotal evidence indicates that immigrants tend to remain in their own communities with other immigrants from their country of origin and thus rarely have daily interactions with natives (Mochizuki, 2019). In addition, the number of immigrants in many parts of Japan is still small, given that Japan's immigrant population amounts to 3% of the population of Japan. This is in contrast with Western European and North American countries, where the percentage of immigrants ranges from 4% (Czech Republic) to 30% (Switzerland; Pew Research Center, 2019). The large share of people with neutral attitudes, as shown in Figure 13.5, suggests that the presence of foreign residents is not large enough to prompt strong reactions against them, leaving the natives indifferent. Furthermore, natives may view foreign workers as staying only temporarily in Japan and thus perceive their presence as not seriously influencing Japanese culture.

The greater presence of immigrants in coming years will likely result in more frequent interactions, which may in turn either induce negative attitudes due to a greater sense of cultural or economic threats, or alternatively generate positive attitudes due to increased familiarity. Sniderman et al. (2004) and Hopkins (2014) show that language fluency is viewed as a sign of "fitting-in" in society, thereby increasing support for immigrants, while those with low fluency are less welcomed. Since acquiring proficiency in Japanese is challenging for many reasons, the greater inflow of immigrants may increase negative attitudes. On the other hand, more frequent personal contact may alleviate negative sentiments (Zhang, 2018; Kobayashi et al., 2015).

Finally, it is important to note that our study, as well as other quantitative studies on this topic in Japan, mostly relied on cross-sectional methods, which do not necessarily reveal a causal effect of the increasing size of immigrants on natives' attitudes. Future studies need to employ more rigorous methodologies that use random assignments of ethnic environments. The anticipated inflow of foreign residents will provide us with a variety of research opportunities.

SUMMARY POINTS

- Studies of inter-ethnic relations argue that a greater presence of immigrants in society increases natives' hostile attitudes towards them, leading to support for a more restrictive immigration policy.
- We investigated whether and how the inflow of immigrants in close proximity changes attitudes towards immigration in Japan, one of the most ethnically and linguistically homogeneous societies in the world, using survey data collected after the 2017 General Election.
- We found that the majority of native-born people in Japan do not show strong negative attitudes towards accepting foreign workers and immigrants. When residing in areas with more immigrants, people tend to accurately perceive the increasing size of immigrants and oppose it but perceive no economic, cultural, or safety threats from their presence.

NOTES

1 Many demonstrations were led by the Association of Citizens against the Special Privileges of Koreans in Japan (*Zaitokukai*). Its aggressive protests have even led to a lawsuit, and one of its members was fined for acts of assault and defamation. In 2016, the first anti-racist law was passed following ordinances to restrict hate speech in various municipalities (Matsui, 2016).

2 We used the version of CSES Module 5 as of October 2019.

3 This log-transformation is necessary because the marginal influences of these variables are considered to be non-linear.

4 The standard errors are clustered by municipality.

SUGGESTED FURTHER READINGS

Hainmueller, J. and Hopkins, D.J., 2014. Public attitudes toward immigration. *Annual Review of Political Science*, 17(1), 225–249.

Hangartner, D., Dinas, E., Marbach, M., Matakos, K., and Xefteris, D., 2019. Does exposure to the refugee crisis make natives more hostile? *American Political Science Review*, 113(2), 442–455.

Mayda, A.M., 2006. Who is against immigration? A cross-country investigation of individual attitudes toward immigrants. *Review of Economics and Statistics*, 88(3), 510–530.

Sniderman, P.M., Hagendoorn, L., and Prior, M., 2004. Predisposing factors and situational triggers: Exclusionary reactions to immigrant minorities. *American Political Science Review*, 98(1), 35–49.

REFERENCES

Blalock, H.M., 1967. *Toward a theory of minority-group relations*. New York and London: John Wiley & Sons, Inc.

Blumer, H., 1958. Race prejudice as a sense of group position. *Pacific Sociological Review*, 1(1), 3–7.

Brader, T., Valentino, N.A., and Suhay, E., 2008. What triggers public opposition to immigration? Anxiety, group cues, and immigration threat. *American Journal of Political Science*, 52(4), 959–978. Available from: http://www.jstor.org/stable/25193860.

Braun, R. and Koopmans, R., 2010. The diffusion of xenophobic violence in Germany: The role of social similarity. *European Sociological Review*, 26, 1–15.

Center for Human Rights Education and Training, 2016. *Report of field survey on hate speeches*. Center for Human Rights Education and Training. Available from: http://www.moj.go.jp/content/001201158.pdf. Vol. 2016.

Citrin, J. and Sides, J., 2008. Immigration and the imagined community in Europe and the United States. *Political Studies*, 56(1), 33–56.

Dancygier, R., 2010. *Immigration and conflict in Europe (Cambridge studies in comparative politics)*. Cambridge University Press. doi: 10.1017/CBO9780511762734.

Dustmann, C. and Preston, I.P., 2007. Racial and economic factors in attitudes to immigration. *The BE Journal of Economic Analysis & Policy*, 7(1), 1–41.

Facchini, G. and Mayda, A.M., 2009. Does the welfare state affect individual attitudes toward immigrants? Evidence across countries. *Review of Economics and Statistics*, 91(2), 295–314. doi: 10.1162/rest.91.2.295.

Giles, M.W. and Hertz, K., 1994. Racial threat and partisan identification. *American Political Science Review*, 88(2), 317–326.

Glaser, J.M., 2003. Social context and inter-group political attitudes: Experiments in group conflict theory. *British Journal of Political Science*, 33(4), 607–620.

Golder, M., 2003. Explaining Variation In The Success Of Extreme Right Parties In Western Europe. *Comparative Political Studies*, 36(4): 432–466.

Green, D., 2017. Immigrant Perception in Japan: A Multilevel Analysis of Public Opinion. *Asian Survey*, 57(2), 368–394.

Green, D.P., Strolovitch, D.Z., and Wong, J.S., 1998. Defended neighborhoods, integration, and racially motivated crime. *American Journal of Sociology*, 104(2), 372–403.

Hainmueller, J. and Hangartner, D., 2013. Who gets a Swiss passport? A natural experiment in immigrant discrimination. *American Political Science Review*, 107(1), 159–187.

Hainmueller, J. and Hiscox, M.J., 2010. Attitudes toward highly skilled and low-skilled immigration: Evidence from a survey experiment. *American Political Science Review*, 104(1), 61–84.

Hainmueller, J. and Hopkins, D.J., 2014. Public attitudes toward immigration. *Annual Review of Political Science*, 17(1), 225–249.

Hainmueller, J. and Hopkins, D.J., 2015. The hidden American immigration consensus: A conjoint analysis of attitudes toward immigrants. *American Journal of Political Science*, 59(3), 529–548.

Hangartner, D., Dinas, E., Marbach, M., Matakos, K., and Xefteris, D., 2019. Does exposure to the refugee crisis make natives more hostile? *American Political Science Review*, 113(2), 442–455.

Higuchi, N., 2020 Chap 5. The 'pro-establishment' radical right – Japan's nativist movement reconsidered. In: D. Chiavacci, S. Grano, and J. Obinge, eds. *Civil society and the state in democratic East Asia: Between entanglement and contention in post high growth*. Amsterdam University Press. doi: 10.2307/j.ctv12sdvjk.

Hopkins, D.J., 2010. Politicized places: Explaining where and when immigrants provoke local opposition. *American Political Science Review*, 104(1), 40–60.

Hopkins, N., 2011. Dual identities and their recognition: Minority group members' perspectives. *Political Psychology*, 32(2), 251–270.

Hopkins, D.J., 2014. One language, two meanings: Partisanship and responses to Spanish. *Political Communication*, 31(3), 421–445.

Igarashi, A., 2018. Territorial conflicts and Japanese attitudes towards East Asian Countries: Natural experiments with foreigners' landings on disputed Islands. *Political Psychology*, 39(4), 977–992.

Key, V., 1949. *Southern politics in state and nation*. New York: Alfred A. Knopf.

Kobayashi, T., Collet, C., Iyengar, S., Hahn, K.S., 2015. Who deserves citizenship? An experimental study of Japanese attitudes toward immigrant workers. *Social Science Japan Journal*, 18(1), 3–22.

Matsui, S., 2016. The challenge to multiculturalism: Hate speech ban in Japan. *University of British Columbia Law Review*, 49(1), 427–484.

Mayda, A.M., 2006. Who is against immigration? A cross-country investigation of individual attitudes toward immigrants. *Review of Economics and Statistics*, 88(3), 510–530.

Mazumi, Y., 2015. What shapes public opinion toward foreign workers in the era of the aging of population in Japan: An analysis using JGSS-2008. *JGSS Research Series* 12, 51–61.

Ministry of Health, Labour and Welfare, 2002. *Foreign workers issue research report* (in Japanese). Government of Japan, Tokyo. Available from: https://www.mhlw.go.jp/topics /2002/07/tp0711-1.html.

Ministry of Health, Labour and Welfare, 2018. Registration overview of foreign worker employment status (as of October 2018) (in Japanese). Government of Japan, Tokyo. Available from: https://www.mhlw.go.jp/stf/newpage_03337.html.

Ministry of Justice, 2019. The number of foreign residents in June 2019 (in Japanese). Government of Japan, Tokyo. Available from: http://www.moj.go.jp/nyuukokukanri/ kouhou/nyuukokukanri04_00083.html.

Mochizuki, H., 2019. *Futatsu no Nihon: Imin Kokka no Tatemae to Genjitsu*. Tokyo: Kodansha Gendai Shinsho.

Nagayosi, K., 2009. Whose size counts? Multilevel analysis of Japanese anti-immigrant attitudes based on JGSS-2006. *JGSS Research Series* 6, 157–174.

Nakazawa, W., 2007. The relationship between the number of foreigners residing in Japan and the Japanese prejudices toward foreigners: Multilevel modeling by using the JGSS data, *Soshioroji* 52(2), 75–91.

Newman, B.J., Hartman, T.K., and Taber, C.S., 2012. Foreign language exposure, cultural threat, and opposition to immigration. *Political Psychology*, 33(5), 635–657.

Nukaga, M., 2006. Xenophobia and the effects of education determinants of Japanese attitudes toward acceptance of foreigners. *JGSS Research Series* 2, 191–202.

Oliver, E.J., 2010. *The paradoxes of integration: Race, neighborhood, and civic life in multiethnic America.* Chicago, IL: The University of Chicago Press.

Olzak, S., 1992. *The dynamics of ethnic competition and conflict.* Stanford: Stanford University Press.

Piatkowska, S.J. and Lantz, B., 2021. Temporal clustering of hate crimes in the aftermath of the brexit vote and terrorist attacks: A comparison of Scotland and England and Wales. *British Journal of Criminology*, 61(3), 648–669. doi: 10.1093/bjc/azaa090.

Quillian, L., 1995. Prejudice as a response to perceived group threat: Population composition and anti-immigrant and racial prejudice in Europe. *American Sociological Review*, 60(4), 586–611.

Scheve, K.F. and Slaughter, M.J., 2001. Labor market competition and individual preferences over immigration policy. *Review of Economics and Statistics*, 83(1), 133–145.

Schneider, S. L., 2008 Anti-Immigrant Attitudes in Europe: Outgroup Size and Perceived Ethnic Threat. *European Sociological Review* 24(1), 53–67.

Sniderman, P.M., Hagendoorn, L., and Prior, M., 2004. Predisposing factors and situational triggers: Exclusionary reactions to immigrant minorities. *American Political Science Review*, 98(1), 35–49.

Swank, D., and Betz, H.-G., 2003. Globalization, the welfare state and right-wing populism in Western Europe. *Socio-Economic Review* 1(2): 215–245.

Taylor, M.C., 1998. How White attitudes vary with the racial composition of local populations: Numbers count. *American Sociological Review*, 63(4), 512–535.

Welch, S., Sigelman, L., Bledsoe, T., and Combs, M., 2001. *Race and place: Race relations in an American city.* Cambridge: Cambridge University Press.

Wong, C., 2007. Little' and 'big' pictures in our heads: Race, local context and innumeracy about racial groups in the U.S. *Public Opinion Quarterly*, 71, 392–412.

Zhang, J., 2018. The Less Favored Foreigners: Public Attitudes toward Chinese and South Korean Residents in Japan. *Journal of Asia-Pacific Studies*, 33: 205–217.

CHAPTER 14

The impact of labour market vulnerability

Explaining attitudes towards immigration in Europe

....

Anthony Kevins

INTRODUCTION

From debates about the shifting political allegiances of blue-collar "rust belt" voters in the United States to discussions of the role "left behind" voters may have played in Brexit, economic vulnerability has been attracting a lot of attention. Behind many of these arguments is the claim that labour market vulnerability – i.e. being more at risk of part-time employment, temporary employment, and/or unemployment – may push native-born workers to become more critical of immigrants and immigration. But to what extent does vulnerability actually shape anti-immigrant stances, and does its effect depend on other key factors, like education (see Chapter 7) and the size of the immigrant population (see Chapter 13)? This chapter explores these questions by building on a body of literature that suggests studying labour market vulnerability can help us to better understand politics and public opinion (see Schwander, 2019).

The chapter begins by highlighting the spread of precarious employment across the Global North over the last few decades, tracing the growing divide between labour market "insiders" – who benefit from more robust employment protections and access to more generous social programmes – and "outsiders" – who do not. As I explain below, there are strong reasons to believe that this division will matter, above and beyond the standard measures of well-being and employment status (such as income, education levels, and employment contract type). I then go on to outline some of the psychological and sociological reasons that may lead labour market vulnerability to shape anti-immigrant sentiment; and, based on these considerations, I lay out the argument that vulnerable workers may be especially sensitive to the size of the immigrant population. The chapter then provides an overview of some of the myriad ways that researchers have conceptualized and measured labour market vulnerability, ranging from "snapshot" approaches – examining an individual's employment status at a given moment – to ones that take a much longer time horizon

DOI: 10.4324/9781003121992-17

– incorporating past experiences on the labour market, or even the likelihood of future employment status changes.

The final sections of the chapter then build on these discussions using original empirical analysis – highlighting under what conditions, and to what extent, different types of labour market vulnerability can help us to understand how Europeans think about immigration. To do so, it uses data from approximately 12,000 responses to the 2014 wave of the European Social Survey, including respondents from 18 countries across Europe (ESS, 2014). I then analyze these data by adapting and breaking down an established measure of vulnerability (Schwander and Häusermann, 2013): measuring exposure to unemployment, fixed-term employment, and part-time employment with the help of data from the European Union Statistics on Income and Living Conditions (Eurostat, 2018). The results presented then range from basic bivariate analyses to full multi-level models that take into account an array of individual- and country-level factors.

The findings from this investigation suggest two major takeaways. First, the type of labour market risk that we focus on makes a difference: overall vulnerability, as well as exposure to unemployment and temporary employment, are associated with greater anti-immigrant sentiment; while exposure to part-time employment, by contrast, has no clear effect. Second, the extent to which vulnerability matters depends on education levels and the size of the immigrant population: specifically, labour market vulnerability has a greater expected impact on individuals with lower levels of education who live in countries with larger foreign-born populations.

LABOUR MARKET VULNERABILITY

Why focus on labour market vulnerability? Researchers since at least the 1970s have been pointing to the spread of labour market precarity (e.g. Berger and Piore, 1980; Doeringer and Piore, 1971), as countries have moved away from the post-war "male-breadwinner" model and towards more "flexible" approaches with weaker protections for workers (see, for example, Weisstanner, 2021). Much of this work has centred around a process labelled labour market "dualization," which is marked by a growing divide between *insiders* – who benefit from strong labour market positions and substantial employment protections – and *outsiders* – who do not (e.g. Emmenegger et al., 2012; Kevins, 2015; Piore, 1980). This shift from "standard" to "atypical" employment has, if anything, increased in recent years: the growth of part-time and fixed-term work has occurred alongside the rise of the so-called "gig economy," with more and more workers pushed outside of the standard employment relationship – and thereby deprived of a wide array of rights and protections (e.g. Crouch, 2019).

Further complicating the situation, the dualization of labour markets has also coincided with a dualization of welfare states (e.g. Kevins, 2017). There are (at least) two mechanisms driving this effect. First, since access to a range of social programmes depends on employment trajectories, a growing number of labour market outsiders have found themselves excluded from the more generous set of "insurance-based" welfare benefits (see Haüsermann and Schwander, 2012). Second, governments have by and large failed to compensate for this trend: instead of increasing benefit coverage in order to benefit the growing class of outsiders, they have typically opted to insulate insiders from retrenchment (e.g. Rueda, 2007). The result is a compounding of economic vulnerability: vulnerable workers are not only more likely to be pushed into repeated stints of unemployment (e.g. Ojala, Nätti, and Lipiäinen, 2018), they are also less likely to have access to generous benefits – if any at all – when they are unemployed (e.g. Rueda, 2014). Indeed, research suggests that deregulated and highly dualized labour markets tend to have lower levels of welfare state redistribution more broadly (see, for example, Fernández-Albertos and Manzano, 2016).

The core argument in this area of the literature, then, is that it is not just the classic measures of deprivation, such as income and wealth, that matter: we should be paying attention to labour market risks as well. At the same time, "labour market vulnerability" is not simply another way of referring to education or skill-levels either – a disconnect that is especially clear in Southern Europe, where older low-skilled workers are often better protected than younger high-skilled ones (see, for example, Häusermann, Kurer, and Schwander, 2015). As a consequence, there are good reasons to believe that labour market vulnerability *per se* is an important subject of study.

Building from these arguments, the remainder of this section discusses why, and under what conditions, labour market vulnerability might be expected to impact anti-immigrant sentiment, before turning to consider how best to conceptualize and measure this phenomenon.

The impact of labour market vulnerability

Research on labour market vulnerability has highlighted a wide range of potential negative consequences, including greater political alienation, an increased likelihood of voting for anti-system parties, and lower levels of generalized trust (e.g. Emmenegger, Marx, and Schraff, 2015; Kevins, 2019). Based on the same logic, whereby labour market experiences generate knock-on attitudinal and behavioural effects, it seems probable that opinions on immigration will also be affected. In this section, I lay out common arguments as to why, and under what conditions, this is likely to be the case.

The basic starting point here is that perceptions of economic threat can shape attitudes towards immigrants and immigration (e.g. Heizmann and Huth, 2021; and as discussed in Chapters 6, 7, and 13, for example). Regardless of whether immigrants actually have any meaningful impact on the lives of native-born workers, more vulnerable individuals are disproportionately likely to worry about the consequences of immigration (e.g. Dancygier and Donnelly, 2012): in a pattern reflecting discourses around immigrants not only "stealing" jobs but also "using up" welfare benefits (Taylor-Gooby et al., 2019), workers with lower skill levels tend to be more concerned about the impact immigrants will have on their economic well-being and their access to the welfare state (Gerber et al., 2017); and labour market vulnerability has been associated with more critical beliefs about the economic consequences of immigration more broadly (see Kevins and Lightman, 2020). Similarly, past work suggests that individuals who feel that "people like them" are worse off than immigrants are more likely, all else being equal, to believe that immigration poses an ethnic threat as well (Meuleman et al., 2020).[1]

It therefore seems likely that the economically vulnerable may express the harshest reactions to immigration. Vulnerable native-born workers are likely to at least perceive, if not actually experience, labour market competition with immigrants – partly because immigrants tend to be de-skilled upon arrival in their new country, pushing them into less attractive segments of the labour market (e.g. Lightman and Good Gingrich, 2018). Increased local labour competition with immigrants has, for example, been tied to anti-immigrant sentiment as well as support for anti-immigrant radical parties (Bolet, 2020; Malhotra, Margalit, and Mo, 2013); but research has come to mixed findings on the relationship between vulnerability and immigration policy preferences more broadly (cf. Pardos-Prado, 2020). Further complicating matters, citizens tend to be remarkably bad at estimating the proportion of immigrants in their country, with perceived sizes far outstripping actual ones (e.g. Duffy, 2014). As a consequence, it is unclear whether (objective) immigration population sizes matter for anti-immigrant sentiment – with existing studies coming to mixed conclusions (cf. Gorodzeisky and Semyonov, 2020; Young, Loebach, and Korinek, 2018; and Chapter 13 in this volume).

Despite the many valuable insights generated by past research, however, it is important to note that only a fraction of this work looks specifically at labour market vulnerability: many of the findings are instead centred around proxies for risk exposure, such as low education and skill levels (Paas and Halapuu, 2012) or less transferable skill sets (Pardos-Prado and Xena, 2019). To address my research questions head-on, the second half of this chapter will therefore directly examine the interplay between labour market vulnerability, a more traditional positional measure (namely, education), and the size of a country's immigrant population. Yet before we can do so, we must first consider how, exactly, to measure labour market vulnerability.

Assessing labour market vulnerability

So far, we have seen that there are good reasons to believe that labour market vulnerability, above and beyond the standard markers of well-being and employment status, may shape anti-immigrant sentiment. But labour market vulnerability does suffer from one major shortcoming relative to measures such as income and education: it is much harder to agree on what, in practice, it actually looks like (see Busemeyer and Kemmerling, 2020).

The classical approach to assessing labour market vulnerability, most commonly used in earlier political science research on the topic (e.g. Rueda, 2005, 2007), was a binary one. These studies start from the position that vulnerable workers are either unemployed or on fixed-term or part-time contracts, whereas non-vulnerable workers benefit from permanent full-time contracts. From there, it is easy to construct a simple dichotomous measure of vulnerability: with basic survey data, protected "insiders" – those with standard employment contracts – can readily be distinguished from unprotected "outsiders" – those with atypical contracts, or those currently lacking employment altogether.

This approach generated interesting findings, and also had the benefit of being straightforward – but it was quickly criticized for being overly simplistic (e.g. Marx and Picot, 2013). At least in certain countries, it seems clear that many workers are neither insiders nor outsiders, but somewhere in between (e.g. Jessoula, Graziano, and Madama, 2010). Further complicating matters, in modern, fluid labour markets, it is not uncommon for workers to shift from one type of contract to another – with or without stints of unemployment in between (see, for example, Ojala, Nätti, and Lipiäinen, 2018). This observation has important implications for research on how labour market vulnerability might shape attitudes: just noting down a person's employment status at a given moment will hide a lot of variation in life trajectories (see Schwander and Häusermann, 2013). It seems probable, for example, that a newly minted "insider" who had spent decades in atypical employment will differ in crucial ways from an "insider" who had spent decades in standard employment; similarly, a long-standing "insider" who has been temporarily laid off (and is thus now labelled an "outsider") should probably be distinguished from a worker whose fixed-term contract just ended.

The best approach to addressing this issue is thus to explicitly account for workers' employment histories. This is most commonly done using panel survey data, which provides data for the same set of respondents over a long period of time – allowing researchers to directly examine the long-term consequences of periods of unemployment, fixed-term employment, and part-time work (e.g. Emmenegger, Marx, and Schraff, 2015; Schraff, 2017). Unfortunately, however, this sort of data is expensive, difficult to collect, and relatively rare. Exclusively measuring labour market vulnerability in this way would restrict us to studying a small subset of countries and attitudes; decisions taken years ago by survey organizers around what questions to ask and what countries to study would dictate what researchers will be able to study for decades to come.

Various workarounds have thus been developed to try to assess the labour market vulnerability of individuals when long-term panel data is not available. Rehm (2009), for example, divides workers up into their occupational categories, calculates unemployment rates within each of those occupations, and then assigns each individual a vulnerability score that reflects the prevalence of unemployment in that person's occupation. Schwander and Häusermann (2013), in turn, devised a more refined version of this approach: workers are divided not only by occupational class (see Kitschelt and Rehm, 2005), but also by key demographic characteristics that have been tied to labour market disadvantage (see Häusermann, Kurer, and Schwander, 2016); and they are then assigned vulnerability scores based on the relative rate of unemployment, part-time employment, and fixed-term employment within their particular (demographic-occupational) grouping.

As should now be clear, there is no single, obviously correct way to study labour market vulnerability, and there are major trade-offs to be made between simplicity, accuracy, and data availability (for a detailed discussion, see Marx and Picot, 2020). Thankfully, there is some research to suggest that, at least with regard to certain outcomes, findings are relatively similar across an array of different measures (see Rovny and Rovny, 2017). In the empirical analysis presented here, I use an adapted version of the Schwander and Häusermann (2013) approach, which I then break into its component parts: this gives us an overall vulnerability score (what they call "outsiderness") as well as vulnerability scores measuring the relative risk of part-time employment, fixed-term employment, and unemployment. I provide full details on what this process looks like in practice in the following.

DATA AND ANALYSIS

The remainder of this chapter empirically explores the dynamics highlighted above, combining survey data from the 2014 round of the European Social Survey (ESS, 2014) and the European Union Statistics on Income and Living Conditions (EU-SILC; Eurostat, 2018). As this section outlines in detail, the ESS data allow us to explore the factors shaping anti-immigrant sentiment, while micro-level data from EU-SILC are needed to construct the measures of labour market vulnerability. Overall, the investigation includes data from 11,773 respondents from across 18 European countries (see Appendix Table 14.A1 for a detailed breakdown). Given the focus of this chapter, the study looks only at respondents born in the country they currently live in (i.e. people who are not themselves immigrants) and who are currently still on the labour market (i.e. people who are not retired, on long-term disability, etc.).

Dependent variable

The analysis centres around anti-immigrant sentiment as measured by a six-item index. The first three questions included in the index broadly reflect items in the Comparative Study of Electoral Systems that were considered in Part 2 chapters of this volume. Respondents were asked to give their opinion as to the impact migrants have on:

The economy: "Would you say it is generally bad or good for [country]'s economy that people come to live here from other countries?"

Culture: "Would you say that [country]'s cultural life is generally undermined or enriched by people coming to live here from other countries?"

Crime: "Are [country]'s crime problems made worse or better by people coming to live here from other countries?"

The three other items record additional related attitudes, asking about how migrants affect:

Employment opportunities: "Would you say that people who come to live here generally take jobs away from workers in [country], or generally help to create new jobs?"

Social services: "Most people who come to live here work and pay taxes. They also use health and welfare services. On balance, do you think people who come here take out more than they put in or put in more than they take out?"

Quality of life: "Is [country] made a worse or a better place to live by people coming to live here from other countries?"

Potential responses to each question ranged from zero to ten, and I reverse the scale ordering so that higher values always equate to greater anti-immigrant sentiment. On average, respondents were most worried about how immigrants might affect crime rates (mean response: 6.35) and least worried about their impact on cultural life (mean response: 4.20).[2]

I then combine these six questions (using principal-component factor analysis) to create an index measuring "anti-immigrant sentiment."[3] Appendix Table 14.A2 provides additional descriptive information on the index and its component parts, as well as on all other variables included in the analysis (including means, standard deviations, ranges, and percentage breakdowns).

Independent variables

To examine how economic vulnerability might shape anti-immigrant sentiment, I home in on three key variables: two at the individual level, focusing on labour market risk and education levels; and one at the country level, accounting for the (pro-portional) size of the immigrant population. I start by outlining the measurement of these three explanatory variables before then listing the various controls that are also included in the models.

As we saw above, assessing an individual's exposure to labour market risk can be complex, and there is no single clear way to best measure labour market vul-nerability. Here I use an adapted version of Schwander and Häusermann's (2013) "outsiderness" scores. In brief, this approach centres on the *relative* labour market risk that individuals face based on their specific labour market profile. In the origi-nal form developed by Schwander and Häusermann, these profiles account for dif-ferences based on an intersection of gender, age (over/under 40), and occupational category (divided into the five post-industrial class groups developed by Kitschelt and Rehm, 2005). The measure of labour market vulnerability used in this chap-ter adapts this calculation process in two ways: first, in light of the focus of this study, I add an additional profile marker based on immigration status (designat-ing whether or not an individual or their family has immigrated to the country); and second, in order to incorporate as wide a range of countries into the investi-gation as possible, I use a simpler measure of occupational category, adapted to the broader groupings in the International Standard Classification of Occupations (International Labour Office, 2012).[4]

The next step in the process is to apply these divisions to the detailed EU-SILC micro-level data (Eurostat, 2018), so as to measure the prevalence of part-time employment, temporary employment, and unemployment for any given profile across each of the countries in the dataset. Subtracting these rates from the corresponding country mean then allows us to calculate the *relative* vulnerability of individuals in each profile group. These scores are then standardized, and their average provides an overall "outsiderness" measure. This leaves us with four different labour market vulnerability scores – reflecting the predominance of part-time work, temporary work, unemployment, and their average (i.e. outsiderness) – for every profile (e.g. young, female, native-born managers/professionals) within every country in the analysis. By applying these scores to ESS respondents based on each individual respondent's profile and country of residence, we can then investigate the impact labour market vulnerability has on anti-immigrant sentiment.

Figure 14.1 provides a first indication of how attitudes towards immigrants might be related to the four labour market vulnerability scores under investigation. The figure lays out average anti-immigrant sentiment across each country in the sample, presenting: (1) mean attitudes among those who had a positive risk score (i.e. the comparatively more vulnerable), illustrated with a hollow circle; (2) mean attitudes among those who had a negative risk score (i.e. the comparatively less vulnerable), illustrated with a solid circle; and (3) mean attitudes within the general population, illustrated with a cross. The longer the line between the two dots, the greater the divide between the anti-immigrant attitudes of low- and high-risk individuals. This exercise is repeated four times per country, to illustrate the potential importance of overall labour market vulnerability as well as its three component parts (i.e. exposure to part-time employment, temporary employment, and unemployment).

Breaking the data down in this way reveals several insights. On the one hand, we see sizeable cross-country differences in anti-immigrant sentiment, with Czechs expressing the highest level and Swedes the lowest. On the other, we see a broad pattern suggesting that more vulnerable individuals were more likely than less vulnerable ones to take a critical view of immigrants. Yet we nevertheless also see important variation based on the type of labour market vulnerability under study: exposure to part-time employment has an especially mixed relationship with anti-immigrant sentiment; whereas exposure to unemployment is the measure that most consistently correlates with higher levels of anti-immigrant sentiment.

The other two key explanatory variables are comparatively easy to investigate. To measure education levels, respondents were asked to provide "the highest level of education [they had] successfully completed" in line with the International Standard Classification of Education (UNESCO Institute for Statistics, 2012). I then divide respondents into three groups to reflect low, medium, and high levels of education: those with less than an upper-secondary degree (15.8% of the sample); those with an upper-secondary and/or a post-secondary non-tertiary degree (46.7% of the sample); and those with a tertiary (i.e. university) degree (37.5% of the sample). The size of the immigrant population, in turn, is measured using data from the United Nations (United Nations Population Division, 2015) and captures the proportion of a country's population that was born abroad.

To properly assess the impact of these variables on anti-immigrant sentiment, I also include a series of individual- and country-level controls that past research

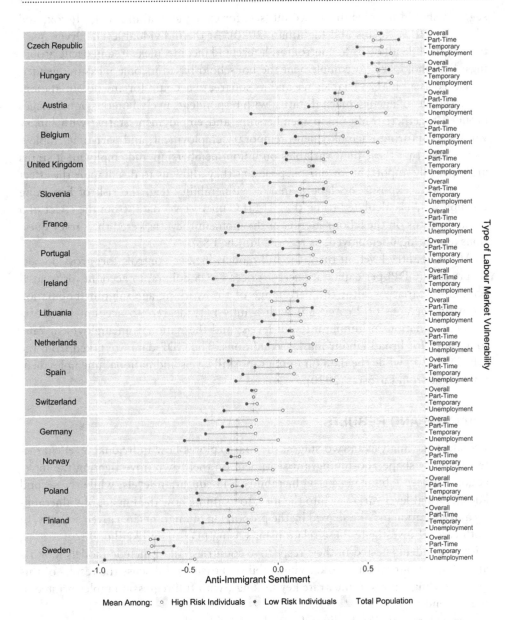

FIGURE 14.1 Mean anti-immigrant sentiment among high-risk individuals, low-risk individuals, and overall, by country and type of labour market vulnerability.

Note: All calculations account for survey design (using post-stratification survey weights) so as to reflect the broader population distribution in each country.

suggests should be taken into account (see, for example, Hainmueller, Hiscox, and Margalit, 2015; Kevins and Lightman, 2020). At the individual level, survey questions in the ESS allow us to control for: household income, measured in decile groupings; household size, to complement the household-based income measure; gender, measured as a binary variable; age and its square, to account for any potential (non-linear) effects of ageing; marital status, with respondents in civil unions or marriages grouped together; trade union membership; and employment status, with binary variables capturing unemployment, temporary employment, and part-time employment. Note that these final variables on union membership and employment status are especially important for our purposes, as they allow us to disentangle the effect of a person's exposure to labour market vulnerability (e.g. the risk of becoming unemployed, as calculated using the EU-SILC micro-level data) from the effect of a person's status on the labour market at the moment they answered the survey questions (e.g. being unemployed, as recorded in the ESS).

At the country-level, in turn, the full models include controls for: gross domestic product (GDP) per capita at current prices in US dollars, to account for general economic scarcity/wealth; the percentage of the working-age migrant population (between the ages of 25 and 69) with a university degree, to account for cross-national variation in immigrant skill levels; and the national unemployment rate, to account for broad labour market conditions. The GDP data are taken from the OECD (2020), while the data on immigrant skill levels and national unemployment rates come from Eurostat (2020).

ANALYSIS AND RESULTS

I conduct the analysis in two stages: the first explores how individual-level characteristics may shape anti-immigrant sentiment on their own, investigating the interaction between labour market vulnerability and education levels; while the second adds national-level variables into the mix, to examine how the impact of vulnerability and education may be shaped by the proportion of migrants in a given country. In both cases, I investigate these relationships using maximum likelihood regressions, with respondents nested in their respective countries; and I include models looking at all four of our labour market vulnerability measures. I discuss the results of this analysis using figures to illustrate key findings, with full regression tables printed in the Appendix.[5]

Turning first to the findings from the individual-level regressions, Figure 14.2 presents the factors that appear to shape anti-immigrant sentiment across the 18 European countries in the sample (see Appendix Table 14.A3 for the underlying regression results). The variables included in the analysis are listed on the left-hand side of the figure, while the panels show the findings for each of the four measures of labour market vulnerability under investigation. Interaction terms are marked with an asterisk (e.g. "Labour Market Vulnerability * Secondary Education") and allow us to examine whether the impact of one variable (e.g. labour market vulnerability)

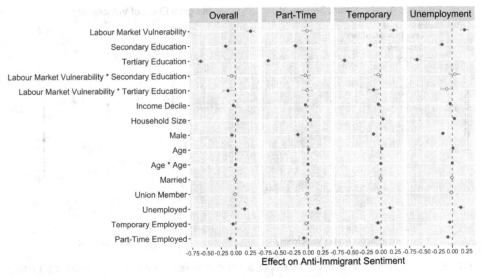

FIGURE 14.2 Factors explaining anti-immigrant sentiment, by type of labour market vulnerability.

Note: Plots are based on the corresponding models found in Appendix Table 14.A3. Figure includes confidence intervals (at the 95 percent confidence level) as well as a dashed vertical line to note the zero marker on the scale.

may change at different values of another variable (e.g. education levels). The circle markers, finally, illustrate the effect a variable has on anti-immigrant sentiment: a hollow circle indicates an effect that we cannot statistically distinguish from zero (i.e. a coefficient that is not statistically significant); while a filled circle indicates an effect that we can conclude with reasonable certainty is above or below zero (i.e. a coefficient that is statistically significant at the $p < 0.05$ level, two-tailed).

Results indicate that among our key control variables, part-time employment is associated with lower anti-immigrant sentiment, whereas unemployment is associated with greater anti-immigrant sentiment (all else being equal). At the same time, and even controlling for other relevant factors, the findings suggest that labour market vulnerability and education levels interact to shape anti-immigrant sentiment: three of our four measures of labour market vulnerability – everything but exposure to part-time work – are associated with stronger anti-immigrant attitudes; while higher education levels are associated with more liberal stances towards immigrants. For both the overall labour market vulnerability and exposure to temporary employment, we also see an additional interactive effect: labour market vulnerability's predicted impact on anti-immigrant sentiment is notably smaller among respondents who have completed university education.

Figure 14.3 digs deeper into this interactive relationship using the results from the regression looking at overall labour market vulnerability (findings vis-à-vis exposure

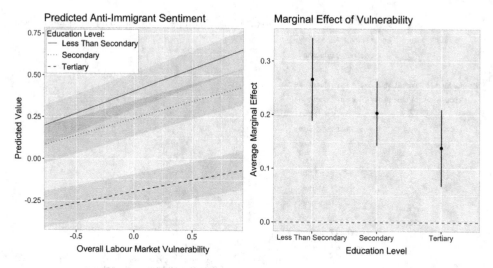

FIGURE 14.3 Relationship between overall labour market vulnerability and anti-immigrant sentiment, by education level.

Note: Plots are based on the "Overall" model found in Appendix Table 14.A3. In the predicted values plot, the x-axis range excludes extreme values of overall labour market vulnerability (below the 5th percentile and above the 95th percentile) to foreground representative effects. The included confidence intervals are: 83.5 percent in the predicted value plot, to highlight where values are statistically distinguishable at the $p < 0.05$ confidence level (overlapping intervals indicate insignificant differences (see Bolsen and Thornton 2014)); and 95 percent in the marginal effect plot, to similarly illustrate statistical significance at the $p < 0.05$ confidence level.

to temporary employment look nearly identical). The figure's left-hand panel shows the predicted level of anti-immigrant sentiment across a range of labour market vulnerability scores (on the x-axis), broken down by education level (illustrated using a solid line for low levels, a dashed line for medium levels, and a dotted line for high levels). The right-hand panel, in turn, illustrates labour market vulnerability's marginal effect on anti-immigrant sentiment, broken down by education level (on the x-axis). This allows us to see the effect that a one-point change in labour market vulnerability would have on anti-immigrant sentiment (i.e. the marginal effect) for three profiles: an "average" respondent with (a) less than secondary education, (b) secondary education, or (c) tertiary education.

Several takeaways emerge from this analysis. First, greater overall labour market vulnerability is associated with stronger anti-immigrant sentiment, regardless of a respondent's education level: the slopes are consistently positive in the predicted values plot, suggesting that as labour market vulnerability increases, so too does anti-immigrant sentiment; and the effect of overall labour market vulnerability is, correspondingly, consistently positive and statistically significant in the marginal effects plot. Second, the predicted values plot highlights that while individuals who completed tertiary education tended to express lower levels of anti-immigrant sentiment, the attitudes of individuals with low and medium levels of education were broadly similar. Indeed, only at high levels of overall labour market vulnerability do the opinions of respondents with low and medium levels of education become statistically distinguishable from one another. Finally, the marginal effects plot indicates that the *size* of labour market vulnerability's effect on anti-immigrant sentiment decreases as education levels increase. Concretely, based on these results we would expect labour market vulnerability's impact on anti-immigrant sentiment to be about twice as large among low-educated individuals as it would be among highly educated ones (with a statistically significant difference between the two effect sizes).

So far, however, I have not yet accounted for potentially relevant differences at the country level. To what extent do these dynamics change if I account for national-level factors, especially when it comes to cross-country differences in immigrant population sizes?

Figure 14.4 lays out how labour market vulnerability, education, and the size of the foreign-born population interact in the models to shape attitudes towards immigration (see Appendix Table 14.A4 for the underlying regression results). The figure illustrates the predicted size of labour market vulnerability's impact on anti-immigrant sentiment across a range of common "migrant stock" levels, with the panels breaking these effects down by education level (i.e. low, medium, and high)

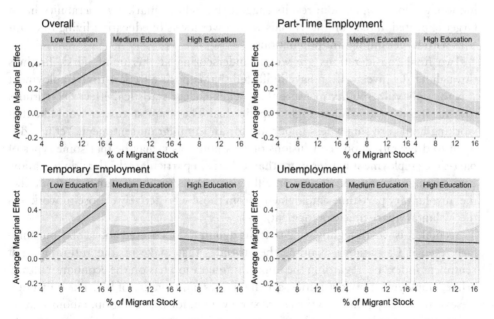

FIGURE 14.4 Impact of labour market vulnerability on anti-immigrant sentiment, by education and immigrant population size (as a percentage of the total population).

Note: Plots are based on the corresponding models found in Appendix Table 14.A4. The x-axis range excludes extreme values of percentage of migrant stock (below the 5th percentile and above the 95th percentile) to foreground representative effects. The figures also include 95 percent confidence intervals, to illustrate statistical significance at the $p < 0.05$ confidence level.

and labour market vulnerability type (i.e. overall, and exposure to part-time employment, temporary employment, and unemployment).

Accounting for national-level variation reveals an important interplay between labour market vulnerability, education levels, and immigrant population sizes. First, the figure points to an even more systematic impact of labour market vulnerability on anti-immigrant sentiment: only with exposure to part-time employment do we see no evidence of an effect. Second, a larger immigrant population magnifies the predicted impact that the other three measures of labour market vulnerability have on anti-immigrant sentiment. Notably, however, this effect is only visible for individuals with low and, in the case of exposure to unemployment, medium levels of education. Lastly, in countries with particularly small immigrant populations (below 5 to 7% of the total population), the predicted impact of labour market vulnerability on anti-immigrant sentiment effectively disappears, becoming statistically indistinguishable from zero.

Results thus suggest that vulnerability does indeed matter and that it does so even after controlling for an array of other labour market– and well-being–related considerations. Overall labour market vulnerability, as well as exposure to unemployment and temporary employment (but not part-time employment), are all associated with higher levels of anti-immigrant sentiment. The scope of this effect, however, depends both on an individual's educational background and on the size of a country's existing foreign-born population: results suggest that labour market vulnerability has a larger expected impact on individuals with lower levels of education living in countries with larger immigrant populations.

Two final considerations are worth underscoring at this point. First, findings throughout the investigation have indicated that exposure to part-time employment was the only vulnerability measure that lacked a clear statistical effect on attitudes towards immigration. What might explain this? The simplest answer would be that working hours are simply less important for anti-immigrant sentiment. Yet it is difficult to draw any strong conclusions on this point, as it may be that some types of part-time employment matter more than others: in particular, the data do not allow us to distinguish individuals who unwillingly work fewer hours than they would like (i.e. involuntary part-time employment) from those who actively choose to work less (i.e. voluntary part-time employment).

Second, it is worth highlighting that the dynamics uncovered above play out similarly even if I separately examine the attitudes that make up the anti-immigrant sentiment index: i.e. regarding the impact immigration has on the economy, culture, crime, employment opportunities, social services, and quality of life. The only notable exception is responses to the *crime* survey item: for this question, labour market vulnerability is only associated with a more anti-immigrant perspective among individuals who have not completed tertiary education; and the size of the immigrant population does not appear to shape the impact of vulnerability among those with less education either. Attitudes on immigrant criminality, then, may be driven by slightly different factors – though even here results suggest that labour market vulnerability and education levels matter.

CONCLUSION

This chapter set out to investigate to what extent, and under what conditions, labour market vulnerability might be an important factor shaping attitudes towards immigrants and immigration. It began by highlighting that labour markets have been marked by increasing precarity in recent decades, reflecting a process typically labelled "dualization" (e.g. Piore, 1980). The interplay between employment status and welfare state access has, in turn, contributed to a growing gap between (relatively) protected insiders and less protected outsiders – generating a variety of attitudinal and behavioural knock-on effects (see Schwander, 2019). It then highlighted why labour market vulnerability might affect anti-immigrant sentiment in particular, and why vulnerable workers might be especially sensitive to the size of the immigrant population. After reviewing various approaches to conceptualizing and assessing vulnerability, the remainder of the chapter empirically examined the relationship between different measures of labour market vulnerability and anti-immigrant sentiment – both directly and in interaction with education and immigration levels.

Extending past work looking at the perceived economic effects of immigration (see Kevins and Lightman, 2020), the empirical analysis highlighted that different types of labour market vulnerability do indeed appear to increase anti-immigrant sentiment. At the same time, the findings also suggested that vulnerability may have an especially strong impact on individuals with lower levels of formal education – a result that chimes with the broad link between education and labour market positions, since risk exposure is likely to be particularly worrisome for low-educated workers. That these same workers were the ones affected by the size of the immigrant population therefore also makes sense. What is more, given how bad citizens tend to be at assessing the size of the immigrant population in their country (e.g. Duffy, 2014), it is noteworthy that the findings indicate that actual (rather than simply perceived) levels of migrant stock may also be shaping the relationship between labour market vulnerability and anti-immigrant sentiment.

SUMMARY POINTS

- This chapter investigated to what extent, and under what conditions, labour market vulnerability may be an important factor shaping attitudes towards immigration.
- After reviewing various approaches to conceptualizing and assessing vulnerability, I examined the relationship between different measures of labour market vulnerability and anti-immigrant sentiment using data from the European Social Survey.
- I found that: (1) the type of labour market risk makes a difference; overall vulnerability, as well as exposure to unemployment and temporary employment, are associated with greater anti-immigrant sentiment, while exposure to part-time employment has no clear effect; and (2) the extent to which vulnerability matters appears to vary based on education levels and the size of the immigrant population: specifically, results suggest that labour market vulnerability has a larger impact on individuals with lower levels of education who live in countries with larger foreign-born populations.

NOTES

1 The relative impact of economic considerations (e.g. perceived self-interest) versus symbolic ones (e.g. perceived ethnic threat) on anti-immigrant sentiment has been subject to considerable debate (see, for example, Hainmueller and Hopkins, 2014). These phenomena are generally difficult to disentangle, however, and very likely to be deeply interconnected (see Baute and Meuleman, 2020).
2 Note that, here and below, all analysis is conducted using survey weights.
3 The Eigenvalue is 3.57, and the proportion of variance explained is 0.59. Factor loadings range from 0.63 (for the *crime* item) to 0.85 (for *quality of life*).
4 These occupational categories are: managers and professionals; technicians and associate professionals; clerical support workers, service and sales workers; skilled agricultural, forestry/fishery workers, and elementary occupations; and craft and related trades workers, plant and machine operators, and assemblers.
5 The figures in this chapter were drawn using several R packages (Kassambara, 2020; Leeper, 2018; Lüdecke, 2018; Wickham, 2016; Wickham et al., 2019). The tables, in turn, were produced using Stargazer (Hlavac, 2018) and Table1 (Rich, 2020).

SUGGESTED FURTHER READINGS

Kevins, A. and Lightman, N., 2020. Immigrant sentiment and labour market vulnerability: Economic perceptions of immigration in dualized labour markets. *Comparative European Politics*, 18(3), 460–484.

Meuleman, B., Abts, K., Schmidt, P., Pettigrew, T.F., and Davidov, E., 2020. Economic conditions, group relative deprivation and ethnic threat perceptions: A cross-national perspective. *Journal of Ethnic and Migration Studies*, 46(3), 593–611.

Pardos-Prado, S., 2020. Labour market dualism and immigration policy preferences. *Journal of European Public Policy*, 27(2), 188–207.

Schwander, H., 2019. Labor market dualization and insider–outsider divides: Why this new conflict matters. *Political Studies Review*, 17(1), 14–29.

REFERENCES

Baute, S. and Meuleman, B., 2020. Public attitudes towards a European minimum income benefit: How (perceived) welfare state performance and expectations shape popular support. *Journal of European Social Policy*, 30(4), 404–420.

Berger, S. and Piore, M.J., 1980. *Dualism and discontinuity in industrial societies*. New York: Cambridge University Press.

Bolet, D., 2020. Local labour market competition and radical right voting: Evidence from France. *European Journal of Political Research*, 59(4), 817–841.

Bolsen, T. and Thornton, J.R., 2014. Overlapping confidence intervals and null hypothesis testing. *The Experimental Political Scientist*, 4(1), 12–16.

Busemeyer, M. and Kemmerling, A., 2020. Dualization, stratification, liberalization, or what? An attempt to clarify the conceptual underpinnings of the dualization debate. *Political Science Research and Methods*, 8(2), 375–379.

Crouch, C., 2019. *Will the gig economy prevail?* Cambridge, UK: John Wiley & Sons.

Dancygier, R.M. and Donnelly, M.J., 2013. Sectoral economies, economic contexts, and attitudes toward immigration. *The Journal of Politics*, 75(1), 17–35.

Doeringer, P. and Piore, M.J., 1971. *Internal labor markets and manpower adjustment*. New York: DC Heath and Company.

Duffy, B., 2014. Perceptions and reality: Ten things we should know about attitudes to immigration in the UK. *The Political Quarterly*, 85(3), 285–288.

Emmenegger, P., Haüsermann, S., Palier, B., and Seeleib-Kaiser, M., 2012. *The age of dualization*. Oxford, UK: Oxford University Press.

Emmenegger, P., Marx, P., and Schraff, D., 2015. Labour market disadvantage, political orientations and voting: How adverse labour market experiences translate into electoral behaviour. *Socio-Economic Review*, 13(2), 189–213.

ESS, 2014. *European social survey round 7 data*. Data file edition 2.2. NSD - Norwegian Centre for Research Data, Norway – Data Archive and distributor of ESS data for ESS ERIC. doi:10.21338/NSD-ESS7-2014

Eurostat, 2018. *Income and living conditions dataset*. Eurostat, ed.

Eurostat, 2020. *European Union – Labour Force Survey*. Luxembourg: Eurostat, the statistical office of the European Union. doi.org/10.2907/LFS1983-2019

Fernández-Albertos, J. and Manzano, D., 2016. Dualism and support for the welfare state. *Comparative European Politics*, 14(3), 349–375.

Gerber, A.S., Huber, G.A., Biggers, D.R., and Hendry, D.J., 2017. Self-interest, beliefs, and policy opinions: Understanding how economic beliefs affect immigration policy preferences. *Political Research Quarterly*, 70(1), 155–171.

Gorodzeisky, A. and Semyonov, M., 2020. Perceptions and misperceptions: Actual size, perceived size and opposition to immigration in European societies. *Journal of Ethnic and Migration Studies*, 46(3), 612–630.

Hainmueller, J. and Hopkins, D.J., 2014. Public attitudes toward immigration. *Annual review of political science*, 17(1), 225–249.

Hainmueller, J., Hiscox, M.J., and Margalit, Y., 2015. Do concerns about labor market competition shape attitudes toward immigration? New evidence. *Journal of International Economics*, 97(1), 193–207.

Häusermann, S., Kurer, T., and Schwander, H., 2015. High-skilled outsiders? Labor market vulnerability, education and welfare state preferences. *Socio-Economic Review*, 13(2), 235–258.

Häusermann, S., Kurer, T., and Schwander, H., 2016. Sharing the risk? Households, labor market vulnerability, and social policy preferences in western Europe. *The Journal of Politics*, 78(4), 1045–1060.

Häusermann, S. and Schwander, H., 2012. Varieties of dualization? Labor market segmentation and insider-outsider divides across regimes. In: P. Emmenegger, S. Haüsermann, B. Palier, and M. Seeleib-Kaiser, eds. *The age of dualization: The changing face of inequality in deindustrializing societies*. Oxford, UK: Oxford University Press, 27–51.

Heizmann, B. and Huth, N., 2021. Economic conditions and perceptions of immigrants as an economic threat in Europe: Temporal dynamics and mediating processes. *International Journal of Comparative Sociology*, 62(1), 56–82.

Hlavac, M., 2018. *Stargazer: Well-formatted regression and summary statistics tables*. Bratislava, Slovakia: Central European Labour Studies Institute (CELSI).

International Labour Office, 2012. *International standard classification of occupations 2008 (ISCO-08)*. Geneva: International Labour Office.

Jessoula, M., Graziano, P., and Madama, I., 2010. 'Selective flexicurity' in segmented labor markets: The case of Italian 'mid-siders.' *Journal of Social Policy* 39(4), 561–583.

Kassambara, A., 2020. *'Ggpubr': 'ggplot2' based publication ready plots*. R package version 0.2.5.

Kevins, A., 2015. Political actors, public opinion, and the extension of welfare coverage. *Journal of European Social Policy*, 25(3), 303–315.

Kevins, A., 2017. *Expanding welfare in an age of austerity: Increasing protection in an unprotected world*. Amsterdam, NL: Amsterdam University Press.

Kevins, A., 2019. Dualized trust: Risk, social trust and the welfare state. *Socio-Economic Review*, 17(4), 875–897.

Kevins, A. and Lightman, N., 2020. Immigrant sentiment and labour market vulnerability: Economic perceptions of immigration in dualized labour markets. *Comparative European Politics*, 18(3), 460–484.

Kitschelt, H. and Rehm, P., 2005. Work, family and politics: Foundations of electoral partisan alignments in postindustrial democracies. Annual Meeting of the American Political Science Association.

Leeper, T.J., 2018. *Margins: Marginal effects for model objects*. R package version 0.3.23.

Lightman, N. and Good Gingrich, L.G., 2018. Measuring economic exclusion for racialized minorities, immigrants and women in Canada: Results from 2000 and 2010. *Journal of Poverty*, 22(5), 398–420.

Lüdecke, D., 2018. Ggeffects: Tidy data frames of marginal effects from regression models. *Journal of Open Source Software*, 3(26), 772.

Malhotra, N., Margalit, Y., and Mo, C.H., 2013. Economic explanations for opposition to immigration: Distinguishing between prevalence and conditional impact. *American Journal of Political Science*, 57(2), 391–410.

Marx, P. and Picot, G., 2013. The party preferences of atypical workers in Germany. *Journal of European Social Policy*, 23(2), 164–178.

Marx, P. and Picot, G., 2020. Three approaches to labor-market vulnerability and political preferences. *Political Science Research and Methods*, 8(2), 356–361.

Meuleman, B., Abts, K., Schmidt, P., Pettigrew, T.F., and Davidov, E., 2020. Economic conditions, group relative deprivation and ethnic threat perceptions: A cross-national perspective. *Journal of Ethnic and Migration Studies*, 46(3), 593–611.

OECD, 2020. *National Accounts Statistics*. Paris: Organisation for Economic Co-Operation and Development. doi.org/10.1787/na-data-en

Ojala, S., Nätti, J., and Lipiäinen, L., 2018. Types of temporary employment: An 8-year follow-up of labour market attachment. *Social Indicators Research*, 138(1), 141–163.

Paas, T. and Halapuu, V., 2012. Attitudes towards immigrants and the integration of ethnically diverse societies. *Eastern Journal of European Studies*, 3(2), 161–176.

Pardos-Prado, S. and Xena, C., 2019. Skill specificity and attitudes toward immigration. *American Journal of Political Science*, 63(2), 286–304.

Pardos-Prado, S., 2020. Labour market dualism and immigration policy preferences. *Journal of European Public Policy*, 27(2), 188–207.

Piore, M.J., 1980. Economic fluctuation, job security, and labor-market duality in Italy, France, and the United States. *Politics & Society*, 9(4), 379–407.

Rehm, P., 2009. Risks and redistribution: An individual-level analysis. *Comparative Political Studies*, 42(7), 855–881.

Rich, B., 2020. Table1. Tables of descriptive statistics in HTML. *R package version 1*.

Rovny, A.E. and Rovny, J., 2017. Outsiders at the ballot box: Operationalizations and political consequences of the insider–outsider dualism. *Socio-Economic Review*, 15(1), 161–185.

Rueda, D., 2005. Insider-outsider politics in industrialized democracies: The challenge to Social Democratic parties. *American Political Science Review*, 99(1), 61–74.

Rueda, D., 2007. *Social democracy inside out: Partisanship and labor market policy in industrialised democracies*. New York: Oxford University Press.

Rueda, D., 2014. Dualization, crisis and the welfare state. *Socio-Economic Review*, 12(2), 381–407.

Schraff, D., 2018. Labor market disadvantage and political alienation: A longitudinal perspective on the heterogeneous risk in temporary employment. *Acta Politica*, 53(1), 48–67.

Schwander, H., 2019. Labor market dualization and insider–outsider divides: Why this new conflict matters. *Political Studies Review*, 17(1), 14–29.

Schwander, H. and Häusermann, S., 2013. Who is in and who is out? A risk-based conceptualization of insiders and outsiders. *Journal of European Social Policy*, 23(3), 248–269.

Taylor-Gooby, P., Hvinden, B., Mau, S., Leruth, B., Schoyen, M.A., and Gyory, A., 2019. Moral economies of the welfare state: A qualitative comparative study. *Acta Sociologica*, 62(2), 119–134.

UNESCO Institute for Statistics, 2012. *International Standard Classification of Education: ISCED 2011*. Montreal: UNESCO Institute for Statistics Montreal.

United Nations, Department of Economic and Social Affairs, Population Division, 2015. Trends in International Migrant Stock: The 2015 Revision. (United Nations database, POP/DB/MIG/Stock/Rev.2015)

Weisstanner, D., 2021. Insiders under pressure: Flexibilization at the margins and wage inequality. *Journal of Social Policy*, 50(4), 725–744.

Wickham, H., 2016. *Ggplot2: Elegant graphics for data analysis*. New York: Springer.

Wickham, H., 2019. Welcome to the Tidyverse. *Journal of Open Source Software*, 4(43), 1686–1692.

Young, Y., Loebach, P., and Korinek, K., 2018. Building walls or opening borders? Global immigration policy attitudes across economic, cultural and human security contexts. *Social Science Research*, 75(April), 83–95.

APPENDIX

TABLE 14.A1 Number of respondents, per country

Country	Observations
Austria	572
Belgium	653
Czech Republic	717
Finland	960
France	748
Germany	1,207
Hungary	511
Ireland	633
Lithuania	656
Netherlands	726
Norway	743
Poland	449
Portugal	413
Slovenia	300
Spain	621
Sweden	738
Switzerland	447
United Kingdom	679
Total	**11,773**

TABLE 14.A2 Descriptive statistics for all variables included in the analysis

	Total (N = 11,773)
Anti-immigrant sentiment	
Mean (SD)	−0.000000000773 (1.00)
Median (min, max)	−0.108 (−2.83, 2.79)
Immigrants harm the economy	
Mean (SD)	4.98 (2.38)
Median (min, max)	5.00 (0, 10.0)
Immigrants harm culture	
Mean (SD)	4.20 (2.48)
Median (min, max)	4.00 (0, 10.0)
Immigrants increase crime	
Mean (SD)	6.35 (1.90)
Median (min, max)	6.00 (0, 10.0)
Immigrants reduce job opportunities	
Mean (SD)	5.19 (2.23)
Median (min, max)	5.00 (0, 10.0)
Immigrants harm social services	
Mean (SD)	5.59 (2.15)
Median (min, max)	5.00 (0, 10.0)
Immigrants bad for the country	
Mean (SD)	4.87 (2.20)
Median (min, max)	5.00 (0, 10.0)
Labour market vulnerability, overall	
Mean (SD)	−0.0110 (0.497)
Median (min, max)	−0.0959 (−1.30, 1.58)
Labour market vulnerability, part-time employment	
Mean (SD)	0.00411 (0.504)
Median (min, max)	−0.193 (−0.717, 1.68)
Labour market vulnerability, temporary employment	
Mean (SD)	−0.0146 (0.496)
Median (min, max)	−0.136 (−1.35, 1.96)
Labour market vulnerability, unemployment	
Mean (SD)	−0.0161 (0.491)
Median (min, max)	−0.103 (−1.14, 2.38)
Education level	
Low education	1,857 (15.8%)
Medium education	5,496 (46.7%)
High education	4,420 (37.5%)
Income decile	
Mean (SD)	6.11 (2.68)
Median (min, max)	6.00 (1.00, 10.0)
Household size	
Mean (SD)	2.74 (1.30)
Median (min, max)	3.00 (1.00, 11.0)
Male	
Female	5,839 (49.6%)
Male	5,934 (50.4%)

(Continued)

TABLE 14.A2 Continued

	Total (N = 11,773)
Age	
Mean (SD)	42.1 (12.8)
Median (min, max)	43.0 (14.0, 87.0)
Union member	
Not in a trade union	8,393 (71.3%)
Union member	3,380 (28.7%)
Unemployed	
Not unemployed	10,822 (91.9%)
Unemployed	951 (8.1%)
Temporary employed	
Not in temporary employment	9,081 (77.1%)
Temporary employed	2,692 (22.9%)
Part-time employed	
Not in part-time employment	9,498 (80.7%)
Part-time employed	2,275 (19.3%)
Married	
Unmarried	6,003 (51.0%)
Married	5,770 (49.0%)
% of migrant stock	
Mean (SD)	11.5 (5.68)
Median (min, max)	12.0 (1.62, 28.8)
GDP per capita	
Mean (SD)	45,100 (21,600)
Median (min, max)	47,800 (14,200, 97,100)
% of skilled migrants	
Mean (SD)	33.1 (8.78)
Median (min, max)	31.3 (13.7, 50.6)
Unemployment rate	
Mean (SD)	8.64 (4.48)
Median (min, max)	8.00 (3.50, 24.4)

TABLE 14.A3 Regression analyses, without country-level variables

| | Dependent variable: anti-immigrant sentiment | | | |
| | Type of labour market vulnerability | | | |
	Overall	Part-time employment	Temporary employment	Unemployment
	(1)	(2)	(3)	(4)
Labour market vulnerability	0.266*** (0.039)	−0.011 (0.049)	0.226*** (0.032)	0.223*** (0.042)
Secondary education	−0.163*** (0.026)	−0.208*** (0.025)	−0.166*** (0.026)	−0.176*** (0.027)
Tertiary education	−0.600*** (0.030)	−0.683*** (0.027)	−0.616*** (0.029)	−0.612*** (0.031)
Labour market vulnerability * secondary education	−0.062 (0.045)	−0.043 (0.047)	−0.034 (0.038)	0.048 (0.052)
Labour market vulnerability * tertiary education	−0.127* (0.050)	−0.012 (0.053)	−0.115** (0.044)	−0.095 (0.059)
Income decile	−0.036*** (0.004)	−0.042*** (0.004)	−0.036*** (0.004)	−0.035*** (0.004)
Household size	0.041*** (0.008)	0.043*** (0.008)	0.040*** (0.008)	0.038*** (0.008)
Male	−0.063** (0.021)	−0.178*** (0.028)	−0.120*** (0.019)	−0.165*** (0.018)
Age	0.016*** (0.005)	0.011* (0.005)	0.018*** (0.005)	0.014** (0.005)
Age * age	−0.0002** (0.0001)	−0.0001* (0.0001)	−0.0002** (0.0001)	−0.0001** (0.0001)
Married	−0.007 (0.021)	−0.003 (0.022)	−0.006 (0.021)	−0.006 (0.021)
Union member	−0.016 (0.024)	−0.021 (0.024)	−0.018 (0.024)	−0.023 (0.024)
Unemployed	0.152*** (0.033)	0.170*** (0.033)	0.156*** (0.033)	0.148*** (0.033)
In temporary employment	−0.050* (0.023)	−0.037 (0.023)	−0.054* (0.023)	−0.048* (0.023)
Part-time employed	−0.101*** (0.023)	−0.077** (0.024)	−0.077*** (0.023)	−0.081*** (0.023)
Constant	0.111 (0.127)	0.386** (0.122)	0.072 (0.126)	0.245* (0.123)
Observations	11,773	11,773	11,773	11,773
Log likelihood	−19,342.770	−19,380.820	−19,338.920	−19,331.220
Akaike inf. crit.	38,721.540	38,797.650	38,713.840	38,698.440
Bayesian inf. crit.	38,854.260	38,930.370	38,846.570	38,831.170

Note: cells contain maximum likelihood regression coefficients, with standard errors in parentheses. All models incorporate population and post-stratification survey design weights. $^+ p<0.10$, $^* p<0.05$, $^{**} p<0.01$, $^{***} p<0.001$.

TABLE 14.A4 Regression analyses, with country-level variables included

	Dependant variable: anti-immigrant sentiment			
	Type of labour market vulnerability			
	Overall	Part-time employment	Temporary employment	Unemployment
	(1)	(2)	(3)	(4)
Labour market vulnerability	0.283*** (0.039)	0.005 (0.053)	0.290*** (0.033)	0.240*** (0.042)
Secondary education	−0.167*** (0.026)	−0.212*** (0.026)	−0.169*** (0.026)	−0.184*** (0.027)
Tertiary education	−0.578*** (0.030)	−0.670*** (0.028)	−0.598*** (0.029)	−0.604*** (0.031)
% of migrant stock (centred)	0.023 (0.020)	0.025 (0.019)	0.013 (0.020)	0.023 (0.020)
Labour market vulnerability * secondary education	−0.062 (0.045)	−0.006 (0.053)	−0.078* (0.038)	0.049 (0.052)
Labour market vulnerability * tertiary education	−0.106* (0.050)	0.045 (0.059)	−0.154*** (0.044)	−0.105+ (0.060)
Labour market vulnerability * % of migrant stock (centred)	0.024** (0.008)	−0.011 (0.012)	0.030*** (0.006)	0.026* (0.011)
Secondary education * % of migrant stock (centred)	−0.006 (0.006)	−0.010+ (0.006)	0.001 (0.006)	−0.005 (0.005)
Tertiary education * % of migrant stock (centred)	−0.035*** (0.006)	−0.035*** (0.006)	−0.027*** (0.006)	−0.032*** (0.007)
Labour market vulnerability * secondary education * % of migrant stock (centred)	−0.030** (0.010)	−0.005 (0.014)	−0.028*** (0.007)	−0.006 (0.013)
Labour market vulnerability * tertiary education * % of migrant stock (centred)	−0.028** (0.011)	−0.0004 (0.016)	−0.034*** (0.008)	−0.027+ (0.015)
Income eecile	−0.037*** (0.004)	−0.042*** (0.004)	−0.037*** (0.004)	−0.036*** (0.004)
Household size	0.043*** (0.008)	0.045*** (0.008)	0.042*** (0.008)	0.041*** (0.008)
Male	−0.047* (0.021)	−0.155*** (0.029)	−0.108*** (0.019)	−0.163*** (0.018)
Age	0.018*** (0.005)	0.012** (0.005)	0.022*** (0.005)	0.016*** (0.005)
Age * age	−0.0002** (0.0001)	−0.0001* (0.0001)	−0.0002*** (0.0001)	−0.0002** (0.0001)

(Continued)

TABLE 14.A4 Continued

	Dependant variable: anti-immigrant sentiment			
	Type of labour market vulnerability			
	Overall	Part-time employment	Temporary employment	Unemployment
	(1)	(2)	(3)	(4)
Married	−0.006 (0.021)	−0.001 (0.021)	−0.007 (0.021)	−0.006 (0.021)
Union member	−0.013 (0.024)	−0.021 (0.024)	−0.014 (0.024)	−0.021 (0.024)
Unemployed	0.154*** (0.033)	0.170*** (0.033)	0.157*** (0.033)	0.148*** (0.033)
In temporary employment	−0.046+ (0.023)	−0.032 (0.023)	−0.048* (0.023)	−0.039+ (0.023)
Part-time employed	−0.105*** (0.023)	−0.081*** (0.024)	−0.079*** (0.023)	−0.087*** (0.023)
GDP per capita (centred)	−0.00001 (0.00001)	−0.00001 (0.00001)	−0.00001 (0.00001)	−0.00001 (0.00001)
% of skilled migrants (centred)	−0.001 (0.009)	−0.002 (0.008)	−0.002 (0.009)	−0.0003 (0.009)
Unemployment rate (centred)	−0.019 (0.018)	−0.021 (0.017)	−0.018 (0.018)	−0.021 (0.018)
Constant	0.034 (0.128)	0.332** (0.123)	−0.034 (0.129)	0.198 (0.125)
Observations	11 773	11 773	11 773	11 773
Log likelihood	−19 348.350	−19 393.860	−19 333.760	−19 336.680
Akaike inf. crit.	38 750.700	38 841.720	38 721.530	38 727.360
Bayesian inf. crit.	38 949.780	39 040.800	38 920.610	38 926.450

Note: cells contain maximum likelihood regression coefficients, with standard errors in parentheses. All models incorporate population and post-stratification survey design weights. $+ p < 0.10$, $* p < 0.05$, $** p < 0.01$, $*** p < 0.001$.

CHAPTER 15

Linguistic cleavages in public opinion

....

Ruth Dassonneville, Nadjim Fréchet, and Baowen Liang

INTRODUCTION

Linguistic diversity is a feature of many democratic countries. In a more limited number of cases, however, language constitutes a social and political cleavage. Given the importance of language in nation-building, such divides often go hand in hand with the linguistic minority calling for independence. But how important is the role of language, and does it extend beyond a connection with attitudes and opinions directly linked with the rights and claims to self-governance of different linguistic groups?

This chapter first offers an overview of earlier work on language as an indicator of social and political differences. Our review of previous literature takes a broad look at the field of public opinion and focuses on linguistic differences in national identity, left–right positions, attitudes on economic issues, post-material issues, and immigration.

In a second section, the chapter zooms in on the dividing role of language in public opinion in Belgium and Canada. We leverage the data from a 2019 election survey in Belgium and the 2019 Canadian Election Study – that both include comparable measures of public opinion – to qualify the strength of the linguistic cleavage in both countries. Our analyses suggest meaningful differences in the political views and attitudes that the language groups hold in both countries. These differences relate to opinions on the future of the country and conceptions of national identity, but we also find differences in terms of other political attitudes – both economic and non-economic. Our analyses also indicate that the role of language in public opinion is comparable to that of other social cleavages, such as education or religion (for more on socioeconomic determinants and religion, see Chapters 7 and 8, respectively). These results signal that to understand public opinion in linguistically divided countries, it is important to consider the role of language. At the same time, our analyses

DOI: 10.4324/9781003121992-18

show a great deal of similarity in the opinions and attitudes of different linguistic groups. The differences are overall too small to characterize the countries as constituting two public opinions.

IS LANGUAGE (STILL) A CLEAVAGE?

Scholars of public opinion and elections have long been interested in how social cleavages shape public opinion and voting behaviour. In particular, the work of Lipset and Rokkan (1967) has drawn attention to the structuring role that cleavages play in societies. They identified four cleavages that they found were present across established democracies: a cleavage between the centre and the periphery, one between state and church, a cleavage distinguishing owners and workers, and a rural-urban cleavage. According to Lipset and Rokkan (1967), the presence of these social cleavages was key to understanding why electoral behaviour and party systems were so stable.

The increase in electoral volatility (Chiaramonte and Emanuele, 2017) and the rise of new challenger parties across established democracies (De Vries and Hobolt, 2020), are sometimes taken as an indication that the impact of cleavages is weakening over time. Such observations have spurred lively debates about the decline of the effects of social class or religion on the vote (Evans, 2000; Knutsen, 2004; Goldberg, 2020). Others have argued that we are witnessing a realignment rather than a dealignment, with new cleavages emerging and structuring citizens' preferences and electoral behaviour. It has been argued that citizens are increasingly divided based on their level of education (Stubager, 2010), age, or ethnic background (Ford and Jennings, 2020). See Chapter 4 for more on the role of age in shaping public opinion.

This chapter focuses on an "old" cleavage that has received comparatively less attention than class or religion: language. The role of language in public opinion can be connected to the centre-periphery cleavage that Lipset and Rokkan (1967) identified. More specifically, they described the centre-periphery cleavage as a "conflict between the central nation-building culture and the increasing resistance of the ethnically, linguistically and religious subject population in the provinces and peripheries" (Lipset and Rokkan, 1967, p. 14). Even though not all centre-periphery cleavages are based on a language conflict, in many countries where an opposition between the centre and more peripheral regions structures party competition and shapes public opinion, the minorities living in the periphery speak a different language than the majority. These minorities become mobilized in reaction to the homogenization policies put in place by the centre. Classic work on linguistic conflicts argues that language differences are particularly divisive when paired with differences in social mobility and when there is one language group that clearly dominates (Inglehart and Woodward, 1967). Examples include the Catalan and Basque minorities in Spain, the Flemish in Belgium, or the Quebecers in the Canadian context. But even in countries that at first sight appear linguistically homogeneous such as Germany, language differences and variation in dialects have been found to correlate with political attitudes and behaviour (Ziblatt, Hilbig, and Bischof, 2020).

Even though linguistic divisions are thus closely connected to Lipset and Rokkan's centre-periphery cleavage, not every linguistic division in a society fundamentally structures politics. Following classic definitions of what constitutes a cleavage, for language to be considered a cleavage, it is essential that there are linguistic groups and that members of the different groups can be distinguished based on their values, leading them to develop an identification with their group. It is also thought essential that organizations or parties are formed to represent the interests of the groups (Bartolini and Mair, 1990; Deegan-Krause, 2007). In many linguistically diverse countries, the organizational condition is fulfilled by the presence and electoral success of parties that represent the minorities, such as Junts per Catalunya or the Basque Nationalist Party in Spain, the New Flemish Alliance in Belgium, or the Bloc Québécois in Canada. But do different linguistic groups also have (strongly) divergent values and political preferences? Work documenting an over-time trend of nationalization of election results across Western democracies (Caramani, 2004) suggest a weakening of such differences.[1] To answer this question, in a first step, we turn to the literature and provide an overview of the state of the art on whether and to what extent linguistic differences correlate with differences in public opinion. Our review of the literature focuses strongly, but not exclusively, on the Belgian and Canadian cases. Following our literature review, we analyze survey data from these two countries in more depth to examine the extent to which public opinion is divided by language.

LANGUAGE DIFFERENCES IN PUBLIC OPINION

Language, national identity, and support for independence

A first aspect of public opinion that has been given much attention by scholars studying the role of language relates to citizens' attitudes towards the nation-state, their region, and preferences for independence. That is not surprising, as these attitudes are closely related to the very reason for the emergence of language cleavages in many democracies.

Work focusing on the Belgian case has studied differences in regional and national identities between the Dutch-speaking Flemish and the francophone Walloons.[2] Such analyses point to important differences in both groups' feelings of identity and their attachment to different territorial units. For example, Billiet, Maddens, and Frognier (2006) show that subnational feelings are much stronger in Flanders than in Wallonia. The flip side of the coin is that the identification with Belgium is stronger in Wallonia. These differences in terms of identities also translate into different levels of support for a further federalization of the country – an issue that the Flemish are more in favour of than the Walloons.

Blais (1991) has characterized the linguistic cleavage in Canada as stronger than that in Switzerland, but not as strong as the Belgian linguistic cleavage. Even so, in the Canadian setting as well, language differences shape national identities. Relatedly, language correlates with citizens' views about the future of the country and support for Québec sovereignty. The connection between language and support for the independence of Québec extends beyond the opposition between those living in the province of Québec and those living in other Canadian provinces. Inside the province as well, speaking French is a strong predictor of support for Québec sovereignty. This holds when focusing on differences between anglophones and francophones in Québec (Bélanger and Perrella, 2008), but the role of language is also visible when focusing on newcomers. Bilodeau (2016), for example, shows that among newcomers, the use of French is positively correlated with identifying with Québec and with support for the independence of Québec. The connection between language and Québec identity and support for independence is further identified in the work of Brie and Ouellet (2020). Using an experimental approach, they show that exposure to English is associated with higher support for the sovereignty of Québec. Along the same lines, it has been shown that Quebecers' perceptions of the vitality of French and their views on whether French is under threat correlate with support for independence (Medeiros, Fournier, and Benet-Martínez, 2017; Medeiros, 2017).

The Catalan case provides another example of a setting where there is a strong connection between language and national identity (Miley, 2007) and support for independence (Orriols and Rodon, 2016; Serrano, 2013). Here as well, the role of language is not limited to what language an individual speaks. Rodon and Guinjoan (2018), for example, show that for those with dual identities, support for the independence of Catalonia increases significantly as more people in one's immediate environment speak Catalan.

Even in the United States, a context that is not typically thought of as a setting characterized by a strong linguistic cleavage, there are indications that language shapes national identity. In particular, the work of Citrin et al. (2007) shows that the fact that Hispanic immigrants assimilate and rapidly lose Spanish leads them to feel more patriotic and to develop a stronger national identification. The connection between speaking a certain language and national identity is not universal, however. Focusing on the case of Taiwan – a context with great linguistic diversity – Dupré (2013, p. 442) argues that "language is not an important component of national identity."

Language and attitudes towards the economy

Turning to the association between language and other attitudes, because linguistic cleavages are often connected to inequalities in social mobility, language is regularly found to correlate with individuals' economic preferences.

Evidence in Belgium shows that the linguistic cleavage might be related to attitudes about income redistribution and the welfare state. Flanders possesses a thriving economy with low unemployment levels, while Wallonia struggles to recover from the decline of the old industrial sector that was particularly developed in the south of the country. As a result, Walloons tend to be more to the left than their Flemish counterparts on economic issues (Béland and Lecours, 2006; de Jonge, forthcoming; De Winter, Swyngedouw and Dumont, 2006; Sinardet and Hooghe, 2009). In addition to being more right-wing on economic issues, Flemings are less supportive of increasing federal social programmes since they view them as benefiting Walloons first. These differences are reflected in the positions of parties on both sides of the language border, with both far-right and more moderate Flemish parties favouring a more confederal union, with distinctive social programmes for both regions of their country (Béland and Lecours, 2006).

In Canada as well, language correlates with economic attitudes. Specifically, French-speaking Quebecers are more prone to support a strong role for provincial governments in the economy than English Canadians. There is, in fact, a strong connection between Québec nationalism and attitudes towards the welfare state. This association finds its origins in the 1960s, when the political elites of Québec saw the development of the welfare state as a tool they could leverage to reduce socioeconomic inequalities between French-speaking Quebecers and English Canada (Béland and Lecours, 2005; Gidengil et al., 2012; Medeiros, Fournier, and Benet-Martínez, 2017).

Overall, linguistic differences in terms of economic attitudes mostly concern disagreement about the extent to which federal and regional governments should be involved in the economy. However, the support for or opposition to specific and symbolic economic policies can also be intrinsically linked to a linguistic group's identity. For example, English Canadians are more strongly opposed to healthcare privatization because this policy has become a source of identity and distinctiveness from the United States (Dufresne, Jeram, and Pelletier, 2014; Gidengil et al., 2012).

Canada and Belgium are not the only countries where linguistic cleavage correlates with citizens' attitudes on the government's involvement in the economy. The association between language and economic attitudes is notable in other contexts, such as the United States or Israel. For instance, the growing presence of a Spanish-speaking population in the south of the United States affects English-speaking Americans' attitudes on key social programmes. Huddy and Sears (1995) find strong evidence that English-speaking Americans oppose government investments in bilingual education programmes since they feel economically threatened by Latinos' growing presence (see also, Guibernau, 2007). These findings suggest that the link between language and economic attitudes relates to each group's (perceptions of) access to state resources. Such group dynamics lead to an impact of linguistic diversity on redistribution that is statistically significant and substantively important (Desmet, Weber, and Ortuño-Ortín, 2009).

Language and cultural and post-material attitudes

There is ample evidence that linguistic cleavages also structure citizens' attitudes towards cultural issues. Many Western democracies have been facing a growing number of immigrants, and concerns about immigration have become even more salient in the wake of the refugee crisis.[3] Work on linguistically diverse countries often finds different opinion patterns from separate language communities regarding immigration policy and racial minorities. In Canada, a traditional strand of research contends that Quebecers hold more negative attitudes towards multiculturalism and immigration than English-speaking Canadians (Bolduc and Fortin, 1990; Lambert and Curtis, 1983). A predominant explanation for this phenomenon is Quebecers' sense of linguistic and cultural insecurity (Bouchard, 2012). However, recent research paints a more nuanced picture. As Québec is gaining more control over its immigration policy, some studies suggest that a more open attitude towards immigration is developing among French-speaking Canadians (Gidengil et al., 2003; Turgeon and Bilodeau, 2014). Nevertheless, other work still reveals important regional and linguistic differences. Bilodeau, Turgeon, and Karakoç (2012) find that among the ten Canadian provinces, Quebecers have the coldest attitudes towards immigrants. Furthermore, French-speaking Quebecers hold even more hostile attitudes towards immigrants and racial minorities than English-speaking Quebecers.

Research on Belgium and Spain reveals similar regional disparities. In Belgium, Flemings' and Walloons' views on immigrants are not strikingly different (De Coninck et al., 2018; de Jonge, forthcoming; Meeusen, Boonen, and Dassonneville, 2017), but they have quite different reasons to be against immigration. Flemings usually feel more threatened in terms of cultural issues, while the French-speaking community in the South is more likely to be preoccupied with competition with immigrants regarding employment and social provisions (Billiet, Maddens, and Frognier, 2006). Work on the Spanish case shows that regional identification is a predictor of anti-immigrant sentiment among Basques, Catalans, and Galicians, with those strongly identifying with their region having more exclusionary attitudes (Escandell and Ceobanu, 2010).

In addition to countries where language has been a source of division for centuries, there is also evidence that language explains opinion divergence in places where linguistic division is a more recent phenomenon. The growing importance of the Hispanic population in the United States leads many researchers to study how the perception and usage of Spanish influence people's attitudes towards immigration. Some work interested in the dominant non-Hispanic white population shows that incidental exposure to the Spanish language increases the perception of cultural threat, which subsequently shapes anti-immigrant sentiments and other policy preferences (Newman, Hartman, and Taber, 2012). Enos (2014) even provides causal evidence from the US context that shows that individuals exposed to a linguistic outgroup (i.e., Spanish-speakers) develop more exclusionary attitudes. Other studies, however, do not find a direct effect of Spanish exposure on restrictive immigration attitudes – but argue that the effect of language is conditional on non-Hispanic white Americans' party identity (Hopkins, 2014), prior contact with Spanish (Hopkins, Tran, and Williamson, 2014), and immigrants' efforts to adhere to American norms (Hopkins, 2015). Studies on Hispanic Americans' opinions also demonstrate that language is a relevant factor, with more frequent use of Spanish-language media leading to more liberal attitudes towards immigration (Kerevel, 2011).

Beyond immigration, language appears to link to opinions on other non-economic issues as well. The linguistic cleavage is sometimes found to correlate with citizens' attitudes towards the place of religion and religious symbols. In Canada, regional differences in opinions regarding religious symbols in the public sphere are particularly strong. Opposition to religious accommodation is higher in Québec than in other Canadian provinces (Bridgman et al., 2021; Dufresne et al., 2019; Turgeon et al., 2019). Moreover, within the province of Québec, it is the largely francophone voters outside Montréal who are most supportive of the Québec Charter of Values – a document that aimed to create a secular society (Tessier and Montigny, 2016). There is also work that shows that individuals who have more liberal attitudes in Québec hold different views towards religious minorities and take a different position in terms of the public display of religious symbols than liberals in other Canadian provinces. More specifically, Turgeon et al. (2019, p. 247) find that in Québec liberalism is associated with "support for restrictions on the wearing of minority religious symbols [...], but it is associated with opposition to such restrictions in the rest of Canada."

There is less systematic research on language differences concerning other non-economic issues. Though for these issues as well, research sometimes discovers different attitudes between linguistic groups. For example, research finds that Flemings are somewhat more in favour of euthanasia than Walloons (Cohen et al., 2012) and less prejudiced towards homosexuals (Meeusen, Boonen, and Dassonneville, 2017). These differences suggest the Flemish have more culturally left-wing attitudes, which contrasts with their position on economic issues. Differences in libertarian and authoritarian positions are also visible in Canada, with Quebecers having more left-liberal values than English-speaking Canada (Baer, Grabb, and Johnston, 1993).

The sources of language differences in public opinion

Previous research has documented important differences in the attitudes and positions of language groups in linguistically diverse countries. Based on previous work, differences are particularly strong for groups' identities and their attitudes towards the future of the country, but differences on economic and cultural issues are not uncommon either.

What do we know about the reasons for the emergence of linguistic differences in public opinion? Previous work has argued that mechanisms of socialization, contact between linguistic groups, media, and elite discourses can all shape and reinforce language differences in public opinion. Some authors conceive language as an identity that results from a socialization process that subsequently shapes political preferences. For example, Davidson et al. (2017, p. 104) who find that both regional and linguistic identities shape Canadian citizens' preferences for redistribution, point to the role of schools in this process of socialization. In the Canadian context, they argue that "provisions for linguistically and religiously differentiated school boards have helped sustain distinct group identities." When language identities form, these can subsequently be strengthened by the lack of interaction between in- and out-groups. More specifically, it has been argued that a lack of contact between the two main language groups in Belgium strengthens the differences in political attitudes and preferences (Thijssen et al., 2021). Context-level factors can also affect the extent to which public opinion is divided along linguistic lines. In this regard, scholars have paid close attention to the role of news media. Mendelsohn and Nadeau (1996) theorize that exposure to broadcast media has the potential to reduce social cleavages, but that media coverage that is directed towards a section of public opinion – which they refer to as narrowcasting – can strengthen such cleavages. In Canada, Mendelsohn and Nadeau (1996) find indications of a reinforcement of the cleavage when the focus is Québec, given that media messages were tailored to the different opinions about the issue in both language communities. Similarly, Sinardet (2013) argues that in Belgium, the "media on both sides of the language border seem to have contributed to the polarization of political positions."

There is, thus, not only much evidence of linguistic differences in public opinion. There are also good theoretical reasons why we observe such differences in many linguistically diverse settings. To more systematically assess the extent to which language groups have different opinions and how important these differences are for different types of issues, we next turn to an empirical analysis of opinion differences in two linguistically diverse countries: Belgium and Canada.

AN EMPIRICAL TEST: LANGUAGE AND PUBLIC OPINION IN BELGIUM AND CANADA

Data

To explore to what extent public opinion in Belgium and Canada is divided along linguistic lines, we use recent election surveys. Both countries held an election in 2019, and in the context of those elections scholars in both countries fielded surveys to study citizens' political attitudes and party preferences. The surveys that we rely on both included the questions of the fifth module of the Comparative Study of Electoral Systems (CSES) project, which are also used in Part 2 of this book. The inclusion of the CSES questions provides us with datasets that share many common questions, facilitating the comparisons between countries. However, we do not limit our analyses to common questions and rely on country-specific ones to study language differences in issues that are particularly salient in either of the two countries.

For Belgium, we rely on a probabilistic survey fielded by the Centre for Citizenship and Democracy at KU Leuven following the 2019 regional and federal elections. Respondents in the two main regions of Belgium (Flanders and Wallonia) were sampled from the National Register,[4] and they were sent a paper survey by regular mail. This procedure resulted in 1,820 completed surveys with a response rate of 22.8%.

For Canada, we use the data from the 2019 Canadian Election Study (CES) phone survey (Stephenson et al., 2020, 2021). While the CES team also fielded an online survey in the context of the 2019 Canadian elections, we focus on the phone survey because its probability sampling (based on random digit dialing) makes it more comparable to the Belgian study. The CES consisted of a pre- and a post-election wave, but given that CSES questions were included in the post-election wave, our focus is mostly on the latter. A total of 4,021 respondents completed the pre-election phone survey of the CES, and the response rate for this initial survey was 5.6%. Of the pre-wave respondents, 2,889 (71.8%) also completed the post-election survey – either over the phone or online.

Given that the response rates are rather low, our analyses consistently rely on weighted data to ensure the samples are representative of their respective populations in terms of sociodemographic characteristics.[5]

Measures and methods

To evaluate whether members of different language groups have different political opinions and preferences, we focus on differences in means and evaluate whether differences are significant using t-tests. In Belgium, we operationalize language based on a survey question asking respondents to indicate which language they often use at home. More than 98% of the respondents indicated that this language was either Dutch (61.6%) or French (36.6%). Given their small numbers, respondents indicating they usually speak another language than Dutch or French at home were dropped from the analyses. For Canada, we similarly break apart language groups using information about the language spoken most at home. Of all respondents who participated in the post-election wave, 78.5% indicated English, and 19.8% indicated French. The remaining 2% of respondents were dropped from the analyses.

In comparing means, our focus is on differences based on respondents' language, not the province or region in which they live – even though there is considerable overlap between language and place of living. In Belgium, a division based on language corresponds closely to an analysis of differences between regions. In Canada, the connection between the place of living and language is weaker. There are important francophone communities that do not live in the province of Québec (Johnston, 2017), and a substantial number of anglophones live in Québec as well. Except for an analysis that focuses specifically on Québec sovereignty, all our analyses of the Canadian data consider the role of language in the country as a whole.

We analyze language differences in public opinion regarding three broad categories of attitudes. A first set of attitudes relates to national identity and positions on the future of the federal state. In Belgium, attitudes about the future of the country were measured using a 0–10 item tapping whether respondents thought the regions and communities should be given more power (0), whether the division of power should stay as is (5) or whether the federal government should be given more power (10). In Canada, we rely on a question asking respondents (those living in Québec only) whether they were very favourable, somewhat favourable, somewhat opposed, or very opposed to Québec sovereignty (coded from 1 = very favourable to 4 = very opposed). We also explore whether the language groups in both countries have different views on what they see as essential elements of national identity. More specifically, respondents in both countries were asked to indicate the importance of having been born in their country, having grandparents that were born in the country, being able to speak one of the country's official languages, and following the country's customs and traditions for being "truly" Belgian/Canadian (we coded the answer scales for these items to run from 1 = not important at all to 4 = very important).

Second, we evaluate whether the language groups in both countries differ in terms of their general left–right positions (measured on a scale from 0 = left to 10 = right in both countries) and concerning their views on redistribution. To capture preferences for redistribution, in Belgium, we use a survey item asking respondents to indicate their agreement with the statement that the government should reduce income differences (coded to run from 1 = completely agree to 5 = completely disagree). In Canada as well, we rely on a survey item asking respondents to indicate whether they agree that the government should take measures to reduce income differences (coded from 1 = strongly agree to 5 = strongly disagree). The coding allows consistently interpreting higher values as more right-wing attitudes.

Third, we explore whether there are differences in the language groups' positions on post-materialist issues. Our focus is on attitudes towards the environment and attitudes about immigration. Respondents' environmental attitudes are captured using questions that tap their preferences for government spending on the environment. In the Belgian survey, we focus on preferences for spending in terms of environmental policies and climate change. We distinguish between respondents indicating they want less (coded as 0), the same (coded 1), or more spending (coded 2) in these areas – and we focus on average spending preferences across these two items (the two items strongly correlate, with a Cronbach's α of 0.77). The Canadian election survey included a similar item asking respondents to indicate whether they think the government should spend more, less or about the same on the environment. Attitudes towards immigration were measured in the same way in the two countries. Both surveys included a battery of items asking respondents to indicate their level of agreement with the items "Immigrants are generally good for [country's] economy," "[country's] culture is generally harmed by immigrants," and "immigrants increase crime rates in [country]." These are the same questions as the ones used in Part 2 of this book. Respondents could indicate their level of agreement on a five-point scale, from strongly disagree to strongly agree. Answers on these items correlate strongly in both countries (Cronbach's α of 0.79 in Belgium and 0.76 in Canada), allowing us to create a scale of anti-immigrant attitudes based on these three items.[6] The anti-immigrant attitude scale was coded, so 1 corresponds to the least anti-immigrant attitudes and 5 corresponds to the most anti-immigrant attitudes.

RESULTS

Support for independence and national identity

Language groups are often at opposite ends on the centre-periphery cleavage, which explains why linguistic minorities regularly favor independence. In Belgium, where subsequent state reforms have transformed the country from a unitary into a federal state, discussions about future reforms are ongoing. Such debates oppose those who think the trend towards federalism – whereby the regions have gained more political power – has gone too far from those who think the state reforms should go further and allow the regions to take control over an even larger number of governing competencies. In the 2019 election survey from Belgium, respondents were asked to take a position on this issue, on a scale from 0 = all competencies to the regions to 10 = all competencies to the federal level. On this scale, a score of five signals that the respondent thinks the distribution of competencies must remain as it is.

Figure 15.1 shows the mean answer of respondents on this survey item, by language group. First, it can be noted that for both groups, the average score is close to 5, which corresponds to a status quo position. However, we also see that the two language groups are on average on opposite sides of that status quo option. The Dutch-speaking Flemish are on average in favour of transferring more competencies to the regions, while the average response among francophones is closer to the re-federalization end of the scale. On this issue, which is at the core of debates about the future of Belgium, differences in opinions between the two linguistic groups are significant ($p < 0.001$).

In Canada, debates about the country's future are more focused on the status of Québec in the Canadian federation. This debate has already led to the organization of two independence referenda (in 1980 and 1995). The pro-independence side has failed to secure a majority of the votes each time, though the 1995 referendum was a particularly close call (50.6% voted no) (Nadeau, Martin, and Blais, 1999). The sovereignty debate is a question that divides public opinion within the province of Québec. Accordingly, the 2019 Canadian Election Survey only asked respondents living in Québec to take a position on this issue.

Figure 15.2 shows the average level of support for Québec independence among francophones and anglophones in Québec, as reported in the 2019 Canadian Election Study. The survey item was scaled from 1 to 4, where 1 signifies that the

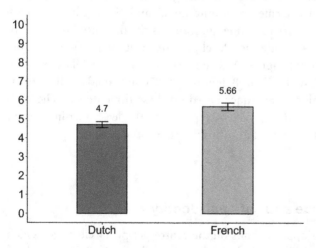

FIGURE 15.1 Attitudes about the future of Belgium.

Note: Bars show average score on a scale from 0 to 10, where 0 means a respondent wants all competencies to be at the regional level and 10 means the respondent wants all governing competencies at the federal level. 95% confidence intervals are added on top.

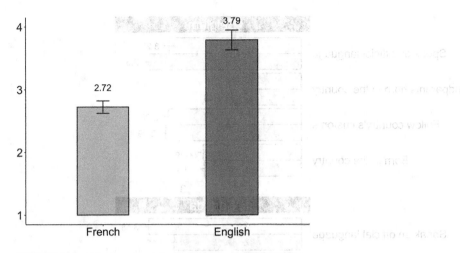

FIGURE 15.2 Attitudes about the independence of Québec.

Note: Bars show average score on a scale from 1 to 4, where 1 means very favourable to Quebec independence and 4 means very opposed. 95% confidence intervals are added on top.

respondent is very favourable to Québec independence, and 4 corresponds to the respondent being very opposed to Québec sovereignty. Higher values thus imply that respondents are more opposed to the idea of an independent Québec. As shown in Figure 15.2, both language groups hold significantly different opinions on the issue of sovereignty. The average score for French respondents in Québec is 2.7, while it is 3.8 for anglophones in Québec. This difference between the two language groups is easily statistically significant (p < 0.001). In short, while francophones in Québec hold somewhat lukewarm attitudes towards the idea of an independent Québec, anglophones living in Québec are strongly opposed to it.

Language differences in linguistically diverse countries correlate not only with citizens' views about the future of the country. The literature has pointed out that language differences can also shape national identities. To examine the role of language in citizens' conceptions of nationalism in Belgium and Canada, we explore how different language groups assess the role of being born in a country, having grandparents that were born in a country, speaking one of the main languages of the country, and following the country's customs and traditions for being considered Belgian/Canadian. In Belgium, we assess differences in attitudes between Dutch-speaking and francophone respondents in the 2019 election survey. In Canada, we turn back to the full sample of the 2019 CES survey and examine the differences between anglophones and francophones across the country.

Starting with conceptions of Belgian national identity, the top panel in Figure 15.3 shows how important Dutch- and French-speaking Belgians consider language, family roots, following the country's customs, and being born in Belgium to be considered Belgian. We see that the two groups hold fairly similar views concerning the importance of different attributes to being Belgian. Overall, speaking an official language

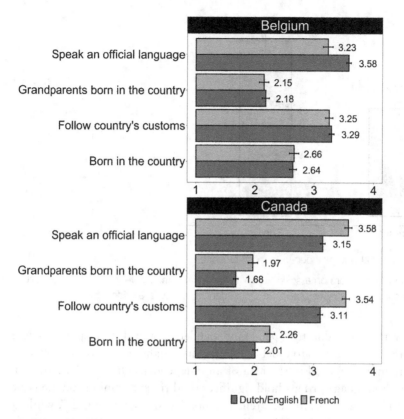

FIGURE 15.3 Importance of different attributes to being Belgian/Canadian.

Note: Bars show average scores on a scale from 1 to 4, where 1 means not important at all and 4 means very important. 95% confidence intervals are added on top.

and following the country's customs are thought of as most important, followed by being born in a country and one's grandparents being born in the country. The degree to which respondents in the two language groups rate these items as important is similar. In fact, there is only one item for which Dutch and French-speaking respondents give answers that differ significantly: the item asking about the importance of speaking an official language. Among francophone respondents, the average importance rating for this item is 3.2, while it is 3.6 for Dutch-speaking respondents (p < 0.001). That the Flemish attach more importance to the role of language in Belgium is not surprising. After all, the use and acceptance of Dutch as one of Belgium's official languages resulted from a long political struggle, and the Flemish Movement is still actively seeking ways to protect Dutch – especially in Brussels, where the Dutch-speaking language group is a minority (Deschouwer, 2012).

Conceptions of national identity appear to differ more strongly between language groups in Canada. This is clear from the bottom panel in Figure 15.3, showing how English- and French-speakers in Canada rate the importance of the same four items.

As can be seen from the graph, for each of the four items, francophones (the light grey bars) seem to attach more importance to it than anglophones (the dark grey bars). This holds for the importance of speaking an official language (3.6 among francophones versus 3.2 among anglophones) and the importance of following the country's customs (3.5 among francophones and 3.1 among anglophones), as well as for individuals and their grandparents being born in the country. Furthermore, the difference in the importance that francophones and anglophones attach to the items, is statistically significant – with p-values < 0.001 – for each survey item.

In both Belgium and Canada, language differences are associated with citizens' views about the future of their country and their conceptions of national identity. Overall, the differences concerning these items seem to be somewhat more important in the Canadian context than what holds for Belgium. Attitudes about the possibility of Québec independence – which are only measured in the province of Québec – differ strongly between francophones and anglophones. Furthermore, conceptions of national identity between the different language groups in Canada differ quite strongly, with French-speakers systematically attaching more importance to language, family roots, following customs, and being born in the country for being considered "truly" Canadian. In Belgium, we also observe differences between Dutch- and French-speakers, but differences are fewer and tend to be smaller.

Left–right positions and economic attitudes

Next, we explore whether the language groups have different opinions when focusing on their general left–right positions and their economic attitudes. Starting with citizens' self-placement on a left–right scale, Figure 15.4 plots the average self-placement of respondents on a 0–10 left–right scale by language group and country. The left-hand panel shows that the Dutch-speaking Flemish, on average, place themselves about 0.8 points more to the right than francophones. This difference is statistically

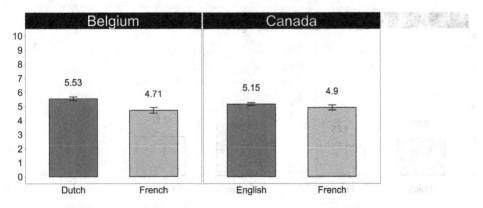

FIGURE 15.4 Left–right positions by language group in Belgium and Canada.

Note: Bars show average score on a scale from 0 to 10, where 0 means left and 10 means right. 95% confidence intervals are added on top.

significant (p < 0.001). In Canada, the two language groups are much more similar in their left–right orientations. The right-hand panel in Figure 15.4 shows that English-speaking Canadians in the 2019 Canadian Election Study, on average, had a left–right self-placement of 5.2, while it was 4.9 for French-speaking Canadians. This difference is statistically significant at the 0.05 level, yet it is substantively small, especially compared to the ideological difference observed in Belgium.

That Flemish voters are significantly and substantively more right-leaning than Walloon voters does not come as a surprise. Election results in Belgium quite systematically show that conservative parties such as the Christian-democratic party and radical right-wing parties perform better in Flanders than in the French-speaking part of Belgium. The francophone socialist and green parties, for their part, have a stronger electoral base in the south than do their Dutch-speaking counterparts in Flanders (Deschouwer, 2012; Pilet, 2021). Such differences in the electoral strength of parties, it seems, are at least in part driven by the fact that public opinion in Flanders is, on average more right-leaning than that in Wallonia.

Traditionally, left and right capture opposing views about the role the state should play in the economy. More specifically, left-wing positions correspond to a view that the state should intervene in the economy to ensure a redistribution of wealth. In contrast, people on the right do not want the government to intervene in the market. Over time, however, this economic interpretation of the left–right division in politics is argued to make a view of left and right as opposing views on cultural issues. Attitudes towards immigration, in particular, are argued to correlate with citizens' self-placement on a left–right dimension (De Vries et al., 2013). As a result, if we want to understand the extent to which different linguistic groups hold similar or different views on economic issues and the role of the state in the economy, it might be better to draw on direct measures of such views.

Both the Belgian and Canadian surveys included survey items that tap citizens' views on government action regarding economic inequalities. In Figure 15.5, we

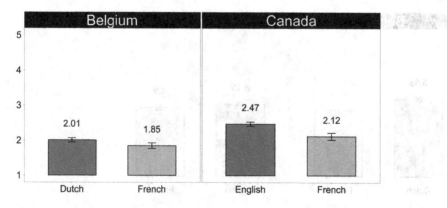

FIGURE 15.5 Positions on income inequality by language group in Belgium and Canada.

Note: Bars show average score on a scale from 1 to 5, where higher values correspond to less government intervention. 95% confidence intervals are added on top.

plot the average scores on such a measure by language group. In both countries, the measures are scaled to run from 1 to 5, whereby 5 corresponds to a preference for less government intervention (i.e. a more economically right-wing attitude).

Figure 15.5 plots the average scores of respondents on these measures for Belgium (left panel) and Canada (right panel). In both countries, the graphs show that French-speakers are economically more left-wing than the other language group. In Belgium, Dutch-speakers have an average score of 2.0 on the two items, while it is 1.9 for francophones. This difference, while small, is significant at the 0.05 level. In Canada, a similar pattern emerges. Here as well, francophones appear to be economically somewhat more left-leaning. The average answer on the item asking Canadian respondents to what extent the government should take measures to reduce income levels is 2.1 for francophones, while it is 2.5 for anglophones. The difference between the two language groups is significant, with $p < 0.001$.

In terms of citizens' left–right orientations, there are noticeable language differences in both countries. Francophones tend to position themselves to the left of the other language group in Belgium and in Canada. The difference is particularly pronounced in Belgium, with French-speakers placing themselves almost a full point (0.8) more to the left than Dutch-speakers. When looking more specifically at citizens' economic positions, we find a pattern consistent with the general ideological one: francophones appear to be economically somewhat more left-wing than Dutch-speakers in Belgium or anglophones in Canada. However, it is noticeable that when focusing on economic positions, the ideological gap between Dutch- and French-speaking Belgians appears to be more muted than what the analysis based on ideological self-placement suggested. For the Belgian case in particular, different economic attitudes only seem to be a part of why the Flemish tend to position themselves in a more right-wing ideological position than francophones. In the Canadian case, the reverse seems to hold, as it seems that the two language groups differ somewhat more in terms of their economic left–right positions than what holds if a general left–right scale is considered. Clearly, to better understand the sources of general ideological differences between the language groups in both countries, we must move beyond a focus on economic issues. In the next section, we, therefore, turn our attention to other types of issues.

Environmental and anti-immigrant attitudes

While a single economic left–right dimension has long been a useful tool to understand voting behaviour and party competition in many established democracies, recent work points to the emergence of a second political fault line (Kriesi, 2010; Hooghe and Marks, 2018). This new political cleavage is sometimes referred to as a GAL/TAN cleavage, whereby GAL stands for green, alternative, and libertarian positions, and TAN captures the traditional, authoritarian, and nationalist end of the dimension (Bakker et al., 2015). In terms of party competition, non-mainstream parties take a strong position on this cleavage, which pits radical-right parties against new left and green parties. To understand the sources of support for such new parties, it is important to look beyond a left–right dimension and to account for measures of public opinion that tap the opposition between GAL and TAN points of view.

The Belgian and Canadian surveys each include measures to capture two elements of this second dimension; environmental attitudes and attitudes towards immigration. Using these items, we examine whether the different language groups in Belgium and Canada can be distinguished in terms of their views about the environment and their anti-immigration attitudes.

Starting with environmental attitudes, we focus on survey items that tap whether respondents want more government spending in terms of environmental policies or to combat climate change. Table 15.1 shows the average responses to those items, that were originally coded so 0 corresponds to wanting less spending, 1 means respondents want spending to remain at current levels, and 2 corresponds to wanting more spending. Table 15.1 also shows the difference in means between the linguistic groups and the p-value for that difference.

As can be seen from Table 15.1, Dutch- and French-speakers in Belgium hold very similar environmental attitudes. On average, both language groups prefer more spending in terms of the environment/to fight climate change, and the difference in opinions between the two groups is not statistically different. In Canada, by contrast, environmental attitudes do seem to differ significantly based on respondents' language. Both language groups have a clear tendency to want more environmental spending, but this preference is significantly more pronounced among francophone Canadians than among anglophones (average score of 1.8 for French-speakers versus 1.6 for anglophones). The difference between the two groups is about 0.2, which is statistically significant.

Finally, we assess whether there is evidence of a language division in terms of public opinion on immigration. Recall that in both countries, the anti-immigration attitude scale was constructed by combining three items, tapping respondents' views on the consequences of immigration in terms of the economy, culture, and crime rates. We coded the scales in such a way that higher levels correspond to more anti-immigrant attitudes.

Figure 15.6 shows the average scores of the different language groups on the anti-immigrant scales in Belgium (left panel) and Canada (right panel). Looking at attitudes in Belgium first, the graph shows that Dutch-speakers, on average, hold significantly more anti-immigrant views than French-speakers (3.4 versus 3.1, p-value < 0.01). This difference in means might be part of why there are viable radical right-wing parties in Flanders, while no such party has emerged in the French-speaking part of the country (de Jonge, forthcoming). In Canada, like in Belgium, the two language groups hold anti-immigrant attitudes that are significantly different (p-value < 0.001). In the

TABLE 15.1 Environmental attitudes by language group in Belgium and Canada

	Dutch/English	French	Difference	p-value
Belgium	1.39	1.41	0.02	0.736
Canada	1.58	1.75	0.17	0.000

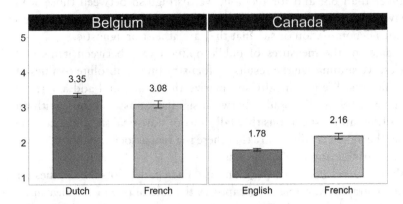

FIGURE 15.6 Anti-immigrant attitudes by language group in Belgium and Canada.

Note: Bars show average score on a scale from 1 to 5, where higher values correspond to more anti-immigrant attitudes. 95% confidence intervals are added on top.

Canadian case, however, francophones hold more anti-immigrant views (2.2) than the other language group (1.8). Both groups, however, appear to be substantially more tolerant towards immigrants than the respondents in the Belgian survey.

The comparative importance of the language cleavage

The results presented in the previous section suggest the important role that language plays in public opinion in Belgium and Canada. It is somewhat difficult to assess the importance of these differences in isolation, however. As a final step, we conducted additional analyses to get a better sense of the importance of language in public opinion in Belgium and Canada, compared to other sociodemographic cleavages.

More specifically, we focus on public opinion concerning themes not specific to language issues, focusing on general left–right views, opinions on income redistribution, environment spending, and anti-immigrant attitudes. We contextualize the role of language by comparing it to the extent to which other social cleavages structure public opinion, with a focus on the effects of gender, education, income, age, and religion. Note that chapters from Part 2 address these other determinants more deeply. Specifically, on gender, see Chapter 5; on education and income, see Chapter 7; on age, see Chapter 4; and on religion, see Chapter 8.

We estimated a series of four multivariate regression models in each country, each time including predictors for six different social cleavages, to explain four different measures of public opinion. To enhance the comparability of the analyses, we assessed the role of each cleavage using a dichotomous indicator. For language, we distinguish between French-speakers and Dutch-speakers in Belgium or anglophones in Canada. For gender, we distinguish between female and male respondents; for education, we focus on the distinction between those with and without a higher education degree; for income, we dichotomize continuous household income variables to distinguish between high and low incomes; for age, we contrast those 65 or older with those younger than 65; and for religion, we distinguish between those who indicate they have a religious denomination and those who either indicate they do not have a religious denomination or say that they are atheist or agnostic.

Because the scales of the measures of public opinion vary between items and between countries, we summarize the results by focusing on the absolute t-values of the cleavage coefficients. We graphically summarize the results and add a vertical line to the graphs at 1.96, to distinguish between significant associations (with an absolute t-value > 1.96) and associations that fall short of statistical significance. The larger the t-value, the more certain we are that there is a real association between the sociodemographic variable and public opinion.

Figure 15.7 shows the results for the Belgian case. Each panel plots the t-values for a specific sociodemographic variable (that captures the role of one of the cleavages) in each of the four regression models. The graphs suggest strong evidence of the education and income cleavages structuring the opinion of Belgian citizens. However, neither of these cleavages shapes general left–right positions. It is the language cleavage that, in fact, appears to be an important societal cleavage in terms of left–right views. In addition, language also significantly predicts Belgian citizens' attitudes

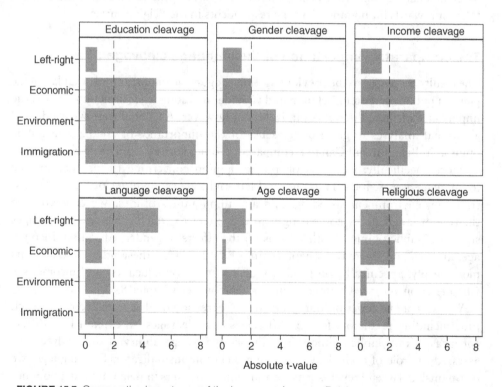

FIGURE 15.7 Comparative importance of the language cleavage, Belgium.

Note: Bars show absolute t-values of four multivariate OLS regression models, with the six cleavage variables as the independent variables and the four measures of public opinion as the dependent variables.

towards immigration. Overall, the role of language in public opinion in Belgium resembles that of gender and religion, while age seems to be the least effective cleavage, accounting only for Belgians' opinion about the environment.

For Canada, we proceed similarly and plot the absolute t-values of dichotomous cleavage indicators, based on four separate OLS models that each time include six cleavage indicators as independent variables. Figure 15.8 suggests that language is one of the most important sociodemographic characteristics. Only language and religion are significantly associated with each of the four measures of public opinion. Furthermore, the size of the absolute t-values suggests that we can have a good deal of certainty in the presence of this association – more so than what holds for the roles that gender, income, or age play in shaping public opinion in Canada.

These additional analyses provide further evidence that language forms a relatively important cleavage. In addition to being connected with citizens' views about the country's future and their conceptions of national identity, the language that citizens in Belgium and Canada speak at home is also associated in meaningful ways with citizens' economic and non-economic opinions. The structuring role of language in public opinion is, in fact, comparable to that of other sociodemographic characteristics, such as education or religion.

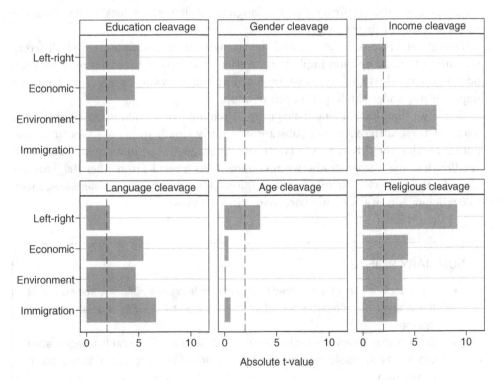

FIGURE 15.8 Comparative importance of the language cleavage, Canada.

Note: Bars show absolute t-values of four multivariate OLS regression models, with the six cleavage variables as the independent variables and the four measures of public opinion as the dependent variables.

CONCLUSION

Sociodemographic characteristics can shape public opinion in important ways. In this chapter, our focus was on the role of language, focusing on the association between language and political attitudes in linguistically diverse countries.

The presence of important differences in the opinions of language groups can be politically consequential. If language groups hold different views on all major issues, this will create a political gridlock or consistently put one group in a minority position. Neither of those outcomes is viable in the long term and might strengthen the push for separation or independence.

Previous work has shown that the language that citizens speak often correlates with the views and opinions they hold. There is even some work that points to the causal effects of language and exposure to a different language on public opinion. Therefore, it is not surprising that we find indications that Dutch- and French-speakers in Belgium, and francophones and anglophones in Canada, hold significantly different positions on some political issues. The differences that we find are generally in line with earlier work that has studied these countries. We find, for example, that the Flemish are more right-leaning than francophone Belgians and that francophones in Canada are more economically left-leaning than anglophone Canadians. We also confirm the role of language in shaping citizens' views about the political future of their country.

Overall, the role of language and the strength of its associations with different measures of public opinion imply that its effect is comparable to that of other sociodemographic cleavages. At least in Belgium and Canada, considering language improves our understanding of public opinion.

While we find that the linguistic groups often hold views that differ significantly, many of these differences are substantively fairly small. In some cases, it is also noticeable that the differences between the language groups in a country are much smaller than the differences between countries. As a result, in neither Belgium nor Canada, there are two distinct public opinions. Instead, linguistic differences, much like religion, education, or income, shape citizens' views.

SUMMARY POINTS

- Many societies are characterized by linguistic heterogeneity and in some instances these language differences take the form of a political cleavage and affect public opinion.
- By analyzing survey data from Belgium and Canada, we found language-based differences in public opinion in both countries, including on attitudes about immigration.
- Our findings suggest that the language cleavage found in Belgium and Canada has an impact comparable to that of other sociodemographic cleavages.

NOTES

1 Though Knutsen (2010) shows that this decline is far from universal, with a strengthening of the regional cleavage in Belgium, Italy, and Spain.
2 It should be noted that the Belgian Federal state is composed of both regions and linguistic communities and that the two do not perfectly overlap. While the Flemish region corresponds quite closely to where the Flemish community lives, francophones live in the Walloon region and constitute a majority in the Brussels capital region (Deschouwer, 2012). Because data on public opinion in Brussels is more difficult to obtain, most work that studies differences between the two language groups opposes the Flemish and francophones in Wallonia. For the same reasons, the small German-speaking minority living in the Walloon region is usually not considered in public opinion research.
3 This increased salience has not resulted in more anti-immigrant attitudes overall (Stockemer et al., 2018), but is associated with a polarization of attitudes towards immigration in Western Europe (van der Brug and Harteveld, 2021).
4 Given the costs of surveying a bilingual region without knowledge of the language of respondents, the Brussels Capital Region is often excluded from sampling frames in Belgium. While the exclusion of this region is unfortunate, a focus on Flanders and Wallonia only still implies that the survey covers about 90% of the Belgian population.
5 For Belgium, the weights ensure the sample is representative of the population in terms of gender, age, and level of education. In the Canadian sample, the weights correct for the province of residence and phone ownership.
6 The statement that immigrants are generally good for the economy was reverse coded so higher values consistently correspond to more anti-immigrant views. The chapters in Part 2 of this book code anti-immigrant attitudes in the exact same way.

SUGGESTED FURTHER READINGS

Hopkins, D.J. 2015. The upside of accents: Language, inter-group difference, and attitudes toward immigration. British Journal of Political Science, 45, 531–557.
Inglehart, R.F. and Woodward, M., 1967. Language conflicts and political community. *Comparative Studies in Society and History*, 10(1), 27–45.
Newman, B.J., Hartman, T.K., and Taber, C.S., 2012. Foreign language exposure, cultural threat, and opposition to immigration. *Political Psychology*, 33(5), 635–657.

REFERENCES

Baer, D., Grabb, E., and Johnston, W., 1993. National character, regional culture, and the values of Canadians and Americans. *Canadian Review of Sociology/Revue Canadienne de Sociologie*, 30(1), 13–36.
Bakker, R., De Vries, C., Edwards, E., Hooghe, L., Jolly, S., Marks, G., Polk, J., Rovny, J., Steenbergen, M., and Vachudova, M.A., 2015. Measuring party positions in Europe: The Chapel Hill expert survey trend file, 1999–2010. *Party Politics*, 21(1), 143–152.
Bartolini, S. and Mair, P., 1990. *Competition to identity. Electoral instability and cleavage persistence in Western Europe 1885–1985*. Cambridge: Cambridge University Press.
Béland, D. and Lecours, A., 2005. The politics of territorial solidarity: Nationalism' and social policy reform in Canada, the United Kingdom, and Belgium. *Comparative Political Studies*, 38(6), 676–703.
Béland, D. and Lecours, A., 2006. Sub-state nationalism and the welfare state: Quebec and Canadian federalism. *Nations and Nationalism*, 12(1), 77–96.
Bélanger, E. and Perrella, A., 2008. Facteurs d'appui à la souveraineté du Québec chez les jeunes: une comparaison entre francophones, anglophones et allophones. *Politique et sociétés*, 27(3), 13–40.

Billiet, J., Maddens, B., and Frognier, A.-P., 2006. Does Belgium (still) exist? Differences in political culture between Flemings and Walloons. *West European Politics*, 29(5), 912–932.

Bilodeau, A., 2016. Usage du français et préférences politiques des néo-Québécois. *Canadian Journal of Political Science*, 49(1), 41–62.

Bilodeau, A., Turgeon, L., and Karakoç, E., 2012. Small worlds of diversity: Views toward immigration and racial minorities in Canadian provinces. *Canadian Journal of Political Science*, 45(3), 579–605.

Blais, A., 1991. Le clivage linguistique au Canada. *Recherches Sociographiques*, 32(1), 43–54.

Bolduc, D. and Fortin, P., 1990. Les francophones sont-ils plus 'xénophobes' que les anglophones au Québec? Une analyse quantitative exploratoire. *Canadian Ethnic Studies – Etudes Ethniques au Canada*, 22(2), 54.

Bouchard, G., 2012. *L'interculturalisme: un point de vue québécois*. Montréal: Éditions Boréal.

Bridgman, A., Ciobanu, C., Erlich, A., Bohonos, D., and Ross, C. 2021. Unveiling: The electoral consequences of an exogenous mid-campaign court ruling. *The Journal of Politics*, 83(3), 1024–1029.

Brie, E. and Ouellet, C., 2020. Exposure to English as a determinant of support for Quebec independence in the 2018 Quebec elections. *French Politics*, 18(3), 238–252.

Caramani, D., 2004. *The nationalization of politics: The formation of national electorates and party systems in Western Europe*. Cambridge: Cambridge University Press.

Chiaramonte, A. and Emanuele, V., 2017. Party system volatility, regeneration and de-institutionalization in Western Europe (1945–2015). *Party Politics*, 23(4), 376–388.

Citrin, J., Lerman, A., Murakami, M., and Pearson, K., 2007. Testing Huntington: Is Hispanic immigration a threat to American identity? *Perspectives on Politics*, 5(1), 31–48.

Cohen, J., Van Wesemael, Y., Smets, T., Bilsen, J., and Deliens, L., 2012. Cultural differences affecting Euthanasia practice in Belgium: One law but different attitudes and practices in Flanders and Wallonia. *Social Science & Medicine*, 75(5), 845–853.

Davidson, A., Lesch, M., Héroux-Legault, M., Whyte, T., Asaf, Z., Czuba, K., and Porisky, A., 2017. Advancing the study of political cleavages through experimentation: Revisiting regionalism and redistributive preferences in Canada. *Regional & Federal Studies*, 27(2), 103–125.

De Coninck, D, Matthijs, K., Debrael, M., Joris, W., Cock, R.D., and d'Haenens, L., 2018. The relationship between media use and public opinion on immigrants and refugees: A Belgian perspective. *Communications*, 43(3), 403–425.

de Jonge, L., 2021. The curious case of Belgium: Why is there no right-wing populism in Wallonia? *Government and Opposition*, 56(4), 598–614.

De Vries, C.E., Hakhverdian, A., and Lancee, B., 2013. The dynamics of voters' left/right identification: The role of economic and cultural attitudes. *Political Science Research and Methods*, 1(2), 223–238.

De Vries, C.E. and Hobolt, S.B., 2020. *Political entrepreneurs. The rise of challenger parties in Europe*. Princeton, NJ: Princeton University Press.

De Winter, L., Swyngedouw, M., and Dumont, P., 2006. Party system(s) and electoral behaviour in Belgium: From stability to balkanisation. *West European Politics*, 29(5), 933–956.

Deegan-Krause, K., 2007. New dimensions of political cleavage. In: R.J. Dalton and H.-D. Klingemann, eds. *Oxford handbook of political behaviour*. Oxford: Oxford University Press, 538–556.

Deschouwer, K., 2012. *The politics of Belgium: Governing a divided society*. Basingstoke: Palgrave Macmillan.

Desmet, K., Ortuño-Ortín, I., and Weber, S., 2009. Linguistic diversity and redistribution. *Journal of the European Economic Association*, 7(6), 1291–1318.

Dufresne, Y., Jeram, S., and Pelletier, A., 2014. The true north strong and free healthcare? Nationalism and attitudes towards private healthcare options in Canada. *Canadian Journal of Political Science*, 47(3), 569–595.

Dufresne, Y., Kilibarda, A., Blais, A., and Bibeau, A., 2019. Religiosity or racism? The bases of opposition to religious accommodation in Quebec. *Nations and Nationalism*, 25(2), 673–696.

Dupré, J.-F., 2013. In search of linguistic identities in Taiwan: An empirical study. *Journal of Multilingual and Multicultural Development*, 34(5), 431–444.

Enos, R.D., 2014. Causal effect of intergroup contact on exclusionary attitudes. *Proceedings of the National Academy of Sciences of the United States of America*, 111(10), 3699–3704.

Escandell, X. and Ceobanu, A.M., 2010. Nationalisms and anti-immigrant sentiment in Spain. *South European Society and Politics*, 15(2), 157–179.

Evans, G., 2000. The continued significance of class voting. *Annual Review of Political Science*, 3(1), 401–417.

Ford, R. and Jennings, W., 2020. The changing cleavage politics of Western Europe. *Annual Review of Political Science*, 23(1), 295–314.

Gidengil, E., Blais, A., Everitt, J., Fournier, P., and Nevitte, N., 2012. *Dominance and decline: Making sense of recent Canadian elections*. Toronto: University of Toronto Press.

Gidengil, E., Blais, A., Nadeau, R., Nevitte, N., and Gagnon, A.G., 2003. La langue française et l'insécurité culturelle. In: A. Gagnon, ed. *Québec: état et société. Tome II*. Montréal: Les Editions Québec/Amérique, 389–412.

Goldberg, A.C., 2020. The evolution of cleavage voting in Four Western countries: Structural, behavioural or political dealignment? *European Journal of Political Research*, 59(1), 68–90.

Guibernau, M., 2007. *The identity of nations*. Cambridge: Polity.

Hooghe, L. and Marks, G., 2018. Cleavage theory meets Europe's crises: Lipset, Rokkan, and the transnational cleavage. *Journal of European Public Policy*, 25(1), 109–135.

Hopkins, D.J., 2014. One language, two meanings: Partisanship and responses to Spanish. *Political Communication*, 31(3), 421–445.

Hopkins, D.J., 2015. The upside of accents: Language, inter-group difference, and attitudes toward immigration. *British Journal of Political Science*, 45(3), 531–557.

Hopkins, D.J., Tran, Van C., and Fisher Williamson, A., 2014. See no Spanish: Language, local context, and attitudes toward immigration. *Politics, Groups, and Identities*, 2(1), 35–51.

Huddy, L. and Sears, D.O., 1995. Opposition to bilingual education: Prejudice or the defense of realistic interests? *Social Psychology Quarterly*, 58(2), 133–143.

Inglehart, R.F. and Woodward, M., 1967. Language conflicts and political community. *Comparative Studies in Society and History*, 10(1), 27–45.

Johnston, R., 2017. *The Canadian party system: An analytic history*. Vancouver, BC: UBC Press.

Kerevel, Y.P., 2011. The influence of Spanish-language media on Latino public opinion and group consciousness. *Social Science Quarterly*, 92(2), 509–534.

Knutsen, O., 2004. Religious denomination and party choice in Western Europe: A comparative longitudinal study from eight countries, 1970–97. *International Political Science Review*, 25(1), 97–128.

Knutsen, O., 2010. The regional cleavage in Western Europe: Can social composition, value orientations and territorial identities explain the impact of region on party choice? *West European Politics*, 33(3), 553–585.

Kriesi, H., 2010. Restructuration of partisan politics and the emergence of a new cleavage based on values. *West European Politics*, 33(3), 673–685.

Lambert, R.D. and Curtis, J.E., 1983. Opposition to multiculturalism among Québécois and English-Canadians. *Canadian Review of Sociology/Revue Canadienne de Sociologie*, 20(2), 193–207.

Lipset, S.M. and Rokkan, S., 1967. *Party systems and voter alignments: Cross-national perspectives*. Toronto: The Free Press.

Medeiros, M., 2017. Refining the influence of language on national attachment: Exploring linguistic threat perceptions in Quebec. *Nationalism and Ethnic Politics*, 23(4), 375–390.

Medeiros, M., Fournier, P., and Benet-Martínez, V., 2017. The language of threat: Linguistic perceptions and intergroup relations. *Acta Politica*, 52(1), 1–22.

Meeusen, C., Boonen, J., and Dassonneville, R., 2017. The structure of prejudice and its relation to party preferences in Belgium: Flanders and Wallonia compared. *Psychologica belgica*, 57(3), 52–74.

Mendelsohn, M. and Nadeau, R., 1996. The magnification and minimization of social cleavages by the broadcast and narrowcast news media. *International Journal of Public Opinion Research*, 8(4), 374–389.

Miley, T.J., 2007. Against the thesis of the civic nation: The case of Catalonia in contemporary Spain. *Nationalism and Ethnic Politics*, 13(1), 1–37.

Nadeau, R., Martin, P., and Blais, A., 1999. Attitude towards risk-taking and individual choice in the Quebec referendum on sovereignty. *British Journal of Political Science*, 29(3), 523–539.

Newman, B.J., Hartman, T.K., and Taber, C.S., 2012. Foreign language exposure, cultural threat, and opposition to immigration. *Political Psychology*, 33(5), 635–657.

Orriols, L. and Rodon, T., 2016. The 2015 Catalan election: The independence bid at the polls. *South European Society and Politics*, 21(3), 359–381.

Pilet, J.-B., 2021. Hard times for governing parties: The 2019 federal elections in Belgium. *West European Politics*, 44(2), 439–449.

Rodon, T. and Guinjoan, M., 2018. When the context matters: Identity, secession and the spatial dimension in Catalonia. *Political Geography*, 63, 75–87.

Serrano, I., 2013. Just a matter of identity? Support for independence in Catalonia. *Regional & Federal Studies*, 23(5), 523–545.

Sinardet, D., 2013. How linguistically divided media represent linguistically divisive issues. Belgian TV-debates on Brussels-Halle-Vilvoorde. *Regional & Federal Studies*, 23(3), 311–330.

Sinardet, D. and Hooghe, M., 2009. *Public opinion in a multilingual society: Institutional design and federal loyalty*. Brussel: Rethinking Belgium/University Foundation.

Stephenson, L.B., Harell, A., Rubenson, D., and Loewen, P.J., 2020. 2019 Canadian election study - Phone survey technical report.pdf. In: *2019 Canadian election study - Phone survey*. Harvard Dataverse. doi: 10.7910/DVN/8RHLG1/1PBGR3.

Stephenson, L.B., Harell, A., Rubenson, D., and Loewen, P.J., 2021. Measuring preferences and behaviours in the 2019 Canadian election study. *Canadian Journal of Political Science*, 54(1), 118–124.

Stockemer, D., Niemann, A., Rabenschlag, J., Speyer, J., and Unger, D., 2018. Immigration, anti-immigrant attitudes and Euroscepticism: A metaanalysis. *French Politics*, 16(3), 328–340.

Stubager, R., 2010. The development of the education cleavage: Denmark as a critical case. *West European Politics*, 33(3), 505–533.

Tessier, C. and Montigny, É, 2016. Untangling myths and facts: Who supported the Quebec charter of values? *French Politics*, 14(2), 272–285.

Thijssen, P., Reuchamps, M., De Winter, L., Dodeigne, J., and Sinardet, D., 2021. Inter-regional contacts and voting behaviour in Belgium: What can we learn from the 2019 elections? *Regional & Federal Studies*, 31(3), 359–380.

Turgeon, L. and Bilodeau, A., 2014. Minority nations and attitudes towards immigration: The case of Quebec. *Nations and Nationalism*, 20(2), 317–336.

Turgeon, L., Bilodeau, A., White, S.E., and Henderson, A., 2019. A tale of two liberalisms? Attitudes toward minority religious symbols in Quebec and Canada. *Canadian Journal of Political Science*, 52(2), 247–265.

van der Brug, W. and Harteveld, E., 2021. The conditional effects of the refugee crisis on immigration attitudes and nationalism. *European Union Politics*, 22(2), 227–247.

Ziblatt, D., Hilbig, H., and Bischof, D., 2020. Wealth of tongues: Why peripheral regions vote for the radical right in Germany. *Working paper*. doi: 10.31235/osf.io/syr84.

CHAPTER 16

The news media organizations and public opinion on political issues

···

Frédérick Bastien

INTRODUCTION

The coevolution of news media and public opinion has attracted much attention. For most citizens, the experience of politics in their everyday life is mediated by news media, and so it is not surprising that theories about the effect of news media on persuasion arose with the spread of mass communications, or that they continue to interest scholars and practitioners. Furthermore, it is hard to believe that public opinion does not play a significant role in democratic regimes. As a consequence, it is expected that news media reflect the diversity of public opinion, either through news organizations that present several points of view (internal pluralism) or through media outlets that highlight a particular viewpoint and compose a media system that is diverse on the whole (external pluralism). This coevolution is of particular interest when it comes to issues that attract a great deal of coverage and seem to be politically important, such as immigration, environmental protection, and economic globalization.

Much of the literature in the field of political communication (for example, Iyengar, 2017; Jamieson, 2017; McNair, 2018) offers a three-stage narrative about the development of theories on the impact of news media on public opinion. Early models, arguably pre-scientific by contemporary standards, claimed that mass media had a direct impact on persuasion, similar to the injection of a substance into a human body through a hypodermic syringe. In the 1950s, initial attempts to scientifically measure the effect of news media on political persuasion and to understand voting behaviour during election campaigns in the United States showed minimal effects, due to social and psychological mechanisms that moderated the impact of political communication. In the following decades, theories emphasizing the effect of news selection by mass media on public opinion have received a great deal of support from empirical research. It has been demonstrated that political communication affects which issues citizens think about (agenda-setting), which cues are criteria

DOI: 10.4324/9781003121992-19

used to make political evaluations (priming), how a political problem is understood (framing), and through which lens citizens perceive the world as a result of long-term exposure to standardized content from mass communication (cultivation), to mention just a few theories. In all of these paradigms, the relationship between the news media and public opinion is seen in terms of causation.

Alternatively, we can see the structure of political opinion in a society as a predictor of the news media system, which may reflect ideological or partisan cleavages. In most democratic countries, political parties play a predominant role in framing debates in the public space. It also happens, to various degrees, that national or regional media landscapes reflect the structure of the political system. Where that is the case, the impact of the news media on public opinion may weaken as citizens have a clearer guide for exposure to content that fits with their political preferences.

In this chapter, I examine the connection between news media and public opinion primarily as a coevolution rather than a one-way causal relationship. To do this, I make use of the concept of parallelism between political and media systems. First, I present an overview, highlighting the degree to which political parallelism in media systems varies across time and in different countries. Then, I present data from two surveys conducted in Canada to show how opinions on immigration – and, to a lesser extent, the environment and economic globalization – are related (or not) to citizens' main news sources. Canada offers an interesting case study for two reasons: first, North American media systems have been classified by some scholars as being less politically oriented than many European ones; second, Canadian political and media systems do not appear to be as polarized as their American counterparts. The results show that, even in such a context, opinions on some political issues are strongly related to exposure to certain news media organizations.

POLITICAL PARALLELISM IN MEDIA SYSTEMS

The degree of connection between news media and political opinions changes over time and in space. In North America, the development of the press during the eighteenth and nineteenth centuries paralleled that of the political parties and ideologies of that era. The writers were commonly publicists promoting a political viewpoint and criticizing opponents. The market was fragmented and comprised a broad range of small outlets advocating for specific causes. A change of "media regime" (Williams and Delli Carpini, 2011) occurred at the turn of the twentieth century. On the one hand, the print press – followed later by radio and television news – became a commercial industry concerned primarily with making a profit. The political colours of the press faded in order to attract a larger and ideologically diverse audience. On the other hand, the development of the doctrine of objectivity, promoted by new training programmes in colleges and universities and by ethics guidelines, fostered the professionalization of journalism. In this context, the level of political parallelism of the media system was low.

In other parts of the Western world, the parallelism between the media and the political fields has been more persistent. For instance, in most European countries, the structure of the media market has largely remained aligned with the prominent ideologies. Hallin and Mancini (2004) observe that in Scandinavian, Dutch, Austrian, and German media systems (which can be broadly classified as Northern Europe), the professionalization of journalism hasn't prevented news media organizations from featuring distinct political orientations, well beyond the editorial pages dedicated to the owners' views, as is the case in North America. In countries such as Greece, Italy, Spain, and Portugal (which can be broadly classified as Southern Europe), political subsidies have played a critical role in supporting the media system, and journalistic norms have been somewhat less professionalized (Hallin and Mancini, 2004).

Although there is some evidence of a convergence of the more politically paralleled European media systems towards the North American liberal model, the American media system shows signs of an increasing politicization, reflecting the polarization of political life in the United States (Nechushtai, 2018). Fox News once appeared to be an exception in the United States media landscape, but cable news channels' programmes have featured specific political orientations, especially since the 2010s. It should also be mentioned that before the rise of Fox News, several talk radio stations were already offering a conservative point of view on public affairs. Parallels between the political and media systems in the United States appear easier to draw today than they were in previous decades.

The term "parallelism" to point out the coevolution of the political and media systems was first coined by the British political scientist Colin Seymour-Ure (1974), who examined the connections between newspapers and party systems, focusing on Britain and making comparisons with several other countries. Seymour-Ure distinguished three dimensions of press–party parallelism: the relationships between newspapers and parties through formal or informal organizational links (such as ownership and management by a party and owners supporting a party); the degree of support for one party's goals in the content of a newspaper; and the partisanship of a paper's readership. Thirty years later, Hallin and Mancini (2004) expanded Seymour-Ure's press–party parallelism to the broader concept of "political parallelism," which is not constrained to connection with a single political party but involves broader ideological trends. They also applied the concept to various kinds of news media organizations rather than limiting its use to the print press.

Aside from some analyses prompted by the rise of cable news channels with obvious political slants in the United States (Arceneaux and Johnson, 2013; Iyengar and Hahn, 2009; Levendusky, 2013), the political profile of the audiences of news media organizations in North America has not been extensively studied, presumably because it was thought that such relationship is unlikely in countries with low parallelism, such as the United States and Canada. It is worthwhile to revisit this question.

NEWS MEDIA EXPOSURE AND OPINION ON IMMIGRATION ISSUES IN CANADA

In this section, I examine the relationship between Canadians' opinions on immigration and exposure to specific news media sources, drawing on data collected during the 2015 Canadian federal election as part of the Making Electoral Democracy Work (MEDW) project (Cross et al., 2017). Conducted in five countries, MEDW examined the political parties' strategies and voters' behaviour across 27 national, supra-national, and sub-national elections through public opinion surveys, experiments, content analyses, and semi-structured interviews (Blais, 2010). In Canada, the survey focused on the three most populous provinces: Ontario, Québec, and British Columbia. Whereas many surveys on politics capture only exposure or attention to types of media (such as television, newspapers, radio, and internet) – as is typically the case for the Canadian Election Study (CES) – MEDW includes measures of exposure to specific news media outlets.

In each province, respondents were presented with a list of news media organizations and asked, "What was (were) your primary source(s) of information about the election? Please check multiple responses if you regularly used more than one source on a daily basis." These outlets included television channels and newspapers (encompassing legacy and online versions) and some news websites. I dropped from each provincial analysis the sources selected by fewer than about 50 respondents,[1] as well as generic categories that cannot be linked to a specific news organization (for example, "local paper," "local commuter paper," "other English language news source," "other non-English language news source").

The dataset includes three measures on immigration issues. First, survey respondents were asked to indicate on a 0–10 scale whether they favour fewer immigrants (0) or more immigrants in Canada (10).[2] Among the respondents, 18% chose the score of 0 and 4% selected 10. To standardize measures used in the analyses below, I recoded on a 0–1 scale (in this case, I divided by 10). The average score is 0.41 with a standard deviation of 0.29, varying from 0.39 in Québec to 0.43 in British Columbia.

Two other measures targeted specific issues in the context of the election campaign. One was about the protection of Syrians amidst the civil war in Syria and the openness of Canada to welcoming Syrian refugees, which was the second-most-covered issue by news media during the campaign (about 10% of print coverage), after the economy (Stephenson et al., 2019, p. 109). It became a prominent issue when a photograph of the body of Alan Kurdi, a three-year-old boy found on a beach in Turkey, was disseminated by news outlets in early September. Political parties framed this issue in different ways.[3] The Conservative Party, led by Prime Minister Stephen Harper, expressed concern with the control of Canadian borders and emphasized law and security components, and advocated fighting the terrorists (specifically, the Islamic State of Iraq and Syria) at the heart of the crisis. In contrast, the Liberal Party and the New Democratic Party framed the issue as a humanitarian crisis and pledged to welcome a large number of refugees (as many as 25,000 by Christmas) (Forest et al., 2017). In the survey, respondents were asked, "Do you approve or disapprove of the current Conservative government's handling of the refugee crisis?" Response choices ranged from "Strongly approve" (0) to "Strongly disapprove" (1). The average score is 0.59 with a standard deviation of 0.35, ranging from 0.57 in Québec to 0.60 in British Columbia.

The right of women to wear a niqab during citizenship oath ceremonies was another campaign issue. On 15 September 2015, the Federal Court of Appeal struck down a lower court ban on wearing a face-covering during oath ceremonies. The Conservative Party and the Bloc Québécois favoured the ban and committed to appealing the decision to the Supreme Court, whereas the Liberal Party and New Democratic Party were opposed to the ban. This issue attracted more media attention in Québec (16% of print coverage) than in British Columbia or Ontario (about 4%) (Stephenson et al., 2019, p. 109). The dataset includes one binary question on the issue, asking whether respondents believe that "women should be allowed to take the citizenship oath when wearing a niqab because respect for minority rights is an important Canadian value" (coded 1) or that "women should not be allowed to take the citizenship oath when wearing a niqab because it is inconsistent with Canadian values" (coded 0). Overall, 63% reported being opposed to wearing a niqab during the citizenship oath and 26% were not; 11% did not know and were coded 0.50. Thus, the average score is 0.31 with a standard deviation of 0.44. This is the lowest mean score of these three measures, and the one that varies the most across the three provinces: 0.42 in British Columbia, 0.38 in Ontario, and 0.14 in Québec.

Figure 16.1 illustrates the difference of mean scores between those whose primary source(s) of information about the election did or did not include a given news media organization. For each issue, Figure 16.1 also indicates whether the difference in means is statistically significant or not. For example, regarding the opportunity to take in more or fewer immigrants, the mean score is 0.49 among those who regularly saw or heard election news on CBC (the English-language Canadian public broadcaster) and 0.37 among those who did not. This 0.12 difference, which is shown at the

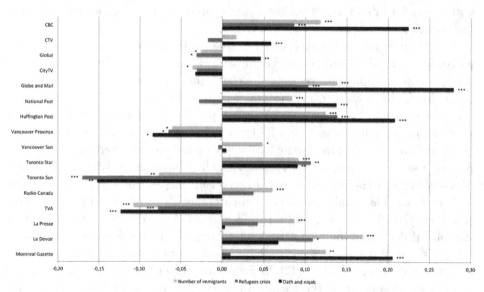

FIGURE 16.1 Opinion about immigration issues by regular exposure to news media sources (differences of means).

Note: *** p < .001, ** p < .01, * p < .05.

Source: Cross et al., 2017.

top of Figure 16.1, is statistically significant ($p < 0.001$). In contrast, on the same issue, the mean score is 0.35 among those who regularly read election news in the *Toronto Sun* (a tabloid) compared with 0.42 among those who did not. This difference of means of -0.07 is also statistically significant ($p < 0.01$), as illustrated by a lower bar.

This first step makes it possible to identify some patterns of political opinions in the news media landscape. Citizens who regularly took in their election news on CBC, in the national newspaper *Globe and Mail*, from the *Huffington Post* website, and in the *Toronto Star* (the highest-circulation broadsheet in the country) were more likely to favour more immigrants, to disapprove of how the Conservative government handled the refugee crisis, and to think women should be allowed to take the citizenship oath while wearing a niqab than were those who did not select these news sources. This is also the case for two of these three opinions among citizens loyal to the broadsheets *National Post*, *Le Devoir* (a French-language high-quality paper available in Québec), and the *Montreal Gazette*. Conversely, those who selected the *Vancouver Province* (another tabloid) and the *Toronto Sun*, as well as TVA (the private French-language television network with the largest market share in Québec), were more likely to favour fewer immigrants, to approve of how the Harper government managed the refugee crisis, and to favour the ban on the niqab during citizenship ceremonies.

One general observation from Figure 16.1 is that opinions regarding immigration issues differ along the lines of news media consumption in most cases. Indeed, 35 out of 48 differences of means are statistically significant. There is not a single news media organization whose audience's opinion on immigration does not differ from that of other citizens for at least one of these issues. However, the consumers of the private English-language television networks CTV and CityTV, the *Vancouver Sun*, and Radio-Canada and *La Presse* (the French-language public television network and the largest-circulation broadsheet in Québec, respectively) appear to be less strongly related to those opinions than do those of consumers of other news media.

Such comparisons are bivariate analyses. They are rudimentary for a couple of reasons. First, about half of the respondents reported having more than one primary source of news. Among the organizations listed, the average number of primary sources was 1.8, with one-quarter of the sample checking three news outlets or more as sources regularly used on a daily basis to get information about the election. Such bivariate analyses do not control for the use of these additional sources. Second, it is likely that opinions about these immigration issues and exposure to specific news media organizations are driven by the same independent variables, whether they are sociodemographic or partisan predictors.

For these reasons, I ran multivariate ordinary least square (OLS) regression analyses. For each immigration issue, Figure 16.2 plots the "impact" of regular exposure to a news media organization, controlling for the effect of being regularly exposed to other outlets among those listed, sociodemographic factors, and party identification. Sociodemographic controls are gender, age, education, generation of immigrants,[4] religiosity,[5] and place of living,[6] all coded from 0 to 1. Party identification captures whether respondents feel closer to the Conservative Party of Canada, the Liberal Party of Canada, the New Democratic Party of Canada, or (in Québec) the Bloc Québécois,

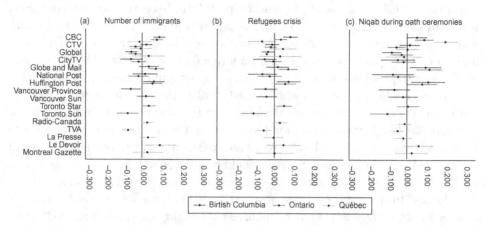

FIGURE 16.2 Relationship between immigration issues and regular exposure to news media sources (coefficient estimates with 95% confidence intervals).

Note: OLS regression coefficients with control for regular exposure to other news media sources, sociodemographic factors, and party identification (Model C in Tables 16.A1 to 16.A3).
Source: Cross et al., 2017.

and for each choice, do they feel very close (1), somewhat close (0.66), not very close (0.33), or not close at all (0). Chapters from Part 2 address most of these other determinants of public opinion. Please refer to them for a greater discussion. Finally, because the structure of media choice is different in each province, I ran separate regression analyses for each province. More comprehensive regression results appear in the appendix.

In Figure 16.2, the value of each regression coefficient is associated with a confidence interval of 95%. In cases where that interval does not overlap zero (the vertical line), there is at least a 95% chance that people who regularly took in their election news from the corresponding outlet have a more positive (or more negative) opinion towards immigration than do citizens who did not get their news from that media organization. For example, the estimates plotted at the top of panel A in Figure 16.2 show regression coefficient values of 0.09 and 0.08 for CBC in British Columbia and Ontario, with confidence intervals clearly higher than zero. This means that among respondents in these provinces, those who regularly got their election news from the CBC had a score of, respectively, 0.09 and 0.08 higher on the 0–1 scale regarding the number of immigrants than did those who were not – exposure to all other news media listed in the model, sociodemographic factors and party identification being equal. However, in Québec, these survey data do not allow for the same conclusion because the regression coefficient is not statistically significant – that is, the difference between CBC users and non-users does not appear to be different from zero.

Thus, most patterns observed through the bivariate comparisons of means still hold. In British Columbia and Ontario, citizens who regularly received their election news from CBC and the *Huffington Post* were more likely to have opinions in favour of cultural and religious diversity for all three issues. This is also the case, in Ontario, for readers of the *Globe and Mail* and the *Toronto Star*. In British Columbia, two out of three coefficients for the *Globe and Mail* fail to reach the statistical significance level once we add controls for party identification, although one remains regarding the niqab issue. In the opposite direction, *Toronto Sun* readers in Ontario and TVA viewers in Québec were still less likely to have positive opinions towards cultural and religious diversity after controlling for sociodemographic factors and partisan identification.

These results are largely congruent with some data from the recent *Canadian Media System Survey* (Thibault et al., 2020, Figure B2.3), which compares the perceptions of scholars – whose expertise is about news media and political communication across all Canadian provinces – of the ideological orientation of the content of major news media organizations. One item of the expert survey focuses on media coverage of religious diversity issues. Similar to the relationships evidenced in this chapter, *Canadian Media System Survey* data show that experts perceive the content of CBC and the *Toronto Star* as being in favour of accommodating religious diversity, with the *Globe and Mail* leaning in the same direction. The *Toronto Sun* and TVA are perceived as being less favourable towards such accommodations, with the *Vancouver Province* also leaning in that direction. Results are congruent for many other news media as well. The main contrast involves the *National Post*: whereas this chapter indicates that readers of the *National Post* are in favour of more immigrants and the right to wear a niqab during oath ceremonies, respondents to the survey perceive *National Post* content as leaning towards opposition to accommodation regarding religious diversity. The reason for this discrepancy remains unclear.

To be sure, the relationship between public opinion about immigration and news media exposure is not constant across the media landscape. Nevertheless, when we sum up the regression coefficients obtained in each of the three provinces for each of the three issues in the model, including control variables for sociodemographic factors and partisan identification, 30 out of 78 are statistically significant with standard confidence intervals of 95% (the proportion increases to 37 out of 78 when we consider confidence intervals of 90%).

Such multivariate analyses with controls for sociodemographic factors and partisan identification are not enough to ensure isolation of the causal effects of news media on opinions about immigration – panel data analyses and experiments would be more effective – but they allow us to rule out a set of rival hypotheses. For example, regression model A, shown in Tables 16.A1, 16.A2, and 16.A3, does not include sociodemographic and party identification controls. In this model, as many as 41 out of 78 regression coefficients are statistically significant with the threshold of 95%. The addition of controls for sociodemographic factors (model B) lowers the value of most regression coefficients, indicating that gender, age, and other variables affect both exposure to some news media and opinions about immigration. However, this impact is not enough to entirely explain why the audience for a certain news outlet is more or less likely to favour immigration, as 40 out of 78 regression coefficients are still statistically significant. In contrast, party identification appears to be a significant driver of both news media exposure and opinion on immigration, as ten of these coefficients are no longer statistically significant in model C. Overall, it is clear from these data that opinions regarding some political issues, such as immigration, and party identification, are related to news media consumption.

IMMIGRATION AND BEYOND: ENVIRONMENT AND ECONOMIC GLOBALIZATION

To what extent are the relations between news media audiences and public opinion dependent on specific issues? I extend my analysis to opinions about environmental protection and economic globalization. Unfortunately, the dataset used in the previous section does not contain items on these issues. Instead, I will use data from another survey conducted in the province of Québec in spring 2018 as part of a project about violent radicalization (Lefebvre et al., 2020).

This dataset includes issue-oriented questions; respondents were asked to indicate how much they agree or disagree with a series of statements on various subjects, including immigration, the environment, and economic globalization. On the immigration issue, I combine two statements: "Québec's cultural life is enriched by immigrants" and "Too many immigrants don't want to fit into Québec society." Once these items are coded in a consistent way on a 0–1 scale (where 0 means the most negative views and 1 the most positive views about immigration), the Pearson correlation coefficient between them is 0.45. For attitudes about environmental protection, I use reactions to the statement "The exploitation of oil resources in Québec is a bad thing for Québec society," where 0 means that the respondent strongly disagrees and 1 means that the respondent strongly agrees. For opinions about economic globalization, I rely on opinions stated regarding the statement "Multinational corporations in Québec make our economy stronger," where 0 and 1 mean that the person strongly disagrees and strongly agrees, respectively.

The survey also taps the frequency of exposure to four French-language news media outlets: the public broadcaster Radio-Canada, the private television network TVA, and the broadsheet *La Presse* (all of which were measured in the MEDW survey), along with the sister regional tabloids *Le Journal de Montréal/Le Journal de Québec*. The tabloids and TVA are owned by the same media organization (Quebecor). In the analyses below, I consider regular consumers to be those who get their news from these media organizations at least three days a week.

Following models similar to those previously introduced, Table 16.A4 (in the appendix) features multivariate analyses of the relationship between regular exposure to these four most popular news media organizations in the province of Québec and opinions about immigration, the environment, and economic globalization (model A), with sociodemographic controls (model B)[7] and with partisan identification controls (model C).[8] Coefficient estimates drawn from the third model for each news media are plotted in Figure 16.3.

The positive coefficients observed for Radio-Canada and *La Presse* in the left-hand panel of Figure 16.3 are consistent with results obtained in most analyses of opinions about the number of immigrants and the Syrian refugee crisis in Figure 16.2. In this case, however, all of the coefficients are statistically significant: Quebecers who

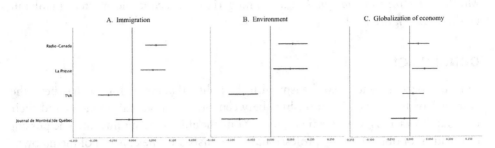

FIGURE 16.3 Relationship between opinion on political issues and regular exposure to news media sources in Québec (coefficient estimates with 95% confidence intervals).

Note: OLS regression coefficients with control for regular exposure to other news media sources, sociodemographic factors and party identification (Model C in Table 16.A4).
Source: Lefebvre et al., 2020.

regularly get their news from Radio-Canada and *La Presse* have a positive opinion about immigrants, even once we control for sociodemographic factors and partisanship. Similarly, the relationship between getting news from TVA and the likelihood of favouring less immigration, agreeing with the Conservatives' management of the refugee crisis, and approving of a ban on wearing the niqab during oath ceremonies (Figure 16.2) is consistent with the coefficients shown for that news media organization in Figure 16.3. On a scale of 0 to 1, regular viewers of news on TVA have a score of 0.06 points lower than do those who do not regularly watch that outlet. Coefficients are also negative for readers of *Le Journal de Montréal/Le Journal de Québec*. This relationship is statistically significant in model A, but it loses that significance once we control for sociodemographic factors (Table 16.A4). To summarize, Figure 16.3 corroborates that exposure to various news media organizations in Québec is related to opinion towards immigration.

This relationship extends to opinions about the exploitation of oil resources in Québec. Those who get their news at least three days a week on Radio-Canada and *La Presse* are more likely to believe that this activity is a bad thing for Québec society. In contrast, those who are regularly exposed to news from TVA and *Le Journal de Montréal/Le Journal de Québec* are less likely to hold this opinion. Of course, a single item is not a comprehensive measure of opinion towards environmental protection, so it would be interesting to test this relationship with additional questions.

However, the parallelism between news media and political opinions is not common to all issues. The media habits captured in these analyses are not related to opinions about the benefits of multinational corporations for the Québec economy. A barely statistically significant relationship appears for *La Presse* once we control for sociodemographic factors. These results for Radio-Canada and *La Presse* are consistent with experts' perceptions about the content of their coverage of economic issues, which is seen as balanced for the former and leaning to the right for the latter. However, these experts also perceive the content of TVA and *Le Journal de*

Montréal/Le Journal de Québec as leaning right on economic matters (Thibault et al., 2020, Figure B2.1).

CONCLUSION

In media systems where parallelism with the political actors is low, as has been the case in North America, relationships between citizens' political opinions and their exposure to various news media organizations should not be significant. The pursuit of the ideal of objectivity by professional journalists and the concern of media owners (and public broadcasters) with reaching the largest audience should mitigate the ideological colouring of the news coverage. On the one hand, audiences apparently select their news sources on the basis of criteria other than ideological orientation, such as emphasis on certain areas of activity, the format used to present the news, or the personality of the news anchors. On the other hand, the effect of specific news media organizations on public opinion should also be limited, as all would strive to present balanced coverage of news issues.

The analyses presented in this chapter challenge these assumptions. On many political issues, there is a relationship between citizens' media use and their opinions, and the relationship works in different directions depending on the news media organization. There is reason to believe the relationship is even stronger in the Canadian media landscape than is indicated by survey data shown here. First, these surveys do not provide data about radio stations from which people get information about current affairs. Yet some stations, especially private talk radio stations, feature clear ideological – often right-leaning – orientations in both Canada (Thibault et al., 2020) and the United States (Berry and Sobieraj, 2011). Second, the news media organizations included in these surveys and my analyses are those with the largest audiences – large enough to be captured in survey sampling. We may hypothesize that news media outlets with small audiences are more likely to ideologically orient their content in order to please a specific niche.

This coevolution of news media and public opinion has two major implications. First, it is important to measure the use of specific news media organizations in surveys designed to understand the role of political communication in public opinion. Questions on attention or exposure to media types such as television, radio, newspapers, and the internet – which are those traditionally used in the American National Election Study (Althaus and Tewksbury, 2007) and the Canadian Election Study – fail to capture the importance of such organizational differences. It is important to get a more comprehensive view of the extent of the relationship between news media consumption and political opinions. The more pervasive this relationship is, the more the news media may contribute to the polarization of society.

Second, it is important to understand what kinds of media content favour parallelism between news organizations and citizens' political preferences. Are there ideological differences in the coverage produced by journalists in various organizations? Are such differences caused by non-journalistic content producers (such as columnists, pundits, and bloggers) who also populate the television news programmes, newspapers, and news websites but do not hew to the same professional standards as those imposed on journalists? In order to foster media literacy, it is important to clarify which kinds of media content citizens should distinguish to assess the quality and diversity of their information diet.

SUMMARY POINTS

- This chapter examined the connection between news media and public opinion primarily as coevolution rather than a one-way causal relationship by adopting the concept of parallelism between political and media systems.
- Using data from two surveys conducted in Canada, we showed that, even in a context where scholars classify the Canadian media system as being less politically oriented than many European ones and where the political and media systems do not appear to be as polarized as their American counterparts, opinions on immigration and environment are related to exposure to news media organizations.
- One important implication of these findings is the importance to measure the use of specific news media organizations – instead of media types such as television, radio, newspapers, and the internet – in surveys designed to understand the role of political communication in public opinion.

NOTES

1 I consequently dropped *The Globe and Mail* and the *National Post* in Québec, Ontario News Watch, Omni TV, Rabble.ca, Buzzfeed, and Vice Canada.
2 The exact wording was, "Some people believe that we should have more immigrants, others believe that we should have fewer. Where would you place yourself on a 0 to 10 scale where 0 means 'very favourable to having more immigrants' and 10 means 'very favourable to having fewer immigrants'?" (Q30e) I reversed and standardized coding from 0 to 1, where 1 means positive attitudes towards immigration. "Don't know" responses were coded in the centre of the scale (0.50).
3 The Canadian federal party system includes four major political parties. Along the left–right spectrum, the Liberal Party generally commands the centre, whereas the New Democratic Party and the Conservative Party are, respectively, on the left and right sides. The Bloc Québécois is slightly to the left; however, as it runs candidates only in Québec, it distinctively advocates for political independence for that province. For an account of the Canadian federal party system, see Johnston (2017). For details about the role of these parties in the 2015 Canadian federal election, see Pammett and Dornan (2016).
4 Respondents born outside Canada were coded 1, second-generation immigrants (operationalized as those born in Canada and whose mother was born outside Canada) were coded 0.50, and those born in Canada and whose mother was also born in Canada were coded 0.
5 The measure of religiosity combines a question asking whether the respondent has a religion or not, and how often he or she attends religious services apart from special occasions such as weddings and funerals.
6 Respondents were asked what best describes the place where they live, with five answer categories ranging from "the countryside" (0) to "a big city" (1).

7 Sociodemographic variables control for gender, age, education, generation of immigrants, and religiosity.
8 Partisan identification variables control for intensity of identification with provincial parties that have members in the National Assembly (Coalition Avenir Québec, Liberal Party, Parti Québécois, and Québec Solidaire).

SUGGESTED FURTHER READINGS

Arceneaux, K. and Johnson, M., 2013. *Changing minds or changing channels? Partisan news in an age of choice*. Chicago, IL: University of Chicago Press.

Hallin, D.C. and Mancini, P., 2004. *Comparing media systems: Three models of media and politics*. Cambridge: Cambridge University Press.

Nechushtai, E., 2018. From liberal to polarized liberal? Contemporary U.S. news in Hallin and Mancini's typology of news systems. *International Journal of Press/Politics*, 23(2), 183–201.

Thibault, S., Bastien, F., Gosselin, T., Brin, C., and Scott, C., 2020. Is there a distinct Quebec media subsystem in Canada? Evidence of ideological and political orientations among Canadian news media organizations. *Canadian Journal of Political Science*, 53(3), 638–657.

REFERENCES

Althaus, S. and Tewksbury, D., 2007. *Toward a new generation of Media use measures for the ANES*. Ann Arbor: Report to the Board of Overseers, American National Election Studies.

Arceneaux, K. and Johnson, M., 2013. *Changing minds or changing channels? Partisan news in an age of choice*. Chicago, IL: University of Chicago Press.

Berry, J.M. and Sobieraj, S., 2011. Understanding the rise of talk radio. *PS: Political Science & Politics*, 44(4), 762–767.

Blais, A., 2010. Making electoral democracy work. *Electoral Studies*, 29(1), 169–170.

Cross, W., Gélineau, F., Gidengil, E., Pruysers, S., Lawlor, A., Blais, A., and Stephenson, L., 2017. *MEDW 2015 Canadian federal election study*. Doi: 10.7910/DVN/ITIJT0.

Forest, D., Bastien, F., Legault-Venne, A., Lacombe, O., and Brousseau, H., 2017. Les mots de la campagne: la fouille de textes appliquée à l'étude de la communication électorale. In: P.-M. Daigneault and F. Pétry, eds. *L'analyse textuelle des idées, du discours et des pratiques politiques*. Québec: Presses de l'Université Laval, 99–122.

Hallin, D.C. and Mancini, P., 2004. *Comparing media systems: Three models of media and politics*. Cambridge: Cambridge University Press.

Iyengar, S., 2017. A typology of media effects. In: K. Kenski and K.H. Jamieson, eds. *The Oxford handbook of political communication*. Oxford: Oxford University Press, 59–68.

Iyengar, S. and Hahn, K.S., 2009. Red media, blue media: Evidence of ideological selectivity in media use. *Journal of Communication*, 59(1), 19–39.

Jamieson, K.H., 2017. Creating the hybrid field of political communication: A five-decade-long evolution of the concept of effects. In: K. Kenski and K.H. Jamieson, eds. *The Oxford handbook of political communication*. Oxford: Oxford University Press, 15–45.

Johnston, R., 2017. Polarized pluralism in the Canadian party system. In: A.-G. Gagnon and A. Brian Tanguay, eds. *Canadian parties in transition*. 4th ed. Toronto, ON: University of Toronto Press: 64–83.

Lefebvre, S., Casoni, D., Bastien, F., Harell, A., Rocheleau, S., and Perreault, J.-P., 2020. *Afraid of what? Violent extremism in Quebec and the media landscape*. Final Report. Québec: Fonds de recherche du Québec – Société et culture.

Levendusky, M., 2013. *How partisan media polarize America.* Chicago, IL: University of Chicago Press.

McNair, B., 2018. *An introduction to political communication.* London: Routledge.

Nechushtai, E., 2018. From liberal to polarized liberal? Contemporary U.S. news in Hallin and Mancini's typology of news systems. *The International Journal of Press/Politics,* 23(2), 183–201.

Pammett, J.H. and Dornan, C., eds., 2016. *The Canadian federal election of 2015.* Toronto, ON: Dundurn.

Seymour-Ure, C., 1974. *The political impact of mass media.* London: Sage.

Stephenson, L.B., Lawlor, A., Cross, W.P., Blais, A., and Gidengil, E., 2019. *Provincial battles, national prize? Elections in a Federal State.* Montreal and Kingston, QC: McGill-Queen's University Press.

Thibault, S., Bastien, F., Gosselin, T., Brin, C., and Scott, C., 2020. Is there a distinct Quebec media subsystem in Canada? Evidence of ideological and political orientations among Canadian news media organizations. *Canadian Journal of Political Science,* 53(3), 638–657.

Williams, B.A. and Delli Carpini, M.X., 2011. *After broadcast news: Media regimes, democracy, and the new information environment.* Cambridge: Cambridge University Press.

APPENDIX

TABLE 16.A1 Opinion about number of immigrants by regular exposure to news media sources

	British Columbia			Ontario			Québec		
	Model A	Model B	Model C	Model A	Model B	Model C	Model A	Model B	Model C
CBC	0.116***	0.103***	0.09***	0.101***	0.088***	0.079***	0.027	-0.02	-0.013
	(.017)	(.017)	(.017)	(.016)	(.016)	(.016)	(.031)	(.032)	(.031)
CTV	0.01	0.011	0.019	-0.041**	-0.038*	-0.036*	0.012	-0.004	-0.008
	(.017)	(.017)	(.017)	(.015)	(.015)	(.015)	(.032)	(.032)	(.031)
Global	-0.065***	-0.059***	-0.06***	-0.05**	-0.04*	-0.038*	0.035	0.013	0.029
	(.016)	(.016)	(.016)	(.019)	(.019)	(.018)	(.048)	(.048)	(.047)
CityTV	-0.069*	-0.057*	-0.06*	-0.007	-0.012	-0.02			
	(.029)	(.029)	(.029)	(.02)	(.02)	(.02)			
Globe and Mail	0.064*	0.051†	0.035	0.101***	0.077**	0.072**			
	(.027)	(.027)	(.026)	(.022)	(.023)	(.022)			
National Post	-0.004	-0.004	0.015	-0.032	-0.039	-0.021			
	(.035)	(.035)	(.035)	(.029)	(.028)	(.028)			
Huffington Post	0.081**	0.073*	0.062*	0.058*	0.065*	0.055*			
	(.029)	(.029)	(.029)	(.026)	(.026)	(.026)			
Vancouver Province	-0.08**	-0.066*	-0.061*						
	(.027)	(.027)	(.027)						
Vancouver Sun	0.04†	0.034	0.02						
	(.024)	(.025)	(.025)						
Toronto Star				0.069***	0.049*	0.034†			
				(.019)	(.019)	(.019)			
Toronto Sun				-0.11***	-0.094**	-0.077*			
				(.031)	(.031)	(.031)			

Radio-Canada							0.049**	0.031†	0.026
							(.017)	(.017)	(.017)
TVA							−0.098***	−0.084***	−0.075***
							(.017)	(.017)	(.017)
La Presse							0.042†	0.036	0.032
							(.022)	(.022)	(.022)
Le Devoir							0.115**	0.095*	0.091*
							(.039)	(.039)	(.038)
Montreal Gazette							0.051	0.032	0.028
							(.043)	(.043)	(.042)
Sociodemog. controls	NO	YES	YES	NO	YES	YES	NO	YES	YES
Party ID controls	NO	NO	YES	NO	NO	YES	NO	NO	YES
Constant	0.401***	0.388***	0.384***	0.377***	0.264***	0.275***	0.394***	0.308***	0.315***
	(.013)	(.031)	(.031)	(.012)	(.027)	(.027)	(.016)	(.03)	(.03)
Adjusted R²	0.095	0.11	0.133	0.092	0.116	0.131	0.062	0.101	0.133
N	1,230	1,230	1,230	1,367	1,367	1,367	1,269	1,269	1,269

Source: Cross et al., 2017.

Note: cells contain OLS regression coefficients (standard errors in parentheses).

*** p < 0.001   ** p < 0.01   * p < 0.05   † p < 0.10

TABLE 16.A2 Opinion about the refugee crisis by regular exposure to news media sources

	British Columbia			Ontario			Québec		
	Model A	Model B	Model C	Model A	Model B	Model C	Model A	Model B	Model C
CBC	0.125*** (.021)	0.123*** (.021)	0.081*** (.018)	0.06** (.02)	0.063** (.02)	0.03† (.018)	-0.061 (.039)	-0.076† (.04)	-0.065† (.037)
CTV	-0.058** (.022)	-0.045* (.021)	-0.013 (.019)	-0.034† (.019)	-0.036† (.19)	-0.021 (.017)	0.022 (.04)	0.047 (.04)	0.042 (.037)
Global	-0.032 (.02)	-0.031 (.02)	-0.034* (.018)	-0.064** (.024)	-0.055* (.023)	-0.045* (.021)	-0.014 (.061)	-0.019 (.06)	0.03 (.056)
CityTV	-0.048 (.036)	-0.042 (.036)	-0.053† (.032)	0.015 (.026)	0.029 (.025)	-0.008 (.023)			
Globe and Mail	0.076* (.034)	0.065† (.033)	0.016 (.029)	0.09** (.028)	0.087** (.028)	0.071** (.025)			
National Post	-0.13** (.045)	-0.139** (.044)	-0.063 (.039)	-0.125** (.036)	-0.108** (.036)	-0.027 (.032)			
Huffington Post	0.133*** (.037)	0.108** (.037)	0.071* (.032)	0.111** (.033)	0.093** (.033)	0.057† (.029)			
Vancouver Province	-0.078* (.037) (.034)	-0.075* (.037) (.034)	-0.047 (.03)						
Vancouver Sun	-0.023 (.031)	0.009 (.031)	-0.042 (.027)						
Toronto Star				0.108*** (.024)	0.104*** (.024)	0.049* (.022)			
Toronto Sun				-0.21*** (.039)	-0.188*** (.038)	-0.11** (.034)			
Radio-Canada							0.036† (.021)	0.035 (.021)	0.024 (.02)
TVA							-0.087*** (.021)	-0.075*** (.022)	-0.058** (.02)

	(1)	(2)	(3)	(4)	(5)	(6)	(7)	(8)
La Presse						0.009	0.005	−0.006
						(.028)	(.028)	(.026)
Le Devoir						0.089†	0.062	0.046
						(.049)	(.049)	(.045)
Montreal Gazette						−0.003	0.001	0.001
						(.054)	(.054)	(.05)
Sociodemog. controls	NO	YES	NO	YES	YES	NO	YES	YES
Party ID controls	NO	NO	NO	NO	YES	NO	NO	YES
Constant	0.574***	0.639***	0.556***	0.503***	0.56***	0.593***	0.532***	0.548***
	(.017)	(.039)	(.015)	(.034)	(.03)	(.019)	(.038)	(.035)
Adjusted R^2	0.064	0.095	0.068	0.099	0.298	0.016	0.039	0.175
N	1,230	1,230	1,367	1,367	1,367	1,269	1,269	1,269

Source: Cross et al., 2017.

Note: cells contain OLS regression coefficients (standard errors in parentheses).

*** $p < 0.001$ ** $p < 0.01$ * $p < 0.05$ † $p < 0.10$

TABLE 16.A3 Opinion about the niqab during oath ceremonies by regular exposure to news media sources

	British Columbia			Ontario			Québec		
	Model A	Model B	Model C	Model A	Model B	Model C	Model A	Model B	Model C
CBC	0.091** (.027)	0.086** (.027)	0.05† (.026)	0.119*** (.026)	0.123*** (.026)	0.089*** (.025)	0.22*** (.032)	0.199*** (.032)	0.201*** (.032)
CTV	-0.019 (.028)	-0.009 (.028)	0.012 (.027)	-0.092*** (.025)	-0.065** (.025)	-0.057* (.024)	0.002 (.032)	0.003 (.032)	-0.001 (.032)
Global	-0.115*** (.026)	-0.077** (.026)	-0.081** (.025)	-0.043 (.03)	-0.04 (.03)	-0.03 (.029)	-0.022 (.049)	-0.028 (.049)	-0.018 (.048)
CityTV	-0.02 (.048)	-0.042 (.047)	-0.05 (.045)	0.008 (.033)	0.002 (.033)	-0.02 (.031)			
Globe and Mail	0.163*** (.044)	0.141** (.043)	0.096* (.042)	0.158*** (.036)	0.13*** (.036)	0.117** (.035)			
National Post	-0.086 (.059)	-0.126* (.057)	-0.075 (.055)	-0.079† (.046)	-0.104* (.046)	-0.048 (.044)			
Huffington Post	0.189*** (.049)	0.141** (.047)	0.11* (.045)	0.141** (.043)	0.115** (.043)	0.077† (.041)			
Vancouver Province	-0.083† (.048)	-0.082† (.047)	-0.068 (.045)						
Vancouver Sun	-0.009 (.041)	0.015 (.041)	-0.022 (.039)						
Toronto Star				0.055† (.031)	0.051 (.031)	0.004 (.03)			
Toronto Sun				-0.196*** (.05)	-0.159** (.049)	-0.104* (.048)			
Radio-Canada							-0.027 (.017)	-0.011 (.017)	-0.013 (.017)
TVA							-0.081*** (.017)	-0.055** (.017)	-0.05**

La Presse							−0.013 (.017)	−0.017 (.017)	−0.02 (.017)
Le Devoir							0.057 (.023)	0.062 (.022)	0.06 (.022)
Montreal Gazette							0.037 (.04)	0.028 (.039)	0.026 (.039)
Sociodemog. controls	NO	YES	YES	NO	YES	YES	NO	YES	YES
Party ID controls	NO	NO	YES	NO	NO	YES	NO	NO	YES
Constant	0.413*** (.022)	0.427*** (.05)	0.412*** (.048)	0.331*** (.019)	0.259*** (.044)	0.293*** (.042)	0.147*** (.016)	0.176*** (.031)	0.177*** (.031)
Adjusted R^2	0.063	0.127	0.199	0.067	0.105	0.177	0.088	0.125	0.135
N	1,230	1,230	1,230	1,367	1,367	1,367	1,269	1,269	1,269

Source: Cross et al., 2017.

Note: cells contain OLS regression coefficients (standard errors in parentheses).

*** $p < 0.001$ ** $p < 0.01$ * $p < 0.05$ † $p < 0.10$

TABLE 16.A4 Opinions regarding political issues by regular exposure to news media sources

	Immigration			Environment			Economic globalization		
	Model A	Model B	Model C	Model A	Model B	Model C	Model A	Model B	Model C
Radio-Canada	0.058***	0.063***	0.06***	0.06**	0.081***	0.056**	0.019	0.009	0.022
	(.014)	(.014)	(.014)	(.019)	(.019)	(.019)	(.014)	(.014)	(.014)
La Presse	0.081***	0.055**	0.052**	0.069**	0.061**	0.05*	0.016	0.033*	0.038*
	(.016)	(.016)	(.016)	(.021)	(.022)	(.022)	(.016)	(.017)	(.016)
TVA	-0.106***	-0.07***	-0.06***	-0.086***	-0.077***	-0.068***	0.015	0.013	0.008
	(.014)	(.014)	(.014)	(.019)	(.019)	(.019)	(.014)	(.014)	(.014)
Journal de Montréal /	-0.046**	-0.018	-0.009	-0.103***	-0.086***	-0.078**	-0.009	-0.012	-0.014
Journal de Québec	(.018)	(.017)	(.017)	(.023)	(.023)	(.023)	(.017)	(.018)	(.017)
Sociodemog. controls	NO	YES	YES	NO	YES	YES	NO	YES	YES
Party ID controls	NO	NO	YES	NO	NO	YES	NO	NO	YES
Constant	0.567***	0.53***	0.527***	0.492***	0.566***	0.546***	.591***	0.546***	0.537***
	(.011)	(.016)	(.017)	(.015)	(.022)	(.024)	(.011)	(.016)	(.018)
Adjusted R²	0.084	0.163	0.201	0.05	0.065	0.115	0	0.017	0.067
N	1,412	1,412	1,412	1,361	1,361	1,361	1,384	1,384	1,384

Source: Lefebvre et al., 2020.

Note: cells contain OLS regression coefficients (standard errors in parentheses).

*** p < 0.001 ** p < 0.01 * p < 0.05 † p < .010

CHAPTER 17

Racial attitudes and opposition to immigration

....

Allison Harell and Robert A. Hinckley

INTRODUCTION

Deciding who becomes a citizen is a core function of government. Historically, the rise of the nation-state was tied intimately to decisions about who belongs in those states. Ethnic nationalism – or the idea that citizenship should be tied to those who share the ethnic, cultural, and linguistic heritage of the nation – continues to colour the ways in which people think about who should be allowed to become a citizen. Over time, explicitly racist immigration policies that denied access to citizenship to black, brown, and Indigenous people have slowly been replaced with policies that are increasingly neutral with respect to race, religion, and cultural heritage.

Today in industrialized democracies, there are three general types of immigration streams: economic, family reunification, and humanitarian. Countries vary in both the places immigrants tend to come from as well as in the balance of immigration flows across these streams. For example, in the United States, Mexico is the largest source country of immigrants by far, followed by China and India (Budiman, 2020). Family reunification as well as undocumented immigrants make up large shares of the immigrant population in the US. While Mexican migrants have made up a large share of undocumented immigrants, from 2017 to 2019 there has been large influxes from Honduras and Guatemala, as measured by apprehensions by the Department of Homeland Security (DHS, 2019). Canada, in contrast, has a comparatively small number of undocumented immigrants in part due to the fact that the only shared border is with the United States. Over half of immigrants in Canada are economic class immigrants, with almost half of all immigrants of Asian origin, as well as a large share from Europe (Statistics Canada, 2016).

Yet, the way in which the public reacts to immigration continues to be influenced by *who* people think about when they think about immigrants. Immigration brings in a diverse group of people to a host society who vary widely in terms of their socioeconomic

DOI: 10.4324/9781003121992-20

backgrounds and their racial, ethnic, and religious backgrounds. People uncomfortable with diversity are likely to prefer immigration policies that favour immigrants like themselves, or to prefer less immigration overall. In this chapter, we focus on exploring the link between immigration attitudes and prejudice. We are particularly interested in understanding immigration as a racialized policy domain. After reviewing the dominant theoretical frameworks for understanding immigration attitudes, we provide an empirical illustration of how immigration is racialized in the minds of Canadians and Americans. First, we show how people's feelings about *immigrants* are strongly predicted by how people feel about ethnic and racial minorities, and that these are in part tied to psychological predispositions. Second, we show that ethnocentric attitudes are also related to lower levels of support for immigration.

CULTURAL VERSUS ECONOMIC PREDICTORS OF IMMIGRATION ATTITUDES

Support for immigration is routinely understood through two dominant frameworks that focus on how host societies assess the potential threat of immigration to both the majority culture and economic prosperity (see, for example, Quillian, 1995; McClaren, 2003). Cultural threat explanations rely on the concept of distance between the majority culture of the host society and that of immigrants. Economic threat focuses on how immigrants may compete for scarce resources like jobs or benefit from government spending (and as a consequence, tax dollars).

We first explore cultural explanations. At its core, cultural explanations are based on the idea that immigrants pose a symbolic threat to the nation. Building on work on symbolic prejudice (Kinder and Sears, 1981), the basic logic is focused on the ways in which newcomers may threaten the cultural dominance of the majority. If immigration is primarily from neighbouring countries that do not differ in meaningful ways from the host society (say, inter-European migration from dominantly Christian societies), integration poses little problem. When immigrants are seen as different from the host society in some salient dimension, the expectation is that support for immigration will be lower because citizens will be uncomfortable with how newcomers will integrate and be seen as a threat to the racial, religious, or cultural status quo leading people to be more hostile towards the inclusion of such immigrants in society (McLaren, 2003).

Empirically, this should have two consequences. First, if immigrants are thought of as culturally different, then attitudes about cultural diversity should be closely tied to attitudes about immigration. If someone is intolerant of diversity, they should dislike immigration because immigration will increase the racial, ethnic, and religious diversity in their country. In other words, we expect two sets of attitudes to be tied closely together: on the one hand, attitudes about cultural diversity and attitudes about immigration. This is often referred to as a "symbolic" threat in the literature, a threat posed to the culture of the majority society rooted in an intergroup dynamic of "us" versus "them." Second, we might expect attitudes towards *specific* immigrants to vary based on their cultural distance.

There is a myriad of support for the first empirical relationship in the literature. For example, using American National Election Study (ANES) data from 1992 and 1996 in the US, Burns and Gimpel (2000) show that racial stereotypes are powerful predictors of attitudes towards immigration policy. Kinder and Kam (2010) similarly show how general measures of ethnocentrism, defined as "a readiness to reduce society to us *versus* them" (p. 8), are strongly related to opposition to immigration in the United States. Valentino and colleagues (2019, p. 22) show that racial resentment in the United States, but also Canada, France, Spain, and the United Kingdom, are powerful determinants of people's willingness to admit immigrants, and in fact, was the *most* powerful predictor.

Yet, this logic might also lead one to expect that citizens will evaluate individual immigrants differently on the basis of their relative cultural distance from the majority of the host society. Ford (2011) finds clear evidence for this in Britain. He shows a clear hierarchy of preferences for immigrants from more culturally proximate countries. The findings are somewhat less consistent when the public is presented with a choice in an increasingly common experimental design where survey respondents are asked to decide between two potential immigrants that vary on a host of characteristics. When they do appear, they tend to be relatively smaller than the effect of general attitudes towards diversity, and especially in comparison to economic cues about the immigration candidates (Harell et al., 2012; Hainmueller and Hopkins, 2015; Valentino et al., 2019). For example, in a cross-national experimental study, Valentino and colleagues (2019) find that publics in eight of the 11 countries studied show bias against Middle-Eastern immigrants, though the size of the effect is greatest in France and the United States. Hainmueller and Hopkins (2015) vary country of origin and find few differences in the US in terms of country of origin (though like Valentino and colleagues, they also find a bias against Middle-Eastern countries in their study). Interestingly, they also show that these preferences are greater among those with ethnocentric attitudes. Stated differently, those with more negative attitudes towards ethnic and racial minorities were more sensitive to cues about cultural difference.

These cultural explanations echo the larger literature on ethnic nationalism, where to be considered *truly* a member of a country is linked in the minds of citizens as sharing history, culture, and language with the dominant majority. People who endorse these more ethnic conceptions of the nation are more likely to see immigrants as a cultural threat (Wright, 2011) and such anti-immigrant sentiment is stronger among those who think of themselves in terms of their Christian identity (Storm, 2011). In a compelling cross-national comparison of attitudes towards immigration in the US and Europe, Sides and Citrin (2007) showed that these symbolic considerations, and notably preference for cultural unity, are powerful predictors of opposition to immigration. In sum, cultural explanations of opposition to immigration tend to focus on how immigration activates considerations of "us" versus "them" as well as stereotypes and racial animus, especially among members of a host society who think of themselves as an ethnic nation and consider themselves as prototypical of that nation.

Cultural explanations, of course, are not by any means the only explanation. Economic explanations tend to focus not on the ethnic or cultural origins of immigrants, but rather focus our attention on how immigrants might compete for scarce resources in the host society, from jobs to welfare benefits (for example see other chapters in this volume on class [Chapter 7] and labour market conditions [Chapter 14]). Building on realistic group conflict theory (Blumer 1958), central to economic explanations is the idea that immigrants are competing with the host society over scarce resources. Similar to cultural explanations, the underlying logic is fundamentally based on intergroup dynamics. "They" are taking "our" jobs, "our" tax dollars, or burdening "our" welfare systems. While this is not the focus of this chapter, it is fundamental to include these components. While the literature finds limited evidence that direct competition drives opposition to immigration (Citrin et al., 1997, though see Esses et al., 2001), there is a clear and consistent preference for higher-skilled immigrants across North America and Europe (Hainmueller and Hiscox, 2010; Harell et al., 2012; Valentino et al., 2019). Evidence points to how citizens view lower-skilled immigrants, especially with families, as a potential burden on the economy, what Valentino et al. (2019, p. 20) call sociotropic economic threat, and that these concerns vary little with the relative socioeconomic status of respondents.

This is in part likely because perceptions of immigrants as a burden are themselves based on stereotypes that often overlap with racial stereotypes, especially as they relate to the perceived work ethic of low-skilled immigrants. Interestingly, Burns and Gimpel (2000) argue that economic downturns activate racial stereotypes. And indeed, Harell, Soroka, and Iyengar (2017) have shown that immigration attitudes are driven in part based on perceptions of stereotypes about the work ethic of immigrants in Canada, the US, and the UK. And in a compelling study by Brader, Valentino, and Suhay (2008), the authors show that cueing the cost of immigration is more powerful when tied to Latino immigrants compared to European immigrants. In sum, there is clear evidence that support for immigration is partly explained by the view that immigrants are low-skilled and potentially pose a burden to the host society's economy. This is reinforced by the fact that myriad studies have shown how unwilling citizens are to share social welfare benefits with immigrants (see, for example, Wright and Reeskens, 2013; Ford, 2015; Soroka et al., 2017). When combined with the association of immigrants to ethnic, racial, and religious minorities, it is not surprising that these *economic* concerns are partly driven by how immigrants' otherness activates racial stereotypes about work ethic.

IMMIGRATION AS A RACIALIZED POLICY DOMAIN

In the remainder of this chapter, we shift to empirically investigating the extent to which immigration is a racialized policy domain. By racialized policy domain, we mean a domain that both activates a racialized conception of who immigrants are and links racial attitudes to support for immigration. In other words, we seek to demonstrate that (1) people *think* about immigrants largely in terms of being ethnic and racial minorities and (2) that negative attitudes to such minorities predict opposition to immigration as a policy.

Racial attitudes and feelings towards immigrants

In this first empirical section, we present evidence that attitudes towards immigrants are strongly tied to attitudes towards racial and other minorities. We draw on data from a comparative study of the USA and Canada, the Rights and Values Survey, collected in 2017 (Harell and Hinckley, 2017), the 2019 Canadian Election Study (Stephenson et al., 2020, 2021), and the 2020 American National Election Study (ANES, 2021).

The Rights and Values Survey asked a sample of Americans and Canadians how closely they identify with the "interests, feelings, and ideas" of immigrants, blacks, whites, Christians, Muslims, and Americans or Canadians. Responses were recorded on a 0 to 10 scale, where 0 meant distant and 10 reflected close identification. The mean levels of identification with immigrants among Americans (M = 5.6, SD = 2.8) and Canadians (M = 5.7, SD = 2.7) were similar. Identification with immigrants was regressed on the items measuring identification with the remaining five groups. Figure 17.1 illustrates the unstandardized OLS regression coefficients for the American and Canadian samples with 95% confidence intervals. When the estimates overlap zero, this means we have no evidence of a relationship. When it is significantly above zero, it implies a positive relationship, and vice versa for negative estimates.

In both countries, identification with blacks and Muslims had the strongest relationships with immigrant identification. This indicates, for instance, that those who strongly identify with blacks also strongly identify with immigrants, and those who feel distant from blacks also feel distant from immigrants. In the US, the coefficients

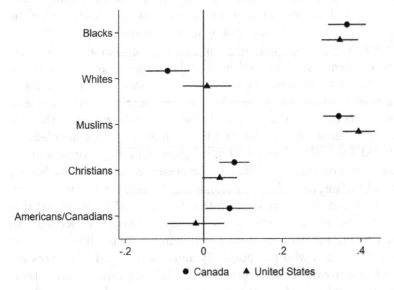

FIGURE 17.1 Regression coefficients: feeling distant/close to immigrants by other groups, Canada and US.

for white, Christian, and American group identifications did not reach the conventional level of statistical significance. In Canada, white identification was weakly and negatively associated with immigrant identification, while identifying as Canadian had a weak positive association.

The ANES 2020 contains other measures that strengthen our claim that attitudes towards immigrants are closely tied to attitudes about race and diversity. For instance, respondents were asked if "increasing diversity made the USA a better or worse place to live." Those who believed that diversity made the USA worse were more likely to have negative out-group attitudes towards immigrants ($r = -0.582$, $p < 0.001$). Perhaps more central to our key claim regarding racialization, a four-item index measuring racial resentment towards blacks is also associated with negative attitudes towards immigrants.[1] The four items are "Blacks should work their way up without special favors," "Blacks have gotten less than they deserve," "past slavery and discrimination have made it difficult for Blacks," and "if Blacks tried harder they'd be as well off as whites." After reverse coding the second and third, these items form a coherent scale (alpha = 0.88) that runs from 4 to 20 (M = 11.2, SD = 4.8), which shows a strong, negative correlation ($r = -553$, $p < 0.001$) with positive out-group attitudes towards immigrants. This strong relationship between racial resentment and attitudes towards immigrants is revealing because the content of the resentment questions does not make any reference to immigrants or immigration.

We take this to mean that how people think about immigrants is largely in terms of who people think immigrants are, and in the minds of most people, immigrants are thought of as ethnic and racial minorities. For this reason, people's feelings towards racial and ethnic minorities are very similar to their attitudes towards immigrants as a group and, as we have shown here, are predictive of each other.

We can take this a step further by looking at how racial attitudes predict evaluations of the cultural and economic threat immigrants pose to society. Using the 2020 ANES, we analyze a trio of questions designed to measure out-group attitudes towards immigrants, particularly views of immigrants as cultural and sociotropic economic threats. The items asked respondents to indicate their degree of agreement or disagreement with the statements, "America's culture is harmed by immigrants," "immigrants are good for America's economy," and "immigrants increase crime in the US." These items are the same that are used in the chapters from Part 2. The coding was reversed for the second item so that an additive index could be computed that runs from 3 to 15 (M = 6.8, SD = 2.8), with higher scores indicating more out-group threat. This measure was regressed on feeling thermometer scores for Asians, blacks, Hispanics, whites, Muslims, and Christians. Figure 17.2 illustrates the unstandardized regression slopes with 95% confidence intervals. The ANES data reveal that negative (positive) feelings about Hispanics, blacks, and Muslims are associated with negative (positive) out-group attitudes towards immigrants. Interestingly, in these data we find that Americans who feel positively about whites and Christians are more likely to have negative out-group attitudes towards immigrants. Overall, these findings from the USA and Canada reaffirm that attitudes towards immigrants are closely tied to feelings about racial and other minority groups.

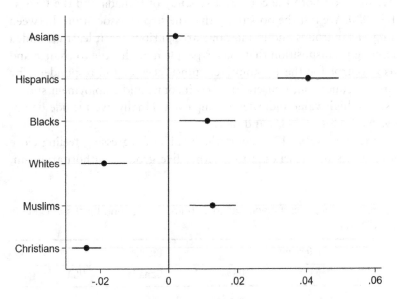

FIGURE 17.2 Regression coefficients: immigrant threat evaluations by feeling thermometer scores for various groups, ANES 2020.

Next, we test multivariate regression models of attitudes towards immigrants that include a range of control variables. Several of these models include two important individual-level dispositions that many studies show are predictors of both attitudes towards racial minorities and immigrants. First, an authoritarian worldview is defined as placing a high value on conformity with social norms and on obeying leaders who are expected to enforce those norms (Hetherington and Weiler, 2009). An authoritarian worldview is associated with negative views of racial and cultural minorities, political intolerance, social intolerance, and the desire to punish rule breakers (e.g. Hetherington and Weiler, 2009; Stenner, 2005). Second, social dominance orientation (SDO) is the tendency to view social hierarchy as natural and desirable (Pratto et al., 1994). Given how attitudes towards immigrants and immigration are shaped by an intergroup "us" and "them" mentality, valuing the enforcement of social conformity and the maintenance of status quo hierarchies are fundamental predispositions that should increase opposition to immigrants, especially when, as we have demonstrated, they are thought about largely in terms of ethnic and racial minorities.

This is not a novel argument. There is a rich literature in psychology tying authoritarianism and SDO to prejudice towards ethnic outgroups (e.g. Duckitt, 2001, 2006; Cohrs and Asbrock, 2009) and anti-immigrant sentiment (e.g. Craig and Richeson, 2014; Yoxon et al., 2019). As this past research makes clear, authoritarianism and SDO should shape views regarding immigrants both directly and indirectly. They contribute directly to negative views of immigrants, and indirectly by fostering a negative view of racial minorities and, subsequently, opinions about immigrants.

Once again, we draw on both the comparative study of Canada and the USA as well as the ANES 2020. We test the possibility that the strong associations between attitudes regarding racial groups and immigrants are spurious, or at least grounded in a deeper underlying predisposition that makes people more hostile to change and diversity. We also control for the economic circumstances of the respondent, by including measures of education, household (HH) income, and employment status, which is coded so the high value indicates unemployed. Finally, we include demographic control variables for sex, age, and race.

The first two models in Table 17.1 report the results of regressing feeling close or distant to immigrants on closeness to the other five groups, authoritarianism,

TABLE 17.1 OLS regression: predicting identification with immigrants and blacks in Canada and USA (2017)

	Immigrants		Blacks	
	Canada	USA	Canada	USA
Blacks	0.366***	0.342***	–	–
	(0.0241)	(0.0243)		
Whites	–0.0663*	0.0147	0.122***	–0.0869**
	(0.0280)	(0.0315)	(0.0296)	(0.0325)
Muslims	0.300***	0.376***	0.377***	0.401***
	(0.0204)	(0.0206)	(0.0194)	(0.0188)
Christians	0.0980***	0.0687**	0.149***	0.202***
	(0.0197)	(0.0229)	(0.0206)	(0.0232)
Canadians/Americans	0.0486	–0.00954	0.181***	0.274***
	(0.0305)	(0.0364)	(0.0321)	(0.0371)
Age	0.0454	–0.00431	0.0979**	–0.0329
	(0.0295)	(0.0324)	(0.0313)	(0.0335)
Authoritarianism	–0.0897**	–0.0935**	–0.0647*	–0.0322
	(0.0306)	(0.0313)	(0.0325)	(0.0323)
SDO	–0.108***	–0.0669**	–0.0416	–0.179***
	(0.0221)	(0.0225)	(0.0235)	(0.0228)
Female	0.119	0.154	0.141	0.0436
	(0.102)	(0.112)	(0.108)	(0.116)
Education	0.225***	0.121**	–0.103**	–0.115**
	(0.0360)	(0.0403)	(0.0382)	(0.0416)
HH income	–0.0145	0.0658	–0.0662	0.0103
	(0.0423)	(0.0459)	(0.0450)	(0.0475)
Unemployed	–0.0232	–0.122	0.189	–0.0582
	(0.175)	(0.172)	(0.186)	(0.178)
Constant	2.564***	2.157***	2.184***	4.008***
	(0.457)	(0.470)	(0.483)	(0.475)
N	1,526	1,593	1,526	1,593
Adjusted-R^2	0.488	0.452	0.365	0.357

Note: Standard errors in parentheses. * $p < 0.05$, ** $p < 0.01$, *** $p < 0.001$.

Source: Rights and Values survey, 2017.

social dominance orientation (SDO), education, income, employment status, and the demographic controls for the Canadian sample (column 1) and the American sample (column 2). The third and fourth models regress identification with Blacks on most of the same predictor variables.

As we saw in the uncontrolled models in Figure 17.1, closeness to blacks and Muslims predicts identification with immigrants in both the Canadian and US samples. Importantly, these relationships persist even after inclusion of the psychological, economic, and demographic control variables. As expected, authoritarianism and SDO also show negative and statistically significant relationships with feeling close or distant to immigrants in both country samples. The third and fourth models in Table 17.1 suggest that authoritarianism and SDO also contribute indirectly to feeling distant from immigrants. Both measures are negatively associated with feeling close to blacks, with authoritarianism significant in Canada and SDO in the US.

The next analysis shifts to the three-item evaluation of immigrant threat measured in the 2020 ANES. The slope estimates for predictors of negative out-group attitudes towards immigrants are available in Appendix Table 17.A3. Model 1 shows the coefficient only for racial resentment, Model 2 includes the economic and demographic control variables, and Model 3 adds authoritarianism as a predictor.[2] Our analysis shows that racial resentment towards blacks remains a strong predictor of negative out-group attitudes towards immigrants. The coefficient is positive and statistically significant, accounting for 30.5% of the variance in attitudes towards immigrants. This relationship persists in the second and third models, despite controls for economic and demographic traits. This relationship is illustrated in Figure 17.3.

Although SDO was not measured in the ANES, the coefficient for authoritarianism indicates that an authoritarian worldview is associated with negative out-group

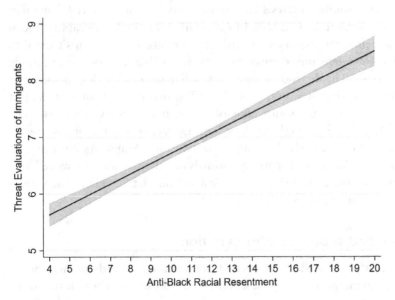

FIGURE 17.3 Immigrant threat evaluations by anti-black racial resentment, ANES 2020.

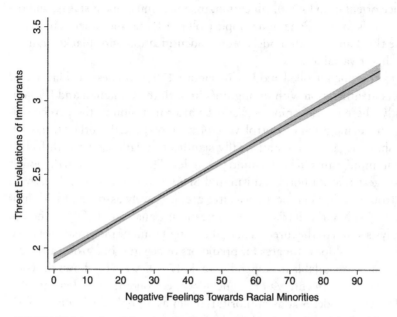

FIGURE 17.4 Immigrant threat evaluations by attitudes towards racial minorities, CES 2019.

attitudes towards immigrants, and its inclusion reduces the size of the effect of racial resentment. This suggests that authoritarianism, as we suspected, is an underlying predisposition that is linked to both prejudicial attitudes towards racial minorities as well as immigrants. It has both a direct and indirect effect on attitudes towards immigrants.

We can conduct a similar analysis in Canada drawing on the 2019 Canadian Election Study (Stephenson et al., 2020). In Appendix Table 17.A4 we capture racial attitudes using a feeling thermometer towards racial minorities that runs from 0 to 100, as well as a four-item index measuring social dominance orientation, along with relevant controls. The dependent variable is a five-item index that includes the three items used in the United States, as well as "Too many recent immigrants just don't want to fit in" and "Immigrants take jobs away from other Canadians." The scale runs from 1 to 5, where higher values indicate seeing immigrants as greater threats. The results mirror closely the analysis in the United States. As illustrated in Figure 17.4, those who feel more negatively towards racial minorities are more likely to see immigrants as a threat and vice versa. We also find that SDO is strongly associated with negative threat perceptions.

Ethnocentrism and support for immigration

In a final set of analyses, we shift the focus from attitudes towards immigrants to attitudes towards immigration as a policy domain. To do so, we again draw on the

2020 ANES and the 2019 CES. In the US, we create a three-item index of pro-immigration attitudes in the ANES based on three questions: whether the person favours
or opposes returning unauthorized immigrants to their native country; favours or
opposes allowing refugees to come to the US; and what should immigration levels be.
In Canada, we combine two items: do you think Canada should admit more, fewer or
about the same number of (1) immigrants and (2) refugees? In both countries, higher
scores indicate more support for immigration. The results are presented in Table 17.2.

As we saw with attitudes towards immigrants, attitudes towards immigration in
the United States and Canada are predicted by racial attitudes and psychological

TABLE 17.2 OLS regression: predicting pro-immigration attitudes in Canada and the US

United States		Canada	
Racial resentment	−0.0192***	Feelings towards racial minorities	−0.004***
	(0.00116)		(0.000)
Authoritarianism	−0.0317***	SDO	−0.111***
	(0.00340)		(0.005)
White	0.0172	White/European descent	−0.004
	(0.00924)		(0.006)
Immigrant	0.0684***	Immigrant	−0.006
	(0.141478)		(0.010)
Age	−0.00123***	Age	0.001***
	(0.000223)		(0.000)
Education	0.0125***	Education	0.071***
	(0.00377)		(0.007)
Female	0.00617	Female	−0.048***
	(0.00736)		(0.006)
Ideology	−0.0143***	Partisanship	
	(0.00203)	Conservative	−0.144***
Partisanship	−0.0183***		(0.008)
	(0.00242)	NDP	0.005
			(0.010)
		BQ	−0.046*
			(0.018)
		Other, none	−0.062***
			(0.009)
HH income	−0.0002	HH income	0.001
	(0.000616)		(0.002)
Unemployed	−0.0382	Unemployed	−0.041***
	(0.0218)		(0.010)
Constant	0.9953***	Constant	0.758***
	(0.0225)		(0.019)
N	4,238		7,573
R-squared	0.501		0.354

Note: Standard errors in parentheses. * $p<0.05$, ** $p<0.01$, *** $p<0.001$.

Source: ANES, 2020; CES, 2019.

predispositions. The more hostile Americans are towards black Americans, the less they favour immigration. And the more they value the enforcement of social conformity, the less likely they are to support immigration. In Canada, we see a very similar pattern emerge. When people report higher levels of dislike towards racial minorities, they are less likely to support immigration. Similarly, those higher on SDO also are less likely to support more immigration.

DISCUSSION AND CONCLUSION

At the individual level, one major source of opposition to immigration and a barrier to their successful integration within a host society is the fact that people think about immigrants as not only foreign, but as ethnically and culturally "Other." As we have argued throughout this chapter, the racialization of immigration is driven by two related processes. First, people often imagine immigrants as ethnic and racial minorities and so attitudes towards one are heavily related to attitudes towards the other. This is captured by cultural explanations of immigration attitudes, but also overlaps economic explanations. Ethnic and racial minority immigrants in the public's imagination are also often low-income or low-skill, and so a whole battery of negative stereotypes driven by racial prejudice are activated when the public thinks about immigrants. Second, and as a consequence, racial attitudes drive immigration attitudes. This is partly rooted in deeper underlying predispositions, which we have captured here through the concepts of authoritarianism and social dominance orientation, but also reflect tensions in how people think about the national community in a country as in part about shared culture, language, and history.

This means that immigration debates, especially when they become politically salient, can be driven by people's discomfort and hostility towards diversity in all its forms. It also means that promoting more inclusive and open attitudes towards newcomers in a society may well require that we target the types of intolerance that ethnic and racial minorities face within these societies, whether they are foreign-born or not.

What can be done? If the fundamental underlying dynamic is one of intergroup relations, then we can look to work in social psychology for possible solutions. While living in diverse contexts can increase hostility towards immigration (as considered in Chapter 13, looking at ethnic heterogeneity in Japan), past research has shown that positive contact within these settings can lessen hostility (McClaren, 2003). Similarly, framing immigration in terms of a common in-group identity can also decrease negative attitudes towards immigrants (Esses et al., 2001). There may also be policy solutions. More selective immigration policies and policies that emphasize integration – and even assimilation – may decrease hostility towards immigration (Citrin and Sides, 2008), though Bloemraad (2006) has argued compellingly that multicultural policies of political incorporation can lead to more cohesive societies. What is clear is that policymakers and social movements that seek to gain support for more open and expansive immigration policies must wrestle with the ways existing racial and ethnic animosity can and is activated when immigration is debated. This stems from existing prejudice, but also underlying psychological predispositions that make prejudice – and opposition to change of any kind – harder for some citizens to accept.

SUMMARY POINTS

- Immigration is a major driver of ethnic and racial diversity. Attitudes towards immigration are heavily influenced by attitudes towards such diversity. Those with prejudicial attitudes are likely to prefer immigration policies that favour immigrants like themselves, or to prefer less immigration overall.
- Drawing on survey data from Canada and the United States, we explored how immigration is a racialized policy domain. We showed that: (1) people's feelings about immigrants as a group are strongly predicted by how people feel about ethnic and racial minorities; and (2) ethnocentric attitudes predict decreased support for immigration as a policy domain.
- Our results suggest that promoting more inclusive and open attitudes towards newcomers in a society requires that we target the types of intolerance that ethnic and racial minorities face within these societies, whether they are foreign-born or not.

NOTES

1 Racial resentment is a measure of symbolic prejudice, as developed by Kinder and Sears (1981), and has become one of the most common measures in studies of racial attitudes in the US (Cramer, 2020).
2 Note that SDO was not available in the ANES 2020.

SUGGESTED FURTHER READINGS

Craig, M.A. and Richeson, J.A., 2014. Not in my backyard! Authoritarianism, social dominance orientation, and support for strict immigration policies at home and abroad. *Political Psychology*, 35(3), 417–429.

Kinder, D.R. and Kam, C.D., 2010. *Us against them: Ethnocentric foundations of American opinion*. Chicago, IL: University of Chicago Press.

Quillian, L., 1995. Prejudice as a response to perceived group threat: Population composition and anti-immigrant and racial prejudice in Europe. *American Sociological Review*, 60(4), 586–611.

Valentino, N.A., Soroka, S.N., Iyengar, S., Aalberg, T., Duch, R., Fraile, M., Hahn, K.S., Hansen, K.M., Harell, A., Helbling, M., Jackman, S.D., and Kobayashi, T., 2019. Economic and cultural drivers of immigrant support worldwide. *British Journal of Political Science*, 49(4), 1201–1226.

REFERENCES

American National Election Studies (ANES), 2021. *ANES 2020 time series study preliminary release: Combined pre-election and post-election data* [Dataset and documentation]. March 24, 2021 version. Available from: www.electionstudies.org.

Bloemraad, I., 2006. *Becoming a citizen: Iincorporating immigrants and refugees in the United States and Canada.* Oakland: University of California Press.

Blumer, H., 1958. Race prejudice as a sense of group position. *Pacific Sociological Review,* 1(1), 3–7.

Brader, T., Valentino, N.A., and Suhay, E., 2008. What triggers public opposition to immigration? Anxiety, group cues, and immigration threat. *American Journal of Political Science,* 52(4), 959–978.

Budiman, A., 2020. Key findings about US immigrants. Pew Research Center (August 20, 2020). Available from: https://www.pewresearch.org/fact-tank/2020/08/20/key-findings -about-u-s-immigrants/.

Burns, P. and Gimpel, J.G., 2000. Economic insecurity, prejudicial stereotypes, and public opinion on immigration policy. *Political Science Quarterly,* 115(2), 201–225.

Citrin, J., Green, D.P., Muste, C., and Wong, C., 1997. Public opinion toward immigration reform: The role of economic motivations. *The Journal of Politics,* 59(3), 858–881.

Citrin, J. and Sides, J., 2008. Immigration and the imagined community in Europe and the United States. *Political Studies,* 56(1), 33–56. doi: 10.1111/j.1467-9248.2007.00716.x.

Cohrs, J.C. and Asbrock, F., 2009. Right-wing authoritarianism, social dominance orientation and prejudice against threatening and competitive ethnic groups. *European Journal of Social Psychology,* 39(2), 270–289.

Craig, M.A. and Richeson, J.A., 2014. Not in my backyard! Authoritarianism, social dominance orientation, and support for strict immigration policies at home and abroad. *Political Psychology,* 35(3), 417–429.

Cramer, K., 2020. Understanding the role of racism in contemporary US public opinion. *Annual Review of Political Science,* 23(1), 153–169.

Department of Homeland Security, 2019. *2019 yearbook of immigration statistics.* Available from: https://www.dhs.gov/immigration-statistics/yearbook/2019.

Duckitt, J., 2001. A dual-process cognitive-motivational theory of ideology and prejudice. *Advances in Experimental Social Psychology,* 33, 41–113.

Duckitt, J., 2006. Differential effects of right wing authoritarianism and social dominance orientation on outgroup attitudes and their mediation by threat from and competitiveness to outgroups. *Personality and Social Psychology Bulletin,* 32(5), 684–696.

Esses, V.M., Dovidio, J.F., Jackson, L.M., and Armstrong, T.L., 2001. The immigration dilemma: The role of perceived group competition, ethnic prejudice, and national identity. *Journal of Social Issues,* 57(3), 389–412.

Ford, R., 2011. Acceptable and unacceptable immigrants: How opposition to immigration in Britain is affected by migrants' region of origin. *Journal of Ethnic and Migration Studies,* 37(7), 1017–1037.

Ford, R., 2015. Who should we help? An experimental test of discrimination in the British welfare state. *Political Studies,* 64(3), 630–650.

Hainmueller, J. and Hiscox, M.J., 2010. Attitudes toward highly skilled and low-skilled immigration: Evidence from a survey experiment. *American political science review,* 104(1), 61–84.

Hainmueller, J. and Hopkins, D.J., 2015. The hidden American immigration consensus: A conjoint analysis of attitudes toward immigrants. *American Journal of Political Science,* 59(3), 529–548.

Harell, A. and Hinckley, R., 2017. *Rights and values survey, Dataset.* Montréal: Université du Québec à Montréal.

Harell, A., Soroka, S., and Iyengar, S., 2017. Locus of control and anti-immigrant sentiment in Canada, the United States and the United Kingdom. *Political Psychology*, 38(2), 245–260.

Harell, A., Soroka, S., Iyengar, S., and Valentino, N., 2012. The impact of economic and cultural cues on support for immigration in Canada and the US. *Canadian Journal of Political Science*, 45(3), 499–530.

Hetherington, M.J. and Weiler, J.D., 2009. *Authoritarianism & polarization in American politics*. London, UK: Cambridge.

Kinder, D.R. and Kam, C.D., 2010. *Us against them: Ethnocentric foundations of American opinion*. Chicago, IL: University of Chicago Press.

Kinder, D.R. and Sears, D.O., 1981. Prejudice and polities: Symbolic racism versus racial threats to the good life. *Journal of Personality and Social Psychology*, 40(3), 414–431.

McLaren, L.M., 2003. Anti-immigrant prejudice in Europe: Contact, threat perception, and preferences for the exclusion of migrants. *Social Forces*, 81(3), 909–936.

Pratto, F., Sidanius, J., Stallworth, L.M., and Malle, B.F., 1994. Social dominance orientation: A personality variable predicting social and political attitudes. *Journal of Personality and Social Psychology*, 67(4), 741–763.

Quillian, L., 1995. Prejudice as a response to perceived group threat: Population composition and anti-immigrant and racial prejudice in Europe. *American Sociological Review*, 60(4), 586–611. doi: 10.2307/2096296.

Sides, J. and Citrin, J., 2007. European opinion about immigration: The role of identities, interests and information. *British Journal of Political Science*, 37(3), 477–504.

Soroka, S., Wright, M., Johnston, R., Citrin, J., Banting, K., and Kymlicka, W., 2017. Ethnoreligious identity, immigration, and redistribution. *Journal of Experimental Political Science*, 4(3), 173–182.

Statistics Canada, 2016. *Census of population, Statistics Canada catalogue no. 98-400-X2016202.*

Stenner, K.L., 2005. *The authoritarian dynamic*. New York: Cambridge University Press.

Stephenson, L.B., Harell, A., Rubenson, D., and Loewen, P.J., 2020. *2019 Canadian election study - Online survey, Harvard Dataverse, V1*. doi: 10.7910/DVN/DUS88V.

Stephenson, L.B., Harell, A., Rubenson, D., and Loewen, P.J., 2021. Measuring preferences and behaviours in the 2019 Canadian election study. *Canadian Journal of Political Science*, 54(1), 118–124. doi: 10.1017/S0008423920001006.

Storm, I., 2011. Christian nations? Ethnic Christianity and anti-immigration attitudes in four Western European countries. *Nordic Journal of Religion and Society*, 24(1), 75–96.

Valentino, N.A., Soroka, S.N., Iyengar, S., Aalberg, T., Duch, R., Fraile, M., Hahn, K.S., Hansen, K.M., Harell, A., Helbling, M., Jackman, S.D., and Kobayashi, T., 2019. Economic and cultural drivers of immigrant support worldwide. *British Journal of Political Science*, 49(4), 1201–1226.

Wright, M., 2011. Diversity and the imagined community: Immigrant diversity and conceptions of national identity. *Political Psychology*, 32(5), 837–862.

Wright, M. and Reeskens, T., 2013. Of what cloth are the ties that bind? National identity and support for the welfare state across 29 European countries. *Journal of European Public Policy*, 20(10), 1443–1463.

Yoxon, B., Van Hauwaert, S.M., and Kiess, J., 2019. Picking on immigrants: A cross-national analysis of individual-level relative deprivation and authoritarianism as predictors of anti-foreign prejudice. *Acta Politica*, 54(3), 479–520.

APPENDIX

TABLE 17.A1 OLS regression: social identification scales and positive identification with immigrants

	Canada	USA
Blacks	0.365***	0.347***
	(0.0245)	(0.0239)
Whites	−0.0917**	0.00925
	(0.0285)	(0.0318)
Muslims	0.344***	0.395***
	(0.0202)	(0.0207)
Christians	0.0782***	0.0411
	(0.0194)	(0.0223)
Americans/Canadiens	0.0660*	−0.0203
	(0.0312)	(0.0368)
Constant	1.799***	1.606***
	(0.253)	(0.243)
N	1,536	1,603
Adjusted R^2	0.455	0.434

Note: Standard errors in parenthese. * $p<0.05$, ** $p<0.01$, *** $p<0.001$.

Source: Rights and Values Survey, 2017.

TABLE 17.A2 OLS regression: feeling thermometer scores and threat evaluations of immigrants

	Model 1
Asians	0.0338***
	(0.00596)
Hispanics	0.0153*
	(0.00660)
Blacks	0.00936
	(0.00597)
Whites	−0.0249***
	(0.00484)
Muslims	0.0226***
	(0.00682)
Christians	−0.0279***
	(0.00277)
Constant	9.255***
	(0.401)
Observations	2,155
Adjusted R^2	0.293

Note: Standard errors in parentheses. Feeling thermometer scores were reversed. * $p<0.05$, ** $p<0.01$, *** $p<0.001$.

Source: ANES, 2020.

TABLE 17.A3 OLS regression: predicting threat evaluations of immigrants (ANES, 2020)

	Model 1	Model 2	Model 3
Racial resentment	0.323***	0.213***	0.180***
	(0.00978)	(0.0143)	(0.0141)
White		−0.0204	0.245*
		(0.109)	(0.104)
Age		−0.00614*	−0.00973***
		(0.00269)	(0.00254)
Education		−0.314***	−0.233***
		(0.0439)	(0.0421)
Female		0.240**	0.223*
		(0.0912)	(0.0870)
Ideology		0.196***	0.143***
		(0.0245)	(0.0230)
Partisanship		0.153***	0.151***
		(0.0294)	(0.0285)
HH income		−0.0386***	−0.0286***
		(0.00760)	(0.00738)
Unemployed		−0.0230	−0.143
		(0.221)	(0.205)
Authoritarianism			0.493***
			(0.0380)
Constant	3.31***	4.25***	3.59***
	(0.113)	(0.281)	(0.266)
N	4,264	4,264	4,264
Adjusted R^2	0.305	0.400	0.441

Note: Standard errors in parentheses. $p<0.05$, ** $p<0.01$, *** $p<0.001$.

Source: ANES, 2020.

TABLE 17.A4 OLS regression: predicting threat evaluations of immigrants (CES, 2019)

	Model 1	Model 2	Model 3
Feeling towards racial minorities	0.023***	0.021***	0.013***
	(0.000)	(0.000)	(0.000)
White/European		−0.011	−0.025
		(0.018)	(0.016)
Immigrant		−0.090**	−0.081**
		(0.031)	(0.027)
Age		−0.008***	−0.006***
		(0.001)	(0.001)
Education		−0.199***	−0.158***
		(0.022)	(0.020)
Female		0.080***	0.138***
		(0.020)	(0.018)
Partisanship (ref = liberal)			
Conservative		0.504***	0.286***
		(0.025)	(0.023)
NDP		0.020	0.076**
		(0.032)	(0.029)
BQ		0.550***	0.394***
		(0.057)	(0.051)
Other, none		0.261***	0.189***
		(0.028)	(0.025)
HH income		−0.025***	−0.033***
		(0.006)	(0.006)
Unemployed		0.178***	0.140***
		(0.031)	(0.028)
SDO			0.587***
			(0.013)
Constant	1.571***	2.013***	0.935***
	(0.017)	(0.055)	(0.054)
N	8,346	7,720	7,720
Adjusted R2	0.311	0.380	0.515

Note: Standard errors in parentheses. * $p<0.05$, ** $p<0.01$, *** $p<0.001$.

Source: CES, 2019.

CHAPTER 18

Conclusion

....

Cameron D. Anderson and Mathieu Turgeon

INTRODUCTION

In this concluding chapter of the volume, we have two central goals. The first is to revisit the determinants, data, and analyses from Part 2. In so doing, we estimate models of immigration opinion using the economy, culture, crime, and index measures. The details of these analyses follow. Our second goal is to review the volume in its entirety and to pull out threads of emphasis and common themes that serve to distinguish the central contributions of the volume.

PUTTING IT ALL TOGETHER

In Part 2, we explored the individual-level determinants of public opinion about immigration using, when available, data from nine Western democracies (Australia, the United Kingdom, Canada, France, Germany, Italy, Portugal, Switzerland, and the US). Specifically, eight chapters from Part 2 were dedicated each to addressing one specific determinant. The individual-level determinants covered in these chapters were: age (Chapter 4), gender (Chapter 5), immigration status (Chapter 6), class (Chapter 7), religion (Chapter 8), personality (Chapter 9), ideology (Chapter 10), and partisanship (Chapter 11). Findings from these chapters indicated that some of these determinants are weakly related to anti-immigration attitudes (e.g. gender and religion), others moderately related (e.g. age, immigration status, and personality), and still others strongly related (e.g. social class, political ideology, and partisanship). Moreover, some of these determinants like ideology and partisanship, for example, are uniformly related to anti-immigration attitudes across all countries. Precisely, those who identify with the political left show systematically less anti-immigration attitudes than those on the political right and that is true in all nine Western democracies examined. Other determinants, however, are sometimes more

DOI: 10.4324/9781003121992-21

strongly related to anti-immigration attitudes in some countries than in others. For example, Italian Catholics show more anti-immigrant attitudes when compared to Italian Protestants, but French Protestants, for their part, have more anti-immigrant views than their fellow Catholics.

Chapters 4 through 11 presented bivariate analyses between the three measures of anti-immigration attitudes (and the composite index) and an individual-level determinant of interest. This type of analysis, however, frequently suffers from omitted variable bias, that is, the bias associated with leaving out a relevant variable from one's analysis. The bias comes from attributing an effect to or an association between the included variables and the dependent variable of interest – the phenomenon under study – when none exists. In our bivariate analyses, it means that we may be attributing an association between said individual-level determinant and anti-immigration attitudes when, in fact, there is no association between the two. One way to attenuate the omitted variable bias is to propose an analysis where we account for multiple determinants at the same time. This can be easily done within a multiple regression analysis framework. This framework allows us to evaluate the association between age and anti-immigration attitudes while accounting for other determinants of anti-immigration attitudes like gender, political ideology, and partisanship, for example.

We proceed with a multiple regression analysis to evaluate which of the individual-level determinants are most strongly associated with anti-immigration attitudes. To do so, however, we must make a few decisions. First, we exclude from our analysis personality traits. As discussed in Chapter 9, only four out of our nine Western democracies had the information necessary to evaluate the association between personality and anti-immigration attitudes (Canada, France, Germany, and the US). Second, we exclude Australia because it was not possible to compute a measure of social class for that country (given limitations on the availability of some variables that make up our measure of social class). As seen in Chapter 7, social class is strongly related to anti-immigration attitudes. We think that it is more appropriate to exclude Australia from our analysis than to exclude social class as a central determinant of anti-immigration attitudes. Third, and finally, for immigration status we only consider the variable about whether the respondent's parents were foreign-born or born in the country. We do this to avoid having to drop one additional country, this time, the US. In the end, we are left with the following eight countries (the United Kingdom, Canada, France, Germany, Italy, Portugal, Switzerland, and the US) and seven individual determinants (age, gender, immigration status, class, religion, ideology, and partisanship) to perform our multiple regression analysis.

Table 18.1 presents four sets of coefficients estimates (with their respective standard errors), one for each of our dependent variables: attitudes about how immigrants are perceived to affect one country's crime (1), culture (2), economy (3), and our immigration index (4). Again, all dependent variables are coded from 1 to 5, with higher values indicating greater anti-immigration attitudes. Also, all independent variables were recoded to range from 0 to 1 to ease interpretation and comparisons. Note, moreover, that age is accounted for by creating two dichotomous variables

TABLE 18.1 Explaining attitudes about how immigrants are perceived to affect a country's economy, culture, and crime (index)

	Crime	Culture	Economy	Immigration index
(Intercept)	2.23***	2.19***	2.08***	2.16***
	(0.08)	(0.10)	(0.08)	(0.07)
Age 35–64	0.15***	0.13***	−0.04	0.08**
	(0.03)	(0.03)	(0.03)	(0.03)
Age 65+	0.24***	0.17***	−0.15***	0.09**
	(0.04)	(0.04)	(0.03)	(0.03)
Women	−0.12***	−0.03	0.14***	−0.00
	(0.03)	(0.03)	(0.02)	(0.02)
Either parent is foreign born	−0.14***	−0.22***	−0.17***	−0.17***
	(0.03)	(0.03)	(0.03)	(0.02)
Social class	−0.26***	−0.34***	−0.22***	−0.27***
	(0.04)	(0.04)	(0.04)	(0.03)
Catholic	0.08+	0.12*	0.14***	0.12***
	(0.05)	(0.05)	(0.04)	(0.03)
Protestant	0.06	0.01	0.12**	0.07+
	(0.05)	(0.05)	(0.04)	(0.03)
Non-religious	−0.01	−0.03	0.05	0.00
	(0.05)	(0.05)	(0.04)	(0.04)
Ideology	1.42***	1.46***	0.84***	1.24***
	(0.07)	(0.07)	(0.06)	(0.06)
Identifies with party from left	−0.34***	−0.35***	−0.24***	−0.31***
	(0.04)	(0.04)	(0.04)	(0.03)
Identifies with party from centre	−0.25***	−0.32***	−0.27***	−0.28***
	(0.04)	(0.04)	(0.03)	(0.03)
Identifies with party from right	0.34***	0.25***	0.22***	0.27***
	(0.04)	(0.04)	(0.04)	(0.03)
F	280.97	170.65	152.32	287.49
Adjusted-R²	0.32	0.24	0.23	0.34
Number of observations	13,618			
+p<0.1, * p<0.05, ** p<0.01, *** p<0.001.				

Note: entries are OLS estimates with standard errors in parentheses. The regression equations also include country dummies to account for country differences.

(variables that take the value 1 for the desired group and 0 otherwise) to identify respondents aged between 35 and 64 and another one for those 65 and more, following the categorization adopted in Chapter 4. The omitted group consists of young respondents (18–34) and the coefficient estimates for our two age variables should be interpreted in comparison to young respondents. Similarly, we created three variables to capture religion, as done in Chapter 8. Specifically, we created one dichotomous variable for respondents who identify as Catholics, another for those who classify themselves as Protestants, and yet another for the non-religious. The omitted group, this time, represents all those who identify with another religion. We also created three additional dichotomous variables for respondents who identify with a party from the left, centre, or right, as done in Chapter 11. The omitted category represents those who do not identify with a political party. For gender and immigration status, we created two dichotomous variables, one indicating women respondents and another one for respondents who have either parent foreign-born. The class variable, as discussed in Chapter 7, runs from 1 to 4 but has been rescaled to go from 0 to 1, with higher values indicating higher social class. Finally, our regression equations also include country dichotomous variables (estimates not shown in Table 18.1) to account for some of the country differences.

The results from Table 18.1 are in line with those presented in Chapters 4 through 11. First, we find that older people are more concerned, as compared to young people, about how immigrants might affect their country's safety and culture. The effect of age on anti-immigration attitudes, however, are relatively small. Interestingly, older people (65+) are less worried, for their part, about the effect of immigrants on the country's economy. This finding is consistent with Chapter 4. Table 18.1 also shows interesting gender differences. Specifically, we find women to be less concerned about the impact of immigrants on safety, when compared to men, but more worried about their impact on the country's economy. This last finding is presumably explained by women's more precarious position in the labour market. Respondents who had either parent foreign-born hold, not surprisingly, less anti-immigration attitudes than those whose parents were both born in the country. But, again, the differences are relatively modest. Also in line with Chapter 7, we find that those who pertain to a higher social class tend to have less anti-immigration attitudes, as compared to those of lower social status. The effect for class is larger than those for age, gender, and immigration status but still fairly moderate. The results for religion are also consistent with those reported in Chapter 8. They show that both Protestants and Catholics are less favourable towards immigrants than those who identify with another religion or identify themselves as non-religious. Catholics, in particular, are more worried about the effect immigrants might have on culture. As found in Chapter 8, however, the relationship between religion and anti-immigration attitudes is mostly country-specific. Finally, the strongest effects are found for both ideology and partisanship. As expected, those who identify with the political right or a party from the right hold systematically more anti-immigration attitudes than those who identify with the left or a party from the left. Again, these findings for ideology and partisanship are also consistent with those reported in Chapters 10 and 11, respectively.

In summary, the results from our multiple regression analysis are consistent with the bivariate analyses presented in Chapters 4 through 11. Some individual-level determinants are only weakly related to anti-immigration attitudes like gender and religion, for example, while others are much more strongly so. Determinants like political ideology and partisanship are particularly strongly related to anti-immigration attitudes. This finding is not surprising given the role that ideology plays in shaping people's and parties' policy preferences. Those that identify with the left and/or a political party from the left hold systematically more favourable attitudes towards immigrants than those that identify with the right and/or a political party from the right. Other individual-level determinants like social class, however, also play a significant role in explaining anti-immigration attitudes. In particular, those that pertain to a lower social class are generally less supportive of immigrants than those with a higher social status. Finally, our multiple regression analysis is less conclusive about the role of religion, in part, because the relationship between religion and anti-immigration attitudes is mostly country-specific. Still, they suggest that Catholics and, to a lesser extent, Protestants hold more anti-immigration attitudes than those who identify with other religions or define themselves as non-religious.

SUMMARY THOUGHTS

Having completed a presentation and discussion of a comprehensive model of results using the CSES data, we now turn to the final tasks for this chapter – providing some summary thoughts about the volume's contributions and acknowledging some limitations. We think that there are a number of things to highlight about the unique contributions of this volume as well as identifying some common themes that wend their way through the volume.

In the first instance, we believe this volume to be a unique contribution to the literature on public opinion in general as well as to the study of public opinion about immigration in specific. While generally pitched at a level for broad consumption, each substantive chapter engages in a sustained treatment of one factor or set of factors that is theorized to influence the shape of public opinion about immigration. The vast majority of chapter contributions are broadly comparative and consider theoretical claims in many empirical contexts. Whether this is done in the more basic analyses of Part 2 chapters or the more advanced chapters of Part 3 (and this chapter as well), a truly comparative approach is taken to exploring public opinion about immigration.

A second unique feature of the volume is the sustained attention to the issue of immigration. There are virtually no books on the market – either for broad consumption or more advanced edited collections – that provide this kind of continued attention to opinions about this issue of public policy. We believe that this persistent focus on immigration throughout the volume provides a treatment of the topic of public opinion and public opinion about immigration that makes a standalone contribution to our understanding of the theoretical precursors to opinion on the issue.

A third unique feature of the volume is the combination of individual-level and contextual factors that are brought to bear on the topic of immigration. Collectively, the chapters in this volume present a picture of the ways in which individual-level factors (like age, class, or party identification) and contextual factors (like party systems, immigration levels, labour market conditions, or news media environments) serve to shape opinion about immigration in the countries included in the volume. We approach the study of public opinion about immigration in a systematic way, moving in Part 2 from individual-level determinants presumably remote from such attitudes like age and gender to others that are much closer like ideology and partisanship. From there, we consider external forces in Part 3, that is, how contexts in which people are embedded also exert an influence on public opinion about immigration.

Collectively, we believe that these three features result in an edited collection of chapters that makes a unique and valuable contribution to the study of and teaching about public opinion and public opinion about immigration.

Beyond these unique features of the volume, we think that there are specific substantive themes and contributions emerging from the collected chapters that should be highlighted. A first theme that emerges is that across the measures of immigration opinion and the countries included for analysis there appear to be evident cross-national differences in public opinion about immigration. When simply looking at average opinion on the various measures (Chapter 3) we observe persistent differences in the average level of positive opinion towards immigrants. For instance, drawing on Figure 3.4, the average opinion on the immigration index for Canadian respondents was 1.86 – the most pro-immigrant public by a good amount. By contrast, the least pro-immigrant public on the same measure was Italy with an average opinion of 3.05 on the 1 to 5 scale. While publics in the other countries included in the analysis are positioned between 2.53 and 2.95, Switzerland (2.95) and Germany (2.88) are closest to Italy in the extent of anti-immigrant sentiment. The chapters from Part 2 also highlight important country differences about how the individual-level determinants are related to immigration opinion. Taken together, these results, in concert with those of the other comparative chapters, demonstrate non-trivial differences in opinion about immigration between the included countries.

A second observation emerges from a consideration of the results in the comparative chapters and is confirmed by the results presented in this chapter (Table 18.1). While there are non-trivial differences in public opinion between these countries, the effects of some of the individual-level factors under consideration have an expected and consistent effect on public opinion in each case. For instance, regardless of whether one considers the nature of public opinion in Australia or Switzerland, the effects of being in a younger age category have a positive effect on pro-immigrant opinion relative to older respondents in both cases (Figure 4.4). The same is also true for many of the other factors under consideration in Part 2 and, in particular, for political ideology and partisanship.

A third concluding observation is that political and social identities matter in the development of public opinion more generally and about immigration in particular. Many of the chapters highlight the effects of a concept that involves a salient political identity such as religion, partisanship, or language. The results of the individual chapters as well as the analyses presented earlier in this chapter highlight the consistent effects of salient political and social identities on public opinion about immigration. For instance, results in this volume show that immigrant status, class position, religious adherence, ideology (e.g. liberal vs. conservative), and party identification, not to mention language group, have important effects on the positions taken about immigrants and immigration. Of course, we know that these kinds of identities have political implications but the point is made all the more salient when we observe these effects in chapter after chapter throughout this volume.

Related to these identities is the emphasis that the volume places on understanding the mechanisms that underlie the impacts of different factors on public opinion about immigration. Here, each chapter sought to explicate an understanding of why their factor of focus would or should influence public opinion. While not an exhaustive list, we can highlight some of the common mechanisms that appeared in these chapters. Many of the chapters detailed a logic of effect that might be termed "economic" in some sense. The chapters on age, gender, class, local presence of immigrants, labour market competition, and language each contain an element, however central, of economic interests which are theorized to structure the development of positions on immigrants and immigration. Other chapters (including those on gender, parental immigrant status, religion, local presence of immigrants, and language) theorize forms of a cultural effect in which group identity defines in- and out-group membership, threats are perceived to social and cultural identities and/or group membership linked fate serve as the theoretical vehicles through which opinion on immigrants and immigration can be shaped.

While economic and cultural themes underlie many of the causal mechanisms discussed, many other chapters highlight mechanisms that relate to context, party systems, and attitudinal complexity as key mechanisms of effect on public opinion. With respect to context, a number of chapters highlight the role of political context as central for influencing opinion about immigration. For instance, the chapter on Japan (Chapter 13) considers the contextual role of the local presence of immigrants on native Japanese opinions about immigrants and immigration. Chapter 16 demonstrates the influence of context through the relationship of media environment (in particular, specific news media organizations) and public opinion in Canada. In particular, this chapter shows that specific new media organizations, rather than media types, coevolve with public opinion on immigration and related issues. Further, Chapter 14 on labour market competition demonstrates the contextual effects of labour market dynamics on public opinion in Europe.

The chapters on party identification and partisan polarization exemplify the impact of political parties and party systems on public opinion. Chapter 11 shows that the most important aspects of partisanship are affective and serve as a highly salient form of political identity. In turn, this identity can shape how partisans evaluate political information, candidates, and policy issues like immigration and adopt opinions that align with the policy positions of their party. Chapter 12 explores how party system polarization influences opinion on immigration and, in particular, opinion about the source countries of immigrants coming into Brazil.

A last summary observation is that many of the chapters specify a nuanced and complex approach to thinking about public opinion. For instance, Chapter 10 on ideology shows how liberals and conservatives tend to take opposing views on immigration and that these positions are grounded in differing values. Going further though, this chapter suggests that while liberals' favourable opinions on immigration are rooted in the values of universalism and benevolence, conservative opposition to immigration can find its basis in the values of tradition and conformity. In a different direction, Chapter 9 shows how personality traits of individual respondents – specifically openness to experience, conscientiousness and emotional stability – can influence opinions about immigration. Finally, Chapter 17 demonstrates that immigration opinion is, in part, a function of attitudes towards racial and ethnic minorities and shows how these attitudes are related to underlying psychological predispositions like social dominance orientation and authoritarianism. We suggest that these values, traits, and predispositions reflect the inherent complexity in understanding the mechanisms of effect on immigration opinion.

Taken together, this volume provides a comprehensive look at public opinion and explores the many dimensions of opinion about immigration. It shows that opinions are influenced from many directions both intrinsic and extrinsic to the individual. It also shows that these influences on opinion have unique and complex pathways to ultimately shaping opinions about immigration.

Finally, we close by pointing to some of the limitations of this book. First, we recognize that its near-exclusive focus on the issue of immigration might sound limiting as public opinion concerns many other issues that wax and wane the public interest like those related to health, education, and the environment, to name a few. The individual-level determinants and contextual factors influencing these other issues of concern may vary greatly and whatever conclusions we have reached about immigration might not apply as well to other issues. Moreover, although we covered a large number of countries in both Parts 2 and 3, we have left out many other "publics." It could be that the conclusions our individual chapters have reached may not travel equally well to other countries, especially those in regions of the world that have been less covered in this book including Africa, the Middle East, Eastern Europe, and Asia. Many countries in these other parts of the world have only more recently democratized and public opinion in these countries may look quite different than that observed in the more established democracies that we have examined (except, admittedly, Brazil). Presumably, public opinion in these countries may be more volatile and less crystallized than in democracies where publics have had greater opportunities to debate and where political parties have been more freely able to contribute to these public debates.

To be sure, the collective contribution of this volume is not that last word on the study of public opinion, a topic that has fascinated many scholars – including ourselves – for decades and is likely to do so for many others. But we think that the volume makes a valuable contribution to the ongoing debates about public opinion, immigration, and the study of political behaviour more generally.

Index

Page numbers in *italics* denote figures. Page numbers in **bold** font denote tables.
Figures and tables that fall within page ranges for a particular topic are not listed separately.

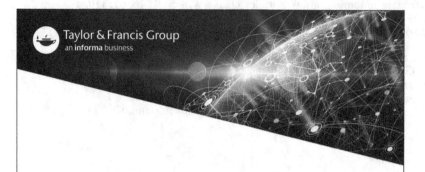